CAMBRIDGE GREEK AND LATIN CLASSICS

GENERAL EDITORS

E. J. KENNEY
Emeritus Kennedy Professor of Latin, University of Cambridge

AND

P. E. EASTERLING
Regius Professor of Greek, University of Cambridge

OVID
HEROIDES
XVI–XXI

EDITED BY
E. J. KENNEY
*Emeritus Kennedy Professor of Latin,
University of Cambridge*

CAMBRIDGE UNIVERSITY PRESS
Cambridge, New York, Melbourne, Madrid, Cape Town, Singapore, São Paulo

Cambridge University Press
The Edinburgh Building, Cambridge CB2 2RU, UK

Published in the United States of America by Cambridge University Press, New York

www.cambridge.org
Information on this title: www.cambridge.org/9780521460729

© Cambridge University Press 1996

This book is in copyright. Subject to statutory exception
and to the provisions of relevant collective licensing agreements,
no reproduction of any part may take place without
the written permission of Cambridge University Press.

First published 1996

A catalogue record for this publication is available from the British Library

Library of Congress Cataloguing in Publication data
Ovid, 43 B.C.–17 or 18 A.D.
[Heroides. 16–21]
Heroides, XVI-XXI/Ovid; edited by E. J. Kenney.
p.   cm. – (Cambridge Greek and Latin Classics)
Includes bibliographical references and index.
ISBN 0 521 46072 7. – ISBN 0 521 46623 7 (pbk.)
1. Epistolary poetry, Latin.   2. Mythology, Classical – Poetry.
3. Love-letters – Poetry.   4. Love poetry, Latin.   5. Women – Poetry.
I. Kenney, E. J.   II. Title.   III. Series.
PA6519.H5   1996
871'.01—dc20   95-17534 CIP

ISBN-13 978-0-521-46072-9 hardback
ISBN-10 0-521-46072-7 hardback

ISBN-13 978-0-521-46623-3 paperback
ISBN-10 0-521-46623-7 paperback

Transferred to digital printing 2005

In grateful and affectionate memory of
PATRICK WILKINSON

CONTENTS

Preface	*page* ix
Abbreviations and references	xii
Introduction	1
1 *The double letters*	1
2 *The three stories: sources, models, treatment*	5
(*a*) Paris and Helen	5
(*b*) Leander and Hero	9
(*c*) Acontius and Cydippe	15
3 *The* 'Gedichtbuch'	18
4 *Style and authorship*	20
5 *Text and transmission*	26
P. OVIDI NASONIS HEROIDVM EPISTVLAE XVI–XXI	29
Commentary	84
Appendix: Greek proper names in *Heroides* 16–21	249
Works cited by short title	252
Indexes	260
1 *Latin words*	260
2 *General*	262

PREFACE

'In considering this strangely neglected topic,' it began. This what neglected topic? This strangely what topic? This strangely neglected what?

Kingsley Amis, *Lucky Jim*

Well might Dr Dixon cringe. This is one of the more grossly overworked topoi of prefatory rhetoric. Yet *Heroides* 16–21 have indeed been strangely neglected in comparison with the single epistles. Still relegated by some scholars to a pseudo-Ovidian penumbra, they have profited less than any other part of the corpus from the renaissance in Ovidian studies that began after the Second World War. That seems strange to me. This is highly original and entertaining, in parts really affecting, poetry, yet another demonstration of the fact that each and every one of Ovid's books, not excepting the poems of exile, represents a fresh *tour de force* of invention (in both the ancient and the modern senses of the word) and creative fantasy. I hope therefore that this commentary may help others to appreciate these brilliant poems as warmly as I have come to do. I hope also that it may serve as a complement to Peter Knox's excellent selection from the single letters in this series. Ovid made for the *Heroides* the adroitly ambiguous claim that he had 'renewed' a genre previously unknown,

ignotum hoc aliis ille nouauit opus.

His creation turned out to be more versatile and influential than even he could have foreseen. The history of the sometimes downright bizarre guises in which, from the twelfth century to the twentieth, the genre which he had founded was again to be renewed and flourish may be followed in Heinrich Dörrie's monumental book, *Der heroische Brief* (Berlin 1968). If Professor Knox and I between us have been able to convey something of the impact which these poems have it in them to make – and have made over the centuries – on the receptive reader, our two books will have earned their place in this series.

It is a pleasure to record the encouragement and assistance received from friends and colleagues. Professor Easterling and Mr A. S. Hollis have read the Introduction, Commentary and Appendix in draft and have contributed many helpful comments and criticisms. Dr Gregory Hutchinson kindly allowed me the use of his notes on Acontius and Cydippe, by which I was able to repair more than one notable omission. Professor W. S. Watt has in correspondence mooted a number of emendations to the text, most of them subsequently published. I have gratefully adopted several of these, conscious that even where I differ, as I sometimes do, from his solutions, their ingenuity and the acumen of his diagnoses never fail to command respect. Dr Peter Godman has probably forgotten the trouble that he took many years ago to verify readings in the Puteaneus by autopsy; I have now at last been able to make belated but thankful use of his collations. I am especially grateful to Dr P. A. M. Thompson, who with great generosity has made me free of his unpublished doctoral dissertation (*Ovid, Heroides 20 and 21: a commentary with introduction.* Oxford 1989). The places where I register a specific obligation to Dr Thompson's work are signalled by the symbol [T.]; they are vastly outnumbered by those where I have drawn without acknowledgement but with his full leave on his ample accumulation of parallels and citations. He has also been kind enough to read the Commentary on these poems in draft, and his comments, not least those offered from the practical perspective of the classroom, have been extremely useful. I, and Acontius and Cydippe, owe him a substantial debt. Finally I must thank those who have assisted in the book's production. Mrs Hazel Dunn again grappled cheerfully with a succession of drafts complicated by authorial corrections and afterthoughts, and with her customary skill and patience finally reduced the Commentary to a presentable form. The proofs have been read by Elaine Fantham and Roland Mayer, to whom I am most grateful for taking time out from their own work on Ovid and Tacitus respectively to do me this friendly office. Pauline Hire and Glennis Foote have as usual – though this is something I hope Cambridge authors will never take for granted – seen the book through the press with care, dispatch and efficiency.

The passages from Leslie Marchand's edition of Byron's Letters and Journals quoted in the Introduction are reproduced by permission of John Murray (Publishers) Ltd.

PREFACE

One of the first harbingers of the reawakening of scholarly and critical interest in Ovid referred to above was Patrick Wilkinson's urbane and sympathetic *Ovid recalled* (Cambridge 1955). The first sentence of the Introduction that follows records his just appreciation of the merits of the poems edited in this book, which I offer as a modest tribute to his memory.

Cambridge
March 1995   E. J. K.

ABBREVIATIONS AND REFERENCES

ANRW (edd.) H. Temporini–W. Haase, *Aufstieg und Niedergang der römischen Welt*. Berlin–New York 1972– .
CHCL (edd.) P. E. Easterling–E. J. Kenney, *The Cambridge History of Classical Literature*. I *Greek Literature* 1985; II *Latin Literature* 1982. Cambridge.
CIL *Corpus Inscriptionum Latinarum*. Berlin 1863–
CP (edd.) J. Diggle–F. R. D. Goodyear, *The classical papers of A. E. Housman*. 3 vols. Cambridge 1972.
EGF (ed.) M. Davies, *Epicorum Graecorum fragmenta*. Göttingen 1988.
FGE (ed.) D. L. Page, *Further Greek epigrams*, rev. and prepared for pubn by R. D. Dawe and J. Diggle. Cambridge 1981.
FLP (ed.) E. Courtney, *The fragmentary Latin poets*. Oxford 1993.
FPL (ed.) W. Morel, *Fragmenta poetarum Latinorum epicorum et lyricorum*. Leipzig 1927, repr. Stuttgart 1963.
GLK (ed.) H. Keil, *Grammatici Latini*. 8 vols. Leipzig 1857–70, repr. 1961.
GP (edd.) A. S. F. Gow–D. L. Page, *The Greek Anthology. The Garland of Philip and some contemporary epigrams*. 2 vols. Cambridge 1968.
HE (edd.) A. S. F. Gow–D. L. Page, *The Greek Anthology. Hellenistic epigrams*. 2 vols. Cambridge 1965.
H–S J. B. Hofmann–A. Szantyr, *Lateinische Syntax und Stilistik*. Munich 1965.
K–S R. Kühner–C. Stegmann, *Ausführliche Grammatik der lateinischen Sprache*. 3. Auflage ed. A. Thierfelder. 2 vols. Leverkusen 1955.
LIMC *Lexicon iconographicum mythologiae classicae*. Zurich–Munich 1981–
LSJ H. G. Liddell–R. Scott, *A Greek–English Lexicon*. New edn H. S. Jones. 2 vols. Oxford 1940 and repr.
N–H R. G. M. Nisbet–Margaret Hubbard, *A commentary on Horace: Odes Book I* 1970; *Book II* 1978. Oxford.
NLS E. C. Woodcock, *A new Latin syntax*. London 1959.
N–W F. Neue–C. Wagener, *Formenlehre der lateinischen Sprache*. 3. Auflage. 4 vols. Leipzig–Berlin 1892–1905.

ABBREVIATIONS AND REFERENCES xiii

*OCD*² (edd.) N. G. L. Hammond–H. H. Scullard, *The Oxford Classical Dictionary*. 2nd edn. Oxford 1970.
OLD (ed.) P. G. W. Glare, *Oxford Latin Dictionary*. Oxford 1982.
Otto A. Otto, *Die Sprichwörter und sprichwörtlichen Redensarten der Römer*. Leipzig 1890.
RE (edd.) A. Pauly–G. Wissowa–W. Kroll, *Real-Encyclopädie der classischen Altertumswissenschaft*. Stuttgart 1893–
Roby H. J. Roby, *A grammar of the Latin language from Plautus to Suetonius*. Part II *Syntax*. London 1896.
ROL (ed.) E. H. Warmington, *Remains of old Latin*. (Loeb Classical Library) 4 vols. Cambridge, Mass. and London 1935–40.
SH (edd.) H. Lloyd-Jones–P. Parsons, *Supplementum Hellenisticum*. Berlin and New York 1983.
TLL *Thesaurus Linguae Latinae*. Munich 1900–
TRF (ed.) O. Ribbeck, *Tragicorum Romanorum fragmenta*. 3rd edn. Leipzig 1897.

To these add two recurrent technical terms:
sedes: position in the metrical scheme of the verse.
ἀπὸ κοινοῦ ('in common'): a form of ellipse in which the sense of a single word or phrase is felt as applying to more than one part of a compound expression. For a selection of Ovidian examples see Kenney, *C.Q.* 8 (1958) 55.
Other technical terms are explained as they occur.

Except where it might occasion ambiguity, the name of the work is omitted from references to the *Heroides*, and the name of Ovid from references to his other works.
See also list of *Works cited by short title*, below pp. 252–9.

INTRODUCTION

1. THE DOUBLE LETTERS

'It is with palates almost ruined by long draughts of the bitter lees of love in the *Heroides*[1] proper (I-XV) that we come to the living wine in XVI-XXI, three letters from heroes with the heroines' replies.'[2] The impetus to embark on this further development of a genre which was substantially Ovid's own creation[3] seems to have come from his friend Sabinus, who furnished some of the single letters with answers, which regrettably do not survive (*Am.* 2.18.27-34). This was a suggestive and fruitful inspiration. *Heroides* 1-14[4] are letters from legendary women complaining of separation from or abandonment by husbands or lovers. It is difficult to rescue them, especially if they are read sequentially, from the charge of monotony. Those are self-contained monologues; the double epistles allow some (admittedly limited) dramatic interaction between the protagonists, somewhat on the lines of a Euripidean *agon*. The difference is analogous to that between the two sorts of declamatory exercise on which Ovid had cut his rhetorical teeth, the *suasoria* and the *controversia*. In the first of these the speaker advised some famous character of history or legend on his course of action in some critical situation; in the second

---

[1] This title is first attested by the sixth-century grammarian Priscian (*GLK* II 544.4); O. himself, presumably referring only to the single letters, uses *Epistula* (*A.A.* 3.345). None of the forms found in the MSS and editions (*Heroides, Heroides siue Epistulae, Heroides Epistulae, Heroidum Epistulae*, etc.) suits 16-21, to which indeed O. may never have given a title (below, §4 *fin.*). In this edition the last form is used *faute de mieux* for the Latin text; elsewhere, for convenience, simply *Heroides*. See Purser *ap.* Palmer (1898) x, Luck (1961) 223-4, Tarrant (1983) 268 n. 1.

[2] Wilkinson (1955) 107 – a welcome contrast to the previous rather lukewarm appraisal of Fränkel (1945) 48-53. See also for a generally appreciative and sympathetic discussion Anderson (1973) 68-81. Mack (1988) 18 disposes of them in two sentences.

[3] *A.A.* 3.346 *ignotum hoc aliis ille nouauit opus*; *nouauit* is ambiguous = either 'invented' or 'renewed', cunningly obscuring without explicitly disclaiming O.'s debt to Propertius' 'Arethusa' (4.3) for the original idea.

[4] It will be taken for granted in this edition that *Her.* 15, the letter of Sappho (*E.S.*), is not by O. See Knox (1995) 12-14, and cf. below, n. 100.

two speakers argued on opposite sides of a question, usually of a legal or quasi-legal nature. The *suasoria* might be deliberative, a soliloquy by the person in the dilemma, and in such cases the exercise became one in the portrayal of character, *prosopopoeia* or *ethopoeia*.[5] The single letters are essentially glorified exercises of this kind. In the double letters Ovid gets the best of both worlds, continuing his exploitation of *ethopoeia* but adding the new dimension offered by the *controversia*, the clash of opposing characters and viewpoints.[6] This is especially evident in the letters of Acontius and Cydippe, where much of the argument turns on legalistic debate about words and intentions.

It was, predictably, the heroines who interested and stimulated him most; Helen, Hero, Cydippe all steal the show: 'our interest focuses on the complex way in which the women respond to new and exciting pressures'.[7] All three heroines as we meet them in these letters are new literary creations. Helen is a brilliant retrojection of Euripides' acid deconstruction; Hero and Cydippe empathetic realizations of characters barely sketched in Ovid's Hellenistic sources.[8].

In generic terms these letters occupy borderline territory between the *Amores* and the *Metamorphoses*. The situation of the lovers is elegiac: wooer and wooed are separated from each other by external obstacles. Their world is the world of Scylla, of Myrrha and Byblis, of Medea and Althaea. Whereas however the dramatic soliloquies of those heroines[9] represent them, like the recipients of *suasoriae*, as poised between alternative courses of action, the roles of Helen, Hero and Cydippe are essentially passive, however dynamic their rhetoric. All are at the mercy of inexorable or irresponsible or vindictive gods. Helen may appear to be a free agent, able to reject Paris' dishonourable advances if she wishes, but (as the reader

---

[5] Bonner (1949) 53, 150. For a useful discussion, and a warning against constructing a simple derivative relationship between these exercises and the *Heroides*, see Jacobson (1974) 325–30.

[6] Kenney (1970c) 405, Sabot (1981) 2610–19.

[7] Anderson (1973) 71; for Hero and Cydippe 'exciting' rather understates the case.

[8] This is certainly true of Cydippe, overwhelmingly probable of Hero; see below, p. 14.

[9] Byblis is given three, the second in the form of a letter (*Met.* 9.530–63); cf. esp. 530–1 *quam nisi tu dederis, non est habitura salutem, | hanc tibi mittit amans* ~ *Her.* 16.2 (n.).

knows) it is already written in the book of the Fates that the Trojan War shall take place and that she shall go down to posterity as the *casus belli*. Hero's happiness depends on unpredictable superhuman forces, the winds and waves that keep Leander from her and will soon destroy him. Cydippe, crushed between the millstones of human and divine obligation, must in the end yield to the decrees of dynastic necessity.[10]

Pace Patrick Wilkinson, these letters are not, at bottom, comfortable reading, often as they may raise a smile. Entertaining as is the verbal fencing of Paris and Helen, the contrast between their self-centred and reckless desire and the train of death, destruction and misery that will follow from it colours the comedy as black as any in the *Metamorphoses*. The story of Hero and Leander is overtly tragic, unrelieved by any kind of humour: romantic love overshadowed by foreboding and doomed to early disaster. The tone of the final pair of letters, those of Acontius and Cydippe, is elusive. When in the end she yields, it is at least in part of her own volition; but it is natural to wonder whether the conclusion of the story, and of the book, is in fact the happy ending that, after what has preceded, one might feel entitled to expect.[11] The mixture of casuistry and violence with which Acontius conducts his wooing is bound to leave an ironical question mark hanging in the air as the book is laid down.

In the double epistles a technical problem inherent in the genre is duplicated: at which points to 'freeze' the action of the story to allow the characters to express their feelings. When Paris takes up his pen the mine has been laid and it only remains to light the fuse. Menelaus is away, the lugger is waiting, the girl (he rightly guesses) is willing; it is now or never. The interval between the receipt of his letter and Helen's reply is no longer than it takes her to write it. She wastes no time; it is at once evident that she has made up her mind. The whole episode is compressed into a few hours. Acontius' letter is also the climax of a long campaign, though how long Ovid is content to leave vague. Cydippe's illnesses have dragged on for many

---

[10] Callim. fr. 75. 50ff. Pf. O. alludes only indirectly to this aspect of the story (20.219–28 and Comm. *ad loc.*), but he would have expected his readers to be aware of it.

[11] Happy endings are notably rare in the *Metamorphoses*: Kenney, *CHCL* II 439–40 = *The age of Augustus* (Cambridge 1982) 143–4.

months (Comm. 20.109–10n.); we are left to wonder whether Acontius has been haunting the back door of her house all that time. Again the interval between his letter and her reply is short: like Helen, though she puts up a more convincing show of resistance, she has already decided to yield. Here too the psychological action is packed into a very short space. The timing of the letters of Leander and Hero is contrived to exploit to the full the tragic ironies of the story. Even while Hero is writing her answer, which will never be sent, Leander, having rashly followed his letter across the sea, already lies dead on the shore below. At dawn she will lie there too: a single day and night will have witnessed the evocation and the extinction of their love.

A second problem is that of putting the reader, where necessary, in possession of the facts of the story. The obvious device of retrospective narration had already been used effectively in the single letters, e.g. those of Ariadne (10.7–58) and Hypermnestra (14.21–84). So far as Paris and Helen were concerned, Ovid was entitled to assume that his readers were conversant with the Trojan legend, that they knew their Homer, and perhaps their Euripides. Paris is made to tell Helen the story of his life, and Helen to recall her abduction by Theseus, not primarily to assist the less well-read but to illuminate the characters of the pair and to provide opportunities for authorial irony. In the case of Acontius and Cydippe acquaintance with Callimachus' treatment could be premised; Ovid's predecessors had already exploited Acontius' soliloquy (below, n.66), and the casual references to Cydippe at *A.A.* 1.455–6 and *Rem.* 382 imply the story was familiar. Readers who did not already know their Callimachus might not grasp at the outset what exactly had happened in the sanctuary of Diana (20.5–12), which does not emerge explicitly until half way through Cydippe's reply (21.107–14), but they had enough to go on to enable them to relish to the full the battle of wills and argument that immediately develops. The theme of first meeting is cleverly dichotomized: Acontius recalls how in the classic manner he was struck all of a heap by the sight of Cydippe (20.203–8), Cydippe demurely affects not to have noticed (21.103–4) – this in passing in the course of a long and extremely effective account of her visit to Delos, designed to throw into relief her present unhappiness (Comm. 21.65–114n.). In the case of Hero and Leander it is doubtful whether

INTRODUCTION 5

Ovid could assume general knowledge of the Greek poem which, as will be argued below, was his model. However, the first fourteen lines of Leander's letter suffice to put the reader abreast of the salient facts: that writer and addressee are on opposite banks of the Hellespont and that their love must be clandestine. Since they alone of the three pairs of lovers have at the time of writing actually consummated their love, the emphasis is made to fall, not on their first meeting, of the circumstances of which we hear nothing, but on their first rendezvous (Comm. 18.55–104n.). Leander's narrative of romantic adventure, activity, endurance and maritime hazards is complemented by Hero's, telling of a different kind of endurance, of enforced domestic passivity, and vicarious fear (19.19–56). None of this is requisite to an understanding of the plot of the story: here too it is the characters of the writers that are illuminated by their recollections.

2. THE THREE STORIES: SOURCES, MODELS, TREATMENT

(a) Paris and Helen[12]

Even today this pair of lovers are a byword, and they certainly needed no introduction to Ovid's readers. The prediction of Homer's Helen that she and Paris would be the subject of song for future generations (*Il.* 6.357–8) had been abundantly fulfilled. Ovid's problem was to select, combine and colour from the wealth of material offered by the poetic tradition. His own unique contribution was to stage the correspondence as a demonstration of the *Ars Amatoria* in action in Mycenaean Greece: the ploys of books I and II deftly advanced by Paris and as deftly countered by Helen with those of book III.[13] There is no great depth to the characterization of Paris: he is driven single-mindedly by lust and the rooted conviction that nothing can avail to stand between him and his promised reward. To all possible objections and obstacles he is blindly and blithely indifferent (Comm. 16.343n.). His rhetoric is that of one possessed by *ate*, divine

---

[12] For a fuller discussion see Kenney (1995).
[13] Belfiore (1980–1) 139–45.

6   INTRODUCTION

infatuation (cf. Hom. *Il.* 6.356). As regards characterization Ovid reserved his best effects, as with Hero and Cydippe, for Helen. Paris, however, posed a technical problem, which it took some care and ingenuity to solve.

The object of Paris' pleading is to impress Helen with the conviction that she has no choice but to go with him. To do this, he tells her the story of his life *in extenso*, to show her that the entire chain of events from Hecuba's pregnancy to the moment when he set sail for Sparta tends to that inevitable conclusion. This entailed combining three legends which were originally distinct: the stories of his birth, exposure and Recognition, the Judgement, and Oenone, his first wife. Oenone makes only a fleeting appearance, providing the opportunity for an epistolary score.[14] To reconcile the other strands in the legend called for more contrivance. For the Recognition story (16.41–52)[15] Ovid drew on Euripides' lost *Alexandros*[16] and on Ennius' adaptation *Alexander*, also lost. For the Judgement and its sequel he used the lost *Cypria*, an epic traditionally ascribed to the early Greek poet Stasinus.[17] The problem was to combine these two stories into a single coherent sequence.

In Paris' narration the Recognition (16.89–92) follows the Judgement (16.52–88), but this cannot represent the chronological order of events in Ovid's sources. In the *Alexandros* the Judgement was evidently foretold by Cassandra towards the end of the play, after Paris (Alexander) had been recognized, a sequence followed faithfully by

---

[14] Comm. 16.97–8, 98, 17.195–8nn. It is probable that she was included only because she had already figured in the single *Heroides* (5); see Comm. 17.196n.

[15] Complementary summaries at Apollod. *Bibl.* 3.12.5.2–5, Hyg. *Fab.* 91.

[16] Comm. 16.51–2, 91nn. That he drew directly on the *Alexandros* cannot be conclusively proved; but (i) given that he had certainly used the *Alexander* (Comm. 16.43–50, 45–6nn.) – *a priori* an unexpected thing for him to have done in view of his expressed disrespect for Ennius' *ars* (*Am.* 1.15.19, *Tr.* 2.424) – it would have been odd not to look at the original; (ii) his characterization of Helen (below, p. 8) clearly owes much to the *Troades*, the last play of the trilogy of which *Alexandros* was the first.

[17] An outline is preserved in the shape of a prose paraphrase in the *Chrestomathia* of the fifth-century philosopher Proclus (*EGF* pp.30–3). For parallels with the *Cypria* see Comm. 16.19, 107–24, 118, 121, 126–7, 303–6nn. – the last particularly piquant.

Ennius.[18] Ovid manipulates the narrative so as to gloze over the discrepancy. Paris had been recognized at some unspecified time (16.91 *post tempora longa*) prior to the Judgement, but where he was and what he had been doing meanwhile (89 *interea*) he does not expressly say. It must be inferred that, even after he had been recognized as a prince of the Trojan royal house, he had remained on Mount Ida tending his father's flocks, as they were now revealed to be. On the face of it this may seem odd, but the apparent anomaly had not worried Euripides or other poets.[19] That the Judgement took place on Ida, the place where it all started, was an unquestioned *datum* of the story (Comm. 16.53n.). These chronological imprecisions conveniently allow Paris to play down his relationship with Oenone by inviting Helen to infer that she came into his life only after the Recognition and then only in the character of a possible not an actual wife (Comm. 16.97–8n.). Helen, needless to say, is not deceived (17.195–8).

Though Helen had her own niche, and a multivalent role, in the mythographical tradition, to reconcile her story with that of Paris posed no special problems. Her previous escapade with Theseus is adroitly turned to account (16.149–62, 327–30, 17.21–34), but as with Oenone serves merely as an occasion for point-scoring. The most surprising feature of Ovid's treatment is the total suppression of the Suitors' Oath (Comm. 16.341n.). He must have known what he was doing here; indeed he goes out of his way to draw attention to the omission by making Paris canvass at some length the chances that an expedition will be mounted to rescue Helen. To have allowed either correspondent to acknowledge that this was in fact a certainty would have created another problem, which in this case Ovid apparently preferred simply to duck. Helen has evidently made up her mind before taking up her pen,[20] and she is not going to complicate things by lodging an objection which she would have had some difficulty in

[18] Coles (1974) 14 and n. 1, 26–7 and n. 24; Enn. *Alex.* 43–6, 47–9 J.; Stinton (1965) 68 n. 3 = (1990) 69 n. 17, Coles (1974) 33 n. 10.

[19] Eur. *Hel.* 29, *I.A.* 76, [Bion] 2.10–11 Gow, Colluthus 72, 104, 139, 198; cf. Stinton (1965) 56 = (1990) 60, Jocelyn (1967) 218 and nn. 1, 2, Hopkinson on Callim. *H.* 6 (Demeter).86.

[20] Rand (1925) 30: 'This [the opening lines of her letter] is surrender; the rest is apology'. Cf. Belfiore (1980–1) 146.

shrugging off. As it is, she does air it in effect, in rather hypothetical terms (17.245-50), rather late in the day. What emerges is the self-centred infatuation of the pair and their willing though uncomprehending acquiescence in their role as instruments of the divine plan.

The most taxing problem with Helen, given that Homer and Euripides had been there first,[21] was to give an original turn to her character. In the *Iliad* neither she nor Paris is entirely a free agent, but neither is a mere puppet at the mercy of *ate*.[22] Helen in particular is drawn with singular delicacy and insight: her reactions to the interventions of Hector and Priam into her uncomfortable relationship with Paris are beautifully managed to excite sympathy and compassion. Far otherwise is the Euripidean Helen, never mentioned by actor or chorus 'without a passing curse of hatred and ill will', portrayed in the *Troades* as 'false, fluent, and self-righteous, engaging with Hecuba in the debate which makes rhetorically articulate all the ambivalence of her actions and moral responsibility'.[23] This, essentially, is Ovid's Helen, 'the woman as she has always been', as Electra calls her in the *Orestes*,[24] imagined as a young woman. 'Following Euripides ... [Ovid] has transformed heroic lovers, playthings of the gods, into human beings.'[25] Euripides had indeed paved the way by his deconstruction of the traditional myth.[26] Ovid's brilliant and sardonic portrayal would surely have appealed to his 'favourite fifth century tragedian'.[27]

---

[21] Not to mention Stesichorus, Gorgias and Isocrates.
[22] See the useful note of Edwards on Hom. *Il.* 19.85-138 (pp. 245-7).
[23] Dale (1967) vii-viii.
[24] Eur. *Or.* 129 ἡ πάλαι γυνή.
[25] Rand (1925) 32. Rand's brilliant summary of her letter (29-31) offers a salutary antidote to the somewhat starry-eyed descriptions of her by e.g. Wilkinson (1955) 111 as 'a young and innocent wife' or by Anderson (1973) as 'a clever, reasonably [!] loyal wife' (70) ... 'morally aware' (78). Nearer the mark are Purser *ap.* Palmer (1898) xxi with 'a regular flirt' or Belfiore (1980-1) 146 and n. 46 with 'a vain, intriguing coquette'. On the whole question of Helen's 'seelischer Konflikt' (a case of 'no contest'?) see Hintermeier (1993) 41-9.
[26] Jouan (1966) 109; cf. Belfiore (1980-1) 138 and n. 13 'In Euripides' account, the "victim" is morally responsible'.
[27] Hinds (1993) 45 n. 79.

INTRODUCTION

(b) *Leander and Hero*[28]

The story as outlined by Servius in his commentary on Virgil's *Georgics* is simple:

> Leander of Abydos and Hero of Sestos loved each other. Leander had been in the habit of visiting her by swimming across the Hellespont,[29] which flows between the two cities. When therefore the young man was drowned in a storm and his body was washed up before her, she threw herself from a tower.[30]

Servius says nothing about the picturesque detail, prominent in Ovid and later writers, of the 'traitor lamp', as Ovid's contemporary Antipater of Thessalonica calls it,[31] though Virgil's *nocte ... caeca* (see below) may hint at its absence to readers expected to be familiar with the story.[32] It is clear from Horace's throwaway reference to 'the strait which runs between neighbouring towers', *freta uicinas inter*

---

[28] So, here only, for the sake of uniformity; 'Hero and Leander' has been standard since Musaeus. See Kost (1971) 117–18, suggesting that the title of the Hellenistic original was probably *Leandros*; and cf. below, pp. 10, 13–14.

[29] Byron's repetition of his feat is well known. 'This morning I *swam* from *Sestos to Abydos*, the immediate distance is not above a mile but the current renders it hazardous, so much so, that I doubt whether Leander's conjugal powers must not have been exhausted in his passage to Paradise' (to Henry Drury, 3 May 1810: *Byron's Letters and Journals*, ed. L. A. Marchand 1 (London 1973) 237). There was an amusing sequel in the shape of a polemical exchange with another Near Eastern traveller, William Turner, on the hazards and technical problems of the crossing (*ibid.* VIII (1978) 80–3). Byron concluded that 'My own experience & that of others bids me pronounce the passage of Leander perfectly practicable; – any young man in good health – and tolerable skill in swimming might succeed in it from *either* side' (*ibid.* 81).

[30] Servius on Virg. *G.* 3.258.

[31] *A.P.* 7.666.4 (*GP* 132); cf. *ibid.* 9.215.5–6 (219–20). In Musaeus' treatment the lamp takes on great significance. It is the theme of the poet's invocation of the Muse, the confidante of the loves of the pair (cf. *Her.* 18.106 and Comm. *ad loc.*), its flame identified with Leander's life (Musaeus 14–15, 217–18, 329–30); see Kost on Musaeus 15 and n. 237, Hopkinson (1994) 138–9. Ovid confines himself to more or less routine word-play (Comm. 18.85–6n.).

[32] Cf. Serv. auctus *loc.cit. Leandri nomen occultauit quia cognita erat fabula.*

currentia turres,³³ that he made a similar assumption. Unfortunately no writer who alludes to the story offers any guidance to its literary antecedents, which must be reconstructed from comparison of the relevant texts.

The key witnesses are Ovid, Virgil, and the late Greek poet Musaeus (fifth century A.D.). The story makes its first certain appearance in European literature in the *Georgics*:

> quid iuuenis, magnum cui uersat in ossibus ignem
> durus amor? nempe abruptis turbata procellis
> nocte natat caeca serus freta, quem super ingens
> porta tonat caeli, et scopulis inlisa reclamant
> aequora; nec miseri possunt reuocare parentes
> nec moritura super crudeli funere uirgo. *G.* 3.258–63

Virgil neither names the protagonists nor fills in all the details. The reference to the young man's parents is inexplicit,³⁴ and the expression *super crudeli funere* characteristically ambiguous.³⁵ In his lines the emphasis falls on the storm and by implication on Leander's folly in attempting the crossing: '... he is driven by this hideous power [love] to do something idiotic, which can only mean death for his beloved and himself and misery for his devoted parents' (Mynors *ad loc.*). So in Ovid's depiction, but by him spelled out at length, the keynote of Leander's character is his headstrong recklessness.

The only extended treatments of the story which survive are those of Ovid and Musaeus. They agree closely enough in specific details³⁶ to make it certain beyond reasonable doubt, given that Musaeus is very unlikely to have read Ovid,³⁷ that both derive from a common

---

³³ *Ep.* 1.3.4, a learned tease, as noted by Mayer *ad loc.* Cf. Kost (1971) 17–18 and n. 32, Gelzer (1975) 304.

³⁴ 'not his parents but the thought of them' (Mynors *ad loc.*); this seems to be borne out by Leander's allusion to them in his letter (18.13–14).

³⁵ See Mynors *ad loc.* Thomas's blunt gloss 'She jumped off the tower' is correct but cannot, in the absence of any mention of a tower, be inferred from Virgil's words. Cf. Musaeus 342 'And Hero lay in death beside her dead bedfellow'.

³⁶ Comm. *passim*; the most striking case is that of 18.148 = Musaeus 255 (see Comm. *ad loc.*).

³⁷ In any case, O. could not have been Musaeus' only model, as will be seen (below, pp. 12–13).

INTRODUCTION

original, presumed to have been a Hellenistic poem. Until recently this remained a largely speculative hypothesis.[38] In 1982 was published a papyrus in which 'some 50 mutilated hexameters dangle before our eyes the debris of a scenario which featured a seascape, an intrepid lover, very significantly a tower (πύργον) and probably a tell-tale lamp, all prominent ingredients in our extant poetic versions'.[39] It may very well be that this is part of the Greek poem which Virgil, Ovid and Musaeus knew; certainly it is the most plausible candidate so far. Its authorship and date of composition continue to be the subject of speculation.[40]

What Ovid and Musaeus made of this postulated original was vastly different. As in the other pairs of letters, Ovid had necessarily to arrest the action at two points, developing the drama through the memories, hopes and fears of the lovers. As with Paris and Helen, the impending tragedy is suggested only by ironical allusion. Musaeus' format is altogether more straightforward, a continuous epic-style[41] narrative culminating in the final union of the lovers in death. What might seem a disproportionate amount of the 343 verses of the poem is taken up with an account of the setting and circumstances of their first meeting (42–220), a theme touched on by Ovid only in the

---

[38] See Gelzer (1975) 304–6 and nn.

[39] Papanghelis (1987) 103–4. For the text see Maehler (1982), *SH* 901A. The papyrus itself is dated to the fourth or fifth century A.D., about contemporary with Musaeus. An earlier papyrus figuring Leander (*SH* 951, first century A.D.) is too fragmentary to allow of any but highly speculative interpretation (Kost (1971) 20–1); but see next n.

[40] An obvious possibility is one of the contemporary Greek *littérateurs* such as Parthenius, 'who in the second half of the first century B.C. resided in Rome as guests or clients of members of refined society' (Gelzer (1975) 306). Mr A. S. Hollis, however, points out (*per litt.*) that in some twenty surviving hexameter endings in *SH* 901A there is not one spondaic fifth foot, a Parthenian trademark (cf. Parth. *Erot. narr.* 11.3 (*SH* 646) with two in six verses), whereas *SH* 951 has one in ten verses. It is equally possible that the poem had been gathering dust in a library for a century or more and was rediscovered and restored to circulation at this time. It is surprising, in view of the romantic appeal of the story, that its diffusion in antiquity was apparently so limited (Gelzer (1975) 307). See now for an up-to-date summary of the source-problem Hintermeier (1993) 58–60.

[41] He begins in the high epic vein with Εἰπὲ θεά 'Tell, goddess' (Kost *ad loc.*); cf. Comm. 18.103–4n.

transformed guise of their first rendezvous (above, p. 5). The most striking discrepancy is that in Musaeus Hero is a priestess of Aphrodite, in whose sanctuary Leander first sees, loves, woos and wins her at one fell swoop. Like Ovid's Hero she lives in a tower by the sea with a single maid for company,[42] this 'by the hateful decision of my parents' (190), who have forbidden her to marry (179–80). Taken with Leander's evident fear in Ovid of parental disapproval (18.13–14), Hero's fear that she may be thought unworthy of him (19.99–100), and the emphasis in both poets on secrecy,[43] this suggests that the social disparity of the lovers was an original element of the story.[44] As with Paris and Helen, and Acontius and Cydippe, though the affair is clandestine and to that extent elegiac, *furtiuus amor*, the plot turns on the issue of marriage and marriageability.[45]

Attempts at reconstructing the Greek original are complicated by the way in which Musaeus has overlaid this simple motivation with elements borrowed from other sources. His description of the two lovers as 'of each of their two cities each the fairest star' (tr. Whitman) echoes Callimachus' introduction of Acontius and Cydippe;[46] and the setting of the festival at which they meet also recalls that story.[47] Twice Hero is described as 'pacing' or 'wandering' about the temple (55, 71) while throngs of young men admire her – odd

[42] Musaeus 187–8 ~ *Her.* 18.97 (Comm. *ad loc.*).

[43] Exaggeratedly emphasized in his description of their wedding that was no wedding (247–83).

[44] Cf. Kost on Musaeus 190.

[45] Musaeus repeatedly stresses the theme of marriage, and Leander calls himself Hero's husband (220 πόσις).

[46] Musaeus 22 ἀμφοτέρων πολίων περικαλλέες ἀστέρες ἄμφω < Callim. fr. 67.8 Pf. καλοὶ νησάων ἀστέρες ἀμφότεροι; cf. Musaeus 200 ~ fr. 67.1 and Kost, Gelzer *ad locc.* See below, nn. 47, 53; and on correspondences with Aristaenetus Kost (1971) 36–43. On the similarities between the two stories see Bopp (1966) 8–12, noting also how Pyramus and Thisbe are likewise compelled by parental opposition to resort to unorthodox expedients in order to meet (Ov. *Met.* 4.60–70).

[47] Musaeus begins the list of worshippers with 'those dwelling in the foothills of the sea-girt islands' (45), mentioning however only Cyprus and Cythera (46), presumably because Aphrodite had important sanctuaries on both. The phrase would better suit a festival at Delos: cf. Thuc. 3.104.3 (Callim. fr. 71 Pf.), Klemm (1889) 13–23 (but his and Knaack's ascription of the original to Callimachus is generally and rightly discredited: Gelzer (1975) 304 n. *c*).

behaviour for a priestess at such a time, especially one previously described as reclusive and devoted to her duties,[48] but entirely appropriate to a visitor like Cydippe, admiring the sights of a great sanctuary and in turn admired by other visitors.[49] A religious festival as the meeting-place of lovers is a stock feature of Greek novels: so Chariton's hero and heroine meet at a festival of Aphrodite (1.1.4–6). The idea of making Hero a priestess may indeed have come to Musaeus from the heroine of another novel, Heliodorus' Chariclea, a virgin priestess of Artemis whose beauty turned all heads when she appeared in public.[50] Resolute chastity is fitting for a priestess of the virgin Artemis; whether priestesses of Aphrodite were generally expected to be chaste, or whether Musaeus thought they were, is an interesting question but for the matter in hand irrelevant. His concern was evidently to create, embellish and exploit a paradox: a priestess of the goddess of love wedded to celibacy and so affording the opportunity for a display of perversely ingenious eloquence on the part of her suitor.

Musaeus' poem ends with a powerful description of the night of storm in which Leander perished (293–330). Given its prominence in Virgil's brief allusion, it is a fair inference that this was an important feature of the original. For obvious reasons Ovid could use it only by way of dramatic irony (Comm. 18.55–104n.). However, not being one to waste anything, he seems to have exploited this part of the original for the descriptions in the *Metamorphoses* of the storm in which Ceyx dies and the sequel in which his body is washed ashore to his waiting wife, who attempts to throw herself on it, *moritura super crudeli funere*.[51]

[48] Musaeus 34–6. When it comes to the crunch we hear no more of that (cf. Hopkinson (1994) on Musaeus 190). On the vagueness of Musaeus' handling of the story see Gelzer (1975) 315–16.

[49] Cf. *Her.* 21.93–104.

[50] Heliod. 2.33.3, 3.4.8. For the recurrent motif of the heroine's beauty and its effect on the beholders see Kost (1971) 223–7 and 55–85nn., Kenney on Apul. *Met.* 4.28.2, 3. Musaeus' description of Hero (55–9) is specifically indebted to Achilles Tatius' of Leucippe (1.4.2–3) (Kost, Hopkinson *ad loc.*). In the context of marriage to a stranger the figures of Jason and Medea, herself a priestess (of Hecate), might also have been present to Musaeus' mind.

[51] *Met.* 11.474–572, 710–31; cf. Pohlenz (1913) 7–8, Schott (1957) 105–8, and Comm. 19.193n. On echoes of the story in Propertius see Papanghelis (1987) 104–10.

Leander's recollection of the song of the halcyons (18.81–2) is a fine example of Ovid's habit of self-reference, at once imparting tragic irony to his story and at the same time inviting the alert reader to admire his deft manipulation of his material.

Musaeus' Hero emerges as largely his own creation, owing little if anything to the original Hero, who was probably as colourless as she was beautiful, like Callimachus' Cydippe. Her characterization, as we have seen, is inconsistent, and the reason which she gives why she cannot be regularly and openly married to Leander is strangely ambiguous: 'it was not pleasing to my parents'.[52] In Ovid it is Leander's parents who would not approve if they knew,[53] and Hero who fears that she may not be good enough for him. Virgil's cryptic reference to Leander's *miseri parentes* suggests that it is Ovid who has kept, and Musaeus who has altered, the motivation of the original here. The folk-tale motif of the girl who lives, alone and inaccessible, in a tower,[54] he domesticates. We hear nothing of Hero's parents or family, but her situation is familiar, that of the housebound female such as Horace's Neobule (*C.* 3.12), with nothing to do but sit indoors and spin while she envies men their freedom to enjoy what the world outside has to offer.[55] The beginning of her letter – 'Euripidean in its simplicity and sentiment'[56] – is beautifully managed so as to bring out the contrast between the protagonists. Leander has all the action; it may at times be painfully exciting, but it is never dull. Hero can only love and suffer.[57] Her long introspective soliloquy, though

---

[52] 180 οὐ γὰρ ἐμοῖς τοκέεσσιν ἐπεύαδεν: the tense seems to suggest that they had already expressed disapproval, not of any marriage, but of this one to a stranger (Kost *ad loc.*).

[53] *Her.* 18.13–14. This again recalls Callimachus, in whom Acontius skulked into the countryside 'fearing to appear before his father' (Aristaen. 1.10.52–4; cf. Callim. fr. 72 Pf.). No such fears trouble Ovid's Acontius.

[54] Cf. Danae, Rapunzel, etc.; Thompson (S.) T. 381 'Imprisoned virgin to prevent knowledge of men ... Usually kept in a tower'.

[55] Comm. 19.9–14n., Kost on Musaeus 190.

[56] Palmer (1898) 468.

[57] Byron again (to Teresa Guiccioli, 25 April 1819): 'Nei distacchi chi parte soffre meno di chi reste. – La distrazione del viaggio, il cangiar' del' Sito, la Campagna – il Moto, forse anche la lontananza dissipa il pensier' ed allegerisce il cuore. – Ma Chi resta si trova circondato dalle medesime cose, domani è come jeri.' (In separation the one who goes away suffers less than the one who stays behind. The distraction of the journey, the change of scene, the land-

INTRODUCTION

occasional coincidences with Musaeus may point to this or that detail in the original, is substantially Ovid's own creation. This is a case-study in egotism versus self-abnegation in love. Hero does indeed love Leander more than he can possibly love her in return (19.17–18). What at the beginning of a love-letter may sound like a routine protestation turns out to be all too tragically accurate. Centrally placed in the triptych, Hero is the most vulnerable of Ovid's three heroines, and the most appealing.

(c) *Acontius and Cydippe*[58]

There is no doubt that Ovid's only source for this story was Callimachus' *Aetia*.[59] As he found it the tale ran as follows:

> Acontius, a beautiful boy from Ceos, fell in love with the equally beautiful Cydippe of Naxos on seeing her at a festival in Delos. He threw in the way of her nurse an apple[60] on which he had written 'I swear by Artemis to marry Acontius'. The nurse picked it up and being unable to read, asked Cydippe to read the inscription, which she did, aloud. She kept the incident to herself and returned to Naxos and to the marriage which her father had already arranged for her.[61] Meanwhile

---

scape, the movement, perhaps even the separation, distracts the mind and lightens the heart. But the one who stays behind is surrounded by the same things; tomorrow is like yesterday.) (*Letters and Journals*, ed. L. A. Marchand VI (London 1976) 115, 177.)

[58] For a fuller treatment of some of the points discussed here see Bopp (1966), Kenney (1970c).

[59] For an admirable brief account of this profoundly influential work and the use made of it by Roman poets see Hopkinson (1988) 85–91; for a text of frr. 67 and 75 and commentary on them see *ibid*. 16–19, 102–10.

[60] Or quince; see Comm. 20.9n. The apple motif, and indeed the plot of Callimachus' story, was appropriated and adapted by Nicander in his story of Hermochares and Ctesylla (Ant. Lib. 1.1 and Papathomopoulos *ad loc.*, Nic. fr. 50 Gow–Scholfield).

[61] If Cydippe was not already betrothed when Acontius first saw her, there was nothing to stop him from seeking her hand in the conventional manner. Ovid's handling of the plot surely requires that her betrothal was antecedent to her oath; otherwise Acontius could have claimed that his *pactum* was prior to his rival's (Kenney (1970c) 411 n. 44). That would have been worth most of his other arguments put together and obviated the need for a great deal of

Acontius had also gone home, where he betook himself into the countryside to lament his situation and carve her name on the trees. In Naxos a day was three times arranged for Cydippe's wedding, but three times she mysteriously fell ill so that it could not take place. The fourth time her father went to Delphi, where Apollo told him of the oath and advised him to fulfil it. So Acontius and Cydippe were married and founded the distinguished clan of the Acontiadae.[62]

In Callimachus' treatment such love-interest as the story possesses is centred on Acontius. He is a pretty boy, courted by youths and men (frr. 68, 69 Pf.). When Ovid's Acontius praises Cydippe's eyes as 'brighter than the stars', he appropriates language which in Callimachus had been used of himself (Comm. 20.55–6, 59nn.); in Callimachus the praise of Cydippe's beauty is relatively perfunctory.[63] When this spoiled minion falls for the beautiful and inaccessible Cydippe his existence is turned upside down: now he knows what it is like to be desperately and hopelessly in love.[64] Now the biter is bit, 'the archer feels the point of an arrow from another's bow'.[65] Having played the trick with the apple he can only return home to await events, which take their inevitable course without any further intervention from him. Of the monologue in which he lamented his frustration only two fragments survive (73, 74 Pf.), but from Aristaenetus

specious rhetoric – the very reason of course why the timing of events postulated here, whether Callimachus had been explicit about it or not, suited Ovid's book.

[62] Callim. frr. 67–75 Pf., supplemented by the epistolographer Aristaenetus (fifth century A.D.), *Epistulae* 1.10. The genealogical *aition* was of course the formal reason for the inclusion of the story in the *Aetia*.

[63] fr. 67.13–14 Pf.; on Aristaenetus' elaboration see Comm. 20.56n.

[64] This is the implication of his carving Κυδίππη καλή 'Cydippe is fair' on the trees (fr. 73 Pf.). He would have been used to seeing his own name written up on the walls by his admirers, Ἀκόντιος καλός. Now he is doing the writing and the name is a girl's (Kenney (1983) 48–9). There is an evidently heartfelt comment on a situation which must have been tolerably frequent in real life in a graffito from Stabiae: εἴ τις καλός γενόμενος | οὐκ ἔδωκε πυγίσαι· ἐκῖνος καλῆς | ἐρασθεὶς μὴ τύχοι βεινήμα|τος (i.e. *si quis formosus noluit paedicari et formosam amauerit, ne contingat ei fututio*). See for text and discussion D'Orsi (1968); πυγίσαι corr. C. P. Jones, *H.S.C.P.* 75 (1971) 82 n. 5: -ῖσαι D'O. (reference owed to Dr Jones, *per litt*.).

[65] Callim. fr. 70 Pf., Aristaen. 1.10.14–17; Comm. 20.231–2n.

and from Pfeiffer's calculation of the number of lost verses it is safe to infer that it formed a prominent element in Callimachus' treatment.[66] What was happening meanwhile to Cydippe back on Naxos is related with impersonal detachment (fr. 75.1–20 Pf.);[67] the dry 'a fourth time her father could stand it no longer' (fr. 75.20 Pf.) suggests annoyance at the thwarting of his plans at least as much as concern for his daughter's welfare. The denouement is sedulously divested of all drama: having heard Apollo's explanation, 'her father went back and questioned the girl herself, and she told him the whole story. And she was well again'. Immediately the spotlight is back on Acontius: 'For the rest, it is your business, Acontius, to go to Naxos ...'.[68] So much for Cydippe and her feelings.

Other Augustan poets had been content with a partial exploitation of the story.[69] Ovid, *more suo*, effected a wholesale transformation. He imposes dramatic unity by transferring the scene to Naxos. Acontius is made to follow Cydippe home and lay siege to her house after the manner of the elegiac *exclusus amator*. The querulous soliloquy delivered to an audience of trees becomes an aggressive presentation of his case direct to the girl in which great play is made with a familiar topic of contemporary rhetoric and advocacy (Comm. 21.133–50n.). The most drastic reshaping is in the article of characterization. In Callimachus both protagonists, after Acontius' one flash of inspiration and the ruse of the apple, play a passive role, waiting on events. Both are very young, Cydippe at her first appearance in the story a mere child, ὀλίγην ἔτι (fr. 67.9 Pf.). Ovid's Acontius is a man, determined, ruthless, obsessed, like Paris and Leander the personification almost to the point of mania of a single-minded drive that will risk anything, not only his own death but even that of the beloved, rather than not have her (see 20.35–6, 51–2, 21.183–8

---

[66] Aristaen. 1.10.56–79, Pfeiffer (1949) 501, Bopp (1966) 25–9. On the influence of this passage on other Augustan poets see Kenney (1983) 45–7.

[67] Cf. the blend of clinical precision and antiquarian scholarship in the comment on her attack of epilepsy (fr. 75.12–14 Pf.) – hardly empathetic writing.

[68] fr. 75.38–41 Pf. The abrupt switch to apostrophizing Acontius, who continues to be addressed for the rest of the episode, shows where for Callimachus the interest of the story lay.

[69] Above, n. 66.

and Comm. *ad locc.*). Cydippe's part in the drama as Ovid rewrites it is passive in so far as, sick and bedridden, she has no hope of influencing events except through pleas which she instinctively knows are bound to fail. The dramatic action takes place in her heart and mind. The outcome is preordained: in spite of herself she senses that she must in the end surrender to Acontius' relentless importunity. The emotional tension is maintained to the last; her resistance finally cracks only when she learns that Apollo as well as Diana is on Acontius' side (Comm. 21.233–4n.). This transformation of a young girl without a speaking part,[70] a *kophon prosopon*, into a tormented and articulate woman is one of Ovid's most remarkable creative feats. In the whole catalogue of his suffering and eloquent heroines Cydippe is the most unexpected and not the least impressive.

3. THE 'GEDICHTBUCH'

It has emerged incidentally from the preceding discussion that these pairs of epistles contrast with and complement each other in various ways. Such correspondences and contrasts are so pervasive that they cannot be regarded as accidental; they clearly form part of a planned overall design. The three stories, of very diverse provenance, were chosen and carefully tailored by Ovid both for their individual interest and as parts of a larger whole. All three turn on the issue of marriage and marriageability. Helen cannot marry Paris without abandoning Menelaus, Hero cannot marry Leander because of the disparity in their social status, Cydippe cannot marry Acontius until a previous engagement is cancelled.[71] In the outermost pairs the emphasis falls on these social barriers, Helen's marriage, Cydippe's prior betrothal, but the elegiac themes of physical separation, enhanced in both cases by proximity, frustrated longing, jealousy of the other man, also figure (16.215ff., 20.133ff.). In the central pair the emphasis falls on the physical barrier of the Hellespont (a 'heroic' version of

[70] Except, presumably, for the words of the oath, though we do not know for a fact that in Callimachus they were in direct speech (Comm. 21.107n.).

[71] It is interesting to see how Ovid rings the changes on the theme of parental opposition: in Paris' case actual but ineffective (16.119–20), in Leander's potential but only too terribly effective (18.13–14), in Cydippe's actual (though unwitting) and effective (20.157–60).

the river in *Am.* 3.6), but disparity of status is the underlying cause of that separation, gnawing always at Hero's confidence (19.99-100).

Similarly with the relationships themselves. Hero and Leander are already lovers, and such happiness as they are fated to enjoy lies in the past, as Hero ends by sensing (19.199-204). Paris and Helen look forward to a brilliant future, which the reader knows will turn out to be an endless vista of disaster. Acontius and Cydippe look forward with differing emotions – joyous anticipation on his part,[72] resignation on hers – to a marriage as to the success of which the reader is left to speculate. Romantic tragedy is framed by ironical comedy.

So too with the protagonists. All three men are in their various ways monomaniacs, blinkered by their obsessions. The vain egotistical Leander, madly pitting himself against elemental forces, is bracketed by Paris and Acontius, each invoking a goddess in support of a spurious or contested claim to a woman pledged to another.[73] Both Helen and Cydippe move in their replies from repudiation to acceptance; each betrays a readiness to yield, hardly concealed in Helen's case, latent but insistent in Cydippe's. Hero moves from impatience to resignation, but in her case too the die has been cast before she takes up her pen.

The structure is subtly underpinned by other linkages. In the outermost pairs the action which precipitates the whole subsequent chain of events is the throwing of an apple.[74] The theme of first meeting recurs in the letters of all three men, elegantly transformed in Leander's case to that of first rendezvous (16.135-6, 20.205-8; Comm. 18.55-104n.; cf. above, p. 5). In all three pairs the course of the psychological drama is significantly affected by intervention *ab extra*, a feature absent from the single *Heroides* except in the disputed case of Deianira.[75] Helen's wish to be taken by force anticipates and

---

[72] Cf. Callim. fr. 75.44-9 Pf.

[73] Comm. 20.49n. That the goddesses in question are those who between them destroyed another hero, Hippolytus, perhaps deserves a moment's thought. On Paris and Acontius cf. Hintermeier (1993) 122-5.

[74] This of course begs a question. The earliest surviving reference to the Apple of Discord is in Hyginus (Stinton (1965) 7 n. 1 = (1990) 22 n. 24). Whether this detail was part of the legend by Ovid's time we do not know.

[75] 17.239-40, 19.193-202; Comm. 21.233-4n.; cf. *Her.* 9.143-4 *scribenti nuntia uenit | fama* eqs. and Vessey (1969) 355.

20   INTRODUCTION

indeed subsumes in four verses the entire story of Cydippe (Comm. 17.185–8n.), to whom this is precisely what happens, though the force is only indirectly physical.

In sum, *Heroides* 16–21 offer another example, one not generally recognized as such, of that characteristically Augustan literary form which scholars, in default of a suitable English term, call the *Gedichtbuch*: a collection of poems designed to be read and appreciated both individually and as a literary whole, each poem or group of poems taking on added significance from the rest. It was a notable *tour de force* even for Ovid, whose entire poetic career can be summarized in the opening words of the *Metamorphoses*, *in noua fert animus*, to bring together and invest with this kind of literary unity three such disparate stories. As he treats them they constitute an extended exploration of the age-old paradox on which all writing about love is predicated, first formulated in the literary tradition by Sappho in her description of Eros as γλυκύπικρον ἀμάχανον ὄρπετον 'bittersweet uncontrollable beast' (fr. 130.2 L–P) – a paradox perhaps embodied in the poetry itself, 'the sweet witty soul of Ovid' casting its enchantment over the hopes and fears of these very disparate pairs of lovers. That the bitter, except in the memories of Hero and Leander, preponderates in these poems over the sweet is no more than we should expect. Hero says it all: *quis enim securus amauit?* 'I long ago come to the conclusion,' says Damon Runyon's Sam the Gonoph, 'that all life is six to five against.' What odds would he have given on Acontius and Cydippe living happily ever after?

4. STYLE AND AUTHORSHIP

'If [the double letters] are not from Ovid's pen, an *ignotus* has beaten him at his own game.'[76] The case has never been more pithily put. That these poems read more like Ovid than any other surviving Latin poet few would dispute. Diction, syntax, expression and versification conform in general to Ovidian usage.[77] However, in dis-

---

[76] Rand (1925) 27; for an eloquent eulogy of 20–21 see van Lennep (1812) 294–5.

[77] See Clark (1908), Tracy (1971). Clark deals adequately with most of the objections that had been raised to date, including many not selected for discussion here, and includes an extended comparative analysis of the metre of the double epistles. Tracy's discussion concentrates on expression and diction.

INTRODUCTION   21

cussions of authorship and authenticity only negative proofs are as a rule cogent. The question is whether the anomalies in metre, style and usage which scholars have purported to detect in these texts cast real doubts on Ovid's authorship. For the purposes of this edition the matter must be handled summarily.[78]

First one unique and striking positive anomaly must be noticed. The use of *nec* = *et* '*ne*' to introduce direct speech (Comm. 16.83, 21.222nn.) is not only seemingly peculiar to Ovid, but is otherwise found only in the *Metamorphoses* and the *Fasti*, the works on which, according to the most probable chronology, he was engaged contemporaneously with *Heroides* 16–21. An imitator who allowed himself an appreciable number of deviations (as severe critics account them) from strict Ovidian usage, but who identified and copied this specifically Ovidian but inconspicuous[79] idiom seems *a priori* an improbable figure.

The negative anomalies of substance[80] that merit consideration may be classified as follows:

(a) Metrical

(i) *Irregular elisions*   Those adduced at 17.97 and 19.29 are demonstrably not unOvidian; *certe ego* at 20.178 certainly is where it is found, but for other reasons cannot in any case be what the poet wrote (see Comm. *ad locc.*).[81]

(ii) *Monosyllables at the end of the hexameter*   See Comm. 16.71n.

(iii) *Polysyllabic pentameter endings*   In all the other elegiacs certainly written by Ovid before his exile he adheres rigidly to the rule that the pentameter should end with a disyllable. In *Heroides* 16–21 the rule is breached three times:

---

[78] A fuller treatment will appear in (edd.) J. N. Adams and R. G. Mayer, *The languages of Latin poetry* (forthcoming).

[79] It appears to have been unremarked or misunderstood until Loers explained it in 1829.

[80] A glance at a discussion such as that of Leyhausen will show why this qualification is in order; cf. below, n. 81. For salutary warnings against hypercriticism of this sort see Müller (1894) 29, Clark (1908) 123.

[81] Critics do not seem to be impelled to call in question the authorship of the *Ars Amatoria* because of the elision of the monosyllabic verb *dem* (3.2), unique, it would appear, not only in O. but in the whole corpus of Latin poetry from Cicero to Silius Italicus (Soubiran (1966) 402–3).

lis est cum forma magna pudicitiae (16.290)

nec sedeo duris torua superciliis (17.16)

unda simul miserum uitaque deseruit (19.202)

In the poems written in exile he allows himself more freedom, but the number of such endings is still comparatively small.[82] In the *Fasti* there are two only:

(gens) et circumfusis inuia fluminibus (5.582)

cantabat maestis tibia funeribus (6.660)

It is possible (but no more) that these verses were added by Ovid in the revision of the *Fasti* that he began but did not complete at Tomis.[83] Though it is not inconceivable that he also began to revise *Heroides* 16–21 there and added the three anomalous pentameters during such a revision, no arguments can be based on such insecure speculations. If the instances in the *Heroides* are to be defended it must be on literary grounds. Benedum's analysis of Ovid's practice in the *Tristia* and *Epistulae ex Ponto* (leaving book IV out of account) demonstrates convincingly that his use of such endings is governed by identifiable and defensible artistic motives. The general quality of the writing in the poems of exile precludes the assumption that this was a mere expedient to which he was driven by failing powers. The same applies to *Heroides* 16–21. Before Ovid we find both *pudicitia* and *supercilium* used to good artistic effect in this position, one to which such words perhaps had a built-in tendency to gravitate;[84] and if the 'rule' be forgotten the first two verses in question are entirely admirable, among Ovid's very best. A quadrisyllabic verb is in a different formal category. Ovid does not elsewhere use polysyllabic verbs in this position before his last work, the *Epistulae ex Ponto*.[85] Comparison with the usage of the other Latin elegists and Callimachus appears to point to this as a specifically neoteric manner-

---

[82] Words of three syllables 6 (of which 3 doubtful); four 29; five 12; six 1 (Platnauer (1951) 16–17). Compare Propertius with 166 of four and 21 of five syllables (*ibid.*).

[83] Courtney (1965) 63–4.

[84] Prop. 4.5.28, Catull. 67.46; cf. Benedum (1967) 136–7.

[85] Courtney (1965) 64.

INTRODUCTION 23

ism.[86] That Ovid should have resorted to it on this one occasion is perhaps surprising, but again in itself the verse and its conclusion need no apology. As the last word of Hero's desolating vision, symbolic of her lover's fate and, implicitly, of her own, *deseruit* carries a powerful emotional charge. What she has dreamed, the reader is invited to infer, has already happened. As she writes, her lover's life has left him and he her – not, as she feared, for another woman (19.95–104), but in reckless pursuit of an unattainable victory over untameable forces. The metrical anomaly is no casual aberration: it underlines the message of the word itself, the tragic isolation of this doomed heroine.

The real puzzle posed by these three verses is why there are only three of them. If Ovid had indeed come to feel that it might have been an artistic mistake to limit the choices open to him of words with which to end the pentameter by rigid conformity to the disyllable rule, the timidity of this experiment is surprising and uncharacteristic.[87] Caution of this order is not usually associated with the poet of whom it was said that he was too much in love with his own genius (Quint. *I.O.* 10.1.88). But if this is an imitator at work, are we most to admire his cunning, his prescience, or his restraint?

(b) Linguistic

(i) *Singularities* Singularity does not in itself constitute a significant negative anomaly.[88] None of the instances of linguistic singularities in the double epistles is any more out of the way than, for instance, *carendus* (1.50) or *reuertendi liber* (1.80) (see Knox *ad locc.*). There is admittedly no very obvious reason why Ovid, who uses the word *causa* some 300 times, should have refrained from using the common idiom *causa* (abl.) + genitive or possessive adjective except in Acon-

[86] Ratios of verbal forms to polysyllabic words at the end of the pentameter (editor's figures): Propertius 3.17%, Tibullus 13%, Catullus 23.4%; Callimachus, *Epigrams* 34.3%, *Hymns* 22.8% (counting participial forms). Cf. Benedum (1967) 137–8.

[87] If it was a mistake, Propertius erred too: from 36% in book I the proportion of polysyllabic endings declined in book IV to 1% (Platnauer (1951) 17).

[88] Cf. above, n. 81.

tius' letter (20.108, 198) – but equally there is no very obvious reason why he should not have. The same applies to the fact that of the forty-four instances of the word *cor* in his works, one only (17.102) is of the (classical and well-attested) sense 'intelligence', 'taste', 'discrimination'. The fact that the phrase *susurrare de aliquo* = 'whisper about somebody' seemingly occurs in the whole corpus of Latin literature only at 19.19,[89] if true, speaks for rather than against Ovidian authorship. The phrase is in itself good and appropriate; *susurro* is in any case rare in poetry, but that Ovid should have extended its range of meaning in this way betokens only a readiness, not confined to him, to experiment with his own language. That is how poetic idiom develops: *sic Latiae creuit facundia linguae*.[90] There is no logic in insisting that a writer is not allowed to do anything unless he does it at least twice.

(ii) *Loose writing* Lachmann complained of a certain diffuseness of style and repetitiveness in these epistles, and there is some substance in the charge.[91] It is certainly noteworthy that, for instance, the words *mora*, *uia* and *unda* each ends a line in Hero's letter no fewer than five times.[92] On the other hand, given that Leander's inability to make his way to her across the sea is what the letter is all about, the fact is not altogether surprising. It is, perhaps, less easy to shrug off the occurrence of four out of the five instances of *unda* in a space of no more than twenty verses (Comm. 19.189n.). Other critics have drawn attention to certain phrases, innocuous in themselves but obtrusively (it is said) frequent: *quod amas/ames* = 'the beloved'; *ut nunc est* = 'as now appears'; *si nescis* = 'let me tell you'.[93] As in the case of monosyllables at the end of the hexameter (above, (*a*) (ii)), each individual instance is natural and appropriate (Comm. 16.50, 85, 246nn.). The same may be said of syntactical phenomena such as the limiting or stipulative use of *ut* ... *sic* and *sic* ... *ut/ne* clauses or *a* = 'after'.

---

[89] Leyhausen (1893) 47.

[90] For other cases in point see Comm. 16.244; 17.203; 18.169; 19.14, 55; 20.99; 21.135, 178, 181nn. Some Ovidian singularities are rather Virgilianisms: see e.g. Comm. 16.57–8, 177, 21.204nn.

[91] See e.g. Comm. 16.17, 23, 18.183nn.

[92] Leyhausen (1898) 52–3.

[93] See Palmer (1898) 436–7. His objection to *iners* is simply inept (Comm. 16.314n.). Cf. Comm. 17.63, 67nn.

INTRODUCTION   25

(iii) *Prosaic, technical and archaic diction and expression* Here it will be sufficient to list the apparent instances and refer to the Commentary for discussion.[94] This is the largest class of ostensible anomalies in the double letters, but as with those noted above ((*b*) (ii)), no single case invites substantial misgivings. Some of these expressions, especially in the letters of Acontius and Cydippe, reflect the kinship of the double letters to *controversiae* (above, §1).

Do these phenomena add up to a case for denying these brilliant poems to Ovid? Is an imitator of such high technical competence, general stylistic consistency, emotional power, lively humour, empathetic sensibility, and unpredictable invention, practising his art on this ample scale, a plausible figure?[95] Nothing in the catalogue discussed above excludes the simple hypothesis advanced by Louis Purser in his modest dissenting judgement from Palmer's condemnation: 'They probably formed a separate volume ... written some years after the others, when Ovid was not so punctilious with regard to his metre as he was in his earlier works, and when he had acquired a greater diffuseness of style'.[96] To this eminently sensible suggestion a rider must be added. One feature not yet mentioned cannot be easily explained away. The anomalous length of Paris' epistle seriously unbalances the otherwise elegant structure of the *Gedichtbuch*. The simple expedient of restoring the balance by pruning it of 106 of its 378 verses by declaring lines 39–144 spurious will not wash.[97] However, the fact and the other phenomena reviewed above are at least consistent with, even if they do not positively enforce, the hypothesis that our text of *Heroides* 16–21 is a draft which at the time of Ovid's exile still lacked his final revision and which was never published in his lifetime.[98] This is a more economical solution than that of (to adapt Max Beerbohm's witticism) 'those incomparable poets

[94] Comm. 16.57–8, 105, 128; 17.29, 37, 69, 127, 165 (cf. above, (ii)), 183, 194, 206, 213; 18.169, 181–2 (the couplet however is almost certainly not by O.); 19.10, 70; 20.29, 36, 74, 127–8, 177–8 (*s.v.l.*), 242; 21.133, 159–60nn.
[95] Cf. Kenney (1979) 430–1.
[96] Purser *ap.* Palmer (1898) xxxii.
[97] It is not the case that '16.39–144 can be bracketed as an interpolation with no ill effect on 16 as a whole' (Tarrant (1983) 271): see Kenney (1979) 397–417.
[98] Cf. Kenney (1995) 200. On the dating of 16–21 the most recent discussion is that of Hintermeier (1993) 190–5.

26   INTRODUCTION

Ovid'. That does not necessarily make it true or even uniquely plausible, and the literary historian must always be uneasily conscious of the vast gaps in the record and the dangers of arguments from silence. Nevertheless there is still much virtue in Occam's Razor: *Magni poetae non sunt multiplicandi praeter necessitatem.*

5. TEXT AND TRANSMISSION[99]

Heroides 1–14, 16–21 have come down to us in a single corpus,[100] and from the evidence now available it is impossible to reconstruct the circumstances of their original publication and transmission in the classical period. Our text goes back to an ancient MS written in capital script which was discovered and copied in the Carolingian period. Of its Carolingian descendants one only survives, Parisinus
P Latinus 8242 (P), written at Corbie in the late ninth century.[101] It lacks 16.39–144 and in all probability originally lacked 21.147–250, but it now ends at 20.175. Two others were evidently still in existence in the fifteenth century. One was a forebear both of P and of a small group of fifteenth-century MSS and editions which are our only
G_u authority for the text of 21.15–146: Wolfenbüttel Gudeanus 297 (G_u)
ρ and the editions of Sweynheim and Pannartz (Rome 1471) (ρ) and
ε Jacobus Rubeus (Venice 1474) (ε).[102] From a second is derived our only authority for the text of 16.39–144 and 21.147–250, the edition of
π Stephanus Corallus (Parma 1477) (π). The rest of the surviving MSS, some 200 in number, which lack both 16.39–144 and 21.15–250, descend from a copy from which both these passages had been lost.[103]

---

[99] The fundamental discussion is that of Dörrie (1960), (1972); see also Kenney (1961), Tarrant (1983).

[100] The non-Ovidian *Epistula Sapphus*, conventionally numbered as 15, is separately transmitted. It was installed between 14 and 16 by Daniel Heinsius in his edition (Leiden 1629). See Tarrant (1983) 272–3, Knox (1995) 36–7.

[101] Bischoff (1961) 53.

[102] Par. Lat. 7997 and Laur. 36.2 are included in this group by Dörrie, but seem to have no independent authority and are ignored in this edition. Cf. Tarrant (1983) 270 n. 8.

[103] Outline stemma (family tree of the MSS) at Kenney (1961) 484. This may be misleading in one respect. A rediscovered text in an unfamiliar script would as a rule be copied from the ancient exemplar only once. We must postulate an intermediary Carolingian MS as the archetype, the common source of the later tradition.

INTRODUCTION

Ovid was a popular author in the Middle Ages, and his copyists freely imported into the text readings from sources other than the exemplars immediately before them, which themselves increasingly came to be liberally embellished with variants. This is the process known to scholars as 'contamination'. Even P, the oldest and best witness, is by no means entirely exempt from its effects; and the bulk of the later MSS, dating from the eleventh century onwards, must be treated by the editor collectively, as a reservoir of readings to be evaluated on their individual merits. 'All inherently plausible readings, whatever their source, must be taken seriously, and sense and usage are the only sure criteria for deciding among them.'[104] A handful of the earlier medieval MSS stand out from the rest: the second hand of P (eleventh century) (p);[105] Wolfenbüttel Extrav. 260 (twelfth century) (G);[106] and (occasionally cited in this edition) the excerpts preserved in Vienna Ser. nov. 107 (twelfth century) (W). A few renderings are quoted from the Greek prose version of the fourteenth-century scholar Maximus Planudes. For the most part later MSS are cited en bloc: ω = all or a majority, ς = a minority. On the authenticity and authorship of the parts of the text transmitted only in π see the full discussion in Kenney (1979). The critical notes appended to the text are highly selective, registering for the most part only those passages where there is room for a sensible difference of opinion as to what Ovid wrote.

p
G
W

Plan.
ω, ς

---

[104] Tarrant (1983) 270.
[105] Unfortunately the activities of this corrector all too frequently obscure the original reading of P.
[106] G is in poor physical shape, and much of its text in these epistles is now almost illegible.

P. OVIDI NASONIS
HEROIDVM EPISTVLAE
XVI–XXI

P. OVIDI NASONIS
HEROIDVM EPISTVLAE

XVI
PARIS HELENAE

Hanc tibi Priamides mitto, Ledaea, salutem
   quae tribui sola te mihi dante potest.

eloquar, an flammae non est opus indice notae
   et plus quam uellem iam meus extat amor?
ille quidem lateat malim, dum tempora dentur   5
   laetitiae mixtos non habitura metus.
sed male dissimulo: quis enim celauerit ignem
   lumine qui semper proditur ipse suo?
si tamen expectas uocem quoque rebus ut addam,
   uror: habes animi nuntia uerba mei.   10
parce, precor, fasso nec uultu cetera duro
   perlege sed formae conueniente tuae.

iamdudum gratum est quod epistula nostra recepta
   spem facit hoc recipi me quoque posse modo.
quae rata sit nec te frustra promiserit opto,   15
   hoc mihi quae suasit mater Amoris iter.
namque ego diuino monitu, ne nescia pecces,
   aduehor, et coepto non leue numen adest.
praemia magna quidem sed non indebita posco:
   pollicita est thalamo te Cytherea meo.   20
hac duce Sigeo dubias a litore feci
   longa Phereclea per freta puppe uias.
illa dedit faciles auras uentosque secundos:
   in mare nimirum ius habet orta mari.
perstet et ut pelagi sic pectoris adiuuet aestum,   25
   deferat in portus et mea uota suos.

32   P. OVIDI NASONIS

attulimus flammas, non hic inuenimus, illas:
　　hae mihi tam longae causa fuere uiae.
nam neque tristis hiems neque nos huc appulit error:
　　Taenaris est classi terra petita meae.　　　　　　　　　　30
nec me crede fretum merces portante carina
　　findere: quas habeo, di tueantur opes.
nec uenio Graias ueluti spectator ad urbes:
　　oppida sunt regni diuitiora mei.
te peto, quam pepigit lecto Venus aurea nostro;　　　　　　35
　　te prius optaui quam mihi nota fores;
ante tuos animo uidi quam lumine uultus;
　　prima tulit uulnus nuntia fama mihi.

nec tamen est mirum si †sicut opporteat arcu†
　　missilibus telis eminus ictus amo.　　　　　　　　　　　40
sic placuit fatis: quae ne conuellere temptes,
　　accipe cum uera dicta relata fide.
matris adhuc utero partu remorante tenebar;
　　iam grauidus iusto pondere uenter erat.
illa sibi ingentem uisa est sub imagine somni　　　　　　　　45
　　flammiferam pleno reddere uentre facem.
territa consurgit metuendaque noctis opacae
　　uisa seni Priamo, uatibus ille refert.
arsurum Paridis uates canit Ilion igni:
　　pectoris, ut nunc est, fax fuit illa mei.　　　　　　　　　　50
　　　*　　*　　*　　*　　*　　*　　*
forma uigorque animi, quamuis de plebe uidebar,
　　indicium tectae nobilitatis erat.

est locus in mediae nemorosis uallibus Idae
　　deuius et piceis ilicibusque frequens,

xvi 38 tulit uulnus *Housman*: dedit u. *dubitanter Kenney*: fuit uultus *codd.*
mihi *Kenney*: tui *codd.*　　39–144 *tradidit sola* π　　39 sic cum polleat arcus
Housman　　49 arsuram *Heinsius; cf.* 17.240　　*post* 50 *lacunam indicauit Scaliger*

qui nec ouis placidae nec amantis saxa capellae 55
  nec patulo tardae carpitur ore bouis.
hinc ego Dardaniae muros excelsaque tecta
  et freta prospiciens arbore nixus eram.
ecce pedum pulsu uisa est mihi terra moueri;
  uera loquar, ueri uix habitura fidem. 60
constitit ante oculos actus uelocibus alis
  Atlantis magni Pleionesque nepos
(fas uidisse fuit, fas sit mihi uisa referre),
  inque dei digitis aurea uirga fuit.
tresque simul diuae, Venus et cum Pallade Iuno, 65
  graminibus teneros imposuere pedes.
obstipui, gelidusque comas erexerat horror,
  cum mihi 'pone metum' nuntius ales ait;
'arbiter es formae: certamina siste dearum,
  uincere quae forma digna sit una duas.' 70
neue recusarem, uerbis Iouis imperat et se
  protinus aetheria tollit in astra uia.
mens mea conualuit subitoque audacia uenit,
  nec timui uultu quamque notare meo.
uincere erant omnes dignae, iudexque querebar 75
  non omnes causam posse tenere suam.
sed tamen ex illis iam tunc magis una placebat,
  hanc esse ut scires unde moueatur amor.
tantaque uincendi cura est, ingentibus ardent
  iudicium donis sollicitare meum. 80
regna Iouis coniunx, uirtutem filia iactat;
  ipse potens dubito fortis an esse uelim.
dulce Venus risit 'nec te, Pari, munera tangant
  utraque suspensi plena timoris' ait;
'nos dabimus quod ames, et pulchrae filia Ledae 85
  ibit in amplexus pulchrior ipsa tuos.'

60 ueri *uel* ueram *Heinsius*: uero π   76 posse tenere *Francius*: uincere posse π   86 ipsa *Bersmanni margo*: illa π

P. OVIDI NASONIS

dixit et ex aequo donis formaque probatis
   uictorem caelo rettulit illa pedem.

interea sero uersis ad prospera fatis
   regius agnoscor per rata signa puer.   90
laeta domus nato post tempora longa recepto est,
   addit et ad festos hunc quoque Troia diem.
utque ego te cupio, sic me cupiere puellae:
   multarum uotum sola tenere potes.
nec tantum regum natae petiere ducumque,   95
   sed nymphis etiam curaque amorque fui.
†quas super oenonem facies mutarer in orbem†
   nec Priamo est a te dignior ulla nurus.
sed mihi cunctarum subeunt fastidia postquam
   coniugii spes est, Tyndari, facta tui.   100
te uigilans oculis animi, te nocte uidebam,
   lumina cum placido uicta sopore iacent.
quid faceres praesens, quae nondum uisa placebas?
   ardebam, quamuis hic procul ignis erat.

nec potui debere mihi spem longius istam,   105
   caerulea peterem quin mea uota uia.
Troica caeduntur Phrygia pineta securi
   quaeque erat aequoreis utilis arbor aquis;
ardua proceris spoliantur Gargara siluis,
   innumerasque mihi longa dat Ida trabes;   110
fundatura citas flectuntur robora naues,
   texitur et costis panda carina suis.
addimus antemnas et uela sequentia malo,
   accipit et pictos puppis adunca deos;
qua tamen ipse uehar, comitata Cupidine paruo   115
   sponsor coniugii stat dea ficta tui.

---

87 probatis *Heinsius*: probata π   89 sero *Wakker*: credo π   101 animi *Bentley*: animo π   103 faceres *Heinsius*: facies π   115 uehar *Bentley*: uehor π   116 ficta *Palmer*: picta π   tui *Naugerius*: sui π

HEROIDVM EPISTVLA XVI

imposita est factae postquam manus ultima classi,
   protinus Aegaeis ire iubemus aquis.
at pater et genetrix inhibent mea uota rogando
   propositumque pia uoce morantur iter; 120
et soror effusis ut erat Cassandra capillis,
   cum uellent nostrae iam dare uela rates,
'quo ruis?' exclamat; 'referes incendia tecum:
   quanta per has nescis flamma petatur aquas.'
uera fuit uates: dictos inuenimus ignes, 125
   et ferus in molli pectore flagrat amor.

portubus egredior uentisque ferentibus usus
   applicor in terras, Oebali nympha, tuas.
excipit hospitio uir me tuus: hoc quoque factum
   non sine consilio numinibusque deum. 130
ille quidem ostendit quicquid Lacedaemone tota
   ostendi dignum conspicuumque fuit;
sed mihi laudatam cupienti cernere formam
   lumina nil aliud quo caperentur erat.
ut uidi, obstipui praecordiaque intima sensi 135
   attonitus curis intumuisse nouis.
his similes uultus, quantum reminiscor, habebat
   uenit in arbitrium cum Cytherea meum.
si tu uenisses pariter certamen in illud,
   in dubio Veneris palma futura fuit. 140
magna quidem de te rumor praeconia fecit,
   nullaque de facie nescia terra tua est,
nec tibi par usquam Phrygiae nec solis ab ortu

   *   *   *   *   *   *   *

inter formosas altera nomen habet.
credis et hoc nobis? minor est tua gloria uero, 145
   famaque de forma paene maligna tua est.

118 iubemus *uel* iubetur *uel* iubemur *Kenney*: iubebat π   120 pia *Heinsius*: uiae π   128 *fort.* en terris ... tuis   136 intumuisse *D. Heinsius*: intonuisse π: intremuisse *Francius*   143 par ... Phrygiae *Naugerius*: per ... phrygia π   *post hunc u. distichon excidisse ueri simile est*

plus hic inuenio quam quod promiserat illa,
　et tua materia gloria uicta sua est.
ergo arsit merito qui nouerat omnia Theseus,
　et uisa es tanto digna rapina uiro, 150
more tuae gentis nitida dum nuda palaestra
　ludis et es nudis femina mixta uiris.
quod rapuit laudo, miror quod reddidit umquam:
　tam bona constanter praeda tenenda fuit.
ante recessisset caput hoc ceruice cruenta 155
　quam tu de thalamis abstraherere meis.
tene manus umquam nostrae dimittere uellent,
　tene meo paterer uiuus abire sinu?
si reddenda fores, aliquid tamen ante tulissem,
　nec Venus ex toto nostra fuisset iners. 160
uel tua uirginitas esset libata uel illud
　quod poterat salua uirginitate rapi.

da modo te, quae sit Paridis constantia nosces:
　flamma rogi flammas finiet una meas.
praeposui regnis ego te, quae maxima quondam 165
　pollicita est nobis nupta sororque Iouis,
dumque tuo possem circumdare bracchia collo,
　contempta est uirtus Pallade dante mihi.
nec piget aut umquam stulte legisse uidebor:
　permanet in uoto mens mea firma suo. 170
spem modo ne nostram fieri patiare caducam
　deprecor, o tanto digna labore peti.
non ego coniugium generosae degener opto,
　nec mea, crede mihi, turpiter uxor eris.
Pliada, si quaeres, in nostra gente Iouemque 175
　inuenies, medios ut taceamus auos.
regna parens Asiae, qua nulla beatior ora est,
　finibus immensis uix obeunda tenet.

177 regna *Bentley*: sceptra *codd.*　　Asiam *Merchant*

innumeras urbes atque aurea tecta uidebis
 quaeque suos dicas templa decere deos. 180
Ilion aspicies firmataque turribus altis
 moenia Phoebeae structa canore lyrae.
quid tibi de turba narrem numeroque uirorum?
 uix populum tellus sustinet illa suum.
occurrent denso tibi Troades agmine matres, 185
 nec capient Phrygias atria nostra nurus.
o quotiens dices 'quam pauper Achaia nostra est'!
 una domus quaeuis urbis habebit opes.
nec mihi fas fuerit Sparten contemnere uestram:
 in qua tu nata es, terra beata mihi est. 190
parca sed est Sparte, tu cultu diuite digna;
 ad talem formam non facit iste locus.
hanc faciem largis sine fine paratibus uti
 deliciisque decet luxuriare nouis.
cum uideas cultus nostra de gente uirorum, 195
 qualem Dardanias credis habere nurus?

da modo te facilem nec dedignare maritum
 rure Therapnaeo nata puella Phrygem.
Phryx erat et nostro genitus de sanguine, qui nunc
 cum dis potando nectare miscet aquas; 200
Phryx erat Aurorae coniunx, tamen abstulit illum
 extremum noctis quae dea finit iter;
Phryx etiam Anchises, uolucrum cui mater Amorum
 gaudet in Idaeis concubuisse iugis.
nec puto collatis forma Menelaus et armis 205
 iudice te nobis anteferendus erit.
non dabimus certe socerum tibi clara fugantem
 lumina, qui trepidos a dape uertat equos;
nec Priamo pater est soceri de caede cruentus
 et qui Myrtoas crimine signat aquas; 210
nec proauo Stygia nostro captantur in unda
 poma nec in mediis quaeritur umor aquis.

[quid tamen hoc refert si te tenet ortus ab illis?
   cogitur huic domui Iuppiter esse socer.]

heu facinus! totis indignus noctibus ille   215
   te tenet amplexu perfruiturque tuo.
at mihi conspiceris posita uix denique mensa,
   multaque quae laedant hoc quoque tempus habet.
hostibus eueniant conuiuia talia nostris,
   experior posito qualia saepe mero.   220
paenitet hospitii cum me spectante lacertos
   imponit collo rusticus iste tuo.
rumpor et inuideo (quianam non omnia narro?),
   membra superiecta cum tua ueste fouet.
oscula cum uero coram non dura daretis,   225
   ante oculos posui pocula sumpta meos.
lumina demitto cum te tenet artius ille,
   crescit et inuito lentus in ore cibus.
saepe dedi gemitus et te, lasciua, notaui
   in gemitu risum uix tenuisse meo.   230
saepe mero uolui flammam compescere, at illa
   creuit, et ebrietas ignis in igne fuit;
multaque ne uideam uersa ceruice recumbo,
   sed reuocas oculos protinus ipsa meos.

quid faciam dubito: dolor est meus illa uidere,   235
   sed dolor a facie maior abesse tua.
qua licet et possum, luctor celare furorem,
   sed tamen apparet dissimulatus amor.
nec tibi uerba damus: sentis mea uulnera, sentis,
   atque utinam soli sint ea nota tibi.   240

213–14 *secl. Reeve*   214 creditur *Hollis, Watt*   223 ab inuidia *Oudendorp*: et inuidia *Damsté*   quianam non *Kenney*: quidn∗∗ *P*: quid ni tamen *W*: quid ne tamen *Gς*: quid non tamen *ω*: quid nam t., quid nunc t., quid enim non ς   narro *Kenney*: narr∗ *P*: narrem *cett.*

HEROIDVM EPISTVLA XVI

a quotiens lacrimis uenientibus ora reflexi
   ne causam fletus quaereret ille mei!
a quotiens aliquem narraui potus amorem,
   ad uultus referens singula uerba tuos,
indiciumque mei sub ficto nomine feci!   245
   ille ego, si nescis, uerus amator eram.
quin etiam, ut possem uerbis petulantius uti,
   non semel ebrietas est simulata mihi.
prodita sunt, memini, tunica tua pectora laxa
   atque oculis aditum nuda dedere meis,   250
pectora uel puris niuibus uel lacte tuamue
   complexo matrem candidiora Ioue:
dum stupeo uisis (nam pocula forte tenebam),
   tortilis a digitis excidit ansa meis.
oscula si natae dederas, ego protinus illa   255
   Hermiones tenero laetus ab ore tuli.
et modo cantabam ueteres resupinus amores
   et modo per nutum signa tegenda dabam.

at comitum primas, Clymenen Aethranque, tuarum
   ausus sum blandis nuper adire sonis;   260
quae mihi non aliud quam formidare locutae
   orantis medias deseruere preces.
di facerent pretium magni certaminis esses
   teque suo posset uictor habere toro,
ut tulit Hippomenes Schoeneida praemia cursus,   265
   uenit ut in Phrygios Hippodamia sinus,
ut ferus Alcides Acheloia cornua fregit
   dum petit amplexus, Deianira, tuos.
nostra per has leges audacia fortiter isset
   teque mei scires esse laboris opus.   270

---

251 tuamue *Francius*: -que *codd.*   259 at ... Aethranque *Kenney*: et ... -amque *codd.*

nunc mihi nil superest nisi te, formosa, precari
  amplectique tuos, si patiare, pedes.
o decus, o praesens geminorum gloria fratrum,
  o Ioue digna uiro, ni Ioue nata fores,
aut ego Sigeos repetam te coniuge portus   275
  aut hic Taenaria contegar exul humo.
non mea sunt summa leuiter destricta sagitta
  pectora; descendit uulnus ad ossa meum.
hoc mihi (nam repeto fore ut a caeleste sagitta
  figar) erat uerax uaticinata soror.   280
parce datum fatis, Helene, contemnere amorem:
  sic habeas faciles in tua uota deos.

multa quidem subeunt, sed coram ut plura loquamur
  excipe me lecto nocte silente tuo.
an pudet et metuis Venerem temerare maritam   285
  castaque legitimi fallere iura tori?
a nimium simplex Helene, ne rustica dicam!
  hanc faciem culpa posse carere putas?
aut faciem mutes aut sis non dura necesse est:
  lis est cum forma magna pudicitiae.   290
Iuppiter his gaudet, gaudet Venus aurea furtis:
  haec tibi nempe patrem furta dedere Iouem.
uix fieri, si sunt uires in semine morum,
  et Iouis et Ledae filia casta potest.
casta tamen tum sis, cum te mea Troia tenebit,   295
  et tua sim quaeso crimina solus ego;
nunc ea peccemus quae corriget hora iugalis,
  si modo promisit non mihi uana Venus.

ipse tibi hoc suadet rebus non uoce maritus,
  neue sui furtis hospitis obstet, abest.   300

279–80 nam ... figar παρενθετικῶς *Ehwald*   280 figerer est *Heinsius*   294 potest ς: potes *Gω*: *de P incert.*   299 ipse tibi hoc *rec. unus sicut coni. Francius*: sed tibi hoc *P*ς: sed tibi et hoc *Gω*: hoc etiam *Diggle*

HEROIDVM EPISTVLA XVI

non habuit tempus quo Cresia regna uideret
   aptius: o mira calliditate uirum!
†esset et† 'Idaei mando tibi' dixit iturus
   'curam pro nobis hospitis, uxor, agas.'
neglegis absentis, testor, mandata mariti: 305
   cura tibi non est hospitis ulla tui.
huncine tu speras hominem sine pectore dotes
   posse satis formae, Tyndari, nosse tuae?
falleris: ignorat nec, si bona magna putaret
   quae tenet, externo crederet ille uiro. 310
ut te nec mea uox nec te meus incitet ardor,
   cogimur ipsius commoditate frui,
aut erimus stulti, sicut superemus et ipsum,
   si tam securum tempus abibit iners.
paene suis ad te manibus deducit amantem: 315
   utere mandantis simplicitate uiri.
sola iaces uiduo tam longa nocte cubili,
   in uiduo iaceo solus et ipse toro.
te mihi meque tibi communia gaudia iungant:
   candidior medio nox erit illa die. 320
tunc ego iurabo quaeuis tibi numina meque
   astringam uerbis in tua iura tuis;
tunc ego, si non est fallax fiducia nostri,
   efficiam praesens ut mea regna petas.

si pudet, et metuis ne me uideare secuta, 325
   ipse reus sine te criminis huius ero.
nam sequar Aegidae factum fratrumque tuorum:
   exemplo tangi num propiore potes?

---

303 esset et *P*ς: esset ut *G*: iuit et ς: ipse abiit ς: ipse et 'ut ...' *Heyworth*: 'res et
ut ...' *Madvig*   322 in tua iura ς: in tua iussa *G*ς: in sacra iura *p*ς
tuis ς: meis *pG*ω   *de P incert.*   323 nostri ς: nostra *PG*ω   328 num *Heinsius*:
non *codd.*

te rapuit Theseus, geminas Leucippidas illi:
  quartus in exemplis annumerabor ego. 330
Troica classis adest armis instructa uirisque;
  iam facient celeres remus et aura uias.
ibis Dardanias ingens regina per urbes
  teque nouam credet uulgus adesse deam,
quaque feres gressus, adolebunt cinnama flammae 335
  caesaque sanguineam uictima planget humum.
dona pater fratresque et cum genetrice sorores
  Iliadesque omnes totaque Troia dabit.
ei mihi, pars a me uix dicitur ulla futuri:
  plura feres quam quae littera nostra refert. 340

nec tu rapta time ne nos fera bella sequantur,
  concitet et uires Graecia magna suas.
tot prius abductis ecqua est repetita per arma?
  crede mihi, uanos res habet ista metus.
nomine ceperunt Aquilonis Erecthida Thraces, 345
  et tuta a bello Bistonis ora fuit.
Phasida puppe noua uexit Pagasaeus Iason,
  laesa neque est Colcha Thessala terra manu.
te quoque qui rapuit, rapuit Minoida Theseus;
  nulla tamen Minos Cretas ad arma uocat. 350
terror in his ipso maior solet esse periclo,
  quaeque timere licet, pertimuisse pudet.

finge tamen, si uis, ingens consurgere bellum:
  et mihi sunt uires et mea tela nocent.
nec minor est Asiae quam uestrae copia terrae; 355
  illa uiris diues, diues abundat equis.
nec plus Atrides animi Menelaus habebit
  quam Paris aut armis anteferendus erit.

352 quaeque ς: quaque Pω: quodque Gς   licet ς: libet PGω

paene puer caesis abducta armenta recepi
  hostibus et causam nominis inde tuli;   360
paene puer iuuenes uario certamine uici,
  in quibus Ilioneus Deiphobusque fuit.
neue putes non me nisi comminus esse timendum,
  figitur in iusso nostra sagitta loco.
num potes haec illi primae dare facta iuuentae?   365
  instruere Atriden num potes arte mea?
omnia si dederis, numquid dabis Hectora fratrem?
  unus is innumeri militis instar erit.
quid ualeam nescis, et te mea robora fallunt;
  ignoras cui sis nupta futura uiro.   370

aut igitur nullo belli repetere tumultu
  aut cedent Marti Dorica castra meo.
nec tamen indigner pro tanta sumere ferrum
  coniuge: certamen praemia magna mouent.
tu quoque, si de te totus contenderit orbis,   375
  nomen ab aeterna posteritate feres.
spe modo non timida dis hinc egressa secundis
  exige cum plena munera pacta fide.

XVII
HELENA PARIDI

* * * * * * *

nunc oculos tua cum uiolarit epistula nostros,
  non rescribendi gloria uisa leuis.
ausus es hospitii temeratis aduena sacris
  legitimam nuptae sollicitare fidem.
scilicet idcirco uentosa per aequora uectum   5
  excepit portu Taenaris ora suo,

xvii 1 *ante hunc u. distichon excidisse ueri simile est*

nec tibi, diuersa quamuis e gente uenires,
    oppositas habuit regia nostra fores.
esset ut officii merces iniuria tanti,
    qui sic intrabas, hospes an hostis eras?   10

nec dubito quin haec, cum sit tam iusta, uocetur
    rustica iudicio nostra querela tuo.
rustica sim sane, dum non oblita pudoris
    dumque tenor uitae sit sine labe meae.
si non est ficto tristis mihi uultus in ore   15
    nec sedeo duris torua superciliis,
fama tamen clara est et adhuc sine crimine uixi,
    et laudem de me nullus adulter habet.
quo magis admiror quae sit fiducia coepti
    spemque tori dederit quae tibi causa mei.   20
an, quia uim nobis Neptunius attulit heros,
    rapta semel uideor bis quoque digna rapi?
crimen erat nostrum si delenita fuissem;
    cum sim rapta, meum quid nisi nolle fuit?
non tamen ex facto fructum tulit ille petitum: 25
    excepto redii passa timore nihil.
oscula luctanti tantummodo pauca proteruus
    abstulit, ulterius nil habet ille mei.
quae tua nequitia est, non his contenta fuisset:
    di melius! similis non fuit ille tibi.   30
reddidit intactam minuitque modestia crimen,
    et iuuenem facti paenituisse patet.
Thesea paenituit, Paris ut succederet illi,
    ne quando nomen non sit in ore meum?

nec tamen irascor (quis enim succenset amanti?),   35
    si modo quem praefers non simulatur amor.

---

16 toruis dura *Bentley*   30 tibi *P (marg.)* ς: tui *P (text.) Gς*

HEROIDVM EPISTVLA XVII

hoc quoque enim dubito, non quo fiducia desit
  aut mea sit facies non bene nota mihi,
sed quia credulitas damno solet esse puellis
  uerbaque dicuntur uestra carere fide. 40
at peccant aliae matronaque rara pudica est:
  quid prohibet raris nomen inesse meum?
nam mea quod uisa est tibi mater idonea, cuius
  exemplo flecti me quoque posse putes,
matris in admisso falsa sub imagine lusae 45
  error inest: pluma tectus adulter erat.
nil ego, si peccem, possum nescisse, nec ullus
  error qui facti crimen obumbret erit.
illa bene errauit uitiumque auctore redemit:
  felix in culpa quo Ioue dicar ego? 50
quod genus et proauos et regia nomina iactas,
  clara satis domus haec nobilitate sua est.
Iuppiter ut soceri proauus taceatur et omne
  Tantalidae Pelopis Tyndareique decus,
dat mihi Leda Iouem cycno decepta parentem, 55
  quae falsam gremio credula fouit auem.
i nunc et Phrygiae late primordia gentis
  cumque suo Priamum Laomedonte refer.
quos ego suspicio, sed qui tibi gloria magna est
  quintus, is a nostro nomine primus erit. 60
sceptra tuae quamuis rear esse potentia Troiae,
  non tamen haec illis esse minora puto.
si iam diuitiis locus hic numeroque uirorum
  uincitur, at certe barbara terra tua est.
munera tanta quidem promittit epistula diues, 65
  ut possint ipsas illa mouere deas.
sed si iam uellem fines transire pudoris,
  tu melior culpae causa futurus eras.

37 quo ς: quod *PGω*   41 formosaque *Bentley*   42 quid *Heinsius*: qui *P*: quis *Gω*   51 quod ς: quid ς: et *pGω*: ea *P*: sed *Housman*   61 regna *Palmer*   troiae *P (marg.) G²ω*: terrae *P (text.) G¹*

aut ego perpetuo famam sine labe tenebo
  aut ego te potius quam tua dona sequar. 70
utque ea non sperno, sic acceptissima semper
  munera sunt, auctor quae pretiosa facit.
plus multo est quod amas, quod sum tibi causa laboris,
  quod per tam longas spes tua uenit aquas.

illa quoque, apposita quae nunc facis, improbe, mensa, 75
  quamuis experiar dissimulare, noto,
cum modo me spectas oculis, lasciue, proteruis,
  quos uix instantes lumina nostra ferunt,
et modo suspiras, modo pocula proxima nobis
  sumis quaque bibi tu quoque parte bibis. 80
a quotiens digitis, quotiens ego tecta notaui
  signa supercilio paene loquente dari,
et saepe extimui ne uir meus illa uideret,
  non satis occultis erubuique notis,
saepe uel exiguo uel nullo murmure dixi 85
  'nil pudet hunc', nec uox haec mea falsa fuit!
orbe quoque in mensae legi sub nomine nostro
  quod deducta mero littera fecit, AMO,
credere me tamen hoc oculo renuente negaui;
  ei mihi, iam didici sic ego posse loqui! 90
his ego blanditiis, si peccatura fuissem,
  flecterer, his poterant pectora nostra capi.
est quoque, confiteor, facies tibi rara, potestque
  uelle sub amplexus ire puella tuos.
altera sed potius felix sine crimine fiat 95
  quam cadat externo noster amore pudor.
disce meo exemplo formosis posse carere:
  est uirtus placitis abstinuisse bonis.
quam multos credis iuuenes optare quod optas?
  qui sapiant oculos an Paris unus habes? 100

69 tuebor *Palmer* (φυλάττω *Plan.*)   95 sed ω: uel *P*ς: *de G incert.*: sic *Kenney*

HEROIDVM EPISTVLA XVII

non tu plus cernis sed plus temerarius audes,
  nec tibi plus cordis sed nimis oris adest.

tunc ego te uellem celeri uenisse carina,
  cum mea uirginitas mille petita procis.
si te uidissem, primus de mille fuisses: 105
  iudicio ueniam uir dabit ipse meo.
ad possessa uenis praeceptaque gaudia serus:
  spes tua lenta fuit; quod petis alter habet.
ut tamen optarim fieri tua, Troice, coniunx,
  inuitam sic me nec Menelaus habet. 110
desine molle, precor, uerbis conuellere pectus
  neue mihi, quam te dicis amare, noce;
sed sine quam tribuit sortem Fortuna tueri
  nec spolium nostri turpe pudoris aue.

at Venus hoc pacta est, ut in altae uallibus Idae 115
  tres tibi se nudas exhibuere deae,
unaque cum regnum, belli daret altera laudem,
  'Tyndaridos coniunx' tertia dixit 'eris.'
credere uix equidem caelestia numina possum
  arbitrio formam supposuisse tuo. 120
utque sit hoc uerum, certe pars altera ficta est,
  iudicii pretium qua data dicor ego.
non est tanta mihi fiducia corporis ut me
  maxima teste dea dona fuisse putem.
contenta est oculis hominum mea forma probari; 125
  laudatrix Venus est inuidiosa mihi.
sed nihil infirmo, faueo quoque laudibus istis:
  nam mea uox quare quod cupit esse neget?
nec tu succense nimium mihi creditus aegre:
  tarda solet magnis rebus inesse fides. 130

109 optarim ... Troice *Bentley*: optarem ... troica *codd.*   114 nec] et
Reeve   aue *Palmer*: habe *codd.*   115 ut *Heinsius*: et *codd.*   119 numina *uet.*
edd.: corpora *codd.*   127–8 *secl. Bentley*   128 nam, mens, uox quare *eqs. Goold*

prima mea est igitur Veneri placuisse uoluptas,
 proxima me uisam praemia summa tibi
nec te Palladios nec te Iunonis honores
 auditis Helenae praeposuisse bonis.
ergo ego sum uirtus, ego sum tibi nobile regnum: 135
 ferrea sim, si non hoc ego pectus amem.
ferrea, crede mihi, non sum; sed amare repugno
 illum quem fieri uix puto posse meum.
quid bibulum curuo proscindere litus aratro
 spemque sequi coner quam locus ipse negat? 140
sum rudis ad Veneris furtum nullaque fidelem
 (di mihi sunt testes) lusimus arte uirum.
nunc quoque quod tacito mando mea uerba libello,
 fungitur officio littera nostra nouo.
felices quibus usus adest: ego nescia rerum 145
 difficilem culpae suspicor esse uiam.

ipse malo metus est: iam nunc confundor et omnes
 in nostris oculos uultibus esse reor.
nec reor hoc falso: sensi mala murmura uulgi,
 et quasdam uoces rettulit Aethra mihi. 150
at tu dissimula, nisi si desistere mauis;
 sed cur desistas? dissimulare potes.
lude, sed occulte: maior, non maxima, nobis
 est data libertas quod Menelaus abest.
ille quidem procul est ita re cogente profectus; 155
 magna fuit subitae iustaque causa uiae,
aut mihi sic uisum est. ego, cum dubitaret an iret,
 'quam primum' dixi 'fac rediturus eas'.
omine laetatus dedit oscula 'res'que 'domusque
 et tibi sit curae Troicus hospes' ait. 160
uix tenui risum, quem dum compescere luctor
 nil illi potui dicere praeter 'erit'.
uela quidem Creten uentis dedit ille secundis,
 sed tu non ideo cuncta licere puta.

HEROIDVM EPISTVLA XVII

sic meus hinc uir abest ut me custodiat absens: 165
  an nescis longas regibus esse manus?
forma quoque est oneri, nam quo constantius ore
  laudamur uestro, iustius ille timet.
quae iuuat, ut nunc est, eadem mihi gloria damno est,
  et melius famae uerba dedisse fuit. 170
nec quod abest hic me tecum mirere relicta:
  moribus et uitae credidit ille meae.
de facie metuit, uitae confidit, et illum
  securum probitas, forma timere facit.

tempora ne pereant ultro data praecipis utque 175
  simplicis utamur commoditate uiri.
et libet et timeo, nec adhuc exacta uoluntas
  est satis; in dubio pectora nostra labant.
et uir abest nobis et tu sine coniuge dormis,
  inque uicem tua me, te mea forma capit; 180
et longae noctes et iam sermone coimus
  et tu, me miseram, blandus et una domus,
et peream si non inuitant omnia culpam;
  nescio quo tardor sed tamen ipsa metu.
quod male persuades, utinam bene cogere posses! 185
  ui mea rusticitas excutienda fuit.
utilis interdum est ipsis iniuria passis:
  sic certe felix esse coacta forem.
dum nouus est, potius coepto pugnemus amori;
  flamma recens parua sparsa residit aqua. 190
certus in hospitibus non est amor: errat, ut ipsi,
  cumque nihil speres firmius esse, fugit.
Hypsipyle testis, testis Minoia uirgo est,
  de non exhibitis utraque questa toris.

---

167 forma *Bentley* (τὸ κάλλος *Plan.*): fama *codd.*   190 residit *Heinsius*: resedit *codd.*   194 de *Francius*: in *codd.*   questa *Heinsius*: iusta *Pς*: lusa *Gς*: iuncta ω

tu quoque dilectam multos, infide, per annos   195
  diceris Oenonen destituisse tuam.
nec tamen ipse negas et nobis omnia de te
  quaerere, si nescis, maxima cura fuit.
adde quod, ut cupias constans in amore manere,
  non potes: expediunt iam tua uela Phryges.   200
dum loqueris mecum, dum nox sperata paratur,
  qui ferat in patriam iam tibi uentus erit.
cursibus in mediis nouitatis plena relinques
  gaudia; cum uentis noster abibit amor.

an sequar, ut suades, laudataque Pergama uisam,   205
  pronurus et magni Laomedontis ero?
non ita contemno uolucris praeconia famae,
  ut probris terras impleat illa meis.
quid de me poterit Sparte, quid Achaia tota,
  quid gentes Asiae, quid tua Troia loqui?   210
quid Priamus de me, Priami quid sentiet uxor,
  totque tui fratres Dardanidesque nurus?
tu quoque qui poteris fore me sperare fidelem
  et non exemplis anxius esse tuis?
quicumque Iliacos intrauerit aduena portus,   215
  is tibi solliciti causa timoris erit.
ipse mihi quotiens iratus 'adultera' dices
  oblitus nostro crimen inesse tuum!
delicti fies idem reprehensor et auctor;
  terra precor uultus obruat ante meos.   220

at fruar Iliacis opibus cultuque beato
  donaque promissis uberiora feram:
purpura nempe mihi pretiosaque texta dabuntur
  congestoque auri pondere diues ero.

---

204 uelis *Francius*   210 asiae ς: aliae *PGω*: aliud *Kenney*   220 precor *Gω*: procul *Pς*

HEROIDVM EPISTVLA XVII

da ueniam fassae, non sunt tua munera tanti: 225
 nescioquo tellus me tenet ipsa modo.
quis mihi, si laedar, Phrygiis succurret in oris?
 unde petam fratres, unde parentis opem?
omnia Medeae fallax promisit Iason:
 pulsa est Aesonia num minus illa domo? 230
non erat Aeetes ad quem despecta rediret,
 non Idyia parens Chalciopeue soror.
tale nihil timeo, sed nec Medea timebat;
 fallitur augurio spes bona saepe suo.
omnibus inuenies, quae nunc iactantur in alto, 235
 nauibus a portu lene fuisse fretum.
fax quoque me terret, quam se peperisse cruentam
 ante diem partus est tua uisa parens;
et uatum timeo monitus, quos igne Pelasgo
 Ilion arsurum praemonuisse ferunt. 240
utque fauet Cytherea tibi, quia uicit habetque
 parta per arbitrium bina tropaea tuum,
sic illas uereor, quae, si tua gloria uera est,
 iudice te causam non tenuere duae.

nec dubito quin, te si prosequar, arma parentur: 245
 ibit per gladios, ei mihi, noster amor.
an fera Centauris indicere bella coegit
 Atracis Haemonios Hippodamia uiros,
tu fore tam iusta lentum Menelaon in ira
 et geminos fratres Tyndareumque putas? 250
quod bene te iactes et fortia facta loquaris,
 a uerbis facies dissidet ista tuis.
apta magis Veneri quam sunt tua corpora Marti:
 bella gerant fortes; tu, Pari, semper ama.

226 ipsa *PGς*: ista *ς*   230 num *PGς*: non ω   232 Chalciopeue *Bentley*: -que *codd.*   239 quibus *Kenney*   240 arsurum *PGω*: arsuram *ς*. *cf.* 16.49 praecinuisse *Kenney*

P. OVIDI NASONIS

Hectora quem laudas pro te pugnare iubeto: 255
militia est operis altera digna tuis.
his ego, si saperem pauloque audacior essem,
uterer: utetur, si qua puella sapit.
aut ego deposito sapiam fortasse pudore
et dabo cunctatas tempore uicta manus. 260

quod petis ut furtim praesentes ista loquamur,
scimus quid captes colloquiumque uoces.
sed nimium properas, et adhuc tua messis in herba est;
haec mora sit uoto forsan amica tuo.
hactenus; arcanum furtiuae conscia mentis 265
littera iam lasso pollice sistat opus.
cetera per socias, Clymenen Aethranque, loquamur
quae mihi sunt comites consiliumque duae.

XVIII
LEANDER HERONI

[Mittit Abydenus quam mallet ferre salutem,
si cadat unda maris, Sesta puella, tibi.]

si mihi di faciles et sunt in amore secundi,
inuitis oculis haec mea uerba leges.
sed non sunt faciles: nam cur mea uota morantur, 5
currere me nota nec patiuntur aqua?
ipsa uides caelum pice nigrius et freta uentis
turbida perque cauas uix adeunda rates.
unus, et hic audax, a quo tibi littera nostra
redditur, a portu nauita mouit iter. 10
ascensurus eram, nisi quod, cum uincula prorae
solueret, in speculis omnis Abydos erat.

267 aethramque *codd.*; *u.* 16.259   **xviii** 1–2 *om. PW: secl. Bentley*   2 Sesti *Heinsius*

HEROIDVM EPISTVLA XVIII

non poteram celare meos uelut ante parentes,
 quemque tegi uolumus non latuisset amor.

protinus haec scribens 'felix i littera' dixi: 15
 'iam tibi formosam porriget illa manum.
forsitan admotis etiam tangere labellis,
 rumpere dum niuea uincula dente uolet.'
talibus exiguo dictis mihi murmure uerbis
 cetera cum charta dextra locuta mea est. 20
at quanto mallem, quam scriberet, illa nataret
 meque per assuetas sedula ferret aquas!
[aptior illa quidem placido dare uerbera ponto,
 est tamen et sensus apta ministra mei.]

septima nox agitur, spatium mihi longius anno, 25
 sollicitum raucis ut mare feruet aquis.
his ego si uidi mulcentem pectora somnum
 noctibus, insani sit mora longa freti.
rupe sedens aliqua specto tua litora tristis
 et, quo non possum corpore, mente feror. 30
lumina quin etiam summa uigilantia turre
 aut uidet aut acies nostra uidere putat.
ter mihi deposita est in sicca uestis harena,
 ter graue temptaui carpere nudus iter.
obstitit inceptis tumidum iuuenalibus aequor 35
 mersit et inuersis ora natantis aquis.
at tu, de rapidis immansuetissime uentis,
 quid mecum certa proelia mente geris?
in me, si nescis, Borea, non aequora, saeuis:
 quid faceres, esset ni tibi notus amor? 40
tam gelidus quod sis, num te tamen, improbe, quondam
 ignibus Actaeis incaluisse negas?

23–4 om. *PG*_u: *secl. Lehrs*   36 inuersis *rec. unus*: adinuersis *P*: aduersis *G*ω

gaudia rapturo si quis tibi claudere uellet
   aerios aditus, quo paterere modo?
parce, precor, facilemque moue moderatius auram: 45
   imperet Hippotades sic tibi triste nihil.
uana peto: precibusque meis obmurmurat ipse
   quasque quatit nulla parte coercet aquas.
nunc daret audaces utinam mihi Daedalus alas,
   Icarium quamuis hinc prope litus abest.   50
quicquid erit, patiar, liceat modo corpus in auras
   tollere quod dubia saepe pependit aqua.

interea, dum cuncta negant uentique fretumque,
   mente agito furti tempora prima mei.
nox erat incipiens (namque est meminisse uoluptas),   55
   cum foribus patriis egrediebar amans.
nec mora, deposito pariter cum ueste timore
   iactabam liquido bracchia lenta mari.
luna fere tremulum praebebat lumen eunti
   ut comes in nostras officiosa uias.   60
hanc ego suspiciens 'faueas, dea candida' dixi
   'et subeant animo Latmia saxa tuo.
non sinit Endymion te pectoris esse seueri:
   flecte, precor, uultus ad mea furta tuos.
tu dea mortalem caelo delapsa petebas;   65
   uera loqui liceat, quam sequor ipse dea est.
neu referam mores caelesti pectore dignas,
   forma nisi in ueras non cadit illa deas.
a Veneris facie non est prior ulla tuaque;
   neue meis credas uocibus, ipsa uide.   70
quantum, cum fulges radiis argentea puris,
   concedunt flammis sidera cuncta tuis,
tanto formosis formosior omnibus illa est;
   si dubitas, caecum, Cynthia, lumen habes.'

66 ipse *P*: ipsa *pGω*

HEROIDVM EPISTVLA XVIII 55

haec ego uel certe non his diuersa locutus 75
  per mihi cedentes sponte ferebar aquas.
unda repercussae radiabat imagine lunae,
  et nitor in tacita nocte diurnus erat,
nullaque uox usquam, nullum ueniebat ad aures
  praeter dimotae corpore murmur aquae. 80
Alcyones solae memores Ceycis amati
  nescioquid uisae sunt mihi dulce queri.

iamque fatigatis umero sub utroque lacertis
  fortiter in summas erigor altus aquas;
ut procul aspexi lumen, 'meus ignis in illo est, 85
  illa meum' dixi 'litora lumen habent',
et subito lassis uires rediere lacertis
  uisaque quam fuerat mollior unda mihi.
frigora ne possim gelidi sentire profundi,
  qui calet in cupido pectore praestat amor. 90
quo magis accedo propioraque litora fiunt
  quoque minus restat, plus libet ire mihi.
cum uero possum cerni quoque, protinus addis
  spectatrix animos ut ualeamque facis.
nunc etiam nando dominae placuisse laboro 95
  atque oculis iacto bracchia nostra tuis.
te tua uix prohibet nutrix descendere in altum
  (hoc quoque enim uidi, nec mihi uerba dabam),
nec tamen effecit, quamuis retinebat euntem,
  ne fieret prima pes tuus udus aqua. 100
excipis amplexu feliciaque oscula iungis,
  oscula, di magni, trans mare digna peti,
eque tuis demptos umeris mihi tradis amictus
  et madidam siccas aequoris imbre comam.

76 sponte *Francius*: nocte *codd.*   81 *fort.* Ceycos   84 *fort.* e summis ... aquis   98 dabam *Bentley, Nodell*: dabas *codd.*   103 eque *PGω*: deque *ς*

cetera nox et nos et turris conscia nouit 105
  quodque mihi lumen per uada monstrat iter.
non magis illius numerari gaudia noctis
  Hellespontiaci quam maris alga potest.
quo breuius spatium nobis ad furta dabatur,
  hoc magis est cautum ne foret illud iners. 110
iamque fugatura Tithoni coniuge noctem
  praeuius Aurorae Lucifer ortus erat.
oscula congerimus properata sine ordine raptim
  et querimur paruas noctibus esse moras,
atque ita cunctatus monitu nutricis amaro 115
  frigida deserta litora turre peto.
digredimur flentes, repetoque ego uirginis aequor
  respiciens dominam dum licet usque meam.
si qua fides uero est [ueniens huc esse natator,
  cum redeo, uideor naufragus esse mihi. 120
hoc quoque si credis], ad te uia prona uidetur,
  a te cum redeo, cliuus inertis aquae.
inuitus repeto patriam (quis credere possit?),
  inuitus certe nunc moror urbe mea.

ei mihi, cur animis iuncti secernimur undis, 125
  unaque mens, tellus non habet una duos?
uel tua me Sestos uel te mea sumat Abydos:
  tam tua terra mihi quam tibi nostra placet.
cur ego confundor quotiens confunditur aequor?
  cur mihi, causa leuis, uentus obesse potest? 130
iam nostros curui norunt delphines amores,
  ignotum nec me piscibus esse reor.
iam patet attritus solitarum limes aquarum
  non aliter multa quam uia pressa rota.
quod mihi non esset nisi sic iter ante querebar, 135
  at nunc per uentos hoc quoque deesse queror.

119–21 ueniens ... credis *secl. Housman*

fluctibus immodicis Athamantidos aequora canent,
  uixque manet portu tuta carina suo.
hoc mare, cum primum de uirgine nomina mersa
  quae tenet est nanctum, tale fuisse puto;   140
et satis amissa locus hic infamis ab Helle est,
  utque mihi parcat, nomine crimen habet.
inuideo Phrixo, quem per freta tristia tutum
  aurea lanigero uellere uexit ouis.
nec tamen officium pecoris nauisue requiro,   145
  dummodo quas findam corpore dentur aquae.
parte egeo nulla, fiat modo copia nandi:
  idem nauigium nauita uector ero.
nec sequor aut Helicen aut qua Tyros utitur Arcton:
  publica non curat sidera noster amor.   150
Andromedan alius spectet claramque Coronam
  quaeque micat gelido Parrhasis Vrsa polo;
at mihi, quod Perseus et cum Ioue Liber amarunt,
  indicium dubiae non placet esse uiae.
est aliud lumen, multo mihi certius istis,   155
  non errat tenebris quo duce noster amor.
hoc ego dum spectem, Colchos et in ultima Ponti
  quoque uiam fecit Thessala pinus eam,
et iuuenem possim superare Palaemona nando
  miraque quem subitum reddidit herba deum.   160

saepe per assiduos languent mea bracchia motus
  uixque per immensas fessa trahuntur aquas:
his ego cum dixi 'pretium non uile laboris,
  iam dominae uobis colla tenenda dabo',
protinus illa ualent atque ad sua praemia tendunt,   165
  ut celer Eleo carcere missus equus.
ipse meos igitur seruo, quibus uror, amores
  teque, magis caelo digna puella, sequor.

144 tergore *Francius*   147 parte *Pς*: arte *pGω*   158 quoque *Kenney*: quaque *codd.*   160 morsaque *Jortin, Bentley*   subitum *Heinsius*: subito *codd.*

digna quidem es caelo, sed adhuc tellure morare,
    aut dic, ad superos et mihi qua sit iter.   170
hic es et exigue misero contingis amanti,
    cumque mea fiunt turbida mente freta.
quid mihi, quod lato non separor aequore, prodest?
    num minus haec nobis tam breuis obstat aqua?
an malim dubito toto procul orbe remotus   175
    cum domina longe spem quoque habere meam.
quo propius nunc es, flamma propiore calesco,
    et res non semper, spes mihi semper adest.
paene manu quod amo (tanta est uicinia) tango,
    saepe sed heu lacrimas hoc mihi 'paene' mouet.   180
[uelle quid est aliud fugientia prendere poma
    spemque suo refugi fluminis ore sequi?]

ergo ego te numquam nisi cum uolet unda tenebo
    et me felicem nulla uidebit hiems,
cumque minus firmum nil sit quam uentus et unda,   185
    in uentis et aqua spes mea semper erit?
aestus adhuc tamen est: quid cum mihi laeserit aequor
    Plias et Arctophylax Oleniumque pecus?
aut ego non noui quam sim temerarius aut me
    in freta non cautus tum quoque mittet amor.   190
neue putes id me, quod abest, promittere, tempus,
    pignora polliciti non tibi tarda dabo.
sit tumidum paucis etiamnunc noctibus aequor,
    ire per inuitas experiemur aquas.
aut mihi continget felix audacia saluo   195
    aut mors solliciti finis amoris erit.
optabo tamen ut partes expellar in illas
    et teneant portus naufraga membra tuos.
flebis enim tactuque meum dignabere corpus
    et 'mortis' dices 'huic ego causa fui.'   200

169 quidem es caelo *Kenney*: q. caes *PG*$_u$: q. caelo *G*ω: q. caelo es *Merkel*   adhuc] nunc *Palmer*   181–2 *secl. Kenney*

scilicet interitus offenderis omine nostri
   litteraque inuisa est hac mea parte tibi.
desino: parce queri, sed uti mare finiat iram,
   accedant, quaeso, fac tua uota meis.
pace breui nobis opus est dum transferor isto;   205
   cum tua contigero litora, perstet hiems.
istic est aptum nostrae nauale carinae
   et melius nulla stat mea puppis aqua.
illic me claudat Boreas ubi dulce morari est;
   tunc piger ad nandum, tunc ego cautus ero.   210
nec faciam surdis conuicia fluctibus ulla,
   triste nataturo nec querar esse fretum.
me pariter uenti teneant tenerique lacerti,
   per causas istic impediarque duas.

cum patietur hiems, remis ego corporis utar,   215
   lumen in aspectu tu modo semper habe.
interea pro me pernoctet epistula tecum,
   quam precor ut minima prosequar ipse mora.

XIX
HERO LEANDRO

[Quam mihi misisti uerbis, Leandre, salutem,
   ut possim missam rebus habere, ueni.]

longa mora est nobis omnis quae gaudia differt:
   da ueniam fassae, non patienter amo.
urimur igne pari sed sum tibi uiribus impar;   5
   fortius ingenium suspicor esse uiris.
ut corpus teneris ita mens infirma puellis:
   deficiam, parui temporis adde moram.

203 uti *Palmer*: ut et *Pς*: et ut ς: ut hoc *Gς*: ut hanc ς: ut ς   **xix** 1–2 *secl. Vahlen*

uos modo uenando, modo rus geniale colendo
 ponitis in uaria tempora longa mora.   10
aut fora uos retinent aut unctae dona palaestrae,
 flectitis aut freno colla sequacis equi;
nunc uolucrem laqueo, nunc piscem ducitis hamo;
 diluitur posito serior hora mero.

his mihi summotae, uel si minus acriter urar,   15
 quod faciam, superest praeter amare nihil.
quod superest facio teque, o mea sola uoluptas,
 plus quoque quam reddi quod mihi possit amo.
aut ego cum cara de te nutrice susurro
 quaeque tuum miror causa moretur iter,   20
aut mare prospiciens odioso concita uento
 corripio uerbis aequora paene tuis,
aut, ubi saeuitiae paulum grauis unda remisit,
 posse quidem sed te nolle uenire queror;
dumque queror, lacrimae per amantia lumina manant,   25
 pollice quas tremulo conscia siccat anus.
saepe tui specto si sint in litore passus,
 impositas tamquam seruet harena notas,
utque rogem de te et scribam tibi, si quis Abydo
 uenerit aut quaero si quis Abydon eat.   30
quid referam quotiens dem uestibus oscula quas tu
 Hellespontiaca ponis iturus aqua?

sic ubi lux acta est et noctis amicior hora
 exhibuit pulso sidera clara die,
protinus in summo uigilantia lumina tecto   35
 ponimus, assuetae signa notamque uiae,
tortaque uersato ducentes stamina fuso
 feminea tardas fallimus arte moras.

11 dona] mane *Bentley*   19 cana *Francius*   29–30 *post* 32 *Heinsius*

HEROIDVM EPISTVLA XIX   61

quid loquar interea tam longo tempore quaeris?
  nil nisi Leandri nomen in ore meo est.   40
'iamne putas exisse domo mea gaudia, nutrix,
  an uigilant omnes et timet ille suos?
iamne suas umeris illum deponere uestes,
  Pallade iam pingui tinguere membra putas?'
annuit illa fere, non nostra quod oscula curet,   45
  sed mouet obrepens somnus anile caput.
postque morae minimum 'iam certe nauigat' inquam
  'lentaque dimotis bracchia iactat aquis',
paucaque cum tacta perfeci stamina terra,
  an medio possis quaerimus esse freto;   50
et modo prospicimus, timida modo uoce precamur
  ut tibi det faciles utilis aura uias.
auribus incertas uoces captamus et omnem
  aduentus strepitum credimus esse tui.

sic ubi deceptae pars est mihi maxima noctis   55
  acta, subit furtim lumina fessa sopor.
    *   *   *   *   *   *   *
forsitan inuitus mecum tamen, improbe, dormis
  et quamquam non uis ipse uenire uenis.
nam modo te uideor prope iam spectare natantem,
  bracchia nunc umeris umida ferre meis,   60
nunc dare quae soleo madidis uelamina membris,
  pectora nunc nostro iuncta fouere sinu,
multaque praeterea linguae reticenda modestae,
  quae fecisse iuuat, facta referre pudet.
me miseram, breuis est haec et non uera uoluptas,   65
  nam tu cum somno semper abire soles.
firmius o cupidi tandem coeamus amantes
  nec careant uera gaudia nostra fide!

42 homines *duo recc. sicut coni. Bentley*   53 incertas *P ex corr. (de m¹ non liquet)*:
incertis *rec. unus*: interdum ω: *de G incert.*   57–8 *hic uix apti; uu. aliquot ex-
cidisse etiam suspiceris*   62 nostro iuncta *Merkel*: iuncto nostra *codd.*

cur ego tot uiduas exegi frigida noctes?
  cur totiens a me, lente morator, abes?   70
est mare, confiteor, non iam tractabile nanti,
  nocte sed hesterna lenior aura fuit.
cur ea praeterita est? cur non uentura timebas?
  tam bona cur periit nec tibi rapta uia est?
protinus ut similis detur tibi copia cursus,   75
  hoc melior certe quo prior illa fuit.

at cito mutata est iactati forma profundi:
  tempore, cum properas, saepe minore uenis.
hic puto deprensus nil quod querereris haberes
  meque tibi amplexo nulla noceret hiems.   80
certe ego tum uentos audirem laeta sonantes
  et numquam placidas esse precarer aquas.
quid tamen euenit cur sis metuentior undae
  contemptumque prius nunc uereare fretum?
nam memini cum te saeuum ueniente minaxque   85
  non minus aut multo non minus aequor erat,
cum tibi clamabam 'sic tu temerarius esto
  ne miserae uirtus sit tua flenda mihi.'
unde nouus timor hic quoque illa audacia fugit?
  magnus ubi est spretis ille natator aquis?   90
sis tamen hoc potius quam quod prius esse solebas
  et facias placidum per mare tutus iter,
dummodo sis idem, dum sicut scribis amemur,
  flammaque non fiat frigidus illa cinis.
non ego tam uentos timeo mea uota morantes   95
  quam similis uento ne tuus erret amor,
neu non sim tanti superentque pericula causam
  et uidear merces esse labore minor.

---

70 morator *PW*: natator *pω*: uiator *rec. unus*: de *G incert.*   71 non iam *Watt*:
non nunc *Bentley*: nondum *pGω*: de *P incert.*   77 pacati *Bentley*   81 laeta
PGω: lenta *ς*   97 neu *Dousa*: ne *codd.*

interdum metuo patria ne laedar et impar
  dicar Abydeno Thressa puella toro.   100
ferre tamen possum patientius omnia quam si
  otia nescioqua paelice captus agis,
in tua si ueniunt alieni colla lacerti
  fitque nouus nostri finis amoris amor.
a potius peream quam crimine uulnerer isto,   105
  fataque sint culpa nostra priora tua!
nec quia uenturi dederis mihi signa doloris
  haec loquor aut fama sollicitata noua,
omnia sed uereor. quis enim securus amauit?
  cogit et absentes plura timere locus.   110
felices illas, sua quas praesentia nosse
  crimina uera iubet, falsa timere uetat!
me tam uana mouet quam facta iniuria fallit,
  incitat et morsus error uterque pares.
o utinam uenias aut ut uentusue paterue   115
  causaque sit certe femina nulla morae!
quodsi quam sciero, moriar, mihi crede, dolendo:
  iamdudum pecca si mea fata petis.

sed neque peccabis frustraque ego terreor istis,
  quoque minus uenias inuida pugnat hiems.   120
me miseram, quanto planguntur litora fluctu
  et latet obscura condita nube dies!
forsitan ad pontum mater pia uenerit Helles,
  mersaque roratis nata fleatur aquis.
an mare ab inuiso priuignae nomine dictum   125
  uexat in aequoream uersa nouerca deam?
non fauet, ut nunc est, teneris locus iste puellis:
  hac Helle periit, hac ego laedor aqua.
at tibi flammarum memori, Neptune, tuarum
  nullus erat uentis impediendus amor,   130

100 ducar *Heinsius*   115 ut *PGω*: hic *ς*: heu *Courtney*: o *Watt, Kenney*

si neque Amymone nec laudatissima forma
    criminis est Tyro fabula uana tui
lucidaque Alcyone Calyceque Hecataeone nata
    et nondum nexis angue Medusa comis
flauaque Laodice caeloque recepta Celaeno   135
    et quarum memini nomina lecta mihi.
has certe pluresque canunt, Neptune, poetae
    molle latus lateri composuisse tuo.
cur igitur totiens uires expertus amoris
    assuetum nobis turbine claudis iter?   140
parce, ferox, latoque mari tua proelia misce;
    seducit terras haec breuis unda duas.
te decet aut magnas magnum iactare carinas
    aut etiam totis classibus esse trucem.
turpe deo pelagi iuuenem terrere natantem,   145
    gloriaque est stagno quolibet ista minor.
nobilis ille quidem est et clarus origine sed non
    a tibi suspecto ducit Vlixe genus.
da ueniam seruaque duos: natat ille, sed isdem
    corpus Leandri, spes mea pendet aquis.   150

sternuit en lumen (posito nam scribimus illo),
    sternuit et nobis prospera signa dedit.
ecce merum nutrix faustos instillat in ignes
    'cras'que 'erimus plures' inquit et ipsa bibit.
effice nos plures euicta per aequora lapsus,   155
    o penitus toto corde recepte mihi.
in tua castra redi, socii desertor Amoris;
    ponuntur medio cur mea membra toro?
quod timeas non est: auso Venus ipsa fauebit,
    sternet et aequoreas aequore nata uias.   160
ire libet medias ipsi mihi saepe per undas,
    sed solet hoc maribus tutius esse fretum.

133 Calyceque Hecataeone *Heinsius*: ceuceque et aueone *P*: celiceque et aueone *G*: *minus probabilia* ω   151 en *Heinsius*: et *codd.*

HEROIDVM EPISTVLA XIX 65

nam cur hac uectis Phrixo Phrixique sorore
  sola dedit uastis femina nomen aquis?

forsitan ad reditum metuas ne tempora desint 165
  aut gemini nequeas ferre laboris onus.
at nos diuersi medium coeamus in aequor
  obuiaque in summis oscula demus aquis
atque ita quisque suas iterum redeamus ad urbes:
  exiguum sed plus quam nihil illud erit. 170
uel pudor hic utinam qui nos clam cogit amare
  uel timidus famae cedere uellet amor.
nunc, male res iunctae, calor et reuerentia pugnant:
  quid sequar in dubio est; haec decet, ille iuuat.
ut semel intrauit Colchos Pagasaeus Iason, 175
  impositam celeri Phasida puppe tulit;
ut semel Idaeus Lacedaemona uenit adulter,
  cum praeda rediit protinus ille sua:
tu, quam saepe petis quod amas, tam saepe relinquis,
  et, quotiens graue sit puppibus ire, natas. 180
sic tamen, o iuuenis tumidarum uictor aquarum,
  sic facito spernas ut uereare fretum.
arte laboratae merguntur ab aequore naues:
  tu tua plus remis bracchia posse putas?
quod cupis, hoc nautae metuunt, Leandre, natare; 185
  exitus hic fractis puppibus esse solet.
me miseram, cupio non persuadere quod hortor,
  sisque precor monitis fortior ipse meis,
dummodo peruenias excussaque saepe per undas
  inicias umeris bracchia lassa meis. 190

sed mihi, caeruleas quotiens obuertor ad undas,
  nescioquo pauidum frigore pectus hebet.

---

180 sit *Pς*: fit *Gω*   192 nescioquo ... frigore ... hebet *Reeve*: nescioquid
(-qd = -quod *P*) ... frigore ... habet *Pω*: nescioquae ... frigora ... habent ς

P. OVIDI NASONIS

nec minus hesternae confundor imagine noctis,
    quamuis est sacris illa piata meis.
namque sub auroram, iam dormitante lucerna,   195
    somnia quo cerni tempore uera solent,
stamina de digitis cecidere sopore remissis
    collaque puluino nostra ferenda dedi.
hic ego uentosas nantem delphina per undas
    cernere non dubia sum mihi uisa fide;   200
quem postquam bibulis illisit fluctus harenis,
    unda simul miserum uitaque deseruit.
quicquid id est, timeo, nec tu mea somnia ride
    nec nisi tranquillo bracchia crede mari.
si tibi non parcis, dilectae parce puellae,   205
    quae numquam nisi te sospite sospes erit.
spes tamen est fractis uicinae pacis in undis:
    tum placidas tuto pectore finde uias.
interea, quoniam nanti freta peruia non sunt,
    leniat inuisas littera missa moras.   210

XX
ACONTIVS CYDIPPAE

*   *   *   *   *   *   *

pone metum: nihil hic iterum iurabis amanti;
    promissam satis est te semel esse mihi.
perlege: discedat sic corpore languor ab isto
    quod meus est ulla parte dolere dolor.
quid pudor ora subit? nam, sicut in aede Dianae,   5
    suspicor ingenuas erubuisse genas.
coniugium pactamque fidem, non crimina, posco;
    debitus ut coniunx, non ut adulter, amo.

195 auroram *Heinsius*: aurora *codd.*   198 nostra] sera *Palmer*   199 huc *Kenney*   204 *fort.* corpora   205 *fort.* parces   206 erit ω: ero PGς   207 *fort.* tandem   208 tuto Gς: toto Pω   **xx** 1 *ante hunc u. distichon excidisse ueri simile est*   5 ora ω: ante PGς

HEROIDVM EPISTVLA XX

uerba licet repetas quae, demptus ab arbore fetus,
   pertulit ad castas me iaciente manus: 10
inuenies illic id te spondere, quod opto
   te potius, uirgo, quam meminisse deam.
nunc quoque idem cupio, sed idem tamen acrius illud:
   assumpsit uires auctaque flamma mora est,
quique fuit numquam paruus, nunc tempore longo   15
   et spe, quam dederas tu mihi, creuit amor.
spem mihi tu dederas, meus hic tibi credidit ardor:
   non potes hoc factum teste negare dea.
adfuit et, praesens ut erat, tua uerba notauit
   et uisa est mota dicta tulisse coma.   20

deceptam dicas nostra te fraude licebit,
   dum fraudis nostrae causa feratur amor.
fraus mea quid petiit, nisi uti tibi iungerer uni?
   id te, quod quereris, conciliare potest.
non ego natura nec sum tam callidus usu: 25
   sollertem tu me, crede, puella, facis.
te mihi compositis (si quid tamen egimus) a se
   astrinxit uerbis ingeniosus Amor.
dictatis ab eo feci sponsalia uerbis
   consultoque fui iuris Amore uafer.   30
sit fraus huic facto nomen dicarque dolosus,
   si tamen est quod ames uelle tenere dolus.

en iterum scribo mittoque rogantia uerba;
   altera fraus haec est, quodque queraris habes.
si noceo quod amo, fateor, sine fine nocebo   35
   teque, peti caueas tu licet, usque petam.
per gladios alii placitas rapuere puellas:
   scripta mihi caute littera crimen erit?

---

13 cupio *Bentley*: timeo codd.: alii alia   17 hinc *Thompson*   20 dicta tulisse *PGω*: d. notasse ς: d. probasse *Heinsius ex codd.*: signa dedisse *Slichtenhorst*   23 unum *Burman*   24 te *Bentley*: me codd.   27 a se *Nisbet*: a me *P*: arte *Gω*   36 peti ς: petam *PGω*   tu *PGω*: te ς   usque ς: ipse *Pω*: ipsa *Gς*

di faciant possim plures imponere nodos,
    ut tua sit nulla libera parte fides.   40
mille doli restant; cliuo sudamus in imo;
    ardor inexpertum nil sinet esse meus.
sit dubium possisne capi, captabere certe;
    exitus in dis est, sed capiere tamen.
ut partem effugias, non omnia retia falles,   45
    quae tibi quam credis plura tetendit Amor.
si non proficient artes, ueniemus ad arma,
    inque tui cupido rapta ferere sinu.
non sum qui soleam Paridis reprehendere factum
    nec quemquam qui, uir posset ut esse, fuit.   50
nos quoque – sed taceo: mors huius poena rapinae
    ut sit, erit quam te non habuisse minor.
nata esses formosa minus: peterere modeste;
    audaces facie cogimur esse tua.
tu facis hoc oculique tui, quibus ignea cedunt   55
    sidera, qui flammae causa fuere meae;
hoc faciunt flaui crines et eburnea ceruix
    quaeque precor ueniant in mea colla manus
et decor et uultus sine rusticitate pudentes
    et Thetidi quales uix rear esse pedes.   60
cetera si possem laudare, beatior essem,
    nec dubito totum quin sibi par sit opus.
hac ego compulsus, non est mirabile, forma,
    si pignus uolui uocis habere tuae.

denique, dum captam tu te cogare fateri,   65
    insidiis esto capta puella meis.
inuidiam patiar, passo sua praemia dentur;
    cur suus a tanto crimine fructus abest?
Hesionen Telamon, Briseida cepit Achilles;
    utraque uictorem nempe secuta uirum.   70

53 nata *Watt*: aut *PGω*: o ς   60 Thetidi *Heinsius*: -dis *codd.*

HEROIDVM EPISTVLA XX

quamlibet accuses et sis irata licebit,
  irata liceat dum mihi posse frui.
idem qui facimus, factam tenuabimus iram,
  copia placandi sit modo parua tui.
ante tuos liceat flentem consistere uultus   75
  et liceat lacrimis addere uerba suis,
utque solent famuli, cum uerbera saeua uerentur,
  tendere summissas ad tua crura manus.
ignoras tua iura: uoca; cur arguor absens?
  iamdudum dominae more uenire iube.   80
ipsa meos scindas licet imperiosa capillos,
  oraque sint digitis liuida facta tuis.
omnia perpetiar; tantum fortasse timebo
  corpore laedatur ne manus ista meo.
sed neque compedibus nec me compesce catenis: 85
  seruabor firmo uinctus amore tui.
cum bene se quantumque uolet satiauerit ira,
  ipsa tibi dices 'quam patienter amat!'
ipsa tibi dices, ubi uideris omnia ferre,
  'tam bene qui seruit, seruiat iste mihi.'   90
nunc reus infelix absens agor et mea, cum sit
  optima, non ullo causa tuente perit.

†hoc quoque quod iussit sit scriptum iniuria nostrum;†
  quod de me solo nempe queraris habes.
non meruit falli mecum quoque Delia: si non   95
  uis mihi promissum reddere, redde deae.
adfuit et uidit, cum tu decepta rubebas,
  et uocem memori condidit aure tuam.
omina re careant! nihil est uiolentius illa
  cum sua, quod nolim, numina laesa uidet.   100

---

74 placandi *PGω*: placandae *ς*   76 suis *Gς*: sui *P*: tuis *ς*: meis *ς*: sua
Palmer   87 uoles *Heinsius*   89 ferri *Ruhnken*   93–4 *secl. Heinsius*   93
quoque quod///uissit (*uel* iussit) sit scriptum *P*: q. quod tu uis sit s. *Gς*: q.
quod iussit (*uel* ius sit) s. est *ω*: quod amor iussit s. est *ς*   nostrum *Pς*: nostra
Gς: nostri *ς*

testis erit Calydonis aper, sic saeuus, ut illo
   sit magis in natum saeua reperta parens;
testis et Actaeon, quondam fera creditus illis,
   ipse dedit leto cum quibus ante feras,
quaeque superba parens saxo per corpus oborto   105
   nunc quoque Mygdonia flebilis extat humo.

ei mihi, Cydippe, timeo tibi dicere uerum,
   ne uidear causa falsa monere mea;
dicendum tamen est. hoc est, mihi crede, quod aegra
   ipso nubendi tempore saepe iaces.   110
consulit ipsa tibi neu sis periura laborat
   et saluam salua te cupit esse fide.
inde fit ut, quotiens existere perfida temptas,
   peccatum totiens corrigat illa tuum.
parce mouere feros animosae uirginis arcus;   115
   mitis adhuc fieri, si patiare, potest.
parce, precor, teneros corrumpere febribus artus:
   seruetur facies ista fruenda mihi;
seruentur uultus ad nostra incendia nati
   quique subest niueo lenis in ore rubor.   120
hostibus et si quis ne fias nostra repugnat
   sic sit ut inualida te solet esse mihi!
torqueor ex aequo uel te nubente uel aegra,
   dicere nec possum quid minus ipse uelim.
maceror interdum quod sim tibi causa dolendi,   125
   teque mea laedi calliditate puto,
inque caput nostrum dominae periuria quaeso
   eueniant: poena tuta sit illa mea.

ne tamen ignorem quid agas, ad limina crebro
   anxius huc illuc dissimulanter eo.   130

101–2 *secl. Heinsius*   106 extat *Burman ex codd.*: astat *codd.*   109 ... tamen. hoc, hoc est ... *Palmer*   120 lenis *PGω*: leuis ς   126 *fort.* pudet   127 inque caput *G*ς: in caput *P*: in caput et ς: in caput ut *Ehwald*   127–8 'in'que 'caput ... periuria' clamo | 'eueniant ...' *Hollis*

HEROIDVM EPISTVLA XX

subsequor ancillam furtim famulumue, requirens
 profuerint somni quid tibi quidue cibi.
me miserum, quod non medicorum iussa ministro
 effingoque manus insideoque toro!
et rursum miserum, quod me procul inde remoto 135
 quem minime uellem forsitan alter adest!
ille manus istas effingit et assidet aegrae
 inuisus superis cum superisque mihi,
dumque suo temptat salientem pollice uenam,
 candida per causam bracchia saepe tenet 140
contrectatque sinus et forsitan oscula iungit;
 officio merces plenior ista suo est.
quis tibi permisit nostras praecerpere messes?
 ad sepem alterius quis tibi fecit iter?
iste sinus meus est, mea turpiter oscula sumis; 145
 a mihi promisso corpore tolle manus.
improbe, tolle manus: quam tangis, nostra futura est;
 postmodo si facies istud, adulter eris.
elige de uacuis quam non sibi uindicet alter:
 si nescis, dominum res habet ista suum. 150
nec mihi credideris: recitetur formula pacti;
 neu falsam dicas esse, fac ipsa legat.
alterius thalamo, tibi nos, tibi, dicimus, exi;
 quid facis hic? exi: non uacat iste torus.
nam quod habes et tu gemini uerba altera pacti, 155
 non erit idcirco par tua causa meae.
haec mihi se pepigit, pater hanc tibi, primus ab illa;
 sed propior certe quam pater ipsa sibi est.
promisit pater hanc, haec et iurauit amanti;
 ille homines, haec est testificata deam. 160
ille timet mendax, haec et periura uocari;
 num dubitas hic sit maior an ille metus?

---

131 famulumue *Heinsius*: -que *codd.* 134 assideoque *Heinsius ex 'Regio'* 144 sepem *Heinsius ex 'uno Mediceo'*: spes *PGω*: spem *ς*: segetem *Damsté*: saeptum (*meliusne fuit* saepta ?) *Hollis* 159 et *PGω*: se *ς*

denique, ut amborum conferre pericula possis,
  respice ad euentus: haec cubat, ille ualet.
nos quoque dissimili certamina mente subimus; 165
  nec spes par nobis nec timor aequus adest.
tu petis ex tuto, grauior mihi morte repulsa est,
  idque ego iam, quod tu forsan amabis, amo.
si tibi iustitiae, si recti cura fuisset,
  cedere debueras ignibus ipse meis. 170

nunc quoniam ferus hic pro causa pugnat iniqua,
  ad te, Cydippe, littera nostra redit.
hic facit ut iaceas et sis suspecta Dianae;
  hunc tu, si sapias, limen adire uetes.
hoc faciente subis tam saeua pericula uitae, 175
  atque utinam pro te, qui mouet illa, cadat!
hunc si reppuleris, nec quem dea damnat amabis
  et tu continuo, tunc ego saluus ero.
siste metum, uirgo: stabili potiere salute,
  fac modo polliciti conscia templa colas. 180
non boue mactato caelestia numina gaudent
  sed, quae praestanda est et sine teste, fide.
ut ualeant, aliae ferrum patiuntur et ignes,
  fert aliis tristem sucus amarus opem.
nil opus est istis: tantum periuria uita 185
  teque simul serua meque datamque fidem.
praeteritae ueniam dabit ignorantia culpae:
  exciderant animo foedera lecta tuo.
admonita es modo uoce mea cum casibus istis
  quos, quotiens temptas fallere, ferre soles. 190
his quoque uitatis in partu nempe rogabis
  ut tibi luciferas afferat illa manus.

172 ad te ϛ: ad quid *pGω*: adq; *P*   175–8 *suspectos habuit Dilthey*   175 *post hunc u. desinit P*   177 hunc *Hollis*: quem *codd.*   amabis *rec. unus*: amaris *Gω*   178 tu] tunc *Thompson*   tunc *ex. gr. Kenney post Housman*: certe *codd.*   certa salutis eris *Palmer*   189 at monita es *Maehly*   cum *Gϛ Plan.*: modo ω

audiet et repetens quae sint audita requiret
   iste tibi de quo coniuge partus eat.
promittes uotum: scit te promittere falso;   195
   iurabis: scit te fallere posse deos.

non agitur de me; cura maiore laboro:
   anxia sunt causa pectora nostra tua.
cur modo te dubiam pauidi fleuere parentes,
   ignaros culpae quos facis esse tuae?   200
et cur ignorant? matri licet omnia narres:
   nil tua, Cydippe, facta ruboris habent.
ordine fac referas ut sis mihi cognita primum,
   sacra pharetratae dum facit ipsa deae,
ut te conspecta subito, si forte notasti,   205
   restiterim fixis in tua membra genis
et, te dum nimium miror, nota certa furoris,
   deciderint umero pallia lapsa meo;
postmodo nescioqua uenisse uolubile malum
   uerba ferens doctis insidiosa notis,   210
quod quia sit lectum sancta praesente Diana,
   esse tuam uinctam numine teste fidem.
ne tamen ignoret scripti sententia quae sit,
   lecta tibi quondam nunc quoque uerba refer.
'nube, precor,' dicet 'cui te bona numina iungunt;   215
   quem fore iurasti, sit gener ille mihi.
quisquis is est, placeat, quoniam placet ante Dianae.'
   talis erit mater, si modo mater erit.
sed tamen ut quaerat qui sim qualisque uideto:
   inueniet uobis consuluisse deam.   220
insula, Coryciis quondam celeberrima nymphis,
   cingitur Aegaeo, nomine Cea, mari.

---

198 causa ... tua *Housman*: uita ... tua ς: uitae ... tuae ω: *de G incert.*   201
ignorent *Heinsius*   219 ut *rec. unus*: et ω   qui *recc. duo*: quis ω   uideto
ω: iubeto ς   *de G incert.*

illa mihi patria est, nec, si generosa probatis
    nomina, despectis arguor ortus auis.
sunt et opes nobis, sunt et sine crimine mores,   225
    amplius utque nihil, me tibi iungit Amor.
appeteres talem uel non iurata maritum;
    iuratae uel non talis habendus erat.

haec tibi me in somnis iaculatrix scribere Phoebe,
    haec tibi me uigilem scribere iussit Amor;   230
e quibus alterius mihi iam nocuere sagittae,
    alterius noceant ne tibi tela caue.
iuncta salus nostra est: miserere meique tuique;
    quid dubitas unam ferre duobus opem?
quod si contigerit, cum iam data signa sonabunt,   235
    tinctaque uotiuo sanguine Delos erit,
aurea ponetur mali felicis imago,
    causaque uersiculis scripta duobus erit:
EFFIGIE POMI TESTATVR ACONTIVS HVIVS
    QVAE FVERINT IN EO SCRIPTA FVISSE RATA.   240
longior infirmum ne lasset epistula corpus
    clausaque consueto sit sibi fine, uale.

XXI
CYDIPPE ACONTIO

* * * * * * *

pertimui scriptumque tuum sine murmure legi,
    iuraret ne quos inscia lingua deos.
et puto captasses iterum, nisi, ut ipse fateris,
    promissam scires me satis esse semel.
nec lectura fui, sed, si tibi dura fuissem,   5
    aucta foret saeuae forsitan ira deae.

224 arguar *Thompson*   228 erat *Gω*: erit *ς*: eram *Bentley, Nodell*   235 rata
Cuperus: fort. pia *uel* bona   *fort.* sonarint   240 in eo *ω*: pomo *ς: de G incert.*
242 sibi *Heinsius*: tibi *codd.*   **xxi** 1 *ante hunc u. distichon excidisse ueri simile est*

HEROIDVM EPISTVLA XXI 75

omnia cum faciam, cum dem pia tura Dianae,
 illa tamen iusta plus tibi parte fauet,
utque cupis credi, memori te uindicat ira:
 talis in Hippolyto uix fuit illa suo.   10
at melius uirgo fauisset uirginis annis,
 quos uereor paucos ne uelit esse mihi.
languor enim causis non apparentibus haeret,
 adiuuor et nulla fessa medentis ope.
quam tibi nunc gracilem uix haec rescribere quamque   15
 pallida uix cubito membra leuare puta!
huc timor accessit ne quis nisi conscia nutrix
 colloquii nobis sentiat esse uices.
ante fores sedet haec quid agamque rogantibus 'intus',
 ut possim tuto scribere, 'dormit' ait.   20
mox, ubi secreti longi causa optima somnus
 credibilis tarda desinit esse mora,
iamque uenire uidet quos non admittere durum est,
 excreat et ficta dat mihi signa nota.
sicut erant, properans uerba imperfecta relinquo,   25
 et tegitur trepido littera rapta sinu.
inde meos digitos iterum repetita fatigat:
 quantus sit nobis aspicis ipse labor.
quo peream si dignus eras, ut uera loquamur,
 sed melior iusto quamque mereris ero.   30

ergo te propter totiens incerta salutis
 commentis poenas doque dedique tuis;
haec nobis formae te laudatore superbae
 contingit merces, et placuisse nocet.

13–144 *codd.* = G_{u}ρε 16 puta ρ: putas G_{u}ε 17 huc *Heinsius*: nunc *codd.* 19–20 *dist. Watt*: ... rogantibus (intus | ... scribere) 'dormit' ait *Thompson* 23 cumque *Gronovius* 24 dicta *Burman*: pacta *Palmer*: certa *Kenney*: fida *Watt* 25 erant *Slichtenhorst*: eram *codd.* 26 rapta *Kenney*: cauta *codd.*: coepta *Dilthey*: rupta *Thompson* 28 sis *Naugerius* 29 quo *Heinsius*: que *codd.* 30 ego *Naugerius*

P. OVIDI NASONIS

si tibi deformis, quod mallem, uisa fuissem, 35
 culpatum nulla corpus egeret ope;
nunc laudata gemo, nunc me certamine uestro
 perditis, et proprio uulneror ipsa bono.
dum neque tu cedis nec se putat ille secundum,
 tu uotis obstas illius, ille tuis; 40
ipsa uelut nauis iactor quam certus in altum
 propellit Boreas, aestus et unda refert;
cumque dies caris optata parentibus instat,
 immodicus pariter corporis ardor adest.
ei mihi, coniugii tempus crudelis ad ipsum 45
 Persephone nostras pulsat acerba fores!
iam pudet, et timeo, quamuis mihi conscia non sim,
 offensos uidear ne meruisse deos.
accidere hoc aliquis casu contendit, at alter
 acceptum superis hunc negat esse uirum; 50
neue nihil credas in te quoque dicere famam,
 facta ueneficiis pars putat ista tuis.
causa latet, mala nostra patent: uos pace mouetis
 aspera summota proelia, plector ego.

dic mihi nunc solitoque tibi ne decipe more: 55
 quid facies odio, sic ubi amore noces?
si laedis quod amas, hostem sapienter amabis;
 me, precor, ut serues, perdere uelle uelis.
aut tibi iam nulla est speratae cura puellae,
 quam ferus indigna tabe perire sinis, 60
aut, dea si frustra pro me tibi saeua rogatur,
 qua mihi te iactas, gratia nulla tua est.
elige quid fingas. non uis placare Dianam:
 immemor es nostri; non potes: illa tui est.

45 ei *Heusinger*: nunc p: tunc *rec. unus*: nec $G_u\varepsilon$ 47 iam] et *Francius*   49 hoc ε: haec $G_u\rho$ at *Bentley*: et *codd.*   51 nihil *Heinsius*: mihi *codd.*   55 dic mihi *Bentley*: dicam *codd.*: dic age *van Lennep*   ne *Naugerius*: me *codd.*   56 *fort.* faceres; *cf.* 16.103   58 posse *Burman*   62 qua *Dilthey*: quid *codd.*   iactes *Palmer*

HEROIDVM EPISTVLA XXI 77

uel numquam mallem uel non mihi tempore in illo 65
  esset in Aegaeis cognita Delos aquis!
tunc mea difficili deducta est sidere nauis
  et fuit ad coeptas hora sinistra uias.
quo pede processi, quo me pede limine moui,
  picta citae tetigi quo pede texta ratis? 70
bis tamen aduerso redierunt carbasa uento –
  mentior a demens: ille secundus erat.
ille secundus erat, qui me referebat euntem
  quique parum felix impediebat iter.
atque utinam constans contra mea uela fuisset; 75
  sed stultum est uenti de leuitate queri.
mota loci fama properabam uisere Delon
  et facere ignaua puppe uidebar iter.
quam saepe ut tardis feci conuicia remis
  questaque sum uento lintea parca dari! 80
et iam transieram Myconon, iam Tenon et Andron,
  inque meis oculis candida Delos erat.
quam procul ut uidi, 'quid me fugis, insula?' dixi
  'laberis in magno numquid ut ante mari?'
institeram terrae, cum iam prope luce peracta 85
  demere purpureis sol iuga uellet equis.
quos idem solitos postquam reuocauit ad ortus,
  comuntur nostrae matre iubente comae.
ipsa dedit gemmas digitis et crinibus aurum
  et uestes umeris induit ipsa meis. 90
protinus egressae superis quibus insula grata est
  flaua salutatis tura merumque damus;
dumque parens aras uotiuo sanguine tingit,
  sectaque fumosis ingerit exta focis,
sedula me nutrix altas quoque ducit in aedes, 95
  erramusque uago per loca sacra pede.

67 difficili *Naugerius*: difficilis *codd.*   sidere *Bentley*: aequore *codd.*   77 Delon
edd.: -um *codd.*   89 crinibus *ed. Venet. 1481*: cruribus *codd.*   91 grata G_uP:
sacra ε   94 sectaque *Heinsius*: festaque *codd.*   95 altas *Wakefield*: alias *codd.*

P. OVIDI NASONIS

et modo porticibus spatior, modo munera regum
    miror et in cunctis stantia signa locis;
miror et innumeris structam de cornibus aram
    et te, qua pariens arbore nixa dea est, 100
et quae praeterea (neque enim meminiue libetue
    quicquid ibi uidi dicere) Delos habet.

forsitan haec spectans a te spectabar, Aconti,
    uisaque simplicitas est mea posse capi.
in templum redeo gradibus sublime Dianae; 105
    tutior hoc ecquis debuit esse locus?
mittitur ante pedes malum cum carmine tali –
    ei mihi, iuraui nunc quoque paene tibi!
sustulit hoc nutrix mirataque 'perlege' dixit:
    insidias legi, magne poeta, tuas. 110
nomine coniugii dicto confusa pudore
    sensi me totis erubuisse genis,
luminaque in gremio ueluti defixa tenebam,
    lumina propositi facta ministra tui.
improbe, quid gaudes aut quae tibi gloria parta est 115
    quidue uir elusa uirgine laudis habes?
non ego constiteram sumpta peltata securi,
    qualis in Iliaco Penthesilea solo.
nullus Amazonio caelatus balteus auro,
    sicut ab Hippolyte, praeda relata tibi est. 120
uerba quid exultas tua si mihi uerba dederunt
    sumque parum prudens capta puella dolis?
Cydippen pomum, pomum Schoeneida cepit:
    tu nunc Hippomenes scilicet alter eris.

at fuerat melius, si te puer iste tenebat 125
    quem tu nescioquas dicis habere faces,

---

100 te *Palmer, Damsté*: de *codd.*   122 doli *Heinsius*

HEROIDVM EPISTVLA XXI

more bonis solito spem non corrumpere fraude:
 exoranda tibi, non capienda, fui.
cur, cum me peteres, ea non profitenda putabas
 propter quae nobis ipse petendus eras? 130
cogere cur potius quam persuadere uolebas,
 si poteram audita condicione capi?
quid tibi nunc prodest iurandi formula iuris
 linguaque praesentem testificata deam?
quae iurat, mens est; nil coniurauimus illa; 135
 illa fidem dictis addere sola potest.
consilium prudensque animi sententia iurat,
 et nisi iudicii uincula nulla ualent.
si tibi coniugium uolui promittere nostrum,
 exige polliciti debita iura tori; 140
sed si nil dedimus praeter sine pectore uocem,
 uerba suis frustra uiribus orba tenes.
non ego iuraui: legi iurantia uerba;
 uir mihi non isto more legendus eras.
decipe sic alios, succedat epistula pomo: 145
 si ualet hoc, magnas ditibus aufer opes.
fac iurent reges sua se tibi regna daturos,
 sitque tuum toto quicquid in orbe placet.
maior es hoc ipsa multum, mihi crede, Diana,
 si tua tam praesens littera numen habet. 150

cum tamen haec dixi, cum me tibi firma negaui,
 cum bene promissi causa peracta mei est,
confiteor, timeo saeuae Letoidos iram
 et corpus laedi suspicor inde meum.
nam quare, quotiens socialia sacra parantur, 155
 nupturae totiens languida membra cadunt?

127 bonis *Naugerius*: boni *codd.*   135 nil tum iurauimus *rec. unus*: nil nos i. *Bentley*: sed nil i. *Palmer*   137–8 *secl. Ehwald*   145–248 *tradit sola* π   *emendationes ab omnibus fere receptae silentur*   145 alias *edd.*   146 ditibus *Heinsius*: diuitis π   149 multo *edd.*   153 Letoidos *Thompson*: latoydos π

80   P. OVIDI NASONIS

ter mihi iam ueniens positas Hymenaeus ad aras
  fugit et a thalami limine terga dedit,
uixque manu pigra totiens infusa resurgunt
  lumina, uix moto concutit igne faces.   160
saepe coronatis stillant unguenta capillis
  et trahitur multo splendida palla croco.
cum tetigit limen, lacrimas mortisque timorem
  cernit et a cultu cuncta remota suo,   164
et pudet in tristi laetum consurgere turba,   167
  quique erat in palla, transit in ora rubor;   168
proicit ipse sua deductas fronte coronas   165
  spissaque de nitidis tergit amoma comis.

at mihi, uae miserae, torrentur febribus artus
  et grauius iusto pallia pondus habent,   170
nostraque plorantes uideo super ora parentes,
  et face pro thalami fax mihi mortis adest.
[parce laboranti, picta dea laeta pharetra,
  daque salutiferam iam mihi fratris opem.
turpe tibi est, illum causas depellere leti,   175
  te contra titulum mortis habere meae.
numquid, in umbroso cum uelles fonte lauari,
  imprudens uultus ad tua labra tuli,
praeteriiue tuas de tot caelestibus aras,
  aue mea spreta est uestra parente parens?   180
nil ego peccaui, nisi quod periuria legi
  inque parum fausto carmine docta fui.
tu quoque pro nobis, si non mentiris amorem,
  tura feras: prosint, quae nocuere, manus.

158 a *Ehwald*: e π   160 concutit *Burman*: coripit (sic) π: *alii alia*   164 cuncta *Francius*: multa π   167–8 *post* 164 *Meynck*   167 considere *uel* os ostendere *Watt*: consistere *Burman*   165 sua deductas *Cuperus, Francius*: suas deducta π: sua detractas *Burman*   174 iam] *fort.* tu   180 aue *Bentley*: atque π   mea spreta est uestra *Kenney*: mea est spreta nostra π

HEROIDVM EPISTVLA XXI

cur, quae succenset quod adhuc tibi pacta puella   185
  non tua sit, fieri ne tua possit agit?
omnia de uiua tibi sunt speranda: quid aufert
  saeua mihi uitam, spem tibi diua mei?
nec tu credideris illum, cui destinor uxor,
  aegra superposita membra fouere manu.   190
assidet ille quidem quantum permittitur, ipse
  sed meminit nostrum uirginis esse torum.
et iam nescioquid de te sensisse uidetur,
  nam lacrimae causa saepe latente cadunt,
et minus audacter blanditur et oscula rara   195
  appetit et timido me uocat ore suam.
nec miror sensisse, notis cum prodar apertis:
  in dextrum uertor, cum uenit ille, latus,
nec loquor, et tecto simulatur lumine somnus,
  captantem tactus reicioque manum.   200
ingemit et tacito suspirat pectore meque
  offensam, quamuis non mereatur, habet.
ei mihi, quod gaudes et te iuuat illa simultas!
  ei mihi, quod sensus sum tibi fassa meos!
quod nisi lenta foret, tu nostra iustius ira,   205
  qui mihi tendebas retia, dignus eras.

scribis ut inualidum liceat tibi uisere corpus:
  es procul a nobis, et tamen inde noces.

185–6 *sic fere edd.*: succenses … facta … | … sed fieri … agis π *distichon post*
188 *Hollis*   185 quae] qui *Hickey*: quia *Diggle* (*seruato utrubique* succenses
… agis)   191 ipse *Dilthey*: ipsi π: aegrae *Heinsius*: usu *Hollis*   193 et iam
Kenney: et quoque iam π: iam quoque *Heinsius*   de te sensisse *Heinsius*: de-
sensisse π: de me s. *Ald.¹*: de se s. *Palmer*   196 appetit *Palmer*: accipit π: oc-
cupat *Watt*   198 uertor *Francius*: uersor π   203 me *Thompson*   illa
Kenney: ista π   simultas *Heinsius*: uoluptas π   205 quod nisi lenta foret
(*sc.* ira) *ex. gr. Kenney praeeunte Watt* (at nisi lenta forem; forem iam *Gronouius*): at
mihi lingua foret π: si mens aequa foret *van Lennep*

P. OVIDI NASONIS

mirabar quare tibi nomen Acontius esset:
　quod faciat longe uulnus, acumen habes.　　　　　210
certe ego conualui nondum de uulnere tali,
　ut iaculo scriptis eminus icta tuis.
quid tamen huc uenias? anne ut miserabile corpus,
　ingenii uideas magna tropaea tui?
concidimus macie, color est sine sanguine, qualem　　　215
　in pomo refero mente fuisse tuo,
candida nec mixto sublucent ora rubore:
　forma noui talis marmoris esse solet;
argenti color est inter conuiuia talis,
　quod tactum gelidae frigore pallet aquae.　　　　220
si me nunc uideas, uisam prius esse negabis,
　'arte nec est' dices 'ista petita mea',
promissique fidem, ne sim tibi uincta, remittes,
　et cupies illud non meminisse deam.
forsitan et facies, iurem ut contraria rursus,　　　　225
　quaeque legam mittes altera uerba mihi.

sed tamen aspiceres uellem, uelut ipse rogabas,
　†et discast† sponsae languida membra tuae:
durius et ferro cum sit tibi pectus, Aconti,
　tu ueniam nostris uocibus ipse petas.　　　　　230
ne tamen ignores, ope qua reualescere possim
　quaeritur a Delphis fata canente deo.
is quoque nescioquem, quantum uaga fama susurrat,
　neglectam queritur testis habere fidem.
hoc deus, hoc uates, hoc ei mihi carmina dicunt;　　235
　at desunt uoto numina nulla tuo.

213 anne ut *Heinsius*: sane π: sane ut *Burman*　　214 magna *Dilthey*: bina π: uana *Meurig Davis*　　216 *fort.* repeto　　222 petita *Dilthey*: petenda π　　223 uincta *Micyllus*: uita π: iuncta *rec. unus*　　225 ut *fort. delendum*　　227 uelut *Francius*: prout π: quod ut *Bentley*　　228 quam dicis *Hollis*　　229 et *Heinsius*: ut π　　230 petes *ed. Venet. 1492*　　233 is *Heinsius ex cod.*: et π　　nescioquem quantum *Kenney praeeunte Fisher* (nescio quem nunc ut): nescioquantum nunc π　　235 hoc uates *Bentley*: & u. π　　ei mihi *Kenney*: & mea π: et mihi *Burman*: edita *Bentley*　　236 numina *Dilthey*: carmina π

HEROIDVM EPISTVLA XXI

unde tibi fauor hic, nisi si noua forte reperta est
  quae capiat magnos littera lecta deos?

* * * * * * *

teque tenente deos numen sequor ipsa deorum
  doque libens uictas in tua uota manus.   240

* * * * * * *

fassaque sum matri deceptae foedera linguae
  lumina fixa tenens plena pudoris humo.
cetera cura tua est: plus hoc quoque uirgine factum,
  non timuit tecum quod mea charta loqui.
iam satis inualidos calamo lassauimus artus,   245
  et manus officium longius aegra negat.
quid, nisi, quod cupio mihi iam contingere tecum,
  restat, ut ascribat littera nostra uale?

237 nisi si noua forte *Housman*: nisi forte noua π   238, 240 *post hos uu. non-*
nulla excidisse ueri simile est   247 quod *add. Ald.*[1]   248 ascribat *Ald.*[1]: -as π

COMMENTARY

xvi
Paris to Helen

1 Hanc ... salutem 'This (wish for) your health'; the conventional greeting (*OLD* s.v. 8) is identified with the letter itself: cf. *Tr.* 5.13.1, *Ex P.* 1.3.1, 2.2.3.

Priamides ... Ledaea 'son of Priam ... daughter of Leda'. Later on Paris spreads himself on his own family (199ff.), Helen's parentage he touches on only in passing (85–6, 214). The formal identification of the two correspondents underlines the portentous consequences of this letter, from which the Trojan War and its vast legacy of suffering were to flow. See Introd. pp. 2–3, 7–8.

2 sola ... te ... dante 'only if you grant it'. Cf. 168n. For the sentiment cf. 4.1–2 *quam nisi tu dederis, caritura est ipsa, salutem | mittit Amazonio Cressa puella uiro.*

3 eloquar, an ... ? ~ Virg. *Aen.* 3.39 *eloquar an sileam?*
notae '(since it is already) known'.

5 lateat malim: the ellipse of *ut* after *malo, uolo, nolo*, etc. is common; cf. e.g. 2.59–60 *mallem suprema fuisset | nox mihi*, 21.65–6; below, 303–4n.

6 non habitura 'which will not have'; the fut. part. stands for a relative clause. Cf. 60 *uix habitura fidem.*

7 quis ... celauerit? 'who could hide?'; cf. *Am.* 2.1.29–30 *quid mihi profuerit uelox cantatus Achilles? | quid pro me Atrides alter et alter agent ... ?*, Hor. *C.* 1.6.13–14 *quis ... digne scripserit?*, *Pan. Mess.* 89ff. *quis ... iecerit aut perfregerit ... aut ... possit?*, Juv. 2.24 *quis tulerit Gracchos de seditione querentes?*, Cic. *De or.* 1.36 *quis enim tibi hoc concesserit?*, *Fin.* 4.48, *Div.* 2.103 *quis hoc non dederit?*, *Rep.* 1.71 *quis ... te potius ... de maiorum dixerit institutis?*, Val. Max. 1 *Praef. quis enim omnis aeui gesta modico uoluminum numero comprehenderit* eqs.? The pf. subj. is used interchangeably with the present (cf. *Am., Pan. Mess.* above) in such potential clauses, but much less commonly in questions than in statements (Blase (1903) 203–5); cf. 189 *nec ... fuerit* and n. See McKeown on *Am.* 1.14.33.

COMMENTARY: 16.10–21

10 animi nuntia uerba mei 'the message [in fact one ominous word (49–50n.)] that tells my feelings', *nuntia* predicative.

11–12 uultu ... formae conueniente tuae 'with an expression that suits your beauty'.

conueniente: adjectival for the more usual (prose) abl. in -*i*, cf. e.g. 31, 284, 17.82, 89, 21.232; but the 'rule' was never rigidly observed, especially by poets in want of a short final syllable (cf. Sommer (1948) 377). So e.g. *Am.* 1.8.20 *nec tamen eloquio lingua nocente caret*)(*Met.* 14.56–7 *latices radice nocenti* | *spargit.* Cf. 279–80n. on *caeleste.*

duro: emphasized by its position at the end of the verse (the 'normal' epithet-noun order *duro ... uultu* in some MSS).

13 iamdudum gratum est 'I'm already grateful'; he clearly anticipates more favours to come (*OLD* s.v. *gratus* 2d). The first hurdle at all events has been cleared: cf. *A.A.* 1.469–70 *si non accipiet scriptum illectumque remittet,* | *lecturam spera propositumque tene.*

13–14 recepta ... recipi: for the special sense of *recipio* absolute = 'receive a lover' on which Paris plays cf. Prop. 2.14.28 *tota nocte receptus amans,* Ov. *Am.* 1.8.78 *audiat exclusi uerba receptus amans,* 3.7.47 *optabam certe recipi: sum nempe receptus, Her.* 2.29 *unum in me scelus est quod te, scelerate, recepi.* See 19.156n. For *recepta* cf. 18.139–40n.

15 nec = *et ne*; cf. 83n.

17 ego: a metrical 'filler'? The emphasis is on *diuino monitu.* The word occurs in *Her.* 16–21 in 3.7% of verses (1–14: 2.9%; *A.A.* 1.1%). Cf. 23n., Introd. p. 24.

ne nescia pecces 'so that you may make no mistake through ignorance', but also 'so that when you fall from grace ⟨which I shall now convince you is inevitable⟩, you will know why'. On the two senses of *pecco* played on see *OLD* s.v. 1, 3. For *ne* cf. 363n.

18 non leue 'most potent', litotes.

19 non indebita: owed to him for adjudicating the prize of beauty to Venus. This indeed is Paris' trump card, repeatedly played (35, 85–6, 165–8; cf. 41n.). The emphasis on Venus' role as stage-manageress seems to go back to the *Cypria* (*EGF* p. 31. 12, 14–15, 22–3); cf. Eur. *Tro.* 940–1, Wentzel (1890) XII, XVI.

21 Sigeo 'Trojan' by synecdoche (the part for the whole); cf. 275 *Sigeos,* 16.187, 17.209 *Achaia* 'Greece', 17.248 *Atracis* 'Thessalian',

16.346 *Bistonis* 'Thracian', 16.30, 17.6 *Taenaris*, 16.276 *Taenaria* 'Spartan', 18.152 *Parrhasis* 'Arcadian', 20.106 *Mygdonia* 'Phrygian'. Sigeum, on the Aegean coast N.W. of Troy, was famous in classical times as the burial-place of Achilles and Patroclus. Conversely (the whole for the part) 16.198, *al. Phryx*, 16.186, *al. Phrygius* 'Trojan'.

22 Phereclea: like Sigeum a name with an ironical resonance. The ships built by Phereclus were 'the initiators of evil (ἀρχεκάκους) that became the ruin of all the Trojans [including Phereclus, whose death the passage records] and of Paris himself, since he did not regard the decrees of the gods' (Hom. *Il.* 5.63–4). Cf. 107–24n.

uias 'journey'; for the pl. cf. 7.116 *feror in dubias hoste sequente uias*, 18.60, 19.52, 21.68, *Met.* 3.12 *hac duce carpe uias*. It appears to be motivated in these exx. solely by metrical convenience; but see 332n.

23 faciles auras uentosque secundos: the doublet *aura* ... *uentus* is characteristic (McKeown on *Am.* 1.8.106), but *faciles* (cf. *OLD* s.v. 9c) ... *secundos* is mere tautology (hence *undas* Oudendorp). Contrast *A.A.* 3.694 *lenibus ... Zephyris auraque salubri* 'the refreshing breath of gentle Zephyr', a real hendiadys. Perhaps an example of the 'molestam quandam et exuberantem orationis abundantiam' of which Lachmann ((1876) 58) complained in these epistles? Cf. Introd. p. 24. On Paris' voyage see 126–7n.

24 orta mari 'being born of the sea'; 'Aphrodite she is called because she grew in the foam (ἐν ἀφρῶι)', Hes. *Theog.* 195–7. One of her cult names was Εὔπλοια 'She who gives a fair voyage'. The same conceit at 7.57–60, 19.159–60, *E.S.* 213; cf. Gaetulicus (?first c. A.D.), *A.P.* 5.17 (*FGE* 175–80). In similar vein is Meleag. *A.P.* 12.119.3 (*HE* 4100) on Bacchus, 'born in fire you cherish the fire of love'.

25 aestum 'tide' and 'fire (of love)' (*OLD* s.v. 8a, 5a).

26 et: postponement of conjunctions by the Latin poets, after the example of their Hellenistic models, begins with Catullus (Fordyce on 23.7); for O.'s elegiac practice see Platnauer (1951) 93–6, and cf. Knox (1986) 88–90. *et* is postponed more frequently in *Her.* 16–21 than in 1–14 and the *amatoria*, but not more than in the *Tristia*. Cf. Haupt I (1875–6) 124–6. Here the placing of *et* serves to emphasize *mea uota*: as Paris has literally, so may his prayers metaphorically make port. Cf. *A.A.* 2.9–10 *quid properas, iuuenis? mediis tua pinus in undis | nauigat, et longe quem peto portus abest*.

27 attulimus flammas ... illas: he had fallen in love with her before he ever saw her (35–40).

29 tristis hiems 'bad weather'.

30 Taenaris: 21n.

classi ... meae: dat. of the agent; the fleet is as eager as its commander.

petita: emphatic, 'the chosen goal'.

31 merces portante carina: the 'goods' (sought not brought, but *porto* can = 'carry off'; cf. Hor. *C.* 1.26.3) will prove to be Helen. In a hexameter fragment preserved on a papyrus more or less contemporary with O. Paris is described as λαθρέμπορος 'furtive-dealing', sc. in other men's wives (*SH* 952.3).

33 ueluti spectator: as young Romans of good family, such as O. himself, would have done; tourism in the Mycenaean age is an amusing anachronism. So Phyllis refers to Athens as a university city, *doctas ... Athenas* (2.83). This was evidently the reason he gave to Menelaus, who duly takes him off sightseeing (131–2); cf. Wentzel (1890) XLIV.

33–4 urbes ... oppida: used by the poets without distinction of sense as metrical convenience dictated.

36 prius ... quam ... nota fores 'before you could have been known to me' (*NLS* §228(*b*)). *fores*, as usual in O., is 'a convenient metrical stand-by' (Brink on Hor. *A.P.* 289) for *esses*; cf. e.g. 274, 17.188, 18.110, 21.6, *al.*

37–40 On the problems of this passage see Kenney (1979) 411, 414–15.

37–8 This element of the story is already found in Hesiod's *Eoeae*: one of Helen's many suitors 'longs to wed Helen of the lovely hair, never having seen her, but hearing the story from others' (fr. 199.2–3 M–W); cf. Colluthus (fifth c. A.D.), *Rape of Helen* 193 (Paris) 'yearning with love in quest of a woman he had never seen'.

tuos ... uultus 'your features'; the pl. of *uultus* is frequent in O., e.g. 10.134, 13.152, 16.137, 244, *al.*

lumine 'eyes'; for the sing. cf. e.g. 21.199 and see Bömer on *Met.* 5.545; apparently a Catullan innovation (64.86 and Fordyce *ad loc.*).

prima tulit uulnus nuntia fama mihi: Housman's *tulit uulnus* produces effective sense in the shape of an explicit statement of the claim hinted at above (27); the transmitted text merely restates line 37, ineptly repeating *uultus* with an even more inept variation of number. *tui* is otiose and may be due to reminiscence of line 10; *mihi* (Kenney), though in itself colourless, rounds off the sense. However, this reconstruction must be treated as a *pis aller*, since *uulnus ferre* commonly means *u. accipere* rather than *dare* (Reeve (1973) 335 n. 1). Perhaps read *dedit uulnus*?

39–144 This part of the text is transmitted only in the Parma edition of 1477 (π). See Introd. p. 26, and for a full discussion Kenney (1979).

39–40 The second half of line 39 is hopelessly corrupt, but the general tenor of the couplet is apt enough in the context: 'I fell in love with the mere report of your beauty. Do not be surprised: it was the will of Fate' (Kenney (1979) 414).

nec tamen is connective, not adversative; *tamen* is often no stronger than Greek δέ (Kenney (1979) 401 n. 23, 410 n. 48). Cf. 115.

41 conuellere 'overthrow', a strong word, pertly picked up by Helen in her reply (17.111n.). This pompous exordium to Paris' narrative ironically underlines his unawareness of the full implications of Hecuba's dream. What the Fates had in store was something infinitely more momentous than the union of these two: O.'s educated readers knew that according to the *Cypria* (*EGF* p. 35) Zeus decided to start the Trojan War to relieve the Earth of surplus population. For other explanations of the divine motivation see Apollod. *Epit.* 3.1. According to one variant of the legend Helen's mother was Nemesis (*Cypria*, *EGF* pp. 37–8, Apollod. *Bibl.* 3.10.7.2–3 and Frazer *ad loc.*).

42 Cf. 60; the solemn and minatory tone suggests that Helen will disregard this at her peril.

accipe ... dicta: an epicism; cf. Enn. *Ann.* 187 Sk. *hoc simul accipe dictum*, Virg. *Aen.* 3.250, 10.104 *accipite ergo animis atque haec mea figite dicta*.

relata = *quae (tibi) refero*; the aspect of the pf. part., as often, is contemporaneous (Kenney on Lucret. 3.171).

43–128 The history of Paris as told by himself. For the sequence of events followed by O. and his reconciliation of the other authorities see Introd. pp. 6–7.

43–50 Hecuba's dream. He plunges dramatically *in medias res*: *ad*-

COMMENTARY: 16.43-45

huc (43) underlines the implication that his was from the very beginning a special destiny. O.'s indebtedness to Ennius' *Alexander* is clear:

> mater grauida parere se ardentem facem
> uisa est in somnis Hecuba. quo facto pater
> rex ipse Priamus somnio mentis metu
> perculsus curis sumptus suspirantibus
> exsacrificabat hostiis balantibus.
> tum coniecturam postulat pacem petens,
> ut se edoceret obsecrans Apollinem
> quo sese uertant tantae sortes somnium.
> ibi ex oraclo uoce diuina edidit
> Apollo puerum primus Priamo qui foret
> postilla natus temperaret tollere;
> eum esse exitium Troiae, pestem Pergamo.   (50–61 Jocelyn)

43 partu remorante: suggesting perhaps reluctance on the part of Fate to set in motion the train of events that would follow his birth if he were allowed to live. The dream offers a last chance to avert these consequences.

44 iusto pondere 'its full weight' (*OLD* s.v. *iustus* 6b); the birth was overdue (cf. 46 *pleno ... uentre*).

45–6 ingentem ... flammiferam: by O.'s time it was a recognized solecism to qualify one noun with two attributes: Serv. on *Aen.* 2.392 *duo epitheta, quod apud Latinos uitiosum est*. The 'rule' was not rigidly observed (Munro on Lucret. 1.258, Williams on Virg. *Aen.* 3.69–70, H–S 160–1); but O.'s breach of it here seems to be a conscious Ennianism (cf. however Skutsch on *Ann.* 141), as suggested independently by Jacobson (1968) 303 n. 21 and White (1968) 190–1. Cf. 223, 17.237–8nn., Introd. p. 6. *ingentem* should certainly not be emended away: the word is used elsewhere of larger-than-life apparitions (*TLL* s.v. 1540.60ff., esp. Lucan 1.186 *ingens uisa duci patriae trepidantis imago*), and it is nothing if not apposite of a *fax* which symbolizes the conflagration of Troy (cf. *Met.* 13.169, 505); cf. 353 *ingens ... bellum*.

sub imagine somni 'in a dream' (= *Met.* 8.824, 9.686). *sub imagine* is an Ovidian cliché (19x); on that and other phrases with *imago* in O. see Bömer on *Met.* 9.464.

flammiferam: cf. Enn. *Alcmeo* 25 J. *flammiferam hanc uim quae me* *excruciat*; not attested again until O., and probably an Ennian coinage (Jacobson, White *locc. cit.*).

47 territa consurgit = *F*. 1.435.

47–8 metuenda ... noctis opacae uisa ~ Lycophr. *Alex.* 224–5 'the nightwalking fears (νυκτίφοιτα δείματα) of Aesacus' oracles'.

uatibus 'seers'. In the Euripidean version, followed by Ennius (above; cf. Jocelyn (1967) 222–3), the dream was referred to the oracle of Apollo. O.'s imprecision may be designed to demonstrate to the alert reader his own awareness of divergencies in his literary sources. Cf. 49n.

ille: O. follows Ennius (cit. 43–50n.) in making Priam rather than Hecuba take this action: 'no Roman *paterfamilias* would have allowed a woman to interfere in so important a matter' (Jocelyn (1967) 221).

49–50 O. makes Paris pun on the literal and metaphorical senses of *ignis* in order to impose his own light-hearted interpretation on the obvious meaning of this ominous response. Cf. Polyphemus' similarly flippant reception of Telemus' prophecy at *Met.* 13.772–5. Helen is justifiably sceptical (17.237–40). The conceit is exploited again at 123–6 – more *molesta abundantia* (23n.)? There are twenty-seven allusions to fire in the letter (Sabot (1981) 2613 n. 106).

49 arsurum: here and at 17.240 Heinsius emended to *arsuram*; but (especially given the quality of the MS tradition) it is often impossible to decide between *Ilios* (f.) and *Ilion* (n.).

uates: possibly (as already suggested by Ciofanus (1582)) Cassandra's brother Aesacus, styled *uates* by Servius (on *Aen.* 2.32 = Euphorion fr. 55 Powell) and identified by Apollodorus (*Bibl.* 3.12.5.2) and Lycophron (*Alex.* 224–8) as having advised Priam to expose Paris or put him to death (cf. Kenney (1993) 465–7). Cassandra's intervention is reserved for later (121–4); according to Apollodorus (*Bibl.* 3.12.5.6) she was born some time after Paris. The repetition of *uates* immediately after *uatibus* = 'one of them' is distinctly awkward; did O. write *canit Aesacus*, *uates* having been supplied as a gloss and then having ousted the name?

50 ut nunc est 'as now appears' = 17.169, 19.127. Why O. should have had this phrase on the brain, as he apparently did when writing these epistles, there is no telling; but the fact is not evidence for non-Ovidian authorship (Kenney (1979) 398, Introd. p. 24).

51–2 Some verses have been lost before this couplet, as Scaliger

COMMENTARY: 16.52-3

first pointed out, in which Paris told how, as a result of the seers' advice, he was exposed at birth, rescued, and brought up by herdsmen on Mt Ida (Apollod. *Bibl.* 3.12.5.4–5, Hyg. *Fab.* 91). Cf. 359–62, where he refers to this period of his life in passing, and see Introd. p. 6.

For the thought cf. *F.* 2.397–8 (Romulus and Remus) '*si genus arguitur uultu, nisi fallit imago,* | *nescioquem in uobis suspicor esse deum*', Cic. *Rep.* 2.37 (Servius Tullius) *non latuit scintilla ingenii quae tum elucebat in puero; sic erat in omni uel officio uel sermone sollers*, and Zetzel *ad loc.* (citing *Fin.* 5.43), Livy 1.39 esp. 4 *iuuenis euasit uere indolis regiae*. That princely birth will out is a traditional belief: Thompson (S.) (1955–8) H.41.5, P.35. Cf. the story of Cyrus (Hdt. 1.114.1–2, 115.2; Coles (1974) 33 n. 10). There is probably an echo of Eur. *Alex.* here; cf. frr. 52, 53 N.² (=40, 41 Snell) on 'nobility of birth' (εὐγένεια), *Hypoth.* i.13–14 'the boy seemed to be ⟨? well-born as to [see Coles (1974) 19 n. 13]⟩ his nature'. In the *Alexandros* 'the other shepherds, on account of the arrogance of his relationship towards them, bound and brought him before Priam' (*Hypoth.* i.15–17 Coles). The unattributed fragment 'how like to the sons of Priam is the neatherd' (*adesp.* 286 N.²) is allotted to the *Alexandros* by Snell (fr. 25).

52 nobilitatis: O. has a penchant for quadrisyllabic nouns in -*itas*, esp. in this *sedes*; cf. in this epistle 162, 302, 312, 316, 376, and see McKeown on *Am.* 1.8.43–4 (pp. 223–4). Many of them would have sounded prosaic to his contemporaries.

erat: as not uncommonly, the verb takes the number of the predicate (*indicium*); cf. e.g. *A.A.* 3.222 *quas geritis uestes, sordida lana fuit*, *Am.* 1.7.60 *sanguis erat lacrimae, quas dabat illa, meus* and McKeown *ad loc.*, Virg. *Ecl.* 8.58 *omnia uel medium fiat mare* and Clausen *ad loc.* Cf. 362n.

53–88 The Judgement. While the gods were making merry at the wedding-breakfast of Peleus and Thetis, a dispute arose between Hera (Juno), Athena (Minerva), and Aphrodite (Venus) as to who was the most beautiful. The dispute was referred by Zeus (Jupiter) to the arbitration of Paris, then still herding his flocks on Ida (*EGF* p.31, 9, paraphrasing the *Cypria*; Hyg. *Fab.* 92). *Nota fabula*, as Servius remarks (*Aen.* 1.27); but why Paris should have been singled out for this honourable but highly invidious assignment is obscure. It was apparently left to Lucian to motivate Zeus's choice: 'because he is himself handsome and skilled in love (σοφὸς τὰ ἐρωτικά)' (35.1 Macleod; cf. 78.7.2). Paris modestly protests that he is a better judge of goats and heifers (*ibid.* 35.7); but as Mr Weller senior sagely observed, 'The man as can form a ackerate judgment of a animal, can form a ackerate judgment of anythin'.' O.'s Paris has apparently enjoyed better opportunities than Lucian's (93–6).

53–6 The idyllic peace of this pastoral retreat, as with many another Ovidian *locus amoenus* (e.g. *A.A.* 3.687–94; see Segal (1969) *passim*), contrasts ironically with the dire consequences of what happens there (next n.). Cf. for a comparable description of the setting of the Judgement Eur. *I.A.* 1294–9.

53 est locus: the conventional formula to introduce an *ecphrasis*. Ida, the place where it all began, was 'the very ἀρχή [origin]' of the Trojan War (Stinton (1965) 32–3 = (1990) 42). Cf. 303–4 *Idaei ... hospitis* and n., 19.177n.

54 deuius: cf. Eur. *Andr.* 281–3 the goddesses came 'to the solitary young herdsman and his lonely hearth and home', *I.A.* 573–81.

57–8 hinc ... prospiciens: *tecta nobilitas* instinctively yearning for its birthright?

Dardaniae 'Troy', a Virgilianism; elsewhere in O. only as adj. 'Trojan'.

prospiciens ... eram = *prospiciebam*; cf. e.g. 18.55 *nox erat incipiens*, *Met.* 12.395 *barba erat incipiens*, though neither these nor the other exx. cited by Bömer on *Met.* 4.772–3 are clearly pure periphrases for the usual tense, as is the case here. The construction is at home in comedy and prose (Blase (1903) 256–7); for the problem of classification see Eklund (1970) *passim*, but his doubts as to the existence of 'periphrases with verbal complements ... in pre-Christian Latin' (47) require reconsideration in the light of this passage. Cf. 151–2, 17.68nn.

59 pedum pulsu uisa est mihi terra moueri: this sounds more like the tramp of an armed host or the onset of cavalry (Virg. *Aen.* 6.591, 7.722, 12.334–5, 445; cf. Enn. *Thy.* 305 J.) than the arrival of aspirants for the title of Miss Olympus; but gods and goddesses are of superhuman size and weight (*F.* 2.503, 3.330 and Bömer *ad locc.*), and Paris is laying himself out to impress.

60 habitura: 6n.

ueri ... fidem 'belief in the truth', credibility; cf. *Met.* 3.659–60

COMMENTARY: 16.61-71

uera ... *ueri maiora fide*, *Tr.* 4.1.66 *uera quidem, ueri sed grauiora fide*, *F.* 3.662 *nec a ueri dissidet illa fide.* The gen. is objective.

61 constitit ante oculos: similarly of epiphanies at *A.A.* 3.44 (*a. o. c.*), *E.S.* 162, [Ov.] *Am.* 3.5.10.

uelocibus alis: the *talaria* on his sandals. Though he is escorting the goddesses, who arrive on foot, he needs them for his dramatic exit (72).

62 Hermes (Mercury) was the son of Maia, daughter of Atlas and Pleione. The grand Greek names invest the god, and the occasion, with awe.

63 fas uidisse fuit: generally it was *nefas* to look a god in the face: *F.* 6.7-8, Livy 1.16.6, Sen. *Ep. Mor.* 115.4, Lucan 1.598, *al.*

64 aurea uirga: the caduceus; Virg. *Aen.* 4.242-4 *tum uirgam capit: | hac animas ille euocat Orco | pallentis, alias sub Tartara tristia mittit, | dat somnos adimitque, et lumina morte resignat.* His Homeric epithet is χρυσόρραπις 'golden-wanded'.

67 obstipui: he uses the same word to describe his reaction to the first sight of Helen (135). The verse is a good ex. of adroit Virgilian pastiche: *arrectaeque horrore comae* (*Aen.* 4.280, 12.868) + *obstipui, steteruntque comae* (2.774, 3.48) + *obstipuere animi gelidusque per ima cucurrit | ossa tremor* (2.120-1) + *mihi frigidus horror | membra quatit gelidusque coit formidine sanguis* (3.29-30). Oenone had reacted similarly when Paris told her of it: *attoniti micuere sinus, gelidusque cucurrit, | ut mihi narrasti, dura per ossa tremor* (5.37-8), an even more open Virgilian *furtum*.

gelidusque comas: hexameters with a 'weak' or 'feminine' caesura in the third foot are relatively rare in O.'s elegiacs: the figure for *Her.* 16-21 (3.6%) is markedly lower than that for all but the exile poems (Platnauer (1951) 10). Cf. 337n.

69 es: indic. rather than imperative; after *pone metum* a (reassuring) statement is in order.

69-70 certamina ... quae ... digna sit 'the contentions (as to) which deserves'.

71 neue = *et, ne* (*OLD* s.v. *neue* 2b).

uerbis Iouis 'in Jupiter's name' (*OLD* s.v. *uerbum* 14).

et se: the proportion of hexameters ending in two monosyllables in *Her.* 16-21 is considerably higher than in 1-14: 1.8 as against 0.36 per cent. However, no single instance is in itself anomalous, and the phenomenon is not uncommon in the Latin poets (Hellegouarc'h

(1964) 55–61; Helzle on *Ex P.* 4.2.47). Here it is effective in accentuating the abruptness (*protinus*) of Mercury's departure.

74 uultu ... notare 'to take a careful look at'; for *uultus* = 'gaze' see *OLD* s.v. 3a.

75 iudex 'though I was the judge', and supposedly taking a detached view.

76 posse tenere: this is Francius' correction of the MS *uincere posse*, which has obviously intruded from line 75. *causam tenere* is normal Ovidian Latin (17.244, *Met.* 13.190) for 'win one's case' (*OLD* s.v. *causa* 3c), *causam uincere* excessively rare and unparalleled in O. (*TLL* s.v. *caussa* 694.65–7).

78 'so that one might have known (sc. without being told) that this was the goddess who inspires love'. This use of *scires* is characteristic of O. (*Am.* 1.13.47, *Met.* 1.162 and Bömer *ad loc.*, 6.23, *F.* 2.419, 5.376); only here introduced by consec. *ut*; cf. Suet. *Aug.* 42.1 *sed ut salubrem magis quam ambitiosum principem scires, querentem de inopia et caritate uini populum seuerissima coercuit uoce* (cit. Palmer).

unde = *a qua* (*OLD* s.v. 2a, 8a).

79 tanta ... est, ... ardent = *tanta est, ut ardeant*; the paratactic (coordinating) expression here helps to suggest their urgency.

81 regna ... uirtutem: specifically and respectively, according to Euripides (*Tro.* 925–8), dominion over Europe and Asia, and the conquest of Greece. Helen's specious argument there, contemptuously demolished by Hecuba (971ff.), is predicated on a *color* worthy of O. himself, which we may suspect he enjoyed. *uirtutem* 'martial prowess' (*OLD* s.v. 1b).

82 i.e. *dubito (utrum) potens an fortis esse uelim*; the omission of the first conjunction is normal (*NLS* §182 (4), *OLD* s.v. *an* 4, 7), the hyperbaton (dislocated word-order) a concession to metrical expediency. Cf. *Tr.* 3.1.44 *quam tribuit terris, pacis an ista nota est?*

83 dulce ... risit: recalling her Homeric epithet 'laughter-loving'.

'nec ...' ait = *et ait 'ne ...'*; this trick of dividing the copulative and the negative functions of *nec* between narrative and direct speech is peculiar to O. The construction can be accurately represented according to modern conventions of punctuation only 'by a grotesque employment of inverted commas' (Housman, *CP* 413): ... *risit 'ne'c 'te ...* '. Cf. 21.222, and on the extreme unlikelihood of this feature as the work of an interpolator Kenney (1979) 396, Introd. p. 21. See also 17.159n.

84 suspensi ... timoris 'anxiety and fear' – ironical in view of the consequences of his choice.

85 quod ames 'something to love', final subj. (*NLS* §148); cf. *A.A.* 1.91 *illic inuenies quod ames*. This use of *quod* is characteristic of O. (Booth on *Am.* 2.2.14); its frequency in *Her.* 16–21 (8x as against none in 1–14) has been used as an argument against their authenticity. Given that these epistles have more to do with wooing than the others and have more of the *Amores* and *Ars* about them in consequence, this is not a point of much substance. Cf. also Plaut. *Curc.* 29, 31, 136, 138, 170!

86 ipsa: this is a marginal reading in the edn of G. Bersmann (1582); cf. *Am.* 3.2.32 *sequitur fortes fortior ipsa feras*, Virg. *Ecl.* 5.44 *formosi pecoris custos, formosior ipse*, *Dirae* 33–4 *formosaeque cadent umbrae, formosior illis | ipsa cades. illa* (π) is pointless. Cf. Hor. *C.* 1.16.1 *o matre pulchra filia pulchrior* and N–H *ad loc.*, suggesting an allusion to Stesichorus.

87 ex aequo (= 20.123) 'equally'; O. 'greatly favours such phrases constructed with *ex* and an adjective and bearing the sense of an adverb' (McKeown on *Am.* 1.10.33); cf. 160 *ex toto*, 20.167 *ex tuto*. *OLD*'s classification of this usage under *aequum* (2c) is misconceived.

probatis: Heinsius' correction gives an unambiguous construction, whereas *probata* (π) may be either nom. 'having been approved in respect of both her bribes and her beauty' or abl. 'her bribes and her beauty having been approved', with the participle agreeing grammatically with the nearer noun (362n.). Cf. 205 *collatis forma ... et armis*, 19.163 *uectis Phrixo Phrixique sorore*.

88 uictorem ... rettulit ... pedem 'returned victorious', predicative; for *uictor* as adj. see *OLD* s.v. 3b.

caelo: dat. of direction towards.

89–98 The Recognition. Paris is found to be a prince of the royal house and restored to his fortunes. On O.'s manipulation of the narrative see Introd. pp. 6–7 and cf. next n.

89 interea 'meanwhile'; O.'s chronology is studiously vague, but as he manages the narrative the Recognition and Paris' consequent emergence as an eligible *parti* (93–6) must have preceded the Judgement; otherwise what he says at lines 99–100 would not make sense. For the meaning of *interea* see Kinsey (1979), arguing that in Virgil and Ovid it never means 'and now', 'next', always 'meanwhile', *dum haec geruntur* (Serv. on *Aen.* 1.479, *al.*). The exx. for the connective sense cited by Bömer on *Met.* 2.153 will not pass muster.

sero 'at last' (Wakker), cf. 91 *post tempora longa*; *credo* (π) is only pointed if ironic, but in these epistles the only effective irony is authorial. Paris and Helen must play it straight.

90 rata signa 'tokens duly certified'. This must refer to the rattle (*crepundia*) by which in drama abducted or abandoned children were commonly identified; so in Nero's *Troica* (Serv. on *Aen.* 5.370), Dracontius (*De raptu Helenae* 102 *certa crepundia*), and probably in Euripides' *Alexandros* (Coles (1974) 28 n. 26).

91 post tempora longa ~ Eur. *Alex.* 42 N.² = fr. 2 Snell καὶ χρόνου προύβαινε πούς 'and the foot of time was marching on', *Hypoth.* i.12–14 Coles 'twenty years went by' (?), Enn. *Alex.* 42 J. *multos annos latuit*.

92 A regular Trojan Calendar with public festivals to mark redletter days in the annals of the royal house looks like another Ovidian anachronism (33n.).

et: 26n.

94 multarum uotum 'what so many have longed for'; cf. 106n.

96 ... -que ... -que: 'a feature of epic style, found already in Ennius, who took it over from the Homeric correlation τε ... τε' (Austin on Virg. *Aen.* 1.18, q.v.); in O.'s elegiacs merely a metrical convenience (cf. 21.101n.), as indeed it already was for Ennius (Skutsch on *Ann.* 170).

97–8 The text of line 97 is hopelessly corrupt, but the general drift is clear. Paris' marriage to Oenone and his desertion of her, the subject of *Her.* 5, was too familiar a part of the legend to be passed over in silence, but by the same token did not need to be spelled out, especially when it had been exploited so thoroughly already. This airy throwaway reference is clever and in character: as Paris tells the story Oenone was just one of the many aspirants to his hand, though an exceptionally eligible one. He also fudges the chronology: for to bring in Oenone at this point, especially after 95–6, implies that his acquaintance with her postdated the Recognition, which was very far from the truth; when he married her he was still a simple herdsman, as Oenone had recalled in her own letter: *nondum tantus eras, cum te contenta marito | edita de magno flumine nympha fui. | qui nunc Priamides – absit reuerentia uero! – | seruus eras; seruo nubere nympha tuli* (5.9–12). It will emerge that Helen knows better (17.195–8n.). Cf. Introd. pp. 6–7. There is no case for deleting the couplet as spurious (Kenney (1979) 399 and n. 17).

98 'There is, next to you, none more fit to be Priam's daughter-in-law'; skilfully ambiguous wording, which skates over without actually denying that this was precisely what Oenone was.

a 'after', 'next to' (*OLD* s.v. 13c); cf. 6.156, 18.69, 20.157, Introd. p. 24.

99–126 The main narrative resumes. Paris resolves to carry off Helen. The Shipbuilding and the departure for Sparta.

99 sed ... postquam ... : the chronological progression interrupted by *interea* (89n.) now resumes.

100 Tyndari 'daughter of Tyndareus'.

101 uigilans oculis animi: sequences of three anapaestic words 'unblurred by synaloepha' (Wilkinson (1963) 82) are rare in poetry; in *Her.* at 8.75, 12.27, 57, 13.29, 51, 17.81, 20.35 (*quod amo* virtually one word), 37; cf. also e.g. *Am.* 1.10.17, 11.23 (*opus est* virtually one word), 2.14.11, *A.A.* 1.13, 447, 707 (reading *nimiast*), *Met.* 3.242. See Norden on Virg. *Aen.* 6.290, Clausen on *Ecl.* 1.22, McKeown (1987) 118–19.

animi is Bentley's certain correction of the nonsensical *animo* (π). For *oculis animi* cf. *Met.* 15.64 *oculis ea pectoris hausit, Ex. P.* 1.8.34 *cuncta ... mens oculis peruidet usa suis, Tr.* 3.4.55–6 *sic tamen haec adsunt ut quae contingere non est | corpore; sunt animo cuncta uidenda meo,* 4.2.57 *haec ego summotus qua possum mente uidebo,* Cic. *Or.* 101 *eloquentia ipsa, quam nullis nisi mentis oculis uidere possumus,* Plat. *Symp.* 219a2–3 ἡ ... τῆς διανοίας ὄψις, *Rep.* 7.519b, 533d, Bömer on *Met.* 10.351. The verse takes up and varies line 37 *ante tuos animo uidi quam lumine uultus.* Cf. 20.229–30.

102 lumina cum ... iacent: sc. but the mind is still active. The *cum*-clause qualifies *nocte*, not *uidebam*.

103 quid faceres ...? 'What would you have done (to me)?', impf. for plupf.; cf. 18.43–4, *Met.* 4.704 *quis enim dubitaret?* and Bömer *ad loc., Her.* 12.146 *quis uellet tanti nuntius esse mali?*, Blase (1903) 154. See 156–8n.

104 ~ *Am.* 2.16.12 *quae mouet ardores, est procul; ardor adest.*

hic: in Sparta, where he is now.

105 'I could not go on withholding realization of that hope from myself'. This sense of *debeo* = 'leave unpaid' seems to be otherwise peculiar to Cicero: *OLD* s.v. 3b, Shackleton Bailey on *Att.* 4.2 (74).2.

106 peterem quin 'without seeking', an easy extension of the usual construction with *facere non possum* 'I cannot help but ...' (*OLD* s.v. *quin* 4c, *NLS* §187(*d*)). Cf. H–S 678–9.

mea uota 'the object of my prayers', 'id est te, quam cupiebam & amabam' (Micyllus (1549)); cf. 94n.

107–24 The Shipbuilding and Cassandra's intervention evidently figured in the *Cypria* (*EGF* p. 31, 13–16). The ship was a powerful symbol of human recklessness (N–H on Hor. *C.* 1.3, pp. 43–4); as the building of the Argo was identified as the starting-point of Medea's tragic history (Eur. *Med.* 1–6, Enn. *Med.* 208–16 J.), so the launching of Paris' fleet marks the point of no return for Troy (cf. 1.5–6, Eur. *Hec.* 629–37, Lycophr. *Alex.* 16–27). The motif reappears in Herodotus (5.97.3). Cf. 22n.

107–14 Every verse in this passage except 113 is constructed with two adj.-noun pairs grouped round a verb, three of them (109, 110, 111) in the balanced configuration known since Dryden as 'Golden' ('two substantives and two adjectives with a verb betwixt to keep the peace'): 107 aVbAB, 108 VabBA, 109 abVAB, 110 abVBA, 111 abVAB, 112 VAbBa, 114 VaBbA. Such a concentration of patterned verses seems to be unique in O., but what special effect, if any, is intended is unclear. The mannerism is neoteric: cf. e.g. Catull. 64.63–7, 311–19, Gallus (cit. 19.142n.). The passage may owe something to the stock epic motif of felling trees for a funeral pyre (Williams (1968) 263–7); *proceris* (a word not found in the *Aeneid*) suggests that O. may have had Ennius in mind (*Ann.* 178 Sk. *pinus proceras peruortunt*). This ample treatment contrasts markedly with Oenone's telegraphic brevity: 5.41–2 *caesa abies sectaeque trabes et classe parata | caerula ceratas accipit unda rates* (abVAB). On such verses in Latin poets see Kenney (1984) xlivf., lxiff. Cf. 19.37–8, 21.70nn.

107 Troica ... Phrygia: if this were prose, the adjj. would naturally be read as modifying *securi* and *pineta* respectively. Double enallage (transference of epithets), though not peculiar to O. (Virg. *Aen.* 6.268, 9.455 and Austin, Hardie *ad locc.*), is characteristic of him: cf. *Am.* 3.7.21–2 *sic flammas aditura pias aeterna sacerdos | surgit*, *Met.*

1.39 *flumina* ... *obliquis cinxit decliuia ripis* and Bömer *ad loc.*, Kenney (1973) 131 and nn. 102, 103. Cf. 18.133n.

109 Gargara: one of the peaks of Ida. It was one of the others, Phalacra, that traditionally provided the timber for Paris' fleet (Lycophr. *Alex.* 24, Pfeiffer on Callim. fr. 34).

111–12 'Oaks are bent to form the structure of the swift ships, and the curved hulls receive their framework of ribs'. The couplet is an ex. of theme and variation, describing in summary fashion not two operations but one: the attachment of the frames or ribs (*costae*) to the planking of the hull (*carina* = 'ship' not 'keel'), which was constructed first (Casson (1971) 202–3). It is rash to postulate technical accuracy in such poetic descriptions; though O. may well have been conversant with what must have been an elementary fact, his treatment is heavily indebted to literary models. Cf. esp. for *texitur* Enn. *Alex.* 43–4 J. *iamque mari magno classis cita | texitur*, Catull. 64.10 *pinea coniungens inflexae texta carinae* and Fordyce *ad loc.* (but for 'keel' read 'ship'), Virg. *Aen.* 11.326 *Italo texamus robore naues, al.*; and cf. 21.70n. Technical precision (oak is not readily bent, and indeed was not much used in ship-building (Meiggs (1982) 118); but O. had found the word in Virgil) is sacrificed to ingenious variation: Catullus' *inflexae ... carinae > flectuntur ... naues > panda carina*. Line 111 should perhaps be read as enallage = *robore fundantur flexae naues. suis* = 'its due complement of (ribs)' (*OLD* s.v. *suus* B12a). See on the passage Meijer (1990), who however fails to grasp that the sense of 112 is identical with that of 111, which he is reduced to vaguely paraphrasing (450).

111 citas: a stock epithet originating in the Homeric formulae νῆες θοαί, νηῒ θοῆι, etc.

113 addimus ... malo 'fit to the mast'.

uela sequentia 'the sail that goes with it', i.e. with the yard to which it is attached, as it is hauled up and down, 'its attendant sail', an unparalleled expression but by no means inapt. A Homeric ship had a single mast, yard, and sail: *uela* is common in poetry of a single sail, but *antemnae* is a real plural, used of the two spars that were lashed together to form the yard. Cf. Hor. *C.* 1.14.3–6 *nonne uides ut ... | ... malus celeri saucius Africo | antemnaeque gemant ...?* and N–H *ad loc.*

114 pictos ... deos: not a figurehead, but the *tutela*, an image carried at the stern: *Tr.* 1.4.7–8 (O. on his way to Tomis) *puppi . . . recuruae | insilit et pictos uerberat unda deos.* See N–H on Hor. *C.* 1.14.10.

115–16 The conceit is further embellished by the Ovidianizing poet of *E.S.*: *solue ratem: Venus orta mari* [24n.] *mare praestat amanti. | aura dabit cursum, tu modo solue ratem. | ipse gubernabit residens in puppe Cupido, | ipse dabit tenera uela legetque manu* (213–16).

qua ... uehar 'in which I am to be carried', final subj.

tamen: 39n.

comitata Cupidine paruo = *F.* 2.463 (Dione).

sponsor coniugii ... tui 'as surety for (my) marriage with you', a stately phrase, purporting to solemnize and legitimate Paris' proceedings; cf. 2.33–4 *Hymenaeus ... | qui mihi coniugii sponsor et obses erat.* The legality is bogus, for *sponsores* in Roman law had nothing to do with marriage or betrothal (cf. however 20.11n.) – to say nothing of the fact that Helen is married already. *sponsor* is here fem., like *auctor* at e.g. 14.109–10 *... quorum mihi cana senectu*s | *auctor, A.A.* 1.72 *porticus auctoris Liuia nomen habet, al.,* and other nouns in *-or* (N–W I 908–11).

ficta 'represented'; Palmer's correction is a necessary improvement of *picta* (π), due to *pictos* in 114.

118 Aegaeis ... aquis 'across the Aegean', an extension of the so-called 'abl. *uiae*' (Roby §1176, H–S 131); cf. 18.58, 19.32, Hor. *Sat.* 1.9.1 *ibam forte Via Sacra, A.A.* 2.37 *caelo temptabimus ire* (cf. *Met.* 8.186 *ibimus illac*), 3.747 *mihi nudis rebus eundum est* 'I must negotiate bare subject-matter', *al.*

~~iubemus:~~ this seems the most plausible correction of *iubebat* (π): for the ellipse of the object of the verb cf. 20.80 *iamdudum dominae more uenire iube, Met.* 8.138 *properare iubet,* sc. *me*, though the construction is rare (*TLL* s.v. 577.76–83; but cf. Bömer on *Met.* 8.114). Also possible is *iubetur,* sc. *a me,* with *classis* understood as subject from the preceding verse; less likely *iubemur,* sc. *a Venere,* for which see the *Cypria* (*EGF* p. 31, 13–15), Aphrodite ordering the shipbuilding and the inclusion of Aeneas in the expedition, thus it appears generally in charge (19n.). Other attempts at correction (*iubebar* Itali, *lubebat* Heinsius) are ruled out by the imperfect tense.

121 ut erat 'just as she was', a favourite phrase of O.'s: 10.16, *A.A.* 1.529 *utque erat e somno ... , Met.* 4.474 *Tisiphone canos ut erat turbata capillos, al.,* Bömer on *Met.* 6.237. Cf. 20.19, 21.25nn.

Cassandra: this scene in which she prophesied 'concerning the future' at Paris' departure figured in the *Cypria* (*EGF* p. 31, 15–16). Cf. Pindar, *Paean* 8a '⟨... seeing⟩ him hastening (σπεύδοντ') the inspired heart of the sacred maiden shrieked ...'.

122 uellent 'were about to'; cf. 21.86, 3.57–8 *fama est ... | te dare nubiferis lintea uelle Notis*, *Am*. 1.12.3 *modo cum discedere uellet*, Juv. 10.282 *cum de Teutonico uellet descendere curru* and Courtney *ad loc.*, *OLD* s.v. *uolo*¹ 5d. For the personification of the ships cf. 13.134 *Inachiae uertite uela rates*.

123–6 The prophecy uttered by the *uates* at Paris' birth is repeated by Cassandra, and Paris repeats his flippant interpretation of it (49–50). The words of her outburst echo those of Ennius' Cassandra, *adest adest fax obuoluta sanguine atque incendio* (*Alex*. 41 J.). Cf. Pindar, *Paean* 8a (Cassandra's vision of Hecuba's dream): 'She thought she had borne a fiery hundred-handed Fury, who with harsh might hurled down all Ilium to the ground'.

124 flamma ... aquas: perhaps a glance at the conceit (more Ovidian than Cassandran) that water cannot extinguish the power of love: *Am*. 3.6.25–6 *Inachus in Melie Bithynide pallidus isse | dicitur et gelidis incaluisse uadis*, 41–2 *(Nilus) fertur in Euanthe collectam Asopide flammam | uincere gurgitibus non potuisse suis*, Philostr. *Ep*. 11 'even water is set ablaze by love'.

125 uera fuit uates: richly ironic. Of course she was always right, but it was her fate to be disbelieved. For once she is believed, but only through a wilful misconstruction of her words. Cf. 280 *uerax*.

dictos inuenimus ignes does not contradict 27 *attulimus flammas, non hic inuenimus, illas*, but it is perhaps unfortunate that O. makes Paris use such similar wording to make a different point, viz. that now that he has seen Helen he understands what the *uates* and Cassandra, as *he* interprets their words, were talking about (Kenney (1979) 401). This is the sort of inadvertence which might well have been attended to in revision; see Introd. p. 25.

127–8 egredior ... applicor: no sooner embarked than arrived! See next n.

uentisque ferentibus = *Am*. 3.11.51, *Tr*. 1.2.73 (*OLD* s.v. *ferens* 1). This and 23 *faciles auras uentosque secundos* sound like echoes of the *Cypria* as reported by Herodotus (2.117) εὐαέϊ τε πνεύματι χρησάμενος καὶ θαλάσσηι λείηι 'experiencing [lit. 'using'] a fair wind and a calm sea'. Herodotus however refers this to the return trip, though quoting (2.116.3) Hom. *Il.* 6.289–92, which alludes to a detour on that voyage via Sidon, explained by the *Cypria* (*EGF* p. 31, 25–6) and Apollodorus (*Epit.* 3.4) as the result of a storm sent by Hera. On these discrepancies see Frazer on Apollod., Kirk on Homer *locc. cit.*

128 in: cf. Livy 37.12.10 *in Erythraeam primum classem applicauerunt*; in the sense 'put in at' the regular construction is with dat. (7.117, *Tr.* 3.9.10) or *ad* (*Met.* 3.598). Possibly O. wrote *en terris . . . tuis*?

Oebali: Oebalus was her paternal grandfather. O. uses considerable freedom with Greek proper names, and Οἰβαλίς does not appear to be attested, though Tyndareus is called Οἰβαλίδης at Hes. fr. 199.8 M–W. Cf. 9.50 *Ormeni nympha* and Casali *ad loc.*

nympha: O. alone, and only in *Her.*, uses *nympha* like Greek νύμφη = '(young) wife' (*OLD* s.v. 2). Paris' first wife Oenone really was a nymph: 96–8, 5.9–12 (cit. 97–8n.).

129–30 Menelaus is introduced only to be sidelined; he is merely the complaisant tool of the divine purpose, which is to get Helen into Paris' bed. Presently he will take his complaisance to absurd lengths (299–304n.). Paris does not condescend to name him until line 205.

factum: sc. *est*.

131–2 quidem ostendit: for the elision cf. *Met.* 1.488 *ille quidem obsequitur*, 10.573 *illa quidem immitis*, *Rem.* 359 *multa quidem ex illis* (cf. Soubiran (1966) 236 n. 1). See 17.97n.

quicquid . . . dignum conspicuumque fuit: such as it was (189–92).

Lacedaemone tota 'in all Sparta' (*OLD* s.v. *totus* 3a). For the locative abl. in such phrases cf. *NLS* §51 (iv).

134 i.e. *nil aliud erat quo lumina caperentur*; final-consec. subj.

135 obstipui = 67; he reacts to his first sight of Helen as he had to the appearance of the three goddesses. Cf. 137–8, 20.205–8n.

praecordia . . . intima = Virg. *Aen.* 7.347, Ov. *Met.* 4.507, 6.251 (*i. . . . p.*).

136 intumuisse: Daniel Heinsius' correction of *intonuisse* (π), only here of love, more usually of pride or anger (*OLD* s.v. *intumesco* 4a). O. may have written *intremuisse* (Francius).

137 his 'yours'. For the pl. see 37n.

140 in dubio 'doubtful', an Ovidian cliché: 17.178, 19.174, *Am.* 2.10.6, *Met.* 1.396 and Bömer *ad loc.*, *OLD* s.v. *dubius* 6b, *al.* Cf. 87n.

COMMENTARY: 16.143-150

143-4 The text here printed is a *pis aller*. What O. wrote is past recovery.

nec tibi par usquam Phrygiae (sc. *est*) 'And there is not your equal anywhere in Phrygia', Naugerius' economical restoration of *per ... phrygia* (π), giving good sense but an unexampled extension of the common idiom (*n*)*usquam gentium* 'nowhere/anywhere in the world'.

nec solis ab ortu: a pentameter and hexameter have been lost after 143 with the complementary half of a polar expression 'from east to west'; cf. *Ex. P.* 1.4.29-30 *Caesaris ira mihi nocuit, quem solis ab ortu | solis ad occasus utraque terra tremit* (Kenney (1970*b*) 179-80). For a possibly analogous case in the text of Ennius see Walbank (1967) 57-8 and n. 2.

nomen habet 'deserves to be named', sc. as beautiful. One of O.'s favourite phrases (91x); see McKeown on *Am.* 1.3.21-2. Cf. Prop. 1.4.8 *Cynthia non illas nomen habere sinat*.

145 hoc 'in this', i.e. in what follows. For the construction with dat. of the person believed and acc. of the thing believed in cf. e.g. *Met.* 1.753-4 *matri ... omnia demens | credis*, 13.824-5 *de laudibus harum | nil mihi credideris, F.* 4.857 *quis tunc hoc ulli credere posset?, Tr.* 5.4.23 *si quid credis mihi, al.*, Ter. *Andr.* 497 *credon tibi hoc nunc* : ... ?, Scholte on *Ex P.* 1.1.59f., Bennett II (1914) 202, 207, *OLD* s.v. *credo* 4a, 5a. The impersonal passive version of the construction occurs at *A.A.* 1.387 *si quid modo creditur arti*.

147 illa: *fama* rather than Venus ('the goddess', Showerman-Goold): 147-8 restate and vary 145-6 chiastically, with 148 responding to 145 (*gloria* repeated) and 147 to 146.

148 materia 'material' in the sense of subject-matter or theme (*OLD* s.v. 7). O. is fond of this word (47x), which outside Lucretius is relatively uncommon in poetry: Virgil 1x (*Aen.* 11.328 = 'timber'), Horace 1x in *Odes*, 2x in *A.P.* as technical term, Prop. 0, Tib. 0, Lucan 5x, V.F. 1x, Juv. 6x, *TLL* s.v. 449.2-5.

149 ergo ... merito: so, I see, he knew what he was about (153n.).

omnia 'all your charms', explained below.

150 uisa es: sc. *merito*.

150 uiro ... 152 uiris: the repetition of the same word in this *sedes* in two successive pentameters was something that O. did not go out of his way to avoid. Cf. e.g. 210 *aquas*, 212 *aquis*; 17.108, 110 *habet*; 18.66 *dea est*, 68 *deas*; 19.8 *moram*, 10 *mora*; and in works of undisputed Ovidian authorship *Her.* 2.140, 142 *iuuat*; 5.82, 84 *nurus*; 7.60 *aquis*, 62 *aquas*; 8.32, 34 *auus*, 112 *manu*, 114 *manus*; 14.44 *manu*, 46 *manus*; *Am.* 1.14.34, 36 *manu*; *A.A.* 1.424 *emas*, 426 *emi*, 564 *toro*, 566 *tori*; *Tr.* 1.2.20, 22 *putes*, 5.68 *locis*, 70 *locus*. See Sedlmayer (1880) and on O.'s relative insensitivity (compared with Virgil or Horace) to verbal repetition Kenney (1959) 248. These lists could be lengthened immensely by the inclusion of unemphatic words such as pronouns and parts of *sum*; on the general tendency of O. to relegate such words to this *sedes* see Axelson (1958). Cf. 279–80n.

151–2 That it was Sparta that set the fashion of exercising and competing naked is attested by Thucydides (1.6.5); that Spartan girls exercised with boys scantily clad we learn from Euripides (*Andr.* 595–600 and Stevens *ad loc.*; cf. Pausan. 5.16.2–3); that they wore nothing at all when so engaged (cf. Prop. 3.14.4) may have been wishful thinking (but cf. Plut. *Lycurg.* 47–8). To backdate all this into Mycenaean times is another of O.'s cheerful anachronisms (33, 92nn.). *nudus*, however, like γυμνός, can mean 'stripped for action' rather than stark naked (*OLD* s.v. *nudus* 2).

nitida 'gleaming', sc. with the oil used by the athletes; cf. 19.11 *unctae dona palaestrae*, *Met.* 6.241 *opus nitidae iuuenale palaestrae*, al.

es mixta = *misceris*; the force of *mixtus* is often adjectival, as at 10.38 *uerbera cum uerbis mixta fuere meis*, *A.A.* 2.570 *multa ... cum forma gratia mixta fuit*, *Met.* 8.674 *hic nux, hic mixta est rugosis carica palmis*. Cf. 58 *prospiciens ... eram* and n.; but the cases are probably not on all fours (H–S 306). Barth's *is* is inapt; she was wrestling, not processing.

153 rapuit ... reddidit: he carried her off to Aphidnae in Attica, whence she was rescued by her brothers Castor and Pollux (*EGF* p. 39, F12, Apollod. *Bibl.* 3.10.7.4, *Epit.* 1.23 and Frazer *ad locc.*). According to Apollodorus (*Epit.* 1.23) she was only twelve (Diod. Sic. 4.63.2 says ten) when this happened, but O. does not make Helen avail herself of this point in her rejoinder (17.21–32). The notion that Theseus had confined his attentions to kissing her (17.25–8) is summarily and scornfully dismissed by Oenone (5.129–30).

155 recessisset 'would have parted company' (*OLD* s.v. 5a). Cf. Prop. 2.7.7–8 *nam citius paterer caput hoc discedere collo | quam possem nuptae perdere more faces*, etc.

COMMENTARY: 16.156–164

ceruice cruenta 'bloodily from my neck'; *ceruice* is abl. of separation, *cruenta* predicative.

156–8 abstraherere ... uellent ... paterer: impff. with plupf. sense; cf. 103n.

157 uellent 'would have consented' (*OLD* s.v. 5a).

160 ex toto 'completely' (87n.).

161 libata: for *libare* = 'fere i.q. decerpere' see *TLL* s.v. 1340.1–20, and cf. the Virgilian *oscula libare* (Austin on *Aen.* 1.256). Here however and at 2.115–16 the basic sense 'offer up' (to Venus?) is felt – perhaps an Ovidian extension of a more general image of defloration as death (Fowler (1987)). Cf. Val. Max. 6.1.4 *uirginitatem illibatam* (cit. Barchiesi, q.v. on 2.115).

illud: sc. *puerile*; cf. Plaut. *Pseud.* 780, 786, Mart. 9.67.3 *fessus mille modis illud puerile poposci,* Apul. *Met.* 3.20.3 *mihi iam fatigato de propria liberalitate Photis puerile obtulit corollarium,* Priap. 3.7–8 *quod uirgo prima cupido dat nocte marito, | dum timet alterius uulnus inepta loci,* this last apparently attributed by Seneca (*Contr.* 1.2.22) to O. The implication is 'as I rather think Theseus in fact did', for there was a tradition that this Spartan custom of treating unmarried girls 'like favourite boys' (Athen. 602d–e) was, according to 'Aristotle' (*teste Photio* s.v. κυσολάκων) invented by Theseus and Helen: see Dover (1978) 188, Parker (1993) 327 n. 38. An alternative tradition that Helen had a child by Theseus (Lycophr. *Alex.* 103, Euphorion, fr. 90 Powell; cf. 255–6n.) offered less scope for O.'s sly wit.

162 poterat 'might have been'; the past tenses of *possum* and of other verbs connoting potentiality, obligation, etc. are regularly used with a potential sense in the indicative: H–S 327–8, *NLS* §§125, 200. Cf. 17.92, 170, 186, 18.13, 19.130, 20.170, 21.125, 132.

salua uirginitate 'while leaving your virginity intact'.

163 da ... te = (here: contrast 197) *si te dederis,* imperative standing for the protasis of a conditional sentence. Cf. 18.193n.

164 flamma rogi: more irony; the pyre to which Paris' *constantia* will lead and which he will ignite (49, 123) is that of Troy itself. Cf. Virg. *Aen.* 2.624–5 *tum uero omne mihi uisum considere in ignis | Ilium* and Austin *ad loc.,* 'Troy settled down into the flames like a corpse upon a pyre', Sen. *Tro.* 20–1 *nube ceu densa obrutus | ater fauilla squalet Iliaca dies* and Fantham *ad loc.,* '*Squalet* adds the overtones of human mourning ... the cloud is the pall of mourning that the daylight has put on for Troy'.

una 'only' (*OLD* s.v. 7).

167 dum ... possem 'so long as I might' (*OLD* s.v. *dum* 2).

168 uirtus Pallade dante 'the prowess which Athene offered'. Cf. 2n.

172 deprecor: *vox propria* of praying that something may not happen, may be averted (*OLD* s.v. 3).

tanto ... labore 'at the price of so much effort' – but *labor* can also connote suffering and distress.

173 generosae degener: juxtaposition and etymological wordplay emphasize the point.

174 turpiter: cf. 20.145; the positive form of the adverb is relatively rare (*OLD* s.v.); O. has it 19x, of which 18x in the *amatoria* and *Her.* In general O. is readier than the other poets to use adverbs in *-e*, *-o*, and *-(i)ter* which seem to have been regarded as prosaic: Axelson (1945) 62–3. Cf. 154 *constanter*, 269, 18.84 *fortiter*, 17.153 *occulte*, 18.171 *exigue*, 19.4, 20.88 *patienter*, 19.15 *acriter*, 20.38 *caute*, 20.53 *modeste*, 20.130 *dissimulanter*, 21.57 *sapienter*, 21.195 *audacter*; 16.247 *petulantius*, 17.167 *constantius*, 18.45 *moderatius*, 19.67 *firmius*, 19.101 *patientius*, 17.168, 21.205 *iustius*.

175 Pliada ... Iouemque: the great names bracket the rest of the *gens*, the *medii aui* of the next verse.

Pliada: Dardanus' mother Electra was one of the seven daughters of Atlas and Pleione (62n.).

176 ut taceamus 'to say nothing of' (*OLD* s.v. *ut* 35).

177 regna ... Asiae 'the realm of Asia', a usage unparalleled in O., apparently a Virgilianism; cf. *Aen.* 1.226 *Libyae ... regnis*, 6.694 *Libyae ... regna. Asiam* (Merchant) removes the anomaly, if it is one, but imports a hyperbaton which lacks exact Ovidian parallel, addicted as he is to this figure (Housman, *CP* 139–41, 415–17). *regna* is Bentley's certain correction (approved by Housman) of MS *sceptra*, impossible with *obeunda*, which can only refer to territory.

178 finibus immensis 'by reason of its vast bounds', abl. of cause.

179 aurea tecta: cf. Eur. *Tro.* 994–6 (Hecuba taxing Helen with her real motives) 'You hoped to get quit of Sparta and to overwhelm with your extravagance the city of the Phrygians, flowing with gold'.

180 quae ... dicas 'such as you might say', consecutive-generic subj.

suos: referring to *templa*.

182 Another ominous allusion. Laomedon, king of Troy, hired Apollo and Poseidon to build the city walls, and refused to pay them when the work was done (Apollod. *Bibl.* 2.5.9.9–12 and Frazer *ad loc.*). His treachery figures repeatedly in the Augustan poets as the ultimate source of Troy's and Rome's ills: Virg. *G.* 1.501–2 and Mynors, Thomas *ad loc.*, *Aen.* 4.541–2, Hor. *C.* 3.3.18–24 '*Ilion, Ilion | fatalis incestusque iudex | et mulier peregrina uertit ‖ in puluerem, ex quo destituit deos mercede pacta Laomedon mihi* [sc. Juno] *| castaeque damnatum Mineruae | cum populo et duce fraudulento*', Ov. *Met.* 11.194–215 and Bömer *ad loc.* That the walls built themselves to Apollo's music seems to be Ovidian embroidery (picked up and further embroidered by Martial 8.6.5–6), a borrowing from the story of Amphion and the building of Thebes (Apollod. *Bibl.* 3.5.5.10 and Frazer *ad loc.*).

183 turba ... numeroque 'the thronging multitude', hendiadys.

186 'and you will find that the rooms of the palace are scarcely large enough to hold (*OLD* s.v. *capio* 25a) the brides of Troy', an allusion to Priam's fifty daughters-in-law (Hom. *Il.* 6.244, Virg. *Aen.* 2.503). For this use of the future cf. e.g. 188 *habebit*, 206 *erit*, 357–8 *habebit ... erit*, 368, 17.48, 60, *al.*; K–S I 142–3, Bennett I (1910) 44–5, Blase (1903) 119, Housman on Manil. 2.432, Courtney on Juv. 1.125–6, McKeown on *Am.* 1.2.7.

187 Helen's anticipated amazement seems to have been relocated: in the earlier literary tradition it is the sight of Paris in his Trojan finery that bowls her over: Eur. *Tro.* 991–2, *Cycl.* 182–4 and Seaford *ad loc.*, surmising that this feature of the story may go back to the *Cypria*, Stinton (1965) 51 n. 2 = (1990) 56 n. 2. Cf. 195, which suggests that Paris is not at present dressed to kill.

Achāïä 'Greece' (*OLD* s.v. 3; cf. 21n.). The word is first found with this arbitrary treatment of the Greek quantities at Prop. 2.28.53; the Greek poets use the metrically more tractable Ἀχαιΐς.

189 nec mihi fas fuerit 'However, I ought not to ...'; for the perf. subj. cf. 7, 17.109–10nn. *nec* is, as not infrequently, adversative (*OLD* s.v. *neque* 5).

uestram: hers and her countrymen's, implying shared pride.

191 parca: cf. Eur. *Tro.* (Hecuba to Helen) 993 'You lived in Argos [Greece] poorly (μίκρ' ἔχουσα)'.

sed: on the postponement of conjunctions see 16.26n. O. postpones *sed* less frequently than *et*: in *Am.* at 2.8.2, 2.14.41; not in *A.A.*; in *Her.* 17.95, 18.180, 19.72, 109.

digna: sc. *es*.

192 non facit 'does not suit'; cf. 6.128 *Medeae faciunt ad scelus omne manus*, 14.56 *non faciunt molles ad fera tela manus*, al. (*OLD* s.v. 29b). Apparently an Ovidian innovation: McKeown on *Am.* 1.2.16.

193 hanc faciem 'beauty such as yours'.

195–6 cultus ... qualem: O. uses *cultus* in sing. and pl. indifferently = *ornatus* 'toilette'; the variation in number here seems designed to avoid adding another sibilant to 196.

198 Therapnaeo ... Phrygem: Therapnae was her birthplace and that of her brothers Castor and Pollux. A country girl should think twice before turning down a prince of Troy; but there is a hint of anachronistic defensiveness in Paris' eulogy of his race. In classical times Phrygians were proverbially objects of derision (Otto s.v. *Phryx*, Haüssler (1968) 63), and O.'s readers are also likely to have recollected Remulus' contemptuous outburst at Virg. *Aen.* 9.598–620 (see Hardie *ad loc.*). Cf. Eur. *Andr.* 592 and Stevens *ad loc.*

199–200 Ganymede was carried off to Olympus by Jupiter's eagle – or, in the version preferred by O. (*Met.* 10.155–61), by Jupiter in the guise of an eagle – to be his cupbearer and catamite.

nostro ... de sanguine: the vagueness is no doubt intentional, reflecting O.'s learned awareness that Homer's identification of his father as Tros (*Il.* 20.231–2) was by no means the only one known to the tradition (Bömer on *Met.* 10.155–61, p. 63).

cum dis etc. 'mixes water with nectar for the gods to drink' = *cum nectare dis potando miscet aquas* (Housman, *CP* 439). Edd. generally take *cum dis* together = 'on Olympus' (cf. Enn. *Ann.* 110–11 Sk. *Romulus in caelo cum dis genitalibus aeuom | degit*) and interpret *potando nectare* as 'with nectar (for them) to drink'.

201–2 Tithonus, son of Laomedon, was abducted by Aurora (Eos), goddess of the dawn. He was only one of her victims (West on Hes. *Theog.* 986–91, McKeown on *Am.* 1.13.35–6), and by no means to be envied, for though she secured him immortality she forgot to stipulate for eternal youth also, thus dooming him to everlasting senility.

noctis ... iter ~ *F.* 5.546 *nox ... coartat iter*. For the idea of a

COMMENTARY: 16.203–212

boundary in *finit* cf. *Met.* 4.401, 7.706 *confinia noctis*, 13.592 *noctis confinia*: an Ovidian innovation (Bömer on 4.401).

203–4 The story of the love of Aphrodite (Venus) and Anchises is told at length in the Homeric Hymn to Aphrodite; their son was Anchises, ancestor of the Roman people.

in Idaeis ... iugis: Hom. *Il.* 2.281, Hes. *Theog.* 1010; cf. 53n.

concubuisse: pf. inf. for present, a metrically convenient expedient especially favoured in this *sedes* (Platnauer (1951) 109–12).

205 collatis 'if/when you compare'.

206 anteferendus erit = 358: sc. as you will find when you consider the matter: 186n.

207 socerum: Atreus, who murdered the children of his wife's lover, his brother Thyestes, and served them to him at dinner. In his horror at the sight the sun turned back in his course.

208 qui ... uertat 'such as to turn back', consecutive-generic subj.; cf. e.g. 180, 218.

209–10 Oenomaus, king of Pisa in Elis, offered his daughter Hippodamia to whoever could beat him in a chariot race, unsuccessful suitors to die. Atreus' father Pelops bribed the king's charioteer Myrtilus to remove the linchpins from Oenomaus' chariot, which crashed and killed him. Pelops then murdered Myrtilus by throwing him into the sea named after him (next n.). Pelops was in fact Phrygian, as presently (266) slips out.

Myrtoas ... aquas: the Myrtoan Sea was the part of the Aegean lying between Attica, the Peloponnese, and the Cyclades.

signat: present indic. because the sea is still stigmatized by Pelops' crime, though he is dead; cf. Virg. *Aen.* 9.266 *quem dat Sidonia Dido* 'the gift of Dido' and Henry *ad loc.*, Blase (1903) 107, H–S 306.

211 proauo ... nostro: Tantalus, condemned for divulging the secrets of the gods to eternal torment by hunger and thirst. *proauo* is dat. of the agent with *captantur*; cf. 217 *mihi conspiceris*.

in unda: he stood in a pool of water which sank whenever he tried to drink, under a tree which bent away whenever he tried to eat its fruits.

212 in mediis ... aquis virtually duplicates *in unda*, which indeed is redundant; if the text is sound this is not O. at his best. Contrast *Am.* 2.2.43–4 *quaerit aquas in aquis et poma fugacia captat* | *Tantalus*, 3.7.51–2, *A.A.* 2.605–6.

213–14 Though line 213 is pointed (Paris' indignation is waste of breath since, be his ancestry what it may, Menelaus is in fact married to Helen), line 214, whether punctuated as a question or a statement, is not: that Jupiter, Helen's father by Leda, has been willy-nilly enrolled in this deplorable family has no bearing on the argument – and who forced him anyway? This objection can be met by reading *creditur* (Hollis *per litt.*, Watt (1995) 92), but that does nothing to assist the connexion of thought. Moreover, the repetition of *te tenet* (213, 216) in two different senses but without rhetorical significance is unlike O. Reeve (1973) 333–4 makes out a good case for deleting the couplet.

215 totis ... noctibus 'through whole nights', abl. of duration of time; cf. 18.27–8n. This is the classic self-torment of the *exclusus amator* (*Am.* 1.4.59–70, 1.6 *passim*, *A.A.* 2.523–8, 3.581–2, etc.), heightened by the fact of being under the same roof as the unattainable beloved (cf. Kenney on Apul. *Met.* 6.11.3).

216 perfruiturque: postponement of *-que*, which properly belongs to *amplexu*, to follow a quadrisyllable in this *sedes* is not uncommon in O., though the fashion seems to have been set in the first place by Tibullus (Platnauer (1951) 91). Cf. 17.84, 18.94, 214, 21.200nn. The motive is purely metrical convenience. For *perfruitur* 'enjoys for all he's worth' cf. *OLD* s.v. *per-*.

217 posita ... mensa 'when dinner is on the table' (*OLD* s.v. *pono* 5); cf. 220n.

218 quae laedant 'such as to hurt', consecutive-generic subj

219 hostibus eueniant etc.: cf. 20.121–2, *Am.* 3.11.16 *eueniat nostris hostibus ille pudor*, *A.A.* 3.247 *hostibus eueniat tam foedi causa pudoris*, al. English says 'I wouldn't wish it on my worst enemy'. Cf. 20.127–8n.

220 posito ... mero ~ 217 *posita ... mensa*, rounding off the neat chiastic structure of 217–20, but also introducing the highly diverting scene that follows, Menelaus' maudlin endearments and Paris' hardly less maudlin efforts to control himself. Cf. *Am.* 1.4, where however the lover is in a sense master of the situation, though temporarily thwarted. For the dinner-table as a setting for amatory intrigue see *A.A.* 1.229–44.

221 paenitet hospitii 'I wish I hadn't come'.
me spectante 'before my very eyes'.
222 rusticus iste 'that boor (that you are saddled with)'. *rusticus*

and *rusticitas* in O. connote lack of amatory *savoir-faire*; cf. 20.59, 1.77–8 *forsitan et narres quem sit tibi rustica coniunx, | quae tantum lanas non sinat esse rudes, Am.* 1.8.44 (cit. 285–94n.). Helen is much too good for this oaf. She takes up the word in her reply (17.12). Cf. 287n.

223 rumpor et inuideo 'I cannot contain myself for envy', defensible as a kind of hendiadys, but not really paralleled by 8.57 *rumpor et ora mihi pariter cum mente tumescunt* or Hor. *Sat.* 1.3.136 *rumperis et latras.* O. may have written *r. ab inuidia* (Oudendorp) or *r. et inuidia* (Damsté), for which cf. Virg. *Ecl.* 7.26 *inuidia rumpantur ut ilia Codro,* Mart. 9.97 *rumpitur inuidia* (12x). See Austin–Reeve (1970) 7 n. 5.

quianam non omnia narro? 'Why indeed do I not tell the whole story?' *quianam* (Kenney: *quidn*** P: the other MSS improvise freely) is Ennian and Virgilian (Quint. *I.O.* 8.3.25), but that does not rule it out in this epistle (45–6n.). *narro* (Kenney) is almost certainly what originally stood in P.

224 membra superiecta ... tua ueste fouet 'fondles', [not 'warms' (Riley, Showerman–Goold)] you under (a fold of) his robe'; *membra = corpus* (*OLD* s.v. 2), as often in O. (19.44, 61, 21.16, 156, 190, 228).

225–6 daretis ... posui: similar variations in tense between pf. and historic present occur throughout the passage, but *cum uero* suggests perhaps that this was a peculiarly flagrant provocation on one particular night. Deletion of the couplet (Fischer (1969) 86–7) is uncalled for.

225 non dura = *mollissima* (litotes).
daretis: sc. *inuicem*, 'gave and received'.
227 te tenet = 216; negligence? Cf. 213–14n.
228 crescit ... cibus: cf. Sen. *Ep. Mor.* 82.21 *non in ore creuit cibus, non haesit in faucibus,* Juv. 13.212–13 *inter ... molares | difficili crescente cibo.*

lentus 'obstinately'; the word can connote viscosity (*OLD* s.v. 3), slowness (4, 7), persistence (6), and resistance (8). Cf. 18.58n.

229–30 Helen is well aware of the position (239), but at this stage her reaction as Paris reports it might reflect only disdainful amusement. The subsequent fit of the giggles to which she admits (17.161–2 and n.) gives the game away: she is thoroughly enjoying herself.

232 ~ *A.A.* 1.244 *Venus in uinis ignis in igne fuit.* The thought was proverbial: Otto s.v. *ignis* 3.

233 multaque ne uideam etc. 'and (there are) many (other) things to avoid seeing which ...'.

238 tamen: sc. *quamuis dissimulatus*: cf. e.g. 19.57, *Am.* 1.8.20 *nec tamen eloquio lingua nocente caret* and McKeown *ad loc.*, Housman on Lucan 1.333, Manil. 4.413, Clausen on Virg. *Ecl.* 1.27.

239 uerba damus 'deceive'; cf. 18.98 (*OLD* s.v. *uerbum* 6).

243 aliquem ... amorem 'some tale of love' (*OLD* s.v. *amor* 5).

244 'judging the effect of each word from your expression' (*OLD* s.vv. *refero* 10, *uultus* 1a). For *uultus* pl. cf. 37–8n.

245 indicium ... mei ... feci 'I laid information against myself', 'I gave myself away', *mei* objective gen. The phrase has a legal flavour (*OLD* s.v. *indicium* 2); on O.'s penchant for legal phraseology see Kenney (1969).

246 si nescis 'let me tell you'; the phrase recurs at 17.198 (see n.), 18.39, 20.150, a curiously high incidence but not a cause for suspicion (*pace* Fischer (1969) 116 n. 4). Cf. 50n., Introd. p. 24.

247–8 Paris follows the tactics recommended in the *Ars*: *ebrietas ut uera nocet, sic ficta iuuabit: | fac titubet blaeso subdola lingua sono, | ut, quicquid facias dicasue proteruius aequo, | credatur nimium causa fuisse merum* (1.597–600).

petulantius 'more saucily' sc. than would otherwise have been tolerated (cf. *proteruius aequo*, cit. previous n.). The adverb is nowhere else attested in the poets; cf. 174n.

249–54 This tableau ironically anticipates the famous scene in which Menelaus, about to kill Helen for her treachery, dropped his sword at the sight of her naked breasts: Ar. *Lys.* 155–6 and Σ, Eur. *Andr.* 627–31 and Stevens *ad loc.*

249, 251 pectora: commonly in the pl. for metrical convenience in both literal and metaphorical (278) senses; on poetic plurals of this type (parts of the body) see Löfstedt 1 (1942) 30–1. For the epanalepsis cf. 21.72–3n.

251–2 Such comparisons are traditional: snow + milk [Ov.] *Am.* 3.5.11–14, *Ex P.* 2.5.37–8; milk + swan Callim. *Hec.* fr. 74.15–16 Hollis (260.56–7 Pf.), Ov. *Met.* 13.796; snow Hom. *Il.* 10.437; milk Theoc. 11.20; swan Virg. *Ecl.* 7.37. Cf. Washietl (1883) 121–3.

252 candidiora Ioue: he visited Leda in the shape of a swan; cf. 17.46, 55–6.

COMMENTARY: 16.253-259   113

253-4 ~ Prop. 4.4.21-2 (Tarpeia) *obstipuit regis facie et regalibus armis, | interque oblitas excidit urna manus.*

tortilis ... ansa: this suggests a golden or silver cup of elaborate design, with a decorative handle spirally patterned or perhaps formed from entwined strands. Handles of this latter pattern have eluded detection; O. may have been influenced by a recollection of the twisted collar or torque into which Allecto's serpent is transformed (Virg. *Aen.* 7.351–2 *fit tortile collo | aurum ingens coluber*).

255-6 A variant of another ploy recommended in the *Ars*: see 17.79–80n.

Hermiones: according to Homer (*Od.* 4.12–14; but see Frazer on Apollod. *Bibl.* 3.11.1, and above 161n.) Helen's only child, left behind in Sparta when she eloped (Hom. *Il.* 3.174–5, Alc. fr. 283.7 L–P). Her later history is variously told, notably by Euripides (*Andromache*) and Ovid (*Her.* 8): Jacobson (1974) 43–57.

257 cantabam: this ironically recalls Hector's taunt that if Paris were to meet Menelaus in the field he would not be helped by his musical skills or his gifts as a ladies' man (Hom. *Il.* 3.53–5; cf. Hor. *C.* 1.15.13–15). They are precisely the weapons with which he will win *this* battle.

258 per nutum: cf. *Am.* 1.4.17–18 *me specta nutusque meos uultumque loquacem; | excipe furtiuas et refer ipsa notas*, 2.5.15–16 *multa supercilio uidi uibrante loquentes; | nutibus in uestris pars bona uocis erat*, 3.11.23–4, *A.A.* 1.138.

tegenda 'secret', to be concealed from third parties.

259 at 'however' (Kenney); he has also been taking more active steps in the background. *et* (MSS) connects this approach with the dinner-table scenes, whereas indication of a new departure is wanted.

Clymenen Aethranque: the two maids of honour who in the *Iliad* attend Helen to the famous scene on the city wall (Teichoscopy) (3.144). The approach through a maid was standard comic and elegiac tactics: *Am.* 1.11 and McKeown *ad loc.* (pp. 308–9), *A.A.* 1.351–98 and Hollis *ad loc.* 'Incomparable audacity, the radiant attendants of Helen of the *Iliad* degraded to the circle of Corinna's maids! Bernard Shaw could not shock us more' (Rand (1925) 31–2). Cf. 17.267–8, 20.131–2. On the metrical convenience of the Greek form *Clymenen* see Appendix. Here and at 17.267 O. is likely to have written *Aethran*; cf. 18.151n., *A.A.* 1.53 *Andromedan*, Goold (1965) 95.

261 formidare: sc. *se*.

262 orantis ... deseruere preces: i.e. *orantem in mediis precibus deseruere*.

medias 'before I had finished them' (*OLD* s.v. 7).

263–70 Knight-errant fantasies. More irony: in the *Iliad* a duel between him and Menelaus 'for Helen and all her wealth' (3.70, 91) is actually set up and allowed to proceed until Menelaus is poised for the kill, when Aphrodite steps in and whisks Paris away (3.373–82). Thereafter he does not greatly distinguish himself in the fighting, and indeed as an archer was not generally regarded as a 'real' hero (11.385–95 and Hainsworth *ad loc.*).

263–4 Here the irony is particularly pointed, for the sequel of the unconsummated duel in the *Iliad*, thanks to Aphrodite, was that Paris, the *vanquished*, not the victor, enjoyed Helen in bed (3.437–47).

facerent ... esses ... posset: omission of *ut* after *facio* = 'make happen' (*OLD* s.v. 15a) is extremely common; cf. 5n.

265–6 Both the heroes of these stories won their brides by cheating, and Paris has not long since stigmatized Pelops as a murderer (209–10n.).

Schoeneida: Atalanta, daughter of King Schoeneus. She would only marry the man who could beat her at running, losers to die. Hippomenes won by throwing down golden apples, which she stopped to pick up. The story is told at length at *Met.* 10.560–680.

praemia 'as the reward', predicative.

in Phrygios ... sinus: somewhat weakening, one would have thought, his earlier argument, such as it was.

Hippodamia: 209–10n.

267–8 Hercules wrestled with the river-god Achelous for the hand of Deianira. Finding things going against him, Achelous turned himself successively into a snake and a bull, when Hercules broke off one of his horns and ended the fight (*Met.* 9.1–88). In visualizing himself as a second Hercules Paris has gone from one extreme to the other.

Deianira: in principle such an address to a character in a narrative (apostrophe) raises the emotional temperature; in O. it is often used for purely technical reasons, here because the name (like e.g. Hippodamia) is metrically intractable in the oblique cases.

COMMENTARY: 16.269–279

269–70 'On such terms as these (sc. with you as the prize) my daring would have performed manfully and you would have known that it was *my* toil of which you were the outcome.' *mei ... laboris* is predicative (Terpstra) and emphatic, contrasting with the entreaties and supplications (271–2) which are all he can actually offer.

per has leges ... isset: cf. *A.A.* 3.87 *ite per exemplum ... deorum*, *Tr.* 2.168. For *eo* = 'act (in a particular way)' see *OLD* s.v. *eo*¹ 13.

opus 'achievement': for this sense cf. *Ex P.* 3.4.77 *opus curae ... nostrae*, 4.2.50, *A.A.* 1.266 *praecipuae ... artis opus*, *OLD* s.v. 8, *TLL* s.v. 843.33ff.

271 nunc 'as it is' (*OLD* s.v. 11a).

272 amplecti ... pedes: a gesture of both supplication and of erotic subjection (cf. 20.75–90n.); *Am.* 1.7.61 *ter ... ante pedes uolui procumbere supplex* and McKeown *ad loc.*, *A.A.* 2.533–4 *nec ... puta ... | ... turpe ... ad teneros oscula ferre pedes*. Cf. next n.

273 o decus, o praesens ... gloria: Paris' language reflects her semi-divine status as representative on earth of her deified brothers Castor and Pollux: *OLD* s.vv. *decus* 3, *praesens* 3.

275–6 Sigeos ... Taenaria: 21n. The same alternatives at 18.195–6, 20.51–2 (n.), 167; cf. Musaeus 79, 89. The conceit has a long literary history (Kost *ad locc.*)

te coniuge 'with you as my wife'.

277 summa ... sagitta 'with the tip of the arrow' (*OLD* s.v. *summus* 4a). Though the metaphor of the wound of love is too common to need illustration, this throwaway reference to Cupid's dart without mention of the god himself (apart from the almost equally casual *caeleste* (279–80n.)) is unusual.

278 ad ossa: Theoc. 3.17 '(Love's) slow fires torture me to the very bones', Virg. *G.* 3.258–9 *magnum cui uersat in ossibus ignem | durus amor*, *Her.* 4.70 *acer in extremis ossibus haesit amor*, Prop. 1.9.29 and Fedeli *ad loc.*

279–80 (nam repeto ... figar): Ehwald's punctuation allows *hoc* a natural construction as direct object of *erat uaticinata* and does not breach the sequence of tenses, a problem which troubled Heinsius (who emended *figar erat* to *figerer est*) and Palmer: 'for I (now) recollect that I *am to be* transfixed ...'.

a caeleste sagitta: the arrow meant in the prophecy was that of Philoctetes (Soph. *Phil.* 1425–7), called *caelestis* as having once belonged to Hercules and being guided by Athene (Lycophr. *Alex.* 914–15), but taken by Paris to be Cupid's. Palmer objected to the phrase, but (i) instrumental *ab* is not uncommon in O. (cf. e.g. 5.152 *a nostro saucius igne fuit*, Guttmann (1890) 15ff.); (ii) this abl. form in *-e* is Ovidian (*Met.* 15.743 *specie caeleste recepta*; cf. N–W II 54 and above, 11–12n.); (iii) the repetition of *sagitta* is here essential to the point, and such repetitions (even unmotivated) are by no means rare in O.'s hexameters (Sedlmayer (1880) 295); cf. 150–2n.

uerax: accurate but ironical, as at 125; she is, as always, right and, for once, believed – but misinterpreted.

soror: in ascribing this prophecy to Cassandra, O. follows a tradition represented by Lycophron (*Alex.* 911–15). Calchas (Apollod. *Epit.* 5.8, Q.S. 9.327–9) or Helenus (Soph. *Phil.* 604–13; cf. *EGF* p. 31, 12–13) had foretold more vaguely that Troy could not be taken without the aid of Philoctetes.

281 datum fatis 'allotted by Fate'; cf. Virg. *Aen.* 4.225 *fatisque datas non respicit urbes*. True but profoundly ironical.

282 sic habeas etc.: sc. *si non contemnes*: a standard formulation in prayers, cf. Appel (1909) 152. Cf. 18.46n.

faciles in tua uota 'gracious to fulfil your (own) desires'; for this characteristically Ovidian use of *in* see McKeown on *Am.* 1.1.22.

285–94 an pudet etc. 'It can't really be because ...?' (*OLD* s.v. *an* 1a). Paris' affected incredulity introduces a line of argument straight out of the world of Roman elegy: *Am.* 1.8.39–44 (the speaker is a procuress) *forsitan immundae Tatio regnante Sabinae | noluerint habiles pluribus esse uiris. | nunc Mars externis animos exercet in armis, | at Venus Aeneae regnat in urbe sui. | ludunt formosae: casta est quam nemo rogauit; | aut, si rusticitas non uetat, ipsa rogat* and McKeown *ad loc.*

286 fallere iura 'violate the rights', a phrase paralleled only (*TRF inc. inc.* 60 is doubtfully relevant) at Stat. *Ach.* 1.362–3, apparently an extension of the more familiar *fallere fidem* (7.18, *Am.* 3.3.1; *OLD* s.v. *fallo* 5b).

287 rustica: cf. 222n., McKeown on *Am.* 1.8.43–4 (p. 223). With *dico* = 'use the expression' the word(s) cited may be put into the acc. as the grammatical object of the verb or, as here, be treated as in effect an indeclinable noun: cf. *Ex P.* 4.2.29–30 *paruaque, ne dicam scribendi nulla uoluptas | est mihi*, *OLD* s.vv. *dico* 5, *ne*[1] 13c.

289 non dura 'complaisant'. Contrast 225 = 'voluptuous' (litotes).

COMMENTARY: 16.290–299   117

290 ~ 19.171–3, *E.S.* 121 *non ueniunt in idem pudor atque amor*, Juv. 10.297–8 *rara est adeo concordia formae | atque pudicitiae*. For the polysyllabic ending see Introd. p. 22.

291–2 his ... haec '(just such as) these', i.e. such as I propose.

291 Venus aurea ~ Hom. *Il.* 3.64 χρυσέη Ἀφροδίτη, Virg. *Aen.* 10.16, *al.* As Jupiter was arch-adulterer, so she was arch-adulteress; *aurea* is slyly ironic.

292 nempe 'for indeed'; see 252n. On *nempe* cf. 20.70n.

293 si sunt uires in semine morum 'if character is determined by heredity'. The sense is clear, but the words may be interpreted in two ways: (i) with *morum* as possessive/descriptive gen. 'if the capabilities (*OLD* s.v. *uis* 27) of the character are present in the seed' or (ii) with *morum* as objective gen. 'if there is in the seed power over (to determine) character'. (ii) is preferred by Showerman–Goold, *OLD* s.v. *uis* 25b; but the gen. seems to be unexampled, whereas (i) is supported by phrases such as *uires animi, uires ingenii*. Paris anachronistically touches on a familiar philosophical question.

294 et Iouis et Ledae: another possible anachronism, a hint of awareness of physiological doctrine? It was thought that when the paternal and the maternal seed precisely balanced each other, the offspring resembled both parents (Lucret. 4.1212–17 and Bailey *ad loc.*).

potest has very scanty MS support, but the third person is both more rhetorically effective and more tactful than *potes*, presenting impersonally and as a scientific fact the proposition that no woman with Helen's parentage can reasonably be expected to be chaste.

296 sim quaeso: cf. 20.127–8n.

crimina 'causes for reproach' (*OLD* s.v. 2b), a genuine, not a 'poetic' pl.; the literal sense is 'may all the accusations that can be brought against you be myself alone', the verb being attracted, as often, into the number of the predicate: cf. e.g. *Met.* 15.529 *unum ... erat omnia uulnus* and Bömer *ad loc.*, Ter. *Andr.* 555 *amantium irae amoris integratiost, al.*, K–S I 40–1.

297 ea peccemus quae ... 'let us commit (only) sins which ...'; *ea* (internal acc.) limits and defines. In the *Cypria* they were not married until they arrived in Troy (*EGF* p. 31, 26–7).

299–304 Menelaus' imprudent behaviour, discreetly glossed over by himself in the *Iliad* (13.627), is the subject of bitter reproach by the Euripidean Helen (*Tro.* 943–4; cf. *Andr.* 592–5), and ribald comment by O. elsewhere (*A.A.* 2.359–72, *Rem.* 773–4). Cf. 303–4n.

299 The text is problematic. Most MSS read *sed tibi hoc* (unmetrically) or *sed tibi et hoc*, with *et* awkwardly qualifying *maritus*, 'your husband too'. That difficulty is met by reading *ipse tibi hoc* with one late MS (independently conjectured by Francius); but another remains, unnoticed by editors: *non uoce*, which on the face of it flatly contradicts 303–6 (it is not clear whether Showerman–Goold's 'by deed, if not by word' is an ingenious attempt to gloze over the apparent contradiction). *non uoce* can be defended by construing it elliptically = *non (solum) uoce* (cf. Palmer on 8.5, *Am.* 3.10.46 *quem Iuno (sola)* and Kenney *ad loc.*, 17.134n.); otherwise the choice is between (i) further rewriting, e.g. *rebusque et uoce*, (ii) invoking the lack of a final revision, (iii) excising the couplet as spurious.

300 neue = *et, ne* (71n.).

301 quo ... uideret 'for him to see', final-consecutive subj.

Cresia regna: what they were or why he had to visit them at short notice (17.156 *subitae ... uiae*) O. does not explain; according to Apollodorus (*Epit.* 3.3) it was to bury his maternal uncle Catreus, according to Dictys Cretensis (1.1) it was to claim his share of the estate of his grandfather Atreus.

302 o mira calliditate uirum! 'what a wonderfully astute husband', exclamatory acc. qualified by descriptive abl. On *calliditate* cf. 52n. and below 312, 316; this repeated trick of style somehow enhances the note of mockery.

303–6 Menelaus' injunction to 'look after our guest' is found in the *Odysseus* (17–18) ascribed to Alcidamas (fourth c. B.C.) and evidently went back to the *Cypria* (*EGF* p. 31, 20–1). Paris naturally exploits it for all he is worth.

303 †esset et†: no convincing explanation or correction of the first two words of the verse has been offered.

303–4 mando ... agas 'I charge you to exercise'; cf. *Tr.* 1.1.119 *his mando dicas, Met.* 9.157 *dona det illa uiro mandat* and Bömer *ad loc.*, *Am.* 1.11.17 *aspicias oculos mando frontemque legentis*, al., *OLD* s.v. *mando*[1] 6b. Cf. 5n. On the ironical resonance of *Idaei ... hospitis* cf. 53n.

305 mandata: gleefully and anachronistically Paris explains to Helen that it is her legal duty to cuckold her husband. *mandatum* was in Roman law a special form of contract 'based on a personal relationship of confidence (friendship) between the parties' (Berger (1953) s.v.); in the *Ars* O. had warned that it was liable to abuse: *tuta frequensque uia est, per amici fallere nomen;* | *tuta frequensque licet sit uia, crimen habet.* | *inde procurator nimium quoque multa procurat* | *et sibi mandatis plura uidenda putat* (1.585–8, but the lines are almost certainly misplaced). Paris now proves how right he was; *testor* is high and pompous language, calling gods and men to witness the justice of his plea. See Kenney (1969) 251–3.

307–8 This recalls Ulysses' specious contention that Ajax, *rudis et sine pectore miles*, was unqualified to appreciate the artistic beauties of Achilles' shield (*Met.* 13.288–95); cf. 17.5n. Behind the sophism there perhaps lurks the philosophical commonplace that a man has no right to what he does not understand how to use: Cic. *Rep.* 1.27 *communi lege naturae, quae uetat ullam rem esse cuiusquam nisi eius qui tractare et uti sciat*, Sen. *Phaedr.* 442–3 *perdere est dignus bona* | *quis nescit uti*, Hor. *C.* 4.9.46–50, *Ep.* 1.2.49–50.

sine pectore 'stupid' (*OLD* s.v. *pectus* 3b). Cf. 21.141n.; and for the adnominal use of such phrases with *sine* cf. e.g. 1.97 *sine uiribus uxor*, 20.225 and n., Virg. *Aen.* 2.558 *sine nomine corpus*, 6.292 *tenuis sine corpore uitas*, etc., K–S I 213–15, Bömer on *Met.* 3.250.

satis ... nosse 'properly understand'; Helen is a work of (divine) art demanding intelligent connoisseurship (*OLD* s.v. *nosco* 9a).

309 nec = *non enim*; cf. Lucret. 3.816 and Kenney *ad loc.* See 189n.

311 ut 'even though' (*OLD* s.v. 35).

312 ~ *A.A.* 2.372 *usa est (Helene) humani commoditate uiri*, and cf. 302n.

313 aut 'otherwise' (*OLD* s.v. 7).

314 ~ *A.A.* 3.60 *sic nullum uobis tempus abibit iners.* For *iners*, one of O.'s favourite words (43x), cf. 160, 18.110, 122.

315 suis ad te manibus: the phrasing, with *suis* preceding its noun and juxtaposed with *ad te*, emphasizes Menelaus' idiocy.

deducit: the word is *vox propria* for the ceremonial escorting of a bride to her husband (*OLD* s.v. 10b).

316 mandantis: 305n.

simplicitate: 302n.

317–18 uiduo ... cubili = *Am.* 2.10.17, *uiduo ... toro* = [Ov.] *Am.* 3.5.42, *Her.* 5.106, 10.14, *Tr.* 5.5.48; cf. 1.81 *uiduo ... lecto. uiduus* = 'solitary' (*OLD* s.v. 1b).

317 tam longa nocte 'all the night long', to be understood (ἀπὸ κοινοῦ construction) with the next verse also.

320 candidior 'brighter', with a play on the literal and metaphorical senses (*OLD* s.v. 1, 7) of the word. Cf. Prop. 2.15.1 *o me felicem, o nox mihi candida ...!*

321 quaeuis ... numina: for acc. of what is sworn by see *OLD* s.v. *iuro* 1b.

321–2 meque astringam uerbis in tua iura tuis 'and I shall bind myself to observe your laws in words which you shall dictate'. The text is problematic; the reading printed here is that of a minority of MSS but gives pointed sense. *meque astringam* eqs. is epexegetic of *iurabo*, and *in tua iura* must be construed ἀπὸ κοινοῦ with 321 (cf. 317n.); for *in* + acc. with *iurare* of what the oath-taker swears to observe or support see *OLD* s.v. *in* 18e. For *iura* of the conditions laid down by the elegiac *domina* cf. 20.79–80, Prop. 1.9.3 *ecce iaces supplexque uenis ad iura puellae*, 3.11.2 (*femina*) *trahit addictum sub sua iura uirum*, Ov. *Am.* 2.17.23–4 *tu quoque me, mea lux, in quaslibet accipe leges;* | *te deceat medio iura dedisse foro*; and for a mistress dictating her terms (*formula legis*) cf. Prop. 4.8.73–82. No ancient reader of these lines would fail to remember that lovers' oaths were proverbially worthless: *A.A.* 1.633–6 *Iuppiter ex alto periuria ridet amantum* eqs. and Hollis *ad loc.*, Otto s.v. *amare* 4.

323 fiducia nostri '(my) confidence in myself', objective gen.; cf. 17.19 *fiducia coepti*, 123 *f. corporis*. See 17.209–10n.

325 secuta: sc. *esse*.

326 '(You need feel no shame or fear, since) I shall bear all the blame'.

327 Aegidae: Theseus, son of Aegeus; cf. 153n.

329 geminas Leucippidas: Hilaira and Phoebe, daughters of Leucippus, abducted by the Dioscuri.

332 facient celeres 'will make short work of', *celeres* predicative.

uias 'journeyings'; the pl. is not metrically necessary, as it is at 22 (see n.). The return trip was not in fact direct (126–7n.).

333–8 Cf. Eur. *Tro.* 1020–2 (Hecuba speaking) 'You used to behave insolently in the house of Paris and wished the barbarians to make obeisance to you'. The picture here however is that of the typical heroine (or hero) of Romance, accorded divine honours by a superstitious populace (Kenney on Apul. *Met.* 4.28.3, 29.4). It also recalls

Musaeus' account of the appearance of Hero and its effect on the crowds at the festival of Aphrodite (55–68); see Introd. pp. 12–13. In point of fact Helen was a goddess before she became a heroine (Bethe, *RE* VII 2824–5).

333 ingens regina 'a mighty queen' (*OLD* s.v. *ingens* 4a); cf. *Ex. P.* 2.8.43 *conueniens ingenti nupta marito*.

337 fratresque et: for the elision cf. 21.137, *Am.* 1.6.57 *aut ego iam ferroque ignique paratior ipse*; though it is commonly held that the elision of -*e* was total (Soubiran (1966) 292–4, Richmond (1965)), even a short elided syllable was felt as masking rather than cancelling the caesura ('quasi-caesura': Kenney on Lucret. 3.174, Soubiran (1966) 279–81, 528–33), so that such a verse as this is metrically equivalent to e.g. 16.67 (n.).

340 plura feres 'you will receive more' sc. gifts, but also 'you will suffer more'; she will in fact become the most unpopular woman in the world. See 376n.

341 rapta 'if you are ravished'. Neither he nor Helen (17.245–50) manifests awareness of the oath taken by all her suitors to assist the successful candidate for her hand if she were ever to be abducted again (*A.A.* 1.687–8, Hes. *Eoeae* fr. 204.78–87 M–W, Apollod. *Bibl.* 3.10.9 and Frazer *ad loc.*). See Introd. p. 7.

343 ecqua est repetita per arma?: yes, in precisely the two cases cited by Paris a moment ago: Helen herself, rescued by her brothers (153n.), and the Leucippides, rescued from her brothers by their official lovers Idas and Lynceus. Since in most versions of the latter story Castor was killed (Rose on Hyg. *Fab.* 80, Gow on Theoc. 22 (pp. 383–4), *EGF* p. 31, 29–30), Paris is here on thin exemplary ice.

344 res ... ista 'this business (of abduction)'. Cf. *A.A.* 3.97–8 *nec uos prostituit mea uox, sed uana timere | damna uetat: damnis munera uestra carent*.

345 nomine ... Aquilonis 'in the name of the North Wind'; Paris euhemerizes the story of the abduction of Orithyia by Boreas (cf. 18.37–46 and nn.) – the *doctus poeta* intruding with a vengeance.

Erecthida 'daughter of Erechtheus'; on the spelling in Latin of Greek words with double aspirated consonants see Schulze (1894). This form, for the usual and correctly formed Ἐρεχθηΐς, is found only here and at *Met.* 7.726 (see Bömer on 7.697).

346 et 'and yet' (*OLD* s.v. 14a).
Bistonis 'Thracian' (21n.); the Bistones were a tribe in those parts.
347 Phasida 'the woman of Phasis [the river of Colchis]', as identifying Medea apparently first used by O.; cf. 19.176.
puppe noua: Argo, the first ship; cf. 12.13–14 (Medea speaking) *in nostras ... noua puppis harenas | uenerat.*
Pagasaeus: Pagasae in Thessaly was where the Argo was built and launched.
348 neque 'but ... not': 189n. On the postponement cf. 26n. O. postpones *nec/neque* not infrequently: in *Her.* 4.113, 7.140, 12.154, 18.6, 132, 212, 20.124, 21.217. Here too Paris is economical with the (mythological) truth. If the Colchians did not avenge Medea's abduction, it was not because Aeetes acquiesced in it, but because his troops fell down on the job (Callim. frr. 9–12 Pf., A.R. 4.482–521). In the event both Jason and Medea paid a heavy price for their infatuation.
349 Minoida 'daughter of Minos', i.e. Ariadne; hardly a compelling example, since after being abandoned on Naxos by Theseus she had been taken under the protection of Dionysus (Bacchus) and could not be recovered anyway. Minos was evidently more interested in pursuing the fugitive Daedalus (Apollod. *Epit.* 1.12–15); cf. Mayer on Sen. *Phaedr.* 245.
350 nulla ... ad arma uocat: emphatic for *non uocat ad arma*: cf. 2.105 *nullam ... Phyllida nosti* 'you know no such person as Phyllis', 10.11 *nullus erat* 'he was nowhere to be seen', *OLD* s.v. *nullus* 6, Fordyce on Catull. 17.20.
351 This has a proverbial or sententious ring; cf. perhaps Publ. Syr. P3 *pericla timidus etiam quae non sunt uidet.*
ipso ... periclo 'the actual danger' (*OLD* s.v. *ipse* 5).
352 The form of the verse superficially recalls e.g. 19.64 *quae fecisse iuuat, facta referre pudet, Am.* 3.11.4 *et quae non puduit ferre tulisse pudet*; but the text is uncertain (most MSS have *qua ... libet*) and the point elusive. If Paris is saying 'it is permissible to be apprehensive, but only up to a point', *timere sed non pertimere licet*, then *pertimuisse* is merely a metrically convenient equivalent for the intractable present inf. (203–4n.), and the formulation falls short of the expected Ovidian elegance. If the sense is 'things which (at the time) it is permissible to

fear, one is (later) ashamed of having feared', then the point is obscured by the tense of *pudet* and *per-* is otiose.

354 et mihi sunt uires = Tib. 2.6.10, in the same *sedes*. On Paris' prowess as recorded in the *Iliad* see 263–70n. When he marches out for the duel with Menelaus he is equipped both for archery and for close combat (Kirk on *Il.* 3.17–20) – perhaps an attempt by the poet to reconcile discrepant traditions?

355 uestrae 'of you Spartans'.

357–8 A brilliantly ironical echo of Helen's words to Paris in the *Iliad*: 'You used to boast that you excelled warlike Menelaus in the strength of your hands and your spear' (3.430–1). That Menelaus was not himself in the top flight of warriors we learn from Homer (Edwards on *Il.* 17.24–8), but Paris' naming himself in the 3rd person smacks of arrogance: cf. Turnus at *Aen.* 12.11 (Serv. auct. *plus est 'in Turno' quam si 'in me' dixisset*), 74, 97, 645 (Serv. ἐμφατικῶς *Turnus*), Harrison on *Aen.* 10.73, 825–6. *Atrides* 'for all that he is the son of Atreus'.

habebit ... erit: 186, 206nn.

359, 361 paene 'little more than' (*OLD* s.v. 2).

360 causam nominis inde tuli 'that is why I am called Alexander', the name by which he is most frequently referred to in the *Iliad* (45x: Paris 13x: Kirk on *Il.* 3.16): ἀλέξανδρος = 'warding off men'. Cf. Enn. *Alex.* 64 J. *quapropter Parim pastores nunc Alexandrum uocant*, Apollod. *Bibl.* 3.12.5.5 'He was called Alexander because he drove off the robbers and defended (ἀλεξήσας) the herds.'

361 puer iuuenes: the juxtaposition emphasizes the contrast in ages.

uario certamine: in his own funeral games, celebrated in his memory by Priam. The episode and his subsequent recognition (89–98n.) were the subject of Euripides' *Alexandros* and Ennius' *Alexander* (Stinton (1965) 64–70 = (1990) 66–70, Jocelyn (1967) 202–9), Introd. p. 6.

362 fuit: the verb takes the number of the nearest element of its compound subject (Kenney on Lucret. 3.66).

363 neue putes: for this anticipatory use of *ne* see *OLD* s.v. *ne*¹ 13a. *neue* = *et, ne* (71n.).

363–4 He makes a virtue of what was not usually in the heroic world a subject for boasting (263–70, 354nn.).

iusso 'appointed', 'intended'. Paris himself was fated to perish by the bow of Philoctetes, as O.'s readers well knew (279–80n.).

365 'Can you ascribe (*OLD* s.v. *do*¹ 17a) to him (Menelaus) such exploits of early youth as these (of mine)?'

366 arte mea: archery.

instruere ... num potes ...?: i.e. can you produce a Menelaus qualified as I am?

367 omnia si dederis 'even if you grant him every possible virtue'.

fratrem 'as a brother', predicative.

368 innumeri militis 'a countless host' (*OLD* s.v. *miles* 1b).

erit: 186n.

369–70 A sly hint that his prowess in bed matches that on the battlefield. Cf. 17.256n.

372 Dorica castra = Virg. *Aen.* 2.27, but with a change of meaning from 'encampment' to 'army' (*OLD* s.v. *castra*¹ 1, 2). Cf. 18.175n.

373 nec ... indigner 'Not but what I should be proud', litotes.

tanta connotes importance as much as personal qualities: cf. 5.9 *nondum tantus eras*, 16.150, *Met.* 3.133 *huc adde genus de coniuge tanta*. She is a 'great prize' (374).

sumere ferrum 'take up the sword'.

375 totus ... orbis: his language ironically prefigures the terms in which the Trojan War will go down to posterity: Virg. *Aen.* 1.456–8 *uidet Iliacas ex ordine pugnas | bellaque iam fama totum uulgata per orbem, | Atridas Priamumque et saeuum ambobus Achillem*, 7.222–7 *quanta per Idaeos saeuis effusa Mycenis | tempestas ierit campos, quibus actus uterque | Europae atque Asiae fatis concurrerit orbis, | audiit et si quem tellus extrema refuso | summouet Oceano et si quem extenta plagarum | quattuor in medio dirimit plaga solis iniqui* and Fordyce *ad loc.* See next n.

376 Another brilliantly ironical echo of Helen's own words in Homer, this time to Hector: 'Seeing that your heart is encompassed by trouble on account of me, bitch that I am, and on account of Alexander's infatuation, on whom Zeus has laid an evil fate, that hereafter we shall be a subject of song to the men of the future' (*Il.* 6.355–8). The grand expression ('probably the finest verse in the suspected Epistles', Palmer) compounds the irony. Cf. also *Am.* 1.3.25–6 (the poet-lover to his mistress) *nos quoque per totum pariter can-*

tabimur orbem | iunctaque semper erunt nomina nostra tuis. Helen too is literary *materies*.

posteritate: 302n.

377–8 spe ... non timida, dis ... secundis, cum plena ... fide: the proliferation of abl. adverbial phrases conveying hope and confidence imparts a final touch of irony. *dis ... secundis* is particularly wishful thinking in view of the undying offence given by the Judgement to Juno and Minerva, and the original divine motivation of these events (41n.).

exige 'demand payment of', sc. what he has promised her. Paris cunningly implies that the obligation is somehow on her side.

xvii
Helen to Paris

1 nunc 'as it is' (16.271n.). The abrupt beginning can be defended as dramatically effective, like those of 20 and 21 (see nn. *ad locc.*) and e.g. 7, 10, 12. It is however more probable that, as in those cases and in 18 and 19 (qq. v.) an introductory couplet has been lost, the sense of which was something like 'Had I realized what was in your letter I should have returned it unopened' (cf. Kenney (1961) 485). That supplied in two thirteenth-century MSS is not O.'s (*ibid.*).

uiolarit 'has polluted' (*OLD* s.v. 1c), here with a connotation also of rape (*ibid.* 2c). For metaphorical violation of the senses cf. Cic. *Har.* 26 *uiolatis oculis ... contaminatis manibus*, Petron. 85.2 *uiolari aures meas obsceno sermone nolui*.

2 gloria ... leuis: this seems to imply that what follows will be something she can be proud of. If the lofty indignation of the next couplet were maintained to the end, that would indeed be so. In effect, however, 'this is surrender; the rest is apology' (Rand (1925) 30). Cf. Introd. pp. 7–8.

uisa: sc. *est*.

3 ausus es [= 1.41, 2.93, 9.63 (Casali *ad loc.*), 12.133, 134] ... **aduena** 'you come here and dare ...'; *aduena* is predicative.

hospitii temeratis ... sacris 'by desecrating the sacred laws of hospitality'; cf. 16.42n. *temero* also has sexual connotations (*OLD* s.v. 2). Cf. Hor. *C.* 1.15.1–2 *pastor cum traheret per freta nauibus | Idaeis*

Helenen perfidus hospitam ...; Paris' stock Greek epithet was ξεναπάτης 'host-deceiving' (N–H *ad loc.*).

5 scilicet idcirco 'it was, it seems, for this ...'; so Ulysses on Ajax at *Met.* 13.288 (16.307–8n.).

uentosa per aequora uectum = Virg. *G.* 1.206 (*uectis*), *Aen.* 6.335 (*uectos*) and Austin *ad loc.*

6 Taenaris 'Spartan': 16.21n.

7 diuersa quamuis e gente uenires: an (anachronistic) reference to the xenophobia for which the Spartans were in classical times noted.

9–10 'You who obtained entrance so as to return grievous wrong for so great a service, were you guest or enemy?' *ut* anticipates *sic*; for this construction, in which a subordinate clause is grammatically dependent on a second following subordinate clause cf. 3.39–40 *si tibi ab Atride pretio redimenda fuissem,* | *quae dare debueras, accipere illa negas*, 10.39–40 *si non audires, ut saltem cernere posses,* | *iactatae late signa dedere manus*, Hor. *Sat.* 1.9.1–2, Prop. 4.3.2, [Virg.] *Cat.* 9.25–6, Gratt. *Cyn.* 317–20; Housman, *CP* 477. The vulgate punctuation of this passage, making lines 5–9 one sentence and 10 an independent question, gives inferior sense and rhetoric. Cf. 19.29–30n.

hospes an hostis: cf. 13.43–4 *Dyspari Priamide, damno formose tuorum,* | *tam sis hostis iners quam malus hospes eras*, *F.* 2.787; a common play on words. The original senses of the two words were the same = 'stranger', ξένος (Ernout–Meillet (1959, 1960) s.vv.).

11 cum 'though' (*OLD* s.v.[2] 7a).

12, 13 rustica: 16.222n.

13 oblita: sc. *sim*.

15 'Though I do not feign a severe expression ...'; *si* = *etsi* (*OLD* s.v. 9a).

16 sedeo is almost a technical term to characterize a virtuous matron: *F.* 2.771 (Lucretia) *sic sedit, sic culta fuit, sic stamina neuit*, *Med.* 13–14 *cum matrona premens altum rubicunda sedile* | *assiduo durum pollice nebat opus*, *Tr.* 3.7.3–4 *aut illam inuenies dulci cum matre sedentem* | *aut inter libros Pieridasque suas*; cf. *CIL* VI 11602, 34045 *domiseda*. The old Roman custom was for women to sit at table while the men reclined (Kenney on Apul. *Met.* 6.24.1, Val. Max. 2.1.2). Helen, as we have seen (16.221–8), follows the custom of Ovid's contemporaries.

duris torua: Bentley emended to *toruis dura*, which is attractive:

(i) *toruus* is much more commonly used by O. of *uultus, acies* etc. than of people (but cf. e.g. 2.69 *toruus* ... *Procrustes, A.A.* 2.309 *torua* ... *Medusa*); (ii) Paris has called her *dura* (16.289). For exchange of stems as a cause of corruption see 19.62n. However, there is nothing demonstrably wrong with the text as transmitted; for *duris* ... *superciliis* cf. 16.11 *uultu* ... *duro*. For the polysyllabic ending see Introd. p. 22.

17 sine crimine uixi: the language of sepulchral eulogy; cf. Prop. 4.11.45–6 (Cornelia) *nec mea mutata est aetas, sine crimine tota est: | uiximus insignes inter utramque facem, CIL* I 2.1221.10 *fido fida uiro ueixsit* (*ROL* IV 23), 1206.2 *femina optuma ueixsit* (26), 1732.5–6 *coniuge sum Cadmo fructa Scrateio, | concordesque pari uiximus ingenio* (54). Cf. *OLD* s.v. *uiuo* 9c.

19 quae sit fiducia coepti 'how you can have such confidence in your enterprise' (*OLD* s.v. *qui*[1] 2a). For *coepti* cf. 16.323n.

21 Neptunius ... heros = 4.109, *Met.* 9.1; Theseus (16.153n.) was according to one version of the legend the son of Neptune (Poseidon).

22 rapta 'because I had been abducted'; cf. 16.3n.

bis ... rapi: cf. Lycophr. *Alex.* 513 τῆι δισαρπάγωι κρεκί 'the twice-ravished corncrake'.

23 crimen erat nostrum 'I should have been blameworthy'; for the indic. in the apodosis of a past unreal condition cf. Hor. *C.* 2.17.27–9 *me truncus illapsus cerebro | sustulerat nisi Faunus ictum | dextra leuasset* and N–H *ad loc.*, but here it is difficult to see any motive but metrical convenience at work. See next n.

delenita fuissem = *d. essem*: cf. 91, 21.35; a characteristically Ovidian usage (Bömer on *Met.* 3.228), generally avoided (Livy being a notable exception) by careful stylists (Blase (1903) 220–2, N–W III 142–5). Again the motive for O. was metrical convenience. Cf. 24 *sim* and n.

24 sim: strict syntax demands *essem*; it is difficult to see any reason for the informality, for which parallels are lacking, except – once again – metrical convenience.

meum ... fuit? 'What resource had I but to say "no"?'; for the inf. treated as a neuter noun cf. e.g. 19.16, 145, 185, *Met.* 14.100 *posse queri tantum* ... *reliquit* and Bömer on 2.483, *NLS* §25.

27 proteruus 'in his insolence', predicative.

28 nil ... mei 'nothing of me' partitive genit.; *mei* is genit. of *ego*, not of *meus*.

29 quae ... est 'being what it is' (*OLD* s.v. *qui*[1] 12a); cf. 1.75–6 *haec ego dum stulte metuo, quae uestra libido est, | esse peregrino captus amore potes, Met.* 5.373–4 *et tamen in caelo, quae iam patientia nostra est, | spernimur, Ex P.* 1.7.59, 2.2.21. Apparently a colloquial idiom: Cic. *Epp.*, Hor. *S.* 1.9.54, K–S II 314.

nequitia: a mild term for the innuendo of 16.161–2 (n.); one can imagine (this) Helen dimpling as she writes it.

30 tibi: editors prefer the better-attested *tui*, and in classical Latin the genit. is the regular construction with pronouns. O. however everywhere else (86x) constructs *similis* with dat., and for *tibi* cf. e.g. 12.189 *similes tibi sunt, A.A.* 3.175 *ecce tibi similis, al. tui* is no doubt due to *mei* at 28.

31 modestia 'his restraint'.

32 iuuenem: he was not old enough to know better.

34 in ore 'on (men's) lips'; for the omission of the usual *hominum vel sim.* cf. Cic. *Tusc.* 1.116 *Harmodius in ore ⟨est⟩ et Aristogiton*, Livy 9.10.3 (*s.u.l.*). Cf. 16.376n.

35 quis enim succenset amanti?: a basic (male) premiss of the *Ars Amatoria*: 1.271–4 *uere prius uolucres taceant, aestate cicadae, | Maenalius lepori det sua terga canis, | femina quam iuueni blande temptata repugnet; | haec quoque, quam poteris credere nolle, uolet*, 623 *delectant etiam castas praeconia formae.* Cf. 73–4n.

37 non quo 'not because (as you might think) ...'. Most MSS have *quod*, but the idiom *non quo* + subj. (attributed reason) ... *sed quod/quia* + indic. (actual reason), though apparently found only here in the poets, is well attested in good prose (K–S II 385–6). At *Tr.* 5.11.3–5 *indolui, non tam mea quod fortuna male audit, | qui iam consueui fortiter esse miser, | quam quod cui minime uellem, sum causa pudoris*, the first *quod*-clause states a fact. Corruption of *quo* to *quod* is common in MSS, not so of *quod* to *quo*.

fiducia: sc. *mei* (16.323n.).

39 damno ... esse 'to be their ruin', predicative dat. with *puellis*.

40 uestra 'of you men'.

41 O.'s Rome again: *Am.* 1.8.43–4 (cit. 16.285–94n.) and McKeown *ad loc.* For *matronaque* Bentley temptingly conjectured *formosaque*, comparing 16.290. *at* 'But, you will say' (*OLD* s.v. 4b).

42 quid (Heinsius) not *quis* (MSS) is required in this formula; cf.

10.88 *quid uetat et gladios per latus ire meum?* and Heinsius *ad loc.*, *Am.* 3.7.35 *quid uetat et neruos magicas torpere per artes?*

43 quod 'though', literally 'as to the fact that', a common idiom either, as here, with indic. (familiar in the recurrent *quod scribis* of Cicero's letters, to pick up a point made by a correspondent), of the actual state of affairs alluded to, or with subj. of a presumed or alleged state of affairs; in practice, however, the distinction is by no means clear-cut (251n.). According to context in either construction the sense of the sentence may be confirmatory, deprecatory, adversative or, as here, concessive. Cf. 18.41n., 4.157–61 *quod mihi sit genitor qui possidet aequora Minos, | quod ueniant proaui fulmina torta manu, | quod sit auus radiis frontem uallatus acutis, | purpureo tepidum qui mouet axe diem, | nobilitas sub amore iacet*, *Met.* 7.705–7 *quod sit roseo spectabilis ore, | quod teneat lucis, teneat confinia noctis, | nectareis quod alatur aquis, ego Procrin amabam* (Bömer's n. *ad loc.* is perverse), *A.A.* 1.261 (but see Hollis *ad loc.*), Lucret. 2.532–5, 5.916–19, *Priap.* 6. See further K–S II 277–8, Bennett I (1910) 125–6, 338; and cf. 51, 143, 251, 261, 20.155nn.

44 putes '(such as) you may think'; consecutive-generic subj.

45–6 'In respect of (*OLD* s.v. *in* 42) my mother's offence a mistake is involved (*OLD* s.v. *insum* 4)'.

pluma tectus: 16.252n.

47–8 si peccem ... erit: this variety of mixed condition (the '*sit ... erit*' type) is common in O. (Kenney (1959) 247), so *erit* does not necessarily imply that Helen has already made up her mind. Cf. 16.186n.

crimen obumbret ~ *Ex P.* 3.3.75 *crimen obumbres*.

obumbret '(such as) might obscure', consecutive-generic subj.

49–50 auctore ... Ioue: from the speaker's point of view Jupiter is instrument rather than agent, hence the unaccompanied abl.

49 'She mistook well, and atoned for (*OLD* s.v. *redimo* 3b) her fault through (the identity of) the person responsible (*OLD* s.v. *auctor* 12)': quintessentially Ovidian diction, expression and point.

50 'Where is the Jupiter through whom *I* shall be called fortunate in *my* fault?'

51 quod ... iactas 'for all that you boast of ...': 43n. *quod* is poorly attested but produces much crisper syntax than *et* (most MSS) or *sed* (Housman). Cf. 251n.

53 ut ... taceatur 'to say nothing of'; 16.176n.

soceri proauus '*as* my father-in-law's (Atreus') ancestor', predicative. Helen's trump card is that Jupiter is her father (55, 60).

54 Pelopis Tyndareique decus 'glorious Pelops and Tyndareus'; the phrase is modelled on Greek epic periphrases with βία *et sim.* to describe heroes; cf. Hor. *C.* 3.25.4–5 *Caesaris ... | aeternum ... decus* 'Augustus ever glorious'. In view of Pelops' chequered past (16.209–10n.) irony may be suspected. Tyndareus was only Helen's official father (16.100n.).

55 cycno 'by the swan', dat. of the agent. The spelling *cygnus* still found in modern editions is a barbarism: see Housman, *CP* 1136–46.

parentem 'as a father', predicative.

56 falsam: grammatically feminine but emphatically a male bird; cf. Kenney on Apul. *Met.* 6.15.1.

57–8 i nunc et ... refer 'so much for your recital'; O. is fond of this ironical use of *eo* (*OLD* s.v. 10b): see McKeown on *Am.* 1.7.35–6.

suo 'his dear father' (*OLD* s.v. *suus* B7). There is a suggestion of the patronizing; cf. 61 *tuae ... Troiae* 'this Troy you go on about'.

60 quintus 'as fifth', predicative. The usual tally of intermediaries is Priam-Laomedon-Ilus-Tros-Erichthonius-Dardanus; scholars explain the discrepancy in various ways. O. may be discreetly advertising his awareness of an unfamiliar version of the genealogy, but it is odd that he should apparently make Helen understate her case.

erit: 16.186n.

61 sceptra 'dominion over' (*OLD* s.v. 2). There is no need to emend to *regna* (Palmer) as at 16.177 (q.v.); cf. *Met.* 6.677, *F.* 6.506 *sceptra loci*.

63 si iam 'if, for the sake of argument' (H–S 673, *OLD* s.v. *iam* 7d, *TLL* s.v. *iam* 128.1ff.). It is odd that the phrase should recur within the space of five lines; coming here it weakens the effect of 67, where Helen is making a concession that vitally affects the reader's perception of her probity.

64 barbara: cf. 1.26 *barbara praeda* 'Trojan booty'. A classical attitude; Homer never uses the word βάρβαρος, as Thucydides noted (1.3.3 and Hornblower *ad loc.*). Cf. Eur. *I.A.* 575–8, where the Chorus apostrophize Paris 'piping barbarian strains' while herding on Ida; N–H on Hor. *C.* 2.4.9, Barchiesi on *Her.* 3.2.

65 diues 'with its rich promises' (Palmer).

67 si iam uellem 'if (for the sake of argument) I were inclined

...' (63n.). We have already come some way from her first indignant repudiation; cf. 75, 77n.

fines transire pudoris: cf. Cic. *Verr.* 2.3.220 *si uos semel in iudicando finem aequitatis et legis transieritis* ... , and for the idea of moral boundaries Hor. *C.* 1.18.10–11 *cum fas atque nefas exiguo fine libidinum | discernunt auidi* ... and N–H *ad loc.* citing *inter al.* Livy 39.8.6 *cum uinum animos incendisset et nox et mixti feminis mares, aetatis tenerae maioribus, discrimen omne pudoris exstinxissent.*

68 futurus eras = *esses*, a metrically convenient periphrasis. Cf. e.g. 18.11 *ascensurus eram*, 3.147–8 *me petat ille tuus, qui, si dea passa fuisset, | ensis in Atridae pectus iturus erat*, 13.55–6 *nec rapere ausurus, nisi se defendere posset, | hospes erat, Tr.* 1.7.40 *emendaturus, si licuisset, eram*; Blase (1903) 273–4.

69 famam ... tenebo 'I shall maintain my good name'; cf. Caes. *B.C.* 3.55.2 *Pompeius ... ut famam opinionemque hominum teneret* ... , Livy 39.37.18 *ut ... appareret ... dignitatem suam tenere Romanos non posse.* Palmer ingeniously but gratuitously conjectured *tuebor*, comparing 113 *tueri* and noting that Planudes renders by φυλάττω at both places.

71 ut ... sic 'though ... yet'; for this idiom cf. 109–10n., 241–4, *Met.* 1.15–16, 370 and Bömer *ad loc.*, H–S 633–4. For *sic ... ut/ne* + subj. with a similar limiting nuance cf. 165n.

acceptissima: cf. *Met.* 15.20 *dis acceptissimus*; the superlative otherwise only in prose (cf. 19.131n.). *acceptior* at *Met.* 13.467.

73–4 That women like to be desired has always been generally believed: cf. 35n., 131–6, *A.A.* 1.613–24, Kost on Musaeus 103–4.

spes tua: 'est tu sperans' (Terpstra); cf. 108 *spes tua lenta fuit*, 20.17 *meus ... ardor.* Palmer compared Prop. 1.17.19 *meum ... dolorem = me dolentem.*

75 improbe, 77 lasciue: again (29n.) one senses the giggle which accompanies these ostensibly reproving words.

76 quamuis experiar 'however much I try'.

77–8 ~ Eur. *I.A.* 582–6 (the Chorus to Menelaus) 'Standing before Helen's ivory-inlaid house, gazing straight at her, you inspired love and were yourself by love carried away.'

79–80 ~ *Am.* 1.4.31–2 *quae tu reddideris, ego primus pocula sumam, | et qua tu biberis hac ego parte bibam, A.A.* 1.575–6 *fac primus rapias illius tacta labellis | pocula, quaque bibet parte puella, bibas* and McKeown, Hollis *ad locc.*

proxima nobis 'next after me' (not 'nearest me'), with enallage (16.107n.) for *proximus nobis*.

81–2 ~ Prop. 3.8.25–6 ... *tecta superciliis si quando uerba remittis, | aut mea cum digitis scripta silenda notas*, Am. 1.4.19–20 *uerba superciliis sine uoce loquentia dicam; | uerba leges digitis, uerba notata mero*, 2.5.15–18 *multa supercilio uidi uibrante loquentes; | nutibus in uestris pars bona uocis erat. | non oculi tacuere tui conscriptaque uino | mensa, nec in digitis littera nulla fuit* and Booth *ad loc.*

82 loquente: 16.11–12n.

84 erubuique: 16.216n.

85 nullo murmure 'under my breath'; cf. *Met.* 6.203 *tacito ... murmure.*

87 orbe ... in mensae 'on the round table'; an anachronistic reference to the expensive fashion that came in during the late Republic for round tables (*orbes*) formed from sections of large trees: Juv. 1.137 and Mayor, Courtney *ad loc.*, *OLD* s.v. *orbis* 2f. For the placing of the preposition (anastrophe; cf. 21.31n.) cf. 21.172 *face pro thalami* and e.g. 2.15 *uada ... ad Hebri*, Lucret. 3.1088 *tempore de mortis*, Catull. 69.6 *ualle sub alarum*, Virg. *G.* 3.313 *usum in castrorum*, Ov. *Met.* 4.507 *pectus in amborum*, etc. In such phrases the genitive is equivalent to an attributive adj.: K–S I 587–8, Bömer on *Met.* 5.336.

88 deducta mero littera: cf. 1.31–2 *atque aliquis posita monstrat fera proelia mensa, | pingit et exiguo Pergama tota mero*, Am. 1.4.20 (cit. 81–2n.), *A.A.* 1.571–2 *(licet) blanditias ... leues tenui perscribere uino, | ut dominam in mensa se legat illa tuam.*

89 renuente: 16.11–12n.

91 fuissem: 23n.

92 poterant ... capi 'might have been led captive': 16.162n.

93 quoque qualifies *facies*; he has good looks into the bargain.

94 sub amplexus ire 'share your bed'; *sub* is used = *in* seemingly for metrical convenience, a trick peculiar to O. (*F.* 6.554, *Met.* 7.616 and Bömer *ad loc.*). Contrast 5.100, 16.86, *Rem.* 668, *al.* (*in*), *A.A.* 1.770 (*ad*, s.v.l.).

95 sed: 16.191n. An adversative is not really wanted here; *sic* (Kenney), sc. *sub amplexus tuos eundo*, would give more pointed sense. Cf. 184n.

96 externo 'adulterous', other than her husband's: 5.101–3

(Oenone to Paris) *ut minor Atrides temerati foedera lecti | clamat et externo laesus amore dolet, | tu quoque clamabis*, Prop. 1.3.44 and Fedeli *ad loc.*

97 meo exemplo: this unusual elision of an iambic word before a word other than a monosyllable, and that word a noun, is paralleled in O. only at *Am.* 2.19.20 *saepe time insidias*. Both however can be defended by analogy with elisions in *Met.* of an iambic word before a compound verb, as at 2.315 *iugo eripiunt* (5x): similarly *ex-* and *in-* in the elegiac examples are treated as semi-separable prepositional prefixes (cf. Kenney on Lucret. 3.174, 258 and the analogous treatment of *quidem* (16.131–2n.)). The two instances support each other, since neither can be convincingly emended away; and it is perverse to advance as an argument against Ovidian authorship this rare but specifically Ovidian metrical licence. Cf. 16.83n.

98 Helen demurely and anachronistically plays the Stoic moralist, recommending one of the sect's four cardinal virtues: Cic. *Fin.* 2.60 *transfer idem ad modestiam uel temperantiam, quae est moderatio cupiditatum rationi oboediens*.

abstinuisse: 16.204n.

100 qui sapiant oculos 'eyes that can discern', cf. 101 *cernis*. The old punctuation, still adopted by some editors and unconvincingly defended by Palmer, which makes *qui sapiant?* depend on *iuuenes* in line 99, gives inferior sense, structure and rhetoric. *sapiant* is consecutive-generic subj.

101–2 A fine example of 'theme and variation', with the pentameter repeating but imparting a more arresting turn to the sentiment of the hexameter. The term was coined by the great Virgilian commentator James Henry (1 (1873) 204–7), but the device is, as he remarked, 'almost inseparable from poetry' (745–6). On O.'s use of it see Kenney (1973) 132–5.

nec tibi plus cordis sed nimis oris adest 'It is not sharper wits (*OLD* s.v. *cor* 3) but excess of cheek (*os* 8b) that supports (*adsum* 11a) you'. Assonance – *cordis* (picking up *cernis* from 101) ... *oris* (picking up *temerarius audes*) – sharpens the point. The genitives with *plus* and *nimis* are partitive; cf. 14.82 *sanguinis* ... *parum* 'too little bloodshed'. Elsewhere in O. (43x) *cor* = 'heart'.

104 mille ... procis: though *mille* is often used vaguely = 'many' (*OLD* s.v. 1b), still something of an exaggeration. It is tempting to suspect authorial irony, a dig at the various lists handed down by the mythographical tradition: Hes. *Eoeae* frr. 196–200 M–W, Apollod. *Bibl.* 3.10.8–9, Hyg. *Fab.* 81. Dido, however, makes the same claim for herself (7.123). On O.'s suppression of the Suitors' Oath see 16.341n.

petita: sc. *est*.

106 dabit: sc. if appealed to. We are hardly meant to infer that (at this stage of the affair) she proposes to confide all this to Menelaus when he gets back; or that O. implies a Freudian slip on her part, revealing that she has in fact made up her mind to yield. It would strain the syntax to treat this case as falling under the rubric of the 'future of probability' (16.186n.).

107 possessa ... praecepta: the legal flavour of the words (Berger (1953) s.vv. *Possessio, Praecipere*) is characteristic of O. (Kenney (1969), 16.305n.).

uenis ... serus 'you come too late', predicative.

109–10 'But though I might desire to be your wife, Trojan, it is not against my will that Menelaus holds me.' For this use of correlative *ut ... sic* with concessive sense cf. 71n.; *optarim* is pf. subj. (cf. e.g. *Am.* 2.4.1 *ausim*) of 'cautious assertion' (16.7, 189nn.), not dependent on *ut*. Cf. Eur. *Tro.* 1002–9, where Hecuba accuses her of playing off one lover against the other.

optarim ... Troice: Bentley's palmary corrections of MS *optarem ... troica*; cf. *A.A.* 3.253–4 *Helene, quam non stulte, Menelae, reposcis, | tu quoque non stulte, Troice raptor, habes. tua Troica coniunx* = 'your Trojan wife' is no doubt not impossible Latin, but blunts the antithesis Paris)(Menelaus on which the couplet is articulated.

inuitam ... nec: O. avoids the obvious word-order *sic non inuitam me* so as to (i) emphasize *inuitam*, (ii) associate the negative with the name of Menelaus: *nec* = *ne ... quidem* (*OLD* s.v. *neque* 2), 'neither (= 'and by no means') is M. disagreeable to me', 'M. too has his attractions'. Cf. 233 *nec Medea, Met.* 4.153 *poteris nec morte reuelli* and Bömer *ad loc.*

111 conuellere: a word of unexampled violence to describe an attempt to take the heart of the beloved by storm: Helen playfully picks up and deflates Paris' pomposity at 16.41 (Kenney (1979) 397).

113 sine: sc. *me*.

114 spolium nostri turpe pudoris 'the shameful spoils of my chastity'; *pudoris* is gen. of definition, her chastity *is* the booty. Cf.

5.140 *ille meae spolium uirginitatis habet*, *Met.* 1.600 *rapuit . . . pudorem* and Bömer *ad loc.*, 6.616–17 *quae tibi membra pudorem | abstulerunt*. For the metaphor cf. Catull. 66.14 *uirginis . . . exuuiis*, Hedylus, *A.P.* 5.199.4 (*HE* 1834) παρθενίων ὑγρὰ λάφυρα πόθων 'the scented spoils of maiden love.'

aue: Palmer's correction of MS *habe*, which cannot plausibly be interpreted = 'seek to have'. The sense is pointed, but *aueo* is uncommon in the poets (in. O. only at *Met.* 2.503 *auenti, Ex P.* 4.13.2 *aue* (the greeting)), and it is rarely construed with a direct object. Also deserving consideration is *et . . . habe* (Reeve (1973) 330) 'and consider it shameful to rob me of my honour'; cf. *Met.* 10.325–6 *nec habetur turpe iuuencae | ferre patrem tergo, OLD* s.v. *habeo* 24b.

115 at 'But, you say . . .' (41n.).

ut 'when' (*OLD* s.v. 26a), Heinsius' correction of MS *et*. What follows *pacta est* is not parallel in sense or rhetorical force but adds supporting detail.

116 nudas: this was not mentioned by Paris, but it was one of the features of the story 'known to every schoolboy' – at least to every Roman schoolboy in O.'s day, for that all three goddesses stripped off is first attested by Propertius (2.2.13–14; cf. Wentzel (1890) XLVIII, *LIMC* VII 1.176); cf. 5.35–6 *Venus et Iuno sumptisque decentior armis | uenit in arbitrium nuda Minerua tuum*. It is more likely that O. was negligent than that he meant his readers to infer that Helen, womanlike, leaps to conclusions; in any case lapses of this sort do not support the case for non-Ovidian authorship of 16.39–144 (Kenney (1979) 404). Cf. 237n.

117 una . . . altera: Juno and Minerva.

118 Tyndaridos: O. tends to prefer Greek forms of Greek proper names, whether for metrical reasons (see Appendix) or for the sound. His MSS are not reliable or consistent guides to his usage: e.g. *-idis* here, *-idos* at *Tr.* 2.396. Cf. 18.137 *Athamantidos*, 18.81, 21.77nn.

119 credere uix equidem . . . possum: this recalls Hecuba's scepticism (cf. 16.81n.) about the whole episode at Eur. *Tro.* 969–97: 'L'Europe et l'Asie bouleversées par trois coquettes!' (Jouan (1966) 108).

numina: this is the old vulgate; all MSS appear to have *corpora*, which editors since Heinsius have printed. *caelestia corpora* is in itself unexceptionable as a periphrasis for *caelestes* (*Met.* 15.662, Virg. *Aen.* 11.276; cf. *Her.* 12.30 *corpora Graia*), but is distinctly odd with what follows, unless *formam* is taken = *se* (Kenney on *Moret.* 61). Given the attested propensity of words of this scansion to be confused (Housman, Index to ed. of Manilius s.v. '*dactylicae mensurae uoces inter se confusae*') and the proximity of *corporis* at 123, the correction to *numina* has been strangely slow to impose itself again. For the phrase *caelestia numina* cf. 20.181, *al.*

121 ut 'though' (16.311n.).

123 fiducia corporis 'confidence in my person' (*OLD* s.v. *corpus* 4); cf. 19, 16.323nn.

124 teste dea 'on the word of a goddess'.

126 'Praise from Venus will bring envy on me.' Excessive good fortune was thought of as likely to attract the jealousy of heaven (Otto s.v. *invidia*), but praise from Venus was especially dangerous: Prop. 2.28.9–10 *num sibi collatam doluit Venus? illa peraeque | prae se formosis inuidiosa dea est*. *laudatrix* is predicative; the word is otherwise found in classical Latin only at Cic. *Tusc.* 3.4. Cf. *infirmo* (127n.).

127 nihil 'in no way' (*OLD* s.v. 11a, c).

infirmo 'discredit', sc. *laudes istas* (ἀπὸ κοινοῦ construction). In this technical sense, of disabling an argument, the word is a favourite of Cicero's but occurs nowhere else in classical Latin poetry.

128 uox ... quod cupit: the apparent absurdity of this ('Paullo audacior dictio' Loers) led Bentley to condemn the couplet, indicating as he did so what he took the required sense to be by rewriting *nam cur uox, animus quod cupit, esse neget?* In the same vein is Goold's less ostensibly drastic remedy, *nam, mens, uox quare, quod cupit esse, neget?*; but even by Ovidian standards this hyperbaton is indefensibly harsh (cf. 16.177–8n.). However it is emended the conceit seems feeble, and the couplet is certainly expendable.

129 nimium mihi creditus aegre 'because I have been so reluctant to believe you'.

132 uisam: sc. *esse*.

133 Palladios: i.e. *Mineruae*.

134 auditis 'which you had (only) heard about': Kenney on Lucret. 3.144 and *Addenda*.

bonis 'charms'; cf. *A.A.* 2.112 *ingenii dotes corporis adde bonis*, a special sense peculiar to O. (*OLD* s.v. *bonum* 5*b*).

COMMENTARY: 17.137–151

137 amare repugno 'I fight against loving'; cf. Lucret. 4.1269 *mulier prohibet se concipere atque repugnat*, where Lucretian usage requires that both verbs govern *concipere* ('hinders and stands in the way of her own conceiving' Munro). For *pugno* + inf. cf. 13.77 *uiuere pugna*, *Am.* 1.5.14, *Rem.* 122, *al.* Cf. 20.121 *ne fias nostra repugnat*, itself the only ex. in O. of *repugno* + *ne* and subj.

139–40 ~ 5.115–16 (Oenone quoting Cassandra) *quid facis, Oenone? quid harenae semina mandas? | non profecturis litora bubus aras.* This proverbial image for futile endeavour first figures allusively at Virg. *Aen.* 4.212 (Pease, Austin, *ad loc.*); the Greeks spoke of sowing rocks or the sea (Otto s.v. *harena* 4).

proscindere ... aratro ~ Lucret. 5.209 *proscindere aratris.*

141 ad Veneris furtum 'in illicit love' (*OLD* s.v. *furtum* 2b).

141–2 nulla ... arte 'never by any device'.

143 quod ... mando etc.: cf. 43n. The nuance here is deprecatory: 'This very act of entrusting my words to a secret (*OLD* s.v. *tacitus* 8) letter is for me a new kind of writing'. *littera nostra* = 'my writing' (Riley) rather than 'my letter'; cf. 266.

145 felices: sc. *illas* (cf. 19.111), acc. of exclamation.

quibus usus adest 'who have experience to guide them'; cf. Otto s.v. *usus* 1. This was O.'s own boasted qualification: *A.A.* 1.29–30 *Vsus opus mouet hoc: uati parete perito. | uera canam. coeptis, mater Amoris, ades.*

nescia rerum 'ignorant of the world', but also 'not knowing what the future may hold'.

146 difficilem ... uiam: according to the received wisdom it was the path of righteousness that was steep and stony, that of wrongdoing level and smooth: Hes. *Op.* 287–92 and Sinclair, West *ad loc.*, Otto s.v. *arduus*. In the event she will turn out to be all too right.

147 malo ... est 'is troublesome'; *malo* is predicative dat. A hint of a proverbial idea: Publ. Syr. S12 *semper plus metuit animus ignotum malum*; cf. 1.71–2 *quid timeam ignoro, timeo tamen omnia demens, | et patet in curas area lata meas*, Livy 28.44.3 *maior ignotarum rerum est terror, al.*

iam nunc 'now already' (*OLD* s.v. *iam* 3b), sc. even before I have taken the plunge.

151–2 The pointedly chiastic structure *dissimula ... desistere ... desistas ... dissimulare* is characteristic of O.; cf. 173–4, there with variation of diction, *facie ... uitae ... probitas ... forma/metuit ... confidit ... securum ... timere.*

151 nisi si 'unless indeed'; an originally colloquial pleonasm (H–S 668) favoured by O., often simply = *nisi* (*OLD* s.v. 7), but usually with a trace of irony, as at e.g. 4.111 *nisi si manifesta | negamus*. The other poets avoid it.

153 occulte: 16.174n.

155 re cogente 'because his affairs oblige him'; cf. 16.301n.

158 fac rediturus eas 'go – but hurry back'; not merely Ovidian periphrasis for *redi*. The fut. part. has a strongly predicative force. Cf. 16.263–4n.

159 omine laetatus: events and words uttered at the start of a journey were considered particularly significant (*OLD* s.v. *omen* 2a); cf. 21.69–70n.

'res'que 'domusque ...': this trick of inserting *-que* as a connective into the beginning of direct speech, of which O. is fond, seems to have been his own invention: see Haupt III (1875–6) 510–12, McKeown on *Am.* 1.1.23–4. Cf. the analogous treatment of *nec*, 16.83n. For the collocation *res domusque* cf. Tib. 1.9.72, Hor. *Ep.* 1.2.51. See 20.127–8n.

160 sit curae 'be your care', predicative dat. *sit* agrees with the nearest element of a compound subject (16.362n.).

161–2 The gaff is now blown; so much for her opening protestations. *erit*, one notes, not *erunt*.

163 Creten: acc. of motion towards; islands count as towns in this connexion. Cf. 18.157–8n.

164 non ideo ... puta 'not on that account are you to think'; *non* is occasionally found with the imperative in prohibitions when it qualifies a particular word (K–S I 203, H–S 340; but at *A.A.* 3.129 read *nec*).

165 'Though my husband is away, yet he guards me in his absence'. For this limiting or stipulative use of *ut* + subj. cf. 19.87–8n., 181–2, 20.101–2, Hor. *A.P.* 151–2 and Brink *ad loc.*, H–S 641, Bennett I (1910) 263–7. Contrast correlative *ut ... sic* with similar concessive sense, 109–10n.

166 an nescis etc.: 'You know what they say ...'; the idea is proverbial (Otto s.v. *manus* 4), perhaps of eastern origin: Hdt. 8.140β.2 'the power of the King (sc. Xerxes) is more than mortal and his hand is very long (ὑπερμήκης)'.

167 forma is Bentley's correction of MS *fama*; cf. 9.31 *non honor* *est sed onus species laesura ferentem. fama* 'my fame', i.e. 'the fame of my beauty' (*OLD* s.v. 5), is in itself unexceptionable, but the repetition of the word at 170 in a slightly different sense 'common report', 'reputation' (4, 6a) lacks point. Planudes, who renders τὸ κάλλος, apparently found or thought he found *forma* in his MS.

168 uestro 'of you men'; cf. 40.

169–70 'As things are (16.50n.) this reputation that I enjoy as a beauty is as much a nuisance as a pleasure to me, and it might have been better (16.162n.) to deceive (16.203–4n.) public opinion'; i.e. living up to the reputation for chastity that has been forced on her by Menelaus' jealousy has become a bore now that Paris has shown her what she has been missing all this time.

173–4 Cf. 151–2n. and for the combination of antithesis and chiasmus *Am.* 3.11.37–8 *nequitiam fugio, fugientem forma reducit;* | *auersor morum crimina, corpus amo.*

175 ultro data 'freely offered'; Menelaus has gone out of his way (*OLD* s.v. *ultro* 5) to help. For *tempus* = 'opportunity' see *OLD* s.v. 9.

176 commoditate: 16.302n.

177 exacta 'decided' (*OLD* s.v. *exigo* 10d).

178 in dubio 'in doubt' (16.140n.).

179 uir abest nobis 'my husband is away from me', dat. of dis(?)advantage.

181–2 longae ... blandus ... una: sc. *sunt, es, est.*

181 iam sermone coimus 'we already enjoy intercourse (*OLD* s.v. *coeo* 2) by letter' – sc. so why not in the flesh?

183 peream si 'may I die if', a colloquial expression (*OLD* s.v. *pereo* 3b, Hofmann (1951) 31), something like English 'I'll be hanged if'; in O. only here and at 21.29, and with *nisi, Ex P.* 3.5.45, 4.12.43. It is used by Cicero's correspondents Caelius and Cassius; he himself preferred *moriar si.* Cf. *dispeream si/nisi* (*OLD* s.v. a).

184 sed tamen: for its postponement to this *sedes* cf. 11.106, *Am.* 1.5.14 and McKeown *ad loc.*, [Ov.] *Am.* 3.5.8. Cf. 95n.

185–8 Helen acquiesces in a quintessentially male conviction (*A.A.* 1.671–8), to be shown in successful action in the story of Acontius and Cydippe, which these verses summarize and foreshadow.

185 'If only, what you fail to persuade, you could successfully force me to!' *male* allows that his case is morally bad and his arguments unconvincing, *bene* (*OLD* s.v. 8, 9, 11, 12) that in love might is right.

COMMENTARY: 17.186–194

cogere: sc. *id*, picking up *quod* (*OLD* s.v. *persuadeo* 1a).

186 excutienda fuit 'ought to have been shaken out of me' (16.162n.).

rusticitas: 16.222n.

187 passis: sc. *iniuriam*.

188 certe 'at all events', sc. in my own case (*OLD* s.v. 2a), documenting the generalization (*interdum*) of the previous verse.

189 coepto pugnemus amori ~ Virg. *Aen.* 4.38 *placito ... pugnabis amori?*

190 residit (Heinsius) 'dies down', present of *resido* (*OLD* s.v. 3e). *resedit* (MSS) might formally be pf. of either *resido* or *resideo*; sense in that case would require the former, the tense to be read as 'gnomic' (H–S 318–19), but there is no gain in point to compensate for the ambiguity. The image is not itself proverbial, but illustrates a proverbial idea: *Rem.* 91–2 *principiis obsta: sero medicina paratur, | cum mala per longas conualuere moras*, Otto s.v. *principium*.

191 certus in hospitibus etc.: so in Musaeus (177–8) Hero asks how Leander, 'a stranger and not to be trusted (ξεῖνος ἐὼν καὶ ἄπιστος)' can aspire to her hand. The 'faithless guest' is a recurrent theme in *Her.*: Demophoon (2) (cf. Callim. fr. 556 Pf. νυμφίε Δημοφόων, ἄδικε ξένε), Aeneas (7), Theseus (10); Paris however is the arch-example (Eur. *Tro.* 865–6 and above, 3n.).

errat, ut ipsi: a special case of the familiar general thesis that love is of its nature impermanent: *A.A.* 2.19–20 *et leuis est* (Amor) *et habet geminas quibus auolet alas; | difficile est illis imposuisse modum*, 3.436 *errat et in nulla sede moratur Amor*. Lycophron (*Alex.* 538) styles Paris πλανήτην 'wanderer'.

192 speres 'one hopes', generalizing 2nd person pres. subj. (*NLS* §119).

fugit: cf. 3.42 *quo leuis a nobis tam cito fugit amor?*

193 Hypsipyle: abandoned by Jason, and the writer of *Her.* 6.

Minoia uirgo: Ariadne, daughter of Minos, abandoned by Theseus, and the writer of *Her.* 10.

194 de non exhibitis utraque questa toris 'who both complain of marriages that were not forthcoming'. *de* (Francius) ... *questa* (Heinsius) is the most convincing restoration of MS *in ... iusta/lusa/iuncta*. *Exhibere* has its legal sense 'produce in court' (Berger (1953) s.v.): with the disappearance of their husbands their marriages (*OLD* s.v. *torus*[1] 5b) too were no longer 'there'. Cf. 10.51–2 *saepe torum repeto, qui nos acceperat ambos, | sed non acceptos exhibiturus erat* and Knox *ad loc.*

195–8 Helen was not fooled by Paris' offhand and disingenuous reference to Oenone (16.97–8, 98nn.); and she now reveals that she has been doing some private detective work on her own account. Cf. Dido to Aeneas on the fate of Creusa (7.81–4).

196 diceris 'men say', but also perhaps slyly self-referential, 'you are told of in song' (*OLD* s.v. *dico*[2] 7b), sc. in *Her.* 5. Cf Introd. p. 6.

197–8 'You don't deny it yourself [strictly true], and I have taken some pains, let me tell you, to find out everything I can about you'. This is all very natural and feminine; doubts about the authenticity of the couplet are misconceived (Kenney (1979) 409–10).

199 ut 'though' (16.311n.).

200 expediunt iam tua uela Phryges: this recalls, and may be meant to recall, Aeneas' stealthy preparations for abandoning Dido: cf. esp. Virg. *Aen.* 4.298–9 *eadem impia Fama furenti | detulit armari classem cursumque parari*, 417–18 '*uocat iam carbasus auras, | puppibus et laeti nautae imposuere coronas*'.

Phryges: sc. *tui.*

201 nox: a night of love-making (*OLD* s.v. 3c).

paratur: sc. *tibi*, 'while you plan' (*OLD* s.v. 7c).

202 qui ferat 'to carry you', final-consecutive subj.

203 cursibus in mediis 'in mid-course', uniquely for the usual *in cursu* (5.121, *E.S.* 60, *al.*, *OLD* s.v. 8b). O. uses *cursus* in sing. and pl. more or less interchangeably.

204 cum uentis: cf. 7.8 *idem uenti uela fidemque ferent*. However the point 'our love will depart along with you' is perhaps better conveyed by Francius' *uelis*; cf. 5.55 *abeuntia uela*.

206 pronurus 'granddaughter-in-law'; only here and in the jurists, and perhaps a coinage of O.'s, or an importation by him from legal parlance. Cf. 3.74 *prosocer.*

208 ut ... impleat 'that it should (be allowed to) fill'.

209–10 quid ...?: sc. *nisi probra*; but the ellipse is slightly awkward. The point can be met by reading *aliud* (*aliae* PGω: *asiae* ς) and taking *gentes* = 'the world in general' (*OLD* s.v. 2a, b); though the architecture of the couplet may seem to call for a proper name in each half-verse, cf. the following couplet for a comparable imbalance.

Achaia tota: O. conforms with the general practice of the Augustan poets in avoiding hexameter-endings in which a noun ending in -ă is immediately followed by an attributive epithet agreeing with it. Of the four apparent exx. in *Her.* 16–21 only this one and 18.9 *littera nostra* break the 'rule'; at 16.323 *nostri* should be read as rhetorically superior to the better-supported *nostra*, and at 21.195 *rara* is predicative, 'his kisses are few and far between' (cf. Holmes (1995) nn. 7, 9, 10). The true ratio of such endings is then in line with that in the *Tristia* (*ibid.*). On the prosody of *Achaia* see 16.187n.

211 quid Priamus ...?: O.'s readers would remember his kind and considerate behaviour towards the Homeric Helen (*Il.* 3.161ff.).

212 tot 'all those'.

Dardanides ... nurus 'your Trojan sisters-in-law'; cf. *Met.* 13.412 *Dardanidas matres*.

213 qui ...? 'How?' (*OLD* s.v. *qui*² 1a). Only here in O.; elsewhere in Latin poetry apart from comedy only in Catullus, Lucretius, Horace's hexameters, and Phaedrus. On *quicum* at Virg. *Aen.* 11.822 see Skutsch at Enn. *Ann.* 268.

214 exemplis ... tuis 'because of the example you yourself have set', causal abl. The pl. is purely 'poetic', for the sake of the metre; cf. *Ibis* 400 *exemplis occidit ipse suis*, and *Iliacos ... portus* at 215 below.

216 ~ 8.76 *omnia solliciti plena timoris erant*, 1.12 *res est solliciti plena timoris amor*.

218 'Forgetting that the charge implicates you as well as me'; with *nostro* understand *crimini*.

220 = either 'May I be dead and buried first' or 'may the earth open and swallow me first', the latter an epic motif; cf. 3.63 *deuorer ante, precor, subito telluris hiatu ...* , 6.144 *hiscere nempe tibi terra roganda fuit*, Virg. *Aen.* 4.24–7 *sed mihi uel tellus optem prius ima dehiscat ... | ... ante, pudor, quam te uiolo aut tua iura resoluo*; from the Homeric τότε μοι χάνοι εὐρεῖα χθών (*Il.* 4.182, 8.150).

uultus ... meos 'my blushes'.

221 at 'But, you say ...' (115n.).

222 promissis 'than have been promised'.

225 tanti: sc. *ut patria carere uelim*.

226 tellus ... ipsa 'Sparta itself', i.e. her instinctive attachment to her homeland, irrespective of all other considerations (*OLD* s.v.

ipse 5, 7). *ista*, printed by some editors, cannot = 'this land (of mine)'; contrast 261n. and cf. Kenney (1979) 421 n. 89. For the sentiment cf. *Ex P.* 1.3.35–6 *nescioqua natale solum dulcedine cunctos | ducit et immemores non sinit esse sui.*

tenet 'holds my affection' (*OLD* s.v. 22b).

228 fratres: 16.153n.

230 pulsa est Aesonia ... domo ~ 12.134 *ausus es 'Aesonia' dicere 'cede domo'*; to make room for his new wife Creusa. Aeson was Jason's father, but *Aesonius* here and elsewhere is used = 'Jason's'.

231–2 Aeetes ... Idyia: her father and mother. *Idyia*, Gk ἰδυῖα 'she who knows', a 'speaking' name. Cf. 21.209n.

ad quem ... rediret 'for her to go back to', final-consecutive subj.

233 sed nec Medea 'but neither did Medea' – and look what happened to her. On *nec* cf. 109–10n.

234 'Favourable hopes are often deceived by their own anticipations', an elaborate and sententious version of *A.A.* 1.446 *illa* (Spes) *quidem fallax, sed tamen apta, dea est. Augurium* here is little more than a synonym for *spes* itself = 'expectation' (*OLD* s.v. 2); cf. *Tr.* 3.1.36 *augurium menti ... dabat* 'confirmed my guess'.

235–6 omnibus ... nauibus: dat. of advantage.

237–8 = *fax cruenta, quam se peperisse* eqs.; for the incorporation (here only partial) of the antecedent in the relative clause cf. 21.100n. Reminiscence of Ennius (16.45–6n.) is clearly visible here. (i) The construction *se ... uisa est* for the classical *uisa est* is directly lifted from Enn. *Alex.* 50–1 J. *parere se ardentem facem | uisa est in somnis Hecuba*; see Jocelyn *ad loc.*, Jacobson (1968) 301–2, White (1968) 191 n. 10. (ii) *cruentam* (a detail not mentioned by Paris) is from *Alex.* 41 J. *adest adest fax obuoluta sanguine atque incendio.* Cf. on (ii) 116 *nudas* and n.

239–40 Helen will have none of Paris' flippant interpretation (16.49–50n.) of this portent. She accepts the general view (*ferunt*) that the seers mean what they say. On the alleged difficulties of the passage see Kenney (1979) 407–9.

monitus ... praemonuisse: the repetition lacks point; did O. write *praecinuisse*?

quos: the antecedent is probably *uatum* rather than *monitus*; O. may have written *quibus* (Kenney (1979) 408 n. 44).

arsurum: 16.49n.

241–4 ut ... sic: 71n.

242 bina tropaea: explained in the next couplet.

246 ibit per gladios: cf. 20.37, *Met.* 8.76–7 (Scylla) *ire per ignes | et gladios ausim* and Bömer *ad loc.*, Otto s.v. *ignis* 6. This proverbial boast about overcoming obstacles will be bloodily realized.

ei mihi: elsewhere in O. as a rule at the beginning of the verse even in the middle of a sentence; cf. however 21.235–6n., *Ibis* 30 *qua licet ei misero debitus hostis ero* (*s.v.l.*). For its placing here cf. *Nux* 108 (*s.v.l.*), Prop. 1.3.38, 4.8.48 and *TLL* s.v. *ei* 300.74ff.

247–50 'Do you think that, when Hippodamia provoked war with the Centaurs, Menelaus and my family will be backward in my case?' For the form of the question cf. e.g. 9.147–8 *an tuus in media coniunx lacerabitur Oeta, | tu sceleris tanti causa superstes eris?*, *Met.* 3.559–61 and Bömer *ad loc.* This Hippodamia (cf. 16.209–10n.) was the daughter of Adrastus; at her wedding to Theseus' friend Pirithous the Centaurs, who had been invited as her kinsmen, tried to carry her off, and a bloody fracas ensued. This battle of the Lapiths and Centaurs was a favourite subject in literature (e.g. *Met.* 12.210–535; see McKeown on *Am.* 1.4.7–8) and art (e.g. the Parthenon metopes). Another hint of the unenviable notoriety that Helen is going to bring on herself (16.376n.).

248 Atracis 'Thessalian' (16.21n.); Atrax was a town in Thessaly. *Atracis* only here and at *Am.* 1.4.8; the usual form is in *-ius* (Pfeiffer on Callim. fr. 488, Fedeli on Prop. 1.8.25–6).

Haemonios ... uiros 'the men of Thessaly', the Lapiths.

Hippodamia: called Hippodame by O. at *Met.* 12.210, and by various other names in other allusions to the story (Butler–Barber on Prop. 2.2.9).

249 lentum: to be taken ἀπὸ κοινοῦ with *fratres* and *Tyndareum* following.

tam iusta ... in ira 'with such just cause for anger' (*OLD* s.v. *in* 40b).

251 quod ... iactes ... loquaris 'though you may boast and recite your brave deeds'. Here, as elsewhere in this construction (43n.), the subj. does not convey an assumed or implied state of affairs, for this is precisely what he has been doing. Cf. 51–2, 20.155 for *quod* + indic. with identical sense.

COMMENTARY: 17.252-268

252 Twice in the *Iliad* he is sarcastically addressed by Hector as εἶδος ἄριστε, 'most fair in appearance' (3.39, 13.769); cf. 16.53–88n.

253 apta magis: sc. *sunt*; cf. 18.3, 20.25, *Am.* 2.10.23 *graciles, non sunt sine uiribus artus.*

corpora: 'poetic' pl.

256 militia ... altera 'another kind of warfare'. For the general conceit of love as campaigning see *Am.* 1.9 and McKeown's commentary; here the reference is more specific, to the bed as battlefield (Adams (1982) 158–9). Cf. 16.369–70n.

operis ... tuis 'your services' (*OLD* s.v. *opera* 7a).

257–8 si saperem 'if I knew my business', i.e. if I had the requisite *savoir-faire*. She uses *sapio* in the Ovidian (Pickwickian) sense in which we meet it in the *Amores* and *Ars*, 'know one's (amatory) onions'. Cf. next n.

259 aut ... sapiam fortasse 'or perhaps I *shall* (after all) be wise' (*OLD* s.v. *aut* 6b).

deposito sapiam ... pudore: a fine oxymoron (pointed contradiction).

260 dabo cunctatas ... manus 'I shall finally yield'. *dabŏ* on the analogy of *negŏ, rogŏ, et sim.*; cf. *Tr.* 4.10.130 *erŏ* (Platnauer (1951) 51–2).

261 quod petis 'as for your request ...' (43n.).

ista 'your proposition'.

263 adhuc tua messis in herba est 'your corn is still green' (*OLD* s.v. *herba* 4), proverbial (Otto s.v. *herba* 1); cf. *A.A.* 2.9–10 *quid properas, iuuenis? mediis tua pinus in undis | nauigat, et longe quem peto portus abest.*

265–6 furtiuae conscia mentis littera 'the writing (143n.) that is the confidante of my secret feelings' – but *mens* can also = 'purpose' (*OLD* s.v. 7a). This couplet is a beautiful example of the interlocking construction that is one of the hallmarks of developed Latin poetry: abcB | CdD(V)A. Cf. 16.107–14, 19.37–8nn.

266 lasso pollice 'for my fingers are tired', causal abl.; this not uncommon sense of *pollex*, here used in the poetic sing. = 'hand', is unrecognized by *OLD*. Cf. 19.26, 20.139, *Am.* 2.4.27 *haec habili percurrit pollice chordas* and Booth *ad loc.*

268 comites consiliumque 'my companions and counsellors'

146   COMMENTARY: 18.1-6

(*OLD* s.v. *consilium* 3a). She leaves matters ostensibly in the air, but Paris knows that this is the go-ahead. 'Bref, elle consent à un enlèvement par contrainte' (Frécaut (1972) 209).

xviii
Leander to Hero

Superscription HERONI: the dat. form of the name is not otherwise attested, but *Ioni* is found in Plautus (*Aul.* 556) and Accius (*TRF* 386), and *Didoni* in Servius (N–W 1 525–6); cf. on the analogous treatment of the genitive Charis. p. 79.15–17 B.

1-2 This couplet is not in PW and was deleted by Bentley. Though the play on *salus* is characteristic (16.1n.), the sequence of tenses *mallet ... cadat* is anomalous, and though O. cultivates hyperbaton (16.177n.), the wide separation of *tibi* from *mittit* is awkward writing (Kirfel (1969) 108–9). The main objection, however, is to the content, which feebly anticipates (and has evidently been fabricated from) lines 21–2. The superscriptions to the letters, if authorial (Kenney (1970a) 196 and n. 2), sufficiently identify the writers; but this story can hardly as yet have been generally familiar when O. exploited it, and neither protagonist is identified by name in the body of the epistle, as is the case in all the rest of *Her.* (Kirfel (1969) 109). A genuine introductory couplet has probably been lost: see 19.1–2n. and cf. 17.1, 20.1, 21.1 nn.

Sesta: the proper form is *Sestias* (Musaeus 24 and Kost *ad loc.*, Stat. *Theb.* 6.547). Heinsius emended to *Sesti* on the analogy of *Lesbi puella* at *E.S.* 100 (cf. *Rem.* 262 *Colchi*, 16.100 *Tyndari*), but it is hazardous to 'correct' an unknown and undated interpolator in such a matter.

3 faciles: sc. *sunt* (17.253n.). *in amore* is also to be read ἀπὸ κοινοῦ with both parts of the *si*-clause.

5 mea uota 'the accomplishment of my desires'.

6 currere: frequently used of travel by water (*OLD* s.v. 3a); unexpected of a swimmer, but Leander repeatedly images himself as a ship (207–8n.).

nec: on the postponement see 16.348n. O. could have written *c. nec n. me p.*; the additional postponement lends emphasis, *nec patiuntur* = 'prevent'. Cf. 17.109–10n.

7 pice nigrius ~ *Met.* 12.402, *Ex P.* 4.14.45 *pice nigrior, A.A.* 2.658 *nigrior ... pice*. The comparison is traditional: Hom. *Il.* 4.277, Callim. *Hec.* fr. 74.17 Hollis (260.58 Pf.).

8 per ... cauas ... rates: sc. even by ships, let alone a swimmer. For the ellipse cf. 17.134n. *cauus* is a purely decorative epithet on the model of the Homeric κοῖλος (*OLD* s.v. 3d).

9 et hic: emphatic, just like Eng. 'and he' (*TLL* s.v. *et* 875.22ff.).

10 mouit iter 'has set sail', lit. 'has undertaken the journey' (*OLD* s.v. *moueo* 17a).

11 ascensurus eram = *ascendissem* (17.68n.).

nisi quod 'were it not for the fact that'.

uincula prorae: cf. *Met.* 8.102–3 *classis retinacula solui | iussit*, 15.696 *torta coronatae soluit retinacula nauis*. *prora* probably = 'ship' by synecdoche (*OLD* s.v. b), since it was usual to beach or moor ships stern first for ease of launching (cf. e.g. Virg. *Aen.* 6.3–5).

12 in speculis ... erat 'was watching' (*OLD* s.v. *specula* 1b). Naturally they would have been curious about the motive for this rash exploit.

13–14 Why the affair has to be kept secret from his parents does not appear until Hero's reference, itself by no means explicit, to their social disparity (19.99–100, 147). See Introd. p. 12.

non poteram celare 'I could not have kept them in ignorance'; 16.162n., *OLD* s.v. *celo* 6a.

15–18 For a similar lover's fantasy see O. to his ring, *Am.* 2.15.7–18; cf. *Met.* 8.36–7 (Scylla) *felix iaculum, quod tangeret ille, | quaeque manu premeret, felicia frena uocabat*, and for Gk exx. Anon. *A.P.* 5.83, 84 (*FGE* 1084–7 and Page *ad loc.*).

18 uincula: the linen thread, knotted and sealed with wax, with which the writing-tablets were secured. 'Hero is not willing to wait for a penknife' (Purser).

21 mallem ... nataret ... ferret: 16.5n.

illa: sc. *dextra*.

23–4 This couplet, omitted by PG$_u$, was rightly condemned by Lehrs. The conceit itself might pass muster, but not the expression: (i) *uerbera*, especially juxtaposed with *placido*, is an oddly violent word for swimming strokes, contrasting sharply with the tranquillity described in lines 75–82; (ii) *sensus meus* is not Ovidian (or indeed good) Latin for 'my meaning', though it might = 'my feelings', sc. towards you (21.204, *OLD* s.v. 8a); but in that case *ministra* seems dubiously apt.

25 spatium mihi longius anno: cf. 11.29 *nox erat annua nobis*, Virg. *Ecl.* 7.43 *haec lux toto iam longior anno est* and Clausen *ad loc.*

26 ∼ Musaeus 242 (Leander on the shore) 'Hearing the far echoing thunder of the raving surf' (Whitman).

ut ... feruet 'since it has been boiling' (*OLD* s.v. *ut* 27).

27–8 'If in all these nights any sleep has soothed my heart, may the sea prolong its mad rage.' O.'s Leander, like Musaeus' (233), cannot sleep for thinking of Hero; but the theme is too common (Kost *ad loc.*, McKeown on *Am.* 1.2.1–4) for the coincidence to be of much significance. Cf. Aristaen. 1.10.48–51 on Acontius.

his ... noctibus: the phrase neatly illustrates the ease with which the abl. of 'time within which' developed into the abl. of duration of time, used interchangeably with the regular acc. (16.215n.): K–S I 360–1, Fordyce on Catull. 109.5.

uidi ... somnum: cf. for this idiom Ter. *Haut.* 491, Cic. *Fam.* 7.30.1 and Shackleton Bailey (265) *ad loc.*

insani ... mora ... freti 'the duration (*OLD* s.v. *mora* 7) of the sea's madness.'

30 ∼ 10.135–6 *nunc quoque non oculis, sed, qua potes, aspice mente | haerentem scopulo*, *Tr.* 4.2.57 *haec ego summotus, qua possum, mente uidebo* and Luck *ad loc.*

31 lumina: the leading-light on the top of Hero's tower, that played a central romantic role in the story and was responsible for its tragic denouement: 19.33–6, Antipater of Thessalonica, *A.P.* 7.666.4 (*GP* 132) 'the traitor lamp', Musaeus 5–15, 210–18, 329–30; Hintermeier (1993) 99–102, Introd. p. 9 *lumina* is poetic pl. *uigilantia* (echoed at 19.35) is ironical.

32 acies nostra 'my eyes' (*OLD* s.v. 4b).

uidere putat: sc. *se.* Cf. Virg. *Aen.* 6.454 (< A.R. 4.1479–80) *aut uidet aut uidisse putat per nubila lunam.*

35 iuuenalibus: this youthful rashness is the keynote of Leander's character and the source of the tragedy.

36 inuersis ... aquis 'by its upturned waters'; cf. Hor. *Epod.* 10.5–6 *niger rudentis Eurus inuerso mari | fractosque remos differat* and Mankin *ad loc.*, citing *inter al. Her.* 7.42 *aspice ut euersas concitet Eurus aquas.* This description prefigures the storm in which Leander is fated to die: cf. Musaeus 295–7 'The abysses were dislodged, and the wintry gales with their blowing | Steadily battered the sodden foundations of the sea, | With whirlwind scourging the whole brine' (Whitman), *Met.* 11.497–501 esp. 499 *fuluas ex imo uertit harenas*. See next n., Introd. p. 13. *inuersis* is the reading of P and one late MS; most have *aduersis*, a feeble banalization.

37–46 Leander's prayer to Boreas evidently figured in O.'s Hellenistic original, uttered there in the course of his fatal crossing (36, 42nn.). The situation is the classic one of the locked-out lover, here with Boreas as the hard-hearted doorkeeper. Cf. *Am.* 3.6, where O. upbraids the mountain torrent which bars the way to his mistress. See Kraus (1950–1) 70, Sabot (1981) 2560, Hintermeier (1993) 69–74.

37 rapidis: Terpstra emended to *rabidis*, which may be right, for it is not of Boreas' swiftness but of his violence that Leander complains. For *rapidus* = 'fierce' see *OLD* s.v. 4; but the exx. do not really support the sense here. If, *pace* Lachmann (on Lucret. 4.712), *rapidus* can = *rapax* (a sense which it is difficult to deny at Lucan 3.635: Hunink *ad loc.*), that certainly suits Boreas (42n.).

immansuetissime: such compounds (*in-* + pf. part.) are characteristic of O., and this may have been coined by him (Kenney (1973) 124; but cf. *FPL* p. 179 inc. 46 = *FLP* fr. inc. 24, ascribed to Albinovanus Pedo). He clearly liked the sound of it (3x in *Met.*). On the superlative cf. 19.131n.

38 certa ... mente 'so obstinately'. Hence Italian *certamente*.

39 si nescis 'let me remind you' (16.246n.)

40 For the argument *a minori* cf. 21.56, 14.120 *quid fiet sonti, cum rea laudis agar?*, and McKeown on *Am.* 1.6.31.

41 quod sis 'for all that you are' (17.43n.).

improbe 'you rascal'.

42 ignibus Actaeis 'with love for her of Attica', i.e. Orithyia (16.345n.). Cf. *Am.* 1.6.53–4 *si satis es raptae, Borea, memor Orithyiae, | huc ades et surdas flamine tunde fores*, Musaeus 322 '(Leander) did not leave Boreas unmindful of the Attic girl' and Kost *ad loc.* Cf. Hero's reminder to Neptune (19.129n.), and the catalogue of amorous rivers at *Am.* 3.6.23–48. Ἀκταῖος = 'Attic' seems to have owed its popularity to Callimachus; Ἀκταίη was the first word of his *Hecale* (fr. 1 Hollis, q.v.), in which Boreas evidently figured (fr. 86 Hollis, q.v.).

43–4 uellet ... paterere = *uoluisset ... passus esses* (16.103n.). *uellet* = 'had decided'; for this strong sense of *uolo* see *OLD* s.v. 13.

aditus: in the *Ars* almost a technical term for access to one's mistress (1.163, 229, 721; cf. Tib. 2.4.19). *aerios* plays on Boreas' dual nature as wind and (anthropomorphic) god.

45 moderatius: Latin freely formed comparatives and superlatives from participles (N–W II 214–41); cf. 17.71, 19.83nn. On O.'s use of adverbs cf. 16.174n.

46 Hippotades: Aeolus, son of Hippotes, keeper of the winds. The patronymic was familiar from Homer (*Od.* 10.2, 36) and Apollonius (*Arg.* 4.819, cf. 778); of the Augustan poets only O. uses it (7x: Bömer on *Met.* 4.663).

sic: sc. on condition that you answer my prayer (*OLD* s.v. 8d, N–H on Hor. *C.* 1.3.1); cf. 20.3, 4.147–8 *tolle moras tantum properataque foedera iunge: | qui mihi nunc saeuit, sic tibi parcat Amor.* Cf. 16.282n.

47 obmurmurat 'rumbles against', a rare word which first occurs here and was probably coined by O. The storm is throughout both letters the menacing backdrop to the emotional drama.

48 coercet: for the idea that the winds could actively calm the sea cf. 2.38 *concita qui uentis aequora mulcet* and Barchiesi *ad loc.*, Hor. *C.* 1.3.14–16 *Noti | quo non arbiter Hadriae | maior, tollere seu ponere uult fretum* and N–H *ad loc.*

49–50 Daedalus made artificial wings on which he and his son Icarus escaped from confinement by Minos on Crete: O. tells the story twice elsewhere (*A.A.* 2.21–96, *Met.* 8.183–235). Leander's wish is ominous, as he acknowledges, since Icarus died in the attempt (next n.).

Icarium ... litus: the Icarian Sea, in which Icarus drowned, and the island of Icaria, *tellus a nomine dicta sepulti* (*Met.* 8.235), where he was buried, lie some 180 miles due south of Abydos, a fact of which O. and his readers must have been well aware. A mere *lapsus*, which might have been eliminated in revision, or a learned poet's 'deliberate mistake'? If the latter, the point is elusive. The commentators are discreetly silent. Cf. 21.81–2n.

51 modo 'provided only', i.e. = *si modo, modo si*, a common elliptical usage (*OLD* s.v. 4). Cf. 147, 20.74, 180n., and below, 66n.

52 pependit 'has floated'.

54 furti ... mei 'my secret love' (*OLD* s.v. 2b).

55–104 Musaeus has nothing corresponding to this idyllic description – 'un nocturne en mer' (Ripert (1921) 88) – of Leander's first crossing; he disposes of it summarily in two verses (254–5; Kost *ad loc.*). Nor, at least to judge from the surviving fragments, did the Hellenistic original. The elaboration of O.'s treatment is not gratuitous: (i) This happy recollection is an ironic counterpart to the tragic outcome of Leander's last crossing, not to be described but presumed to be present to the reader's mind and already hinted at (36n.). (ii) Whereas in Musaeus the first meeting of the lovers is treated at great length (84–220), O. leaves his readers totally in the dark on that part of the story (cf. 13–14, 19.99–100nn., Introd. pp. 11–12). This feature may not have been part of the Hellenistic original at all; be that as it may, since the theme is prominent in *Her.* 16–17 and central to 20–21, Leander's recollection here may be seen as an elegant variation, first rendezvous for first meeting.

55 erat incipiens: 16.57–8n.

namque est meminisse uoluptas ~ Virg. *Aen.* 1.203 *forsan et haec olim meminisse iuuabit.*

56 egrediebar amans 'set out on my lover's journey'; *amans* (noun, not part.) is predicative.

57 deposito ... cum ueste timore: a neat and characteristic example of one of O.'s favourite figures, syllepsis, in which a word, here *deponere*, is used with simultaneous literal and metaphorical effect: cf. (almost the converse of this ex.) *Am.* 3.14.27 *indue cum tunicis metuentem crimina uultum.* Musaeus, probably with the Homeric Odysseus (*Od.* 14.349) in mind, has Leander strap his clothes on his head for the crossing. O., following the version which was usual in art (Kost *ad loc.*) allows his hero a more affecting welcome (101–4).

58 liquido ... mari 'over the waters of the sea' (16.118n.).

lenta: the word is quadruply apt, connoting as it does pliancy (*OLD* s.v. 1a), toughness (2), leisurely movement (4a), and persistence (6); cf. 16.228n. If it is also given predicative force, a full translation would be something like 'I drove my strong supple arms slowly and perseveringly through the yielding water'. With sensuous relish (55 *uoluptas*) Leander savours every moment in retrospect.

59 fere 'for most of the time' (*OLD* s.v. 3c), though 77–8 might seem to imply that the night was cloudless.

tremulum 'flickering', 'twinkling' seems on the face of it hardly apt for moonlight, but O. is following Virgil: *Aen.* 7.8–9 *nec candida cursus | luna negat, splendet tremulo sub lumine pontus*, 8.22–4 *sicut aquae tremulum labris ubi lumen aënis | sole repercussum aut radiantis imagine lunae | omnia peruolitat late loca* and Fordyce *ad locc*. It is the reflection on the water that twinkles; cf. 11.75 *ut mare fit tremulum, tenui cum stringitur aura*. Cf. 77n.

60 in nostras officiosa uias 'helping me on my way'; cf. 10.114 *flamina... in lacrimas officiosa meas*. On the pl. *uias* cf. 16.22n.

61–4 The Moon (Greek Selene) fell in love with the shepherd Endymion of Mt Latmos in Caria. He was granted immortality, eternal youth, and eternal sleep (Apollod. *Bibl.* 1.7.6 and Frazer *ad loc.*). With this appeal cf. Philodemus, *A.P.* 5.123 (*GP* 3212–17). Conversely at A.R. 4.57–65 the Moon, observing Medea's elopement, registers sarcastic satisfaction at the sight of a fellow-victim of love. Musaeus less inventively compares Hero directly to Selene (56–7).

62 Latmia saxa = Catull. 66.5 (< Callim. *Aetia*, though the original has been lost at this point).

63 pectoris ... seueri 'of a strict disposition', genitive of description (*NLS* §84). Cf. *A.A.* 3.83 *Latmius Endymion non est tibi, Luna, rubori*. Diana, identified with the Moon, was (supposed to be) a virgin goddess, who might be expected not to favour lovers: *A.A.* 1.261–2 *illa, quod est uirgo, quod tela Cupidinis odit, | multa dedit populo uulnera, multa dabit*. However, in this case she had compromised herself: Prop. 2.15.15–16 *nudus et Endymion Phoebi cepisse sororem | dicitur et nudae concubuisse deae*.

64 flecte ... uultus 'look graciously down'.

66 liceat '(if) it may be allowed', jussive subj. but equivalent to the protasis of a conditional clause. Cf. 51n.

ipse: this is the reading of P alone, giving a rhetorically effective parallel with *tu*: 'you love a mortal, I a goddess'. *ipsa* (all other MSS) lacks point. Housman (*CP* 414) quotes the verse with *ipse*. Musaeus similarly terms Hero a second Aphrodite (33, 68, 135–7); the comparison goes back to Homer, but is especially at home in the Greek novel (Kost on 33, 16.333–8n.). Cf. 169.

67 neu referam 'and to say nothing of', cf. 16.176n.; *neu = et, ne* (16.71n.).

68 non cadit 'does not fall to the lot of' (*OLD* s.v. 16a).

69 a 'next to' (16.98n.).

non est prior ulla: 'compendious comparison' for *non est prior ullius facies*; for this type of construction, which goes back to Homer's κόμαι Χαρίτεσσιν ὁμοῖαι 'hair like (that of) the Graces', cf. e.g. *Am.* 1.8.25 *nulli tua forma secunda est, A.A.* 3.106 *Idaliae similis sit licet illa* (sc. *facies*) *deae*, and see K–S II 566–7, H–S 826. Cf. 19.146n.

tuaque: a politic afterthought!

70 neue = *et, ne* (67n.).

71–2 quantum ... concedunt: cf. *Met.* 12.383–4 *aspice ... | quantum concedant nostro tua cornua ferro. quantum* is acc. of extent (Bömer *ad loc.*, *NLS* §10). This was an encomiastic commonplace from Sappho onwards (N–H on Hor. *C.* 1.12.48).

72 sidera cuncta 'all (the other) heavenly bodies'. Cf. 53 *cuncta*.

74 caecum ... lumen: an untranslatable play on the senses of both words: *caecus* = 'blind' and 'dark' (*OLD* s.v. 1, 6), *lumen* = 'light' and 'eye(sight)' (*OLD* s.v. 1, 9).

75 uel certe non his diuersa: the poet mischievously inserts himself into his character, taking leave *more Thucydideo* (1.22.1–2 and Hornblower *ad loc.*) to improve and embellish the expression while still giving the general sense. Cf. 2.146 *aut hoc aut simili carmine* and Barchiesi *ad loc.*

76 sponte is Francius' palmary correction of MS *nocte*. The word qualifies *cedentes*; on this first crossing all nature (treacherously) conspires to favour him. Contrast 35–6, foreshadowing his last and fatal attempt.

77–82 One of the most memorable descriptive passages in Latin poetry; this is what Macaulay called 'sweet writing'. Cf. Rand (1925) 32.

77 ~ Virg. *Aen.* 8.23 (cit. 59n.).

81–2 The story of the drowning of Ceyx and the transformation of him and his wife Alcyone into birds is the climax of one of the longest and most affecting episodes of the *Metamorphoses* (11.410–748). Leander's crossing took place during the 'halcyon days', when the sea was calm while the birds nested: *Met.* 11.747–8 *tum iacet unda maris: uentos custodit et arcet | Aeolus egressu praestatque nepotibus aequor*. For all its idyllic associations, the reference is ominous.

81 Alcyones ... Ceycis: not only the mythological resonances but also the sounds of the Greek names, with their varied quantities ($\breve{y} \ldots \breve{e}/\bar{e}\bar{y}$) contribute to the sensuous quality of the writing. It is tempting to read *Ceycos* (17.118n.).

83 ~ Musaeus 325–6 (Leander's expiring agonies) 'and the thrust of his feet grew slack, | And profitless was the strength of his unresting hands' (Whitman). Cf. 161–2.

84 fortiter 'manfully', with an effort. See 16.174n.

85–6 lumen ... ignis ... lumen: another play on *lumen* (74n.), here on the senses 'comfort' and 'glory' (*OLD* s.v. 6d, 11a), with *ignis* in its familiar sense of 'beloved' (*OLD* s.v. 9b; cf. e.g. 16.104) providing a transition. In this conceit *lux* is commoner (*OLD* s.v. 6b, 10). Cf. 89–90.

88 uisa: sc. *est*.

89–90 ~ Musaeus 245–7 'yet is the water | The sea's, while the fire of love, lurking within, consumes me. | Seize [?] the fire, my heart, fear not the full-flowing water' (Whitman) and Kost *ad loc.*, Virg. *G.* 3.258–9 *quid iuuenis, magnum cui uersat in ossibus ignem | durus amor?* For similar Hellenistic conceits cf. *FLP* pp. 72–3.

93 cerni quoque 'be seen as well (as see)'.

94 spectatrix 'the fact that you are watching', predicative. Cf. *Am.* 2.12.26 *spectatrix animos ipsa iuuenca dabat*.

ut ualeamque: postponement of *-que* to follow a trisyllable in this *sedes* is relatively uncommon (Platnauer (1951) 91); nearly all the instances are, as here, of a verb preceded by its governing conjunction; cf. e.g. *A.A.* 3.676 *tam sero cur ueniatque roget*. Cf. 16.216, 21.190n.

95 placuisse: 16.203–4n.

96 oculis ... tuis 'for your benefit as you watch', dat. of advantage.

iacto 'move', as at 58 (*OLD* s.v. 7a), but with the senses 'flourish' (6) and 'display', 'show off' (12a) also felt.

97–8 ~ 2.127–8 (Phyllis expecting Demophoon) *in freta procurro uix me retinentibus undis | mobile qua primas porrigit aequor aquas.*

97 nutrix: Musaeus' Hero lives 'with a single maidservant' (188), but she plays no part in the story as he tells it. It seems probable that she figured more prominently in the Hellenistic original: the nurse-confidante was a familiar figure from Homer (Eurycleia), Euripides (*Medea, Hippolytus, Stheneboea, Andromache*), New Comedy, and epyllion (Lyne (1978) 185–6); cf. *Her.* 11.33ff. (Canace), 21.17–24, 109–10 (Cydippe), *Met.* 9.707 (Iphis), 10.382ff. (Myrrha), 14.703 (Anaxarete). Cf. 19.19n.

98 nec mihi uerba dabam 'and my eyes did not play me false' (16.239n.). *dabam* (Bentley, Nodell) gives more pointed sense than MS *dabas*; *uerba dare* connotes intention, and there is no reason why Hero should have wanted to deceive him in the matter, whereas he might well have indulged in wishful thinking.

101 felicia ... oscula 'auspicious kisses', kisses of welcome and good augury (*OLD* s.v. *felix* 2a, 4a). Cf. O.'s imagined reception of Corinna, *Am.* 2.11.45–6 *excipiamque umeris et multa sine ordine* [cf. 113] *carpam | oscula; pro reditu uictima uota cadet.*

101–2 oscula ... oscula: for the epanalepsis cf. 21.72–3n.

103–4 A pleasing and natural scene. In Musaeus Hero takes him, dripping wet as he is, to her room and there, in formal epic manner (Hom. *Od.* 8.424ff., 19.317ff.) bathes and anoints him (260–5).

eque: *demere + e(x)* is attested in other authors, but Ovidian usage suggests *deque* (in a few MSS; *Am.* 1.4.50, *Tr.* 5.2.20, 53) or *aque* (20.9, *A.A.* 3.214).

imbre: abl. of separation. Latin may say 'dries the hair from the brine' where Eng. would say 'the brine from the hair'; cf. *A.A.* 3.224 *nuda Venus madidas exprimit imbre comas.* The construction is analogous to that of verbs such as *soluere, liberare*: *NLS* §41 (8). Similarly *paruis componere magna* and *magnis componere parua* are interchangeable (Clausen on Virg. *Ecl.* 1.23).

105 cetera etc. ~ e.g. *Am.* 1.5.25 *cetera quis nescit?* and McKeown *ad loc.* O.'s masterly but romantic reticence contrasts sharply with Musaeus' pedantic catalogue *à la* Lucan (2.354–71; cf. Fantham *ad loc.*, Bramble, *CHCL* II 544ff.) of the missing concomitants of their secret 'wedding' (274–85 and Kost *ad loc.*).

nouit: 16.362n.

106 lumen: the signal-light does double duty as the lamp in Hero's boudoir at the top of the tower (19.35–8, 151–4); it now takes on its traditional role as voyeur and erotic confidante. Cf. Musaeus 1 'Tell of the lamp, O goddess, the witness of hidden loves' (Whitman) and Kost *ad loc.*, Stat. *Theb.* 6.547 *conscius ignis*; and for the motif e.g. Asclep. *A.P.* 5.7 (*HE* 846–9), Meleag. (?) *A.P.* 5.8 (4348–53), Philod. *A.P.* 5.4 (*GP* 3160–5) and Gow–Page *ad loc.*, Arist. *Eccl.* 7–11. Cf. Introd. p. 9 n. 31.

107–8 Cf. Catull. 61.199–203 *ille pulueris Africi | siderumque micantium | subducat numerum prius, | qui uestri numerare uolt | multa milia ludi* and Fedeli (1972) 108, Fordyce on Catull. 7.3ff. In exile O. repeatedly resorted to such comparisons to excite sympathy for his misfortunes (Kenney (1992) xxv). The substitution of seaweed, elsewhere synonymous with worthlessness (Virg. *Ecl.* 7.42, Hor. C. 3.17.10, *Sat.* 2.5.8), for sand or stars, though clearly suggested by the context (*Hellespontiaci ... maris*), is odd. 'How is sea-weed to be counted?' asks Purser.

110 est cautum ne: legalistic language; cf. *Met.* 5.530–2 *repetet Proserpina caelum, | lege tamen certa, si nullos contigit illic | ore cibos: nam sic Parcarum foedere cautum est* and Bömer *ad loc.* The only other ex. in verse (this one missed) noted by *TLL* s.v. *caueo* 636.72–640.50 is at Lucan 8.824–6 *haud equidem immerito Cumanae carmine uatis | cautum, ne Nili Pelusia tangeret ora | Hesperius miles* (639.2–3). Cf. 17.107n.

iners: cf. *A.A.* 3.60 *sic nullum uobis tempus abibit iners.*

111 Tithoni coniuge: Aurora (16.201–2n.). Ancient poets indulged in innumerable periphrases for dawn and dusk; for this one cf. *Am.* 1.13.1–2 *iam super Oceanum uenit a seniore marito | flaua pruinoso quae uehit axe diem* and McKeown *ad loc.* Cf. 19.33–4, 21.85–6nn.

112 praeuius Aurorae Lucifer ~ Cic. *Alcyones:* ⟨*Lucifer*⟩ [Onions's supplement] *hunc genuit claris delapsus ab astris | praeuius Aurorae, solis noctisque satelles* (*FPL* p. 66, *FLP* pp. 152–3 and Courtney *ad loc.*); cf. *Met.* 4.629–30 *dum Lucifer ignes | euocet Aurorae* and Bömer on *Met.* 2.115. Discreet irony is at work: the Morning and the Evening Star, as the ancients knew well, are, astronomically speaking, the same, the planet Venus. Mythologically 'Lucifer is Venus' favourite star because [as Hesperus] he ushers in the marriage night' (Fordyce on *Aen.* 8.590; cf. Austin on 2.801). Here his reappearance is the signal for lovers to part. Cf. McKeown on *Am.* 1.13 (pp. 337–8).

113 congerimus properata sine ordine raptim: a striking profusion of expressions conveying haste and disorder.

114 The lover's classic complaint; contrast the lonely Helen's *et longae noctes* (17.181).

115 atque ita: sc. kissing and complaining as he put off the final parting. For this characteristic Ovidian idiom cf. 19.169 (n.), 10.27 'having got to the top', *Am.* 3.6.53 'in that posture', 3.6.80 'with her face covered by her dress', *A.A.* 1.129 'as he carried her off', *Rem.*

668 'embracing her', *al.*; see Bömer on *Met.* 3.22. In Virgil the phrase generally (4 of 5 exx.; the exception is *G.* 4.409) introduces a speech.

117 uirginis aequor: the Hellespont, named after Helle, who fell into it and drowned (139–40) while escaping with her brother Phrixus from their stepmother Ino on the back of the ram with the Golden Fleece (143–4): see Apollod. *Bibl.* 1.9.1, Hyg. *Fab.* 1–3. Cf. 19.123–8 and nn.

119 si qua fides uero est 'If the truth can be believed'.

119–21 The bracketed passage was deleted by Housman (*CP* 414–15). His objections to it are unanswerable: (i) *ueniens huc* would make sense only if Leander were writing in Sestos; (ii) the antithesis between *natator* and *naufragus* is absurd: see Hero's own words at 19.185–6; (iii) the repetition *cum redeo ... a te cum redeo* is intolerably feeble; (iv) *credis ad* is impossible prosody for O. (Palmer's correction *credes*, good in itself, is based on the assumption that the passage is genuine).

122 inertis: whereas the water had yielded readily on the outward trip (76n.), it is now resistant, as heavy soil resists the cultivator: Virg. *G.* 1.94 *rastris glaebas ... frangit inertes*, *TLL* s.v. 1311.35–74.

125–6 A variation on the familiar theme that lovers are one soul in two bodies: 13.79–80 *parcite, Dardanidae, de tot precor hostibus uni, | ne meus ex illo corpore sanguis eat*, 19.149–50, 20.4, 233–4, *Met.* 3.473 (Narcissus to his reflection) *nunc duo concordes anima moriemur in una*, 11.388 (Ceyx and Alcyone) *animas ... duas ut seruet in una* and Bömer *ad loc.*, McKeown on *Am.* 1.7.60, Booth on *Am.* 2.13.15–16, Luck on *Tr.* 4.4.71–2, Kenney on Apul. *Met.* 4.34.3.

126 una ... mens ... habet ... duos 'a single mind possesses us'; cf. *Met.* 7.800 *mutua cura duos et amor socialis habebat*, and for the use of *habeo* with emotions as subject see *OLD* s.v. 10, *TLL* s.v. 2431.31–52. The expression is slightly strained – syllepsis bordering on zeugma, perhaps (Bell (1923) 304–14) – in order to exploit the antithesis with *una tellus*.

130 leuis: lit. 'light and insubstantial', but also 'changeable', 'fickle' (*OLD* s.v. 1, 7, 15a). Cf. 185–6n.

131–4 The poet at play. 'Sane condonandum aliquid amatori ad amicam scribenti, nec tam id agenti, ut accurate et ad sanam rationem probabiliter scribat, quam ut plurima et grauissima conditionis suae mala ... vivide et efficaciter exprimat' gravely comments van Lennep (1812) 283 in his elaborate defence of the passage against the hypercritical strictures of Schrader.

131 curui ... delphines = *Met.* 2.265–6; the epithet is *vox propria*, for obvious reasons, of these creatures (Bömer *ad loc.*). Cf. *Tr.* 3.10.43 *pandi ... delphines. delphinĕs* is Greek nom. pl. (cf. 19.199n.).

132 nec: 16.348n.

133 attritus solitarum limes aquarum 'a beaten track across the accustomed sea'; but either adj. suits either noun, and the phrase can be read as a double enallage (16.107n.) = *attritarum solitus limes aquarum*. Cf. 144n. The gen. is one of definition or material; cf. Kenney (1993) 458. Apollonius compares the wake of the Argo to 'a path (ἀτραπός) stretching across a grassy plain' (1.545–6).

135 nisi sic 'except on these terms', sc. by swimming.

137 Athamantidos: Helle (117n.), daughter of Athamas.

139–40 i.e. *cum primum nanctum est de uirgine mersa nomina quae tenet. nomina* is poetic pl., a relatively uncommon (Bömer on *Met.* 5.524, though not all his exx. are relevant) and somewhat arbitrary extension of this metrically convenient expedient; cf. Löfstedt I (1942) 46–8. *de uirgine mersa* 'from the drowning of the girl', the well-known *ab urbe condita* construction (*NLS* §95); cf. 141 *amissa ... ab Helle.* Lycophron (*Alex.* 22) calls the Hellespont παρθενοκτόνον Θέτιν 'maiden-slaying Thetis'.

141 et 'indeed' (*OLD* s.v. 2a).

142 ut 'even though' (*OLD* s.v. 35).

nomine crimen habet 'its name convicts it'.

144 = *lanigera ouis aureo uellere*, double enallage (16.107n.) for metrical convenience: *laniger* cannot = 'woollen' (*OLD* s.v. 3 misleading). *l. uellere* is abl. of description (cf. 16.302). It is possible but unlikely that O. wrote *tergore* (Francius, prob. Bentley), for which cf. Prop. 2.26.6 *aurea quam molli tergore uexit ouis*; the corruption is not easy to account for, and in his other allusions to the story the Fleece (*uellus*) is always explicitly mentioned.

146 quas findam 'for me to cleave', final-consecutive relative clause.

147 parte egeo nulla 'in no respect do I lack (anything)', i.e. (*ab*) *omni parte paratus sum*; cf. *OLD* s.v. *pars* 14d. For this sense of *pars*, common in O., cf. e.g. 20.40, 7.110 *nulla parte pigendus erit, E.S.* 45 *omni*

COMMENTARY: 18.148-152

... *a parte placebam* and Knox *ad loc.*, *Ex P.* 2.6.19-20 *turpe erit in miseris ueteri tibi rebus amico | auxilium nulla parte tulisse tuum*. The alternative reading *arte egeo nulla* 'I need no artificial aid' strains the sense of *ars*, which might apply to a ship, but hardly to the Ram.

fiat modo: 51n.

148 ~ Musaeus 255 (in his two-line account of Leander's crossing) αὐτὸς ἐὼν ἐρέτης αὐτόστολος αὐτόματος νηῦς 'His own oarsman, his own escort, himself his ship' (Whitman). This is easily the most striking piece of evidence for a common (Hellenistic) model for the two poets (Introd. p. 11). That Musaeus drew directly on O. is unlikely (Kost *ad loc.*). For the expression cf. *Am.* 2.12.14 *ipse eques, ipse pedes, signifer ipse fui*, 3.11.18 *ipse tuus custos, ipse uir, ipse comes*.

149-56 ~ Musaeus 212-15 'I shall become Love's vessel, with a star from you, your lamp, | And keeping my watch on that, not on late-setting Boötes, | Nor bold Orion, nor the track of the Wain untouched by the sea, | Let me come to sweet haven in your land on the farther shore' (Whitman). This passage too suggests a common model (Kost *ad loc.*).

149 Helicen ... Arcton: the Greater and the Lesser Bears; cf. *Tr.* 4.3.1-2 *magna minorque ferae, quarum regis altera Graias, | altera Sidonias* [cf. *qua Tyros utitur*], *utraque sicca, rates, F.* 3.107-8.

Tyros = *Tyrii* 'the men of Tyre', standing for the Phoenicians in general, celebrated as seafarers and traders (*OCD*[2] s.v. 'Phoenicians'). For the differing navigational practices of Greek and Phoenician sailors cf. *Tr.* 4.3.1-2 and Luck *ad loc.*, Mayer on Lucan 8.175.

150 publica ... sidera 'the common constellations'; Leander's star is personal to him (155-6), these are available to all and sundry (*OLD* s.v. *publicus* 4). This inevitably recalls Callimachus' expressed distaste for 'everything common' (πάντα τὰ δημόσια) in the context of repudiation of both Homerizing poetry and a shared love (*A.P.* 12.43 (*HE* 1041-6)).

noster amor = 156 (16.150-2n.).

151 Andromedān: for the metrically convenient Greek form cf. *Met.* 4.757 *Andromedan et tanti praemia facti*, 16.259n.

Coronam: the Crown of Ariadne, turned into a constellation when she was rescued and wedded by Bacchus (*A.A.* 1.555-8).

152 Parrhasis Vrsa 'the Arcadian Bear'; Helice (also called Callisto; in his version of the story at *Met.* 2.401-507 O. does not

159

160   COMMENTARY: 18.153–160

name her) came from Arcadia (*OLD* s.vv. *Parrhasis, Parrhasius*, 16.21n.); cf. *F.* 4.577 *Parrhasides stellae, Tr.* 1.3.48 *Parrhasis Arctos*.

153 quod ... amarunt: 16.85n.; here the tone is distinctly dismissive.

Perseus ... Ioue Liber: the lovers respectively of Andromeda, Callisto and Ariadne. Leander declines to rely on second-hand lights-of-love.

156 non errat: tragic irony. For the lamp as guide cf. Musaeus 218 and Kost *ad loc.*

157–8 Variation in the form of a tricolon crescendo on the theme 'as far as Colchis'. Cf. 19.7–8.

Colchos 'to Colchis', acc. of motion towards (17.163n.), freely used in poetry with names of peoples, countries, and places generally; cf. e.g. 19.177, Virg. *Ecl.* 1.64–6 *at nos hinc alii sitientis ibimus Afros, | pars Scythiam et rapidum cretae ueniemus Oaxen | et penitus toto diuisos orbe Britannos* and Clausen *ad loc.*; K–S 1 481, H–S 49–50. For *Colchi* = Colchis cf. 19.175, *OLD* s.v. 2b.

ultima Ponti = *ultimum Pontum* 'the furthest part of the Black Sea'; for this metrically convenient use of the neuter pl. cf. e.g. *Met.* 4.300 *stagni ... ultima, F.* 2.215 *campi ... ultima,* Virg. *Aen.* 1.422 *strata uiarum* and Austin *ad loc.*

quoque 'whither' (Kenney), *-que* being epexegetic = 'that is' (*OLD* s.v. 6a; cf. 21.137n.); the pentameter recapitulates the hexameter (theme and variation). This is neater than *quaque* (MSS; referring to the return route of the Argo? so Hollis *per litt*); *qua* (sc. *uia*) *uiam fecit* is awkward writing.

Thessala pinus: the Argo (16.347n.). Leander implicitly equates himself with Jason and the other heroes. For the Argonauts as heroic prototypes cf. Clausen on Virg. *Ecl.* 4.35.

159 Palaemona: Melicertes, son of Athamas, turned into a sea-god with his mother Ino (*Met.* 4.525–42).

160 mira gives perfectly good sense, but *morsa* (Jortin, Bentley) is tempting; cf. *Met.* 13.942–3 *manuque | pabula decerpsi decerptaque dente momordi.* However, for the repeated emphasis on wonder in O.'s narrative cf. *ibid.* 935, 938, 940.

quem etc.: Glaucus, also changed into a sea-god after eating a magic grass (*Met.* 13.917–65).

subitum reddidit ... deum 'suddenly transformed into a god';

for this characteristically Ovidian trick of style, restored by Heinsius (*subito* MSS), cf. e.g. *Met*. 7.372 *quae subitus celebrauit olor*, F. 3.723–4 *ecce libet subitos pisces Tyrrhenaque monstra | dicere*, *Tr*. 2.389 *fecit amor subitas uolucres cum paelice regem*, Bömer on *Met*. 2.349, *OLD* s.v. *subitus* 4.

161–2 Cf. 83 and n.

163–4 This perhaps recalls Odysseus' repeated adjuration to his heart to be steadfast: Hom. *Od*. 5.298, 355ff. (> Musaeus 243ff.), 407, 464, 20.18 and Russo *ad loc.*

pretium ... laboris: in apposition to the following clause; cf. *Am*. 2.1.34 *ad uatem, pretium carminis, ipsa uenit*, *A.A.* 1.155–6 *protinus, officii pretium, patiente puella | contingent oculis crura uidenda tuis.*

tenenda 'for you to hold' (*NLS* §207 (3)).

166 ~ Tib. 1.4.32 *qui prior Eleo est carcere missus equus*. The 'starting-gate (*OLD* s.v. *carcer* 3) at Elis' refers to the Olympic games (Murgatroyd *ad loc.*).

167 seruo 'watch' (*OLD* s.v. 2), used esp. of observing heavenly bodies; cf. e.g. *Am*. 1.13.11–12 *ante tuos ortus melius sua sidera seruat | nauita*, Virg. *G*. 1.335 *caeli mensis et sidera serua*, *Aen*. 5.25, 6.338.

amores 'my beloved' (*OLD* s.v. 1c).

168 magis: sc. than Andromeda and co.

169 quidem es caelo: the verb, omitted by the MSS, is needed, and *quidem es* (Kenney) is slightly more euphonious than *caelo es* (Merkel). For the prodelision of *es* after *quidem* cf. 19.147.

adhuc ... morare 'stay awhile'; the other exx. of *adhuc* in this sense (*OLD* s.v. 6a, *TLL* s.v. 661.39ff.) are all post-Ovidian, and the construction with imperative apparently unexampled. In such an adventurous writer as O. these are not decisive objections; Palmer's *nunc* is tame. For the sentiment cf. Prop. 2.2.3 (on Cynthia) *cur haec in terris facies humana moratur?*, but the words also recall the stock plea to the *princeps* not to desert mankind just yet, more than once echoed by O. himself: cf. Hor. *C*. 1.2.45–51 *serus in caelum redeas diuque | laetus intersis populo Quirini* eqs. and N–H *ad loc.*

170 et mihi: her mythological studies (19.136, 137nn.) will have acquainted her with a catalogue of mortals who have won to Olympus; he himself has just cited a case in point, Ariadne.

171 et 'and yet' (*OLD* s.v. 14a).

exigue 'rarely': in the poets only here and at Ter. *Haut*. 207, and only here in this sense; cf. 16.174n.

172 The verse is virtually identical with 129 in sense; the expression, however, is recherché = *mens mea cum fretis fit turbida*, an inversion which it is difficult to name or classify.

freta: the elegists avoided ending the pentameter with a short open vowel (Platnauer (1951) 64–6); the only other exx. in *Her.* 16–21 are 174 *aqua*, 20.240 *rata* (see n.); 16.252 *Ioue*, 21.14 (see n.), 36 *ope*, 96 *pede*.

173 quod 'the fact that' (17.43n.).

lato is predicative, 'that it is not a wide expanse of sea that separates us.'

175 dubito toto: exx. of such duplications of syllables (styled by Servius *cacemphaton* 'ill-sounding': see Austin on Virg. *Aen.* 2.27), as at e.g. 216 *aspectu tu*, are too common in O. to be remarkable (Bömer on *Met.* 2.97); triplication is exceptional, but cf. 10.71 *morerere recuruo*.

176 cum domina goes with *spem*; cf. e.g. 20.138.

178 res ... spes: a proverbial antithesis, more cultivated by orators than poets (Otto s.v. *res* (3)).

179 quod amo: 16.85n.

180 sed: 16.191n.

hoc ... 'paene' 'that word "almost"'; cf. Quint. *I.O.* 1.5.22 *ut in hoc 'Camillus'* (*OLD* s.v. *hic*¹ 6a, *TLL* s.v. 2708.55–61). The usage is commoner with *ille* (*OLD* s.v. 13b, *TLL* s.v. 342.53–5). Cf. also Plaut. *Amph.* 530 *id 'actutum' diu est*, *Most.* 71 *istuc 'actutum' sino*. See 21.247–8n.

181–2 This couplet can hardly be by O.: (i) It is not an apt reflection on the idea of 'so near and yet so far'. (ii) The colloquial Ciceronian idiom (Nisbet on *Pis.* 47) *quid est aliud*, sc. *nisi ... ?* is otherwise found in the poets only at Catull. 29.15. (iii) *fugientia ... refugi* is what Housman called 'helpless writing'. (iv) Tantalus (16.211n.) did not stand in a river but a pool. (v) The sentence has no expressed subject and the conceit 'to seek with one's (*OLD* s.v. *suus* B1a) mouth the hope of the retreating stream' is *outré* in a quite unOvidian way. It probably entered the tradition as a scribal gloss on *spes*; on the propensity of copyists to add explanatory verses see e.g. Housman (1938) xxxiiff.

183 ergo 'So it seems ...' (*OLD* s.v. *ergo*² 4).

ego te: see 16.17n.; but *ergo* and *ego* seem to have a natural affinity in O.

184 'and I shall never be happy when the weather is rough'.

185–6 The changeableness of the winds is proverbial: 130, Otto s.v. *ventus* (1). For the collocation *uentus et unda* (generally however apropos of scattered words or dishonoured promises: Otto *ibid.* (2), *aqua* (5)) cf. e.g. Catull. 70.3–4, *Am.* 2.16.45–6, *Tr.* 1.8.35–6.

187 quid: sc. *fiet* (*OLD* s.v. *quis*[1] 13b).

mihi: dat. of disadvantage.

188 Plias ... Arctophylax ... Olenium ... pecus: the Pleiades, Boötes, the Goat, all harbingers of winter gales. *Plias* is collective sing. *Arctophylax* 'Bear-guard' (Arat. *Phaen.* 91–3). *Olenium*: the she-goat Amalthea, who suckled the infant Jupiter, was the daughter of Olenus; but other explanations of the epithet were current in the tradition (Mair on Arat. *Phaen.* 162–4, Bömer on *F.* 5.113).

189 'Either I do not know how far I am prepared to go ...', i.e. 'Either I am less daring than I think, or ...' (Purser). *temerarius* has strong connotations of recklessness.

191 neue putes: 16.363n.

id me etc. = *id me promittere, quod* [because] *tempus abest.*

193 sit: sc. *modo* = *si erit/fuerit*. Cf. 16.163n.

paucis etiamnunc noctibus 'for (only) a few nights more' (*OLD* s.v. *etiamnum* 1b). For the abl. of duration of time cf. 16.215n.

194 inuitas 'whether they like it or not'.

195–6 See 16.275–6n.

195 'Either I shall survive and my daring will be rewarded ...'; *felix, saluo* are both predicative.

197 partes expellar in illas 'may I be washed up on the further shore'. A recurrent fantasy: 2.135–6 (Phyllis) *ad tua me fluctus proiectam litora portent | occurramque oculis intumulata tuis, Met.* 11.563–5 (Ceyx) *illam meminitque refertque, | illius ante oculos ut agant sua corpora fluctus | optat et exanimis manibus tumuletur amicis,* Prop. 3.7.63–4 (Paetus) *at saltem Italiae regionibus euehat aestus; | hoc de me sat erit si modo matris erit.* Cf. Clausen on Virg. *Ecl.* 10 (p. 291); add Prop. 3.16.21–30. The reader of course knows that this is exactly what is going to happen: Virg. *G.* 3.263 *moritura super crudeli funere uirgo* and Servius *ad loc.*, Musaeus 338–43. See Papanghelis (1987) 101–11 and next n., Introd. p. 13 n. 51.

200 mortis ... ego causa fui: 'laus in amore mori' (Prop. 2.1.47) indeed, if this is the epitaph he is to earn. Leander's morbid wish takes us into the world of Propertian love-as-death (Papanghelis (1987) *passim*). Cf. Prop. 1.19.19–20 *quae tu uiua mea possis sentire* *fauilla!* | *tum mihi non ullo mors sit amara loco*, and with *causa fui id.* 1.11.26 *quicquid ero, dicam 'Cynthia causa fuit'*, Virg. *Aen.* 6.458 (Aeneas to Dido) *funeris heu tibi causa fui?* and Norden *ad loc.*

201 scilicet 'I know that ...'.

203 desinŏ: for the prosody cf. Tib. 2.6.41, *Am.* 3.11.35 *oderŏ* (but the couplet is probably spurious), *Ex. P.* 1.1.25 *conferŏ*; *A.A.* 3.410 *Scipiŏ. nesciŏ* (Catull. 85.2) occurs in O. only in *nescioquis*, virtually a single word, and usually written as such.

uti ... finiat depends on *tua uota* (204).

204 accedant ... fac: 16.263–4n.

205 isto 'thither', rare but classical for *istuc* (N–W II 615); also at *Tr.* 5.1.79. *istuc* 5x, all in *Tr.* and *Ex. P*; at *Ex P.* 4.9.131 certified by metre.

207–8 The image of Leander as ship (6, 148, 215, 19.47, 208) here takes on erotic overtones, apparently first detected by Dousa (Burman *ad loc.*, indignantly denying the suggestion). The allusion to his 'keel' being received into Hero's 'dockyard' is too pointed to be overlooked. Cf. Thomas Carew, 'A Rapture':

> Yet my tall pine shall in the Cyprian strait
> Ride safe at anchor, and unlade her freight.
> My rudder with thy bold hand, like a tri'd
> And skilful pilot, thou shalt steer, and guide
> My bark into love's channel, where it shall
> Dance, as the rising waves do rise or fall.   (85–90)

Cf. on erotic seafaring metaphors in general Adams (1982) 167. Musaeus has Leander pray (215) to 'come to sweet haven in your land on the farther shore'; but for πατρίδος 'fatherland' Dilthey proposed Κύπριδος 'in Cypris' haven', which lends more point and gets rid of the difficulty that Sestos was Hero's πατρίς, not his. Cf. 16.161n.

207 istic 'There with you' (*OLD* s.v. *istic*² 1b).

208 stat 'lies at anchor' (*OLD* s.v. 8), but perhaps also with an erotic connotation (5a).

212 nataturo 'when I want to swim' (*NLS* §92(*d*)).

nec: 16.348n.

214 impediarque: 16.216n.

215 remis ... corporis: a variation on the familiar image of wings as oars (Austin on Virg. *Aen.* 6.19).

217 pernoctet ... tecum: he recurs to his opening fantasy (15–18n.).

xix
Hero to Leander

1–2 This couplet was deleted by Vahlen. If 18.1–2 is to be deleted (see n.), this must follow it, being an inferior reworking of the same idea (Kirfel (1969) 110). UnOvidian are (i) *missam*, intended to pick up *quam ... misisti*, but making no sense with *rebus*; (ii) the phrase *rebus (aliquid) habere*, unparalleled in O. or anywhere else. As in 18, a genuine introductory couplet has probably been lost.

4 da ueniam = *si u. dabis* (16.163n.); cf. 8 below.

non patienter amo: so unlike Leander! But there is no irony in Hero's apology. For the expression cf. 20.88 *quam p. amat! Patienter* is one of O.'s favoured adverbs (11x); cf. 16.174n.

6 fortius ingenium 'greater self-control'; Hero seems to accept without question the ancient male view of women as the creatures of their passions: cf. *A.A.* 1.281–2 *parcior in nobis nec tam furiosa libido; | legitimum finem flamma uirilis habet*, Prop. 3.19.1–2 *obicitur totiens a te mihi nostra libido: | crede mihi, uobis imperat ista magis*, Hes. *Op.* 373–4 and West *ad loc.*, Eur. *Hipp.* 405–7.

7 ut corpus: sc. *infirmum (est)*, understood ἀπὸ κοινοῦ from *infirma (est)*.

teneris ... puellis: for this trick of distributing an adj.-noun phrase between two clauses (a form of ἀπὸ κοινοῦ) cf. e.g. 21.188, *Am.* 1.10.19 *nec Venus apta feris Veneris nec filius armis* and McKeown *ad loc.*, *Met.* 1.458 *qui dare certa ferae, dare uulnera possumus hosti*, Housman on Manil. 1.269–70 (+ *addendum*), Juv. 6.495–6.

8 adde = *si addes* (4n.).

9–14 Cf. *A.A.* 3.381–2 *hos ignaua iocos tribuit natura puellis; | materia ludunt uberiore uiri* and the list that follows, also the catalogue of distractions recommended to the unhappy lover in the *Remedia Amoris* (151–210). In Musaeus Hero similarly complains of isolation and boredom (187–93). Cf. Horace's Neobule (*C.* 3.12) and Agathias (sixth c. A.D.), *A.P.* 5.297. When Euripides' Medea complains that wives are denied the extra-domiciliary compensations available to husbands she means of course lovers (*Med.* 244–7 and Page *ad loc.*).

10 ponitis 'lay out' (*OLD* s.v. 14a); with *tempus, dies*, etc., a characteristically Ciceronian usage, in O. otherwise only in the exile poetry (*Ex P.* 1.5.36 and Scholte *ad loc.*). Cf. Hor. *Sat.* 2.7.112–13 *otia recte | ponere*.

in uaria ... mora 'in different pursuits'; for *mora* = 'distraction', 'pastime' (not in *OLD*) cf. *Am.* 2.11.14 *bibuli litoris illa mora est* and Booth *ad loc.*, *Ex. P.* 4.10.12 *placidae saepe fuere morae* ('intervals of peace' Wheeler), *Tr.* 5.1.33–4 *quiesque | nulla nisi in studio est Pieridumque mora* ('devotion to the Muses'), Prop. 4.8.4 *hic ubi tam rarae non perit hora morae*. Planudes renders ἐν ποικίληι τριβῆι 'in varied pursuits'. On the repetition of *mora* after 8 *moram* see 16.150–2n.

11 dona palaestrae 'what the wrestling-school has to offer'; for this use of *donum* no really adequate parallel is forthcoming (van Lennep (1812) 285–6, *TLL* s.v. 2019, 77ff.). Perhaps = 'the gift of wrestling-schools' (*palaestrae* gen. of definition), sc. of Mercury to mankind (N–H on Hor. *C.* 1.10.4); so, ingeniously, Hollis (*per litt.*), and the allusion may not be too difficult for O. Bentley's *mane* (to be taken ἀπὸ κοινοῦ with all three *aut*-clauses) is tempting; cf. 14 *serior hora*.

12 aut: postponed only here in *Her.*; cf. 16.26n.

13 ducitis 'lure' (*OLD* s.v. 17, 18) and 'draw in' (21a), an unobtrusive syllepsis (18.57n.).

14 'You dissipate (lit. wash away) the evening over your wine', an apparently unique extension of this sense of *diluo*, usually of cares or the like (*OLD* s.v. 1b). Cf. 55 *deceptae* and n. *posito* sc. on the table (16.217n.).

15 his mihi summotae 'for me, debarred as I am from these pursuits ...'. 'Hero uses the strong word *summotae*. A woman is told to *stand aside* if she engaged [*sic*] in men's amusements; or at least was told so before the epoch of lawn-tennis, bicycling, and the more healthy amusements of the nineteenth century' (Palmer).

15–16 uel si etc.: i.e. *nil superest quod faciam praeter amare*, (and that would be the case) *uel* [even if] *minus acriter urar*. For *praeter amare* cf. 7.164 *praeter amasse* and Knox *ad loc.*, 17.24n.

acriter: 16.174n.

quod faciam 'for me to do', final-consec. subj.

17–18 A common lover's protestation, here ironically accurate (Introd. p. 15). 'Leander seems to think a great deal more of his athletic feats than he does of Hero. She is a goddess and all that sort of generality; but still his imagination does not picture and sympathize with her loneliness, but always turns to his own swimming and his own troubles' (Purser xxii).

19 cum cara ... nutrice: on the role of the nurse see 18.97n. Francius corrected to *cana* (rec. Goold), but the nurse's age (26, 45–6) seems less relevant here than her closeness to Hero; cf. 45 *oscula*.

21–2 ~ Musaeus 336, 331 'She strained her eyes everywhere over the sea's broad back, | And with great curses reviled the wild-tempered wind' (Whitman; on the transposition see Gelzer, Hopkinson *ad loc.*).

odioso 'tiresome'; O. uses the word exclusively of those interposing obstacles in the path of the lover (*A.A.* 1.489, 2.635, 3.649, *Rem.* 471).

23 saeuitiae paulum 'a little of its savagery', partitive genitive.

24 te: take ἀπὸ κοινοῦ with *posse*.

26 pollice ... tremulo 'with her shaking hand' (17.266n.). The phrase need not imply, as Purser thought, that Hero's establishment could not run to a handkerchief.

29–30 i.e. *quaero si quis Abydo uenerit aut Abydon eat, ut de te rogem et* [*aut* would make this clearer] *tibi scribam.* Cf. 17.9–10n. Heinsius' transposition of the couplet to follow 32 is logically persuasive, but does a logical sequence suit Hero's distracted state of mind?

de te et: O. is not particularly reluctant to elide monosyllabic pronouns (Platnauer (1951) 78), and this is rather prodelision: *te (e)t* not *t(e) et*. For metrical purposes pronouns are proclitic, i.e. they cohere with the word they govern, so that *de te* is in effect a disyllabic word; cf. *F.* 3.585 *primo et*. The objections of Courtney (1965) 64 are overstated.

31–2 This recalls Dido's emotions on seeing the clothes left in her bedroom by Aeneas (*Aen.* 4.648ff.), a passage which in turn recalls similar scenes in tragedy (Pease, Austin *ad loc.*); thus an ominous resonance. Cf. 10.51–4, *E.S.* 147–50.

Hellespontiaca ... aqua: 16.118n.

33–4 ~ Hor. *C.* 3.6.41–4 *sol ... amicum* | *tempus agens abeunte curru.* This expectant evocation of evening complements and contrasts with the unwelcome return of dawn which signals his departure (18.111n.).

35 uigilantia lumina = 18.31 (see n.).

37–8 A characteristically Roman picture of domesticity and a traditional literary motif: Ter. *Haut.* 275–91, Livy 1.57.8–9 and Ogilvie *ad loc.* (Lucretia), Virg. *Aen.* 8.407–13, Tib. 1.3.83–94 and Murgatroyd *ad loc.* (Delia), Prop. 1.3.39–42 (Cynthia), 3.6.16–34 (an imagined monologue by the abandoned *puella*), 4.3.33–42 ('Arethusa' to her absent soldier husband), Ov. *F.* 2.737–58 and Bömer *ad loc.* (Lucretia lamenting her husband's absence at the war), *Met.* 4.218–21. For the patterned structure of the couplet (abVAB | abVAB) cf. 49, 16.107–14n.

37 'Drawing out the twisted threads as the spindle turns (48n.)' ~ *Met.* 4.221 *leuia uersato ducentem stamina fuso*, and cf. *Met.* 6.22 *siue leui teretem uersabat pollice fusum* (both verses patterned like this one abVAB). The ancestor of all such descriptions of spinning in surviving Latin poetry is Catull. 64.311–19.

38 fallimus 'beguile', 'while away' (*OLD* s.v. 7b), an extension of sense first found in O. Cf. 1.9 *spatiosam fallere noctem* (Penelope at her weaving), *al.*, 55n.

40 ~ *Met.* 11.544–5 *Ceycis in ore* | *nulla nisi Alcyone est*, 562–3 *plurima nantis in ore est* | *Alcyone coniunx*; see Introd. pp. 13–14.

41 mea gaudia 'my love' (*OLD* s.v. 3).

42 omnes: sc. all the members of the family rather than the whole town. *homines* (two MSS, independently conjectured by Bentley) gives appropriate and perhaps more pointed sense 'is the world still awake?'; cf. *Met.* 7.185–6 *homines uolucresque ferasque* | *soluerat alta quies*, *Tr.* 1.3.27 *iamque quiescebant uoces hominumque canumque*, Bömer on *Met.* 7.634–5.

suos 'his family'.

44 Pallade: olive oil (*OLD* s.v. *Pallas*¹ 2b); the olive was Athena's tree. This particular metonymy seems to have originated with O.: Haupt II (1876) 168, Bömer on *Met.* 8.275, Luck on *Tr.* 4.5.3f. Long-distance swimmers greased themselves against the cold, as they do now.

45–6 ~ Catull. 61.154–6 *usque dum tremulum mouens* | *cana tempus anilitas* | *omnia omnibus annuit*.

45 curet: subj. as giving an assumed reason (Roby §1744): 'not, I take it, because …'.

46 obrepens somnus ~ Hor. *A.P.* 360 *obrepere somnum*; cf. 195n.

47 nauigat: 18.207–8n.

48 lenta: 18.58n.

dimotis ... aquis 'as he parts the waters'; cf. 37, 16.42n., 18.80. The abl. is instrumental-circumstantial.

49 'When I have spun a few strands and the spindle has touched the ground', at which point the spun thread must be wound up before the next length is spun. This would not take an experienced worker very long; *pauca* underlines her impatience. For the patterned form of the verse (abVAB) cf. 37–8n.

52 uias: 16.22n.

53 incertas is the corrected reading of P (*incertu* apparently the first hand). This gives more pointed sense than the colourless *interdum* of nearly all the other MSS: cf. *F.* 3.273 *incerto ... murmure, TLL* s.v. 881.3ff. One fourteenth-c. copy gives *incertis*, which Merkel printed, but for *auribus* absolute cf. *Met.* 10.62, 14.309.

54 aduentus ... esse tui 'is that of your arrival', possessive gen.

55 sic ... deceptae 'beguiled in this fashion'; cf. *Tr.* 4.10.114 *sic ... absumo decipioque diem*. With this sense of *decipio* (unhelpfully classified by *OLD* s.v. 2a) cf. the analogous use of *fallo* at 38 (n.).

57–8 The couplet seems out of place here. It intervenes oddly between her falling asleep and the dream; and the following *nam* (59) makes no sense. Content and expression are Ovidian; it would fit well e.g. after line 70 or 100. Removing it, however, still leaves *nam* unexplained, and it seems likely that another couplet has been lost or displaced by this one.

57 tamen: sc. *quamuis inuitus* (16.238n.).

58 ipse 'if left to yourself' (*OLD* s.v. 7).

59 uideor: in my dreams. With these phantom pleasures compare those of Sappho at *E.S.* 123–34 (see Knox *ad loc.*).

60 ferre 'support', 'feel the weight of', reliving the feeling of his clinging to her in his exhaustion.

62 pectora ... sinu: the variation in number purely for metrical convenience. *pectora* sc. *tua*.

nostro iuncta is Merkel's neat correction of MS *iuncto nostra*. For examples of this type of error see Housman, *CP* 166, 794, Kenney (1959) 255; at 18.142 some MSS have *crimine nomen* for *nomine crimen*. Cf. 17.16n.

63 linguae ... modestae: dat. of the agent with the gerundive.

64 For the play with tenses cf. *Am.* 3.11.4 (cit. 16.352n.), for the sentiment *Am.* 3.14.7–8 *quis furor est quae nocte latent in luce fateri | et quae* *clam facias facta referre palam?*, *A.A.* 2.607 *praecipue Cytherea iubet sua sacra taceri*.

66 Cf. Theoc. 11.23–4 (Polyphemus to Galatea) 'Why thus, when sweet sleep holds me, do you straightway come to me, and when it leaves me, are you straightway gone?'

67 firmius 'more securely'; cf. 16.174n.

coeamus: cf. 167, 17.181n.

68 uera ... fide 'actuality'; *fides* here connotes both 'truth' (cf. 16.42) and 'fulfilment' of a wish (*OLD* s.v. 3, Bömer on *Met.* 3.527).

69 ~ [Ov.] *Am.* 3.5.42 *frigidus in uiduo destituere toro*, *Her.* 1.7 *non ego deserto iacuissem frigida lecto*, *A.A.* 3.70 *frigida deserta nocte iacebis anus*.

70 morator is attested only by the first hand of P and W; in the sense 'loiterer' required here it is found otherwise only in a Pompeian graffito (*CIL* IV 813 = 704 Diehl). It should clearly be preferred as *lectio rarior* to *uiator* (one MS) or *natator* (the rest).

71 non iam 'no longer' (Watt (1995) 93) gives a more pointed contrast with *nocte ... hesterna* (72) than *nondum* (MSS; but whatever originally stood in P, it was not *nondum*) 'not yet', and is palaeographically and perhaps idiomatically superior to *non nunc* (Bentley) 'not at present'.

72 sed: 16.191n.

73 non uentura 'what was not going to happen'.

74 tam bona ... uia 'so good an opportunity of crossing' (*OLD* s.v. *uia* 5a).

75 ut 'even though'

76 hoc melior ... quo prior 'by as much the better as it was earlier', abl. of the measure of difference (*NLS* §82). *hoc* for the usual (prose) *eo*, for metrical reasons.

77 at 'But, you will say' (16.41n.).

iactati 'so that it has become storm-tossed', proleptic; cf. e.g. *Met.* 1.37 *ambitae* (when it had become encircled) *circumdare litora terrae*. Bentley's *pacati* (rec. Goold) banalizes the expression.

78 tempore ... minore: sc. than the duration of the lull.

79 puto 'I believe', mildly ironical.

deprensus: *vox propria* of mariners caught in a storm; cf. 7.66, *Met.* 11.663, Virg. *G.* 4.421 and Serv. *ad loc.*, Lucret. 6.429, Catull. 25.13, N–H on Hor. *C.* 2.16.2 (*OLD depre(he)ndo* 5a inadequate).

COMMENTARY: 19.80-91

nil quod querereris 'nothing to complain of', consecutive-generic subj.

80 'and in my arms no storm could hurt you', an echo perhaps of Tib. 1.1.45–8 *quam iuuat immites uentos audire cubantem | et dominam tenero continuisse sinu | aut, gelidas hibernus aquas cum fuderit Auster, | securum somnos igne* [v.l. *imbre*] *iuuante sequi!* and Murgatroyd *ad loc.*

81 certe ego = 21.211: a rare elision, but this phrase is an Ovidian cliché (11x, not counting 20.178, q.v.) (Platnauer (1951) 74).

laeta: *lenta* 'unmoved' a few MSS, approved by Hensius, but the point is that she would actually welcome, not merely acquiesce in, the continuance of the storm (cf. Tibullus, cit. previous n.).

83 quid ... euenit cur sis ...? 'what has happened to make you ...?' (*OLD* s.v. *cur* 3).

metuentior: for comparatives formed from participles cf. 18.45n. O. is fond of this type: cf. e.g. *Met.* 1.322–3 *nec amantior aequi | ... aut ... metuentior ... deorum* and Bömer *ad loc., Am.* 2.8.17 *al. praesentior, F.* 4.673 *properantius, Am.* 2.6.23 *simulantior.* Cf. 131n.

85–7 memini cum ... cum 'I remember when'; natural in English, but the construction is rare in Latin: only at *Am.* 1.14.50 *fama tamen memini cum fuit ista mea,* Plaut. *Capt.* 303, Cic. *Fam.* 7.28.1 (*TLL* s.v. *memini* 653.31–3).

86 non minus: sc. *saeuum minaxque.* The sort of hyperbaton that the reader who has become used to the effortless flow of O.'s verse hardly notices as such.

87–8 'Be daring, but not to the point where I have to weep for your bravery'; see 17.165n. and for the negative form of such expressions with *ne* cf. e.g. Hor. *Ep.* 1.13.12–13 *sic positum seruabis onus, ne forte sub ala | fasciculum portes librorum* and Mayer *ad loc., A.P.* 151–2 *sic ueris falsa remisceat, | primo ne medium, medio ne discrepet imum* and Brink *ad loc.* She is picking up his boast at 18.189–90.

87 esto: the 'future' form of the imperative (*NLS* §126 n. (i)), used by O. for emphasis and metrical convenience.

89 quoque 'and whither'.

90 spretis ille natator aquis 'that sea-despising swimmer'; the abl. absolute is descriptive, the aspect of the part. contemporaneous (16.42n.).

91 hoc ... quod: timid and reckless respectively. For the neuter cf. e.g. 11.24 (*cur*) *tibi, non debet quod soror esse, fui?*, 32 *nec noram quid* *amans esset, at illud eram*, *Am.* 3.6.24 *flumina senserunt ipsa, quid esset amor*, *A.A.* 1.130 '*quod matri pater est, hoc tibi' dixit 'ero'*, Virg. *Ecl.* 8.43 *nunc scio quid sit Amor*. The grammarians apparently do not think this idiom worth notice; it is analogous to the predicative use of neuter adjj. as in *Am.* 1.9.4 *turpe senilis amor* (see McKeown *ad loc.*).

esse solebas: it does not in fact appear from his letter that he had made a habit of pushing his luck.

93 sis idem 'do not change'.

amemur 'our love is mutual', i.e. is returned by you; cf. Catull. 45.20 *mutuis animis amant amantur*. The usual form of such reciprocal expressions is with *inter nos* et sim. (K–S I 614–17).

94 ~ *Rem.* 243–4 *lentus abesto,* | *dum perdat uires sitque sine igne cinis* and (there in a simile) *A.A.* 2.439–44; cf. Gow–Page on Callim. *A.P.* 12.139.1–2 (*HE* 1081–2).

96 similis uento: cf. 18.185–6n., 7.51 *tu quoque cum uentis utinam mutabilis esses!*

erret: 17.191n.

97–8 Variations in the form of a tricolon crescendo on the theme 'that I may not be worth it'; cf. 18.157–8. *tanti* is gen. of price. For *merces* 'reward' in such a context cf. *Am.* 2.1.34–5 *ad uatem, pretium carminis, ipsa uenit.* | *magna datur merces*, 18.163 *pretium non uile laboris*.

neu (= *et, ne*: 16.71n.) is Dousa's correction of MS *ne*, a small but worthwhile improvement neglected by edd.

et: sc. *et ne*.

99–100 In Musaeus the disparity between the lovers is to Leander's disadvantage; see Introd. p. 14.

dicar: by whom? Leander is keeping the affair dark. Only if it comes to light will it matter 'what they say' on his side of the water. Hence (presumably) Heinsius' *ducar* (from the *excerpta Vossiana*) 'lest I be considered' (*OLD* s.v. 30), sc. by you; cf. *F.* 2.473 *inde nefas ducunt genus hoc imponere mensis*.

Abydeno Thressa: the juxtaposition emphasizes the disparity. Thrace was not thought of as truly Greek: 'As the Athenians got their policemen from Scythia, so they got their housemaids from Thrace' (Palmer). On the Athenian obsession with 'the supposed desire of foreigners (especially Thracians) to marry into citizen families' see Hall (1989) 109.

102 otia ... agis 'spend your leisure'; cf. *F.* 2.724 *luditur in castris,* *otia miles agit*, 4.926 *otia mundus agit*, Met. 1.100 *mollia securae peragebant otia gentes*, Virg. G. 3.376–7 *secura sub alta | otia agunt terra*. *Otium* will fit into dactylic verse only in the 'poetic' pl.

paelice captus: she is treated grammatically as instrument rather than agent (17.49–50n.).

106 'May my death (*OLD* s.v. *fatum* 6a) happen before you play me false (*culpa* 3b)'. For the pl. *fata* cf. e.g. 118, *Am*. 1.6.14 *non timeo strictas in mea fata manus* and McKeown *ad loc.*, *A.A.* 2.130 *Odrysii fata cruenta ducis*, al., *TLL* s.v. *fatum* 359.38ff.

culpa ... tua: abl. of comparison.

107 nec quia etc. 'Not, however (16.189n.), that you have given me any indication of grief to come', i.e. you have done nothing to make me apprehensive; *dederis* is subj. of an attributed reason (cf. 17.37n.).

109 sed: 16.191n.

quis enim securus amauit?: 'a passionate woman's love is always overshadowed by fear' (George Eliot). Cf. 1.12 *res est solliciti plena timoris amor*, 6.29 *timidum quod amat* (*s.v.l.*: only in E), *Met.* 7.719 *cuncta timemus amantes* and Bömer *ad loc.*, Cic. *Att.* 2.24.1 *non ignoro quam sit amor omnis sollicitus atque anxius*. *amauit* is 'gnomic' pf. (17.190n.).

110 et: 16.26n. Cf. 114, 160.

locus '(their) situation', 'distance'.

111 felices illas: cf. 17.145n.

sua ... praesentia 'the very fact of their being in the same place'. *suus*, as often, refers to the logical rather than the grammatical subject of the sentence (*NLS* §36 n. (i), K–S 1 600–2, H–S 175–6).

112 i.e. *crimina uera timere iubet, crimina falsa timere uetat*, a simple and elegant ex. of the ἀπὸ κοινοῦ construction. However, it seems odd that a woman should feel glad at being *forced* to know about her lover's infidelity; there is some sacrifice of sense to antithesis. Cf. next n.

113–14 'In my case non-existent injuries trouble me, and by the same token I am ignorant of real ones; and each delusion is equally painful.' The correlative structure (*tam ... quam*) of 113 entails a slight ellipse: the sense required is 'I am as much troubled by imaginary injuries as by (possible) real ones of which I am ignorant'.

115 ut has not been satisfactorily explained or emended. It can = *utinam* (*OLD* s.v. 42), but in that sense it occurs nowhere else in O., and in any case with *utinam* preceding it is superfluous. *hic* (some MSS) is a feeble stop-gap. Read *heu* (Courtney (1989) 126) or *o* (independently suggested by Watt (1995) 93)?

116 -que 'or' (*OLD* s.v. 7).
certe femina nulla 'not – please not – a woman'.
117 quodsi quam sciero 'But if I do learn of any such ...'; *quam* is indefinite (*OLD* s.v. *quis*² 1a).
118 'Wrong me at once, if it is my death that you desire'. *Fata petere* lacks an exact parallel; cf. e.g. *Am.* 1.6.14 (cit. 106n.), *Met.* 7.346–7 *quis uos in fata parentis | armat?* and Bömer *ad loc.*, *E.S.* 220 *ut mihi Leucadiae fata petantur aquae* (read *Leucadia ... aqua?*)
119–20 neque ... -que ... -que: styled rare (cf. *OLD* s.v. *neque* 8a, K–S II 48), but not all that uncommon in O.: Scholte on *Ex P.* 1.1.20. The sense of *-que* is, as often, adversative = 'rather' (Bömer on *Met.* 3.524).
quo ... minus = *ne* (*NLS* §150 n. (i)).
inuida pugnat hiems 'it is the envious storm that fights', predicative.
121 fluctu 'waves', collective sing. (*OLD* s.v. 1b); cf. e.g. 201, *Am.* 2.17.4, *Met.* 11.507, 525, 566, *F.* 2.775, *al.*
122 et ... obscura nube 'and with what dark clouds'; *quam* is understood from *quanto* preceding.
123 mater pia ... Helles: the cloud is personified as Nephele (= 'cloud' in Gk) weeping for her dead daughter (18.117n.). O. had exploited the same conceit quite differently at *A.A.* 3.175–6, where the colour of a fabric is compared to a cloud. In Hyg. *Fab.* 1–3 she is called Nebula.
124 roratis ... aquis 'by the water that is showered down'; the aspect of the part. is contemporaneous (16.42n.).
126 nouerca: Ino, who had plotted Helle's death (18.117n.), was subsequently changed into the sea-goddess Leucothea (*Met.* 4.539–42). Having harassed Helle in life she continues to harass (*uexat*) the sea named after her.
127 ~ Antipater of Thessalonica, *A.P.* 9.215.1 (*GP* 215) 'The Hellespont was always an evil sea for women'; see Gow–Page *ad loc.*
ut nunc est: 16.50n.
128 periīt: cf. e.g. *Am.* 3.8.17 *qua periit aliquis*, *A.A.* 3.707 *ut rediit animus*, *Met.* 9.612 *nec petiit horamque animumque uacantem*; not a case of

COMMENTARY: 19.129–133

'lengthening' in arsis, but a revival for metrical convenience of the original vowel quantity (Platnauer (1951) 60–1, with further exx.).

129 tibi ... memori 'if you remembered'; *sum* lacks the present part. which Gk uses in such phrases. *tibi* is dat. of the agent with *impediendus* following.

flammarum ... tuarum: even by the standards of Olympus Neptune was notoriously promiscuous. In Arachne's tapestry anthology of celestial mollocking his score (6) is second only to Jupiter's (9): *Met.* 6.115–20. This list is by no means identical with Arachne's (cf. 136n.). As in Leander's star-catalogue (18.149–52), the poet consciously exploits the sound of the Greek names.

130 erat ... impediendus = *impediri debebat* (16.162n.), with a suggestion of impatience; Neptune ought to have been supportive all along. Cf. 1.108 *nunc erat auxiliis illa tuenda patris* and Barchiesi, Knox *ad loc.*, 21.29n.

131 Amymone: raped while on her way to fetch water (*Am.* 1.10.5–6 and McKeown *ad loc.*).

laudatissima forma ~ *Met.* 9.716–17 *laudatissima formae | dote*. The superlative of *laudatus* occurs nowhere else in classical poetry (Bömer *ad loc.*). Cf. *Met.* 11.637 *consuetissima*, 11.301 *dotatissima (forma)*, 5.60 *iunctissimus*, 9.549, 10.70 *iunctissima*, 9.330 *notissima (forma); Her.* 17.71 *acceptissima* (n.), 18.37 *immansuetissime* (n.), 18.45, 19.83nn. See next n.

132 'are not empty stories laid to your charge'; though grammatically attached to the nearest subject, Tyro (16.362n.), the clause refers to the whole list. *criminis ... tui* lit. 'of your misdoing'.

Tyro: he seduced her disguised as the river Enipeus, with whom she was in love. She leads the parade of heroines introduced to Odysseus in the Underworld (Hom. *Od.* 11.235–59), described there as εὐπατέρεια 'born of a noble father' (235); her superlative in O. has been borrowed from her lover Enipeus, described as 'by far the most beautiful (κάλλιστος) of rivers on earth' (239), a textbook case of *imitatio cum variatione*.

133 Alcyone: one of the Pleiades, daughter of Atlas and Pleione (16.62n.). Cf. 135n.

Calyceque Hecataeone: Heinsius' plausible restoration of P's *ceuceque et aueone*, based on Hyg. *Fab.* 157.2 *(Neptuni filii) Cygnus ex Calyce Hecatonis filia* (see however Rose's sceptical n. *ad loc.*).

134 Medusa: see Hes. *Theog.* 274–81. Pindar (*Pyth.* 12.16) calls her 'fair-faced' (εὐπαράου), but the story that her seduction took place in the temple of Minerva (Athena) and that her beautiful hair was changed to snakes by the goddess as a punishment for this desecration is not attested before O. (*Met.* 4.790–803 and Bömer *ad loc.*). *nexis ... comis* is descriptive abl. For *nondum* cf. Bömer on *Met.* 2.219.

135 Laodice: there were several legendary women of this name, but this is the only reference to a Laodice as one of Neptune's conquests.

caelo ... recepta: as one of the Pleiads; cf. *F.* 4.173 *Neptuno Alcyonen et te, formosa Celaeno (concubuisse ferunt).*

136 memini ... lecta mihi 'I remember to have read'; *mihi* is dat. of the agent.

137 pluresque canunt ... poetae: the *doctus poeta* slyly intrudes; O. implies that he could continue the catalogue *ad lib.*, but will spare the reader the rest. Cf. *Met.* 3.225 (cutting off the list of Actaeon's hounds) *quosque referre mora est, F.* 1.492 (a list of exiles) *et quos praeterea longa referre mora est, Rem.* 461 *quid moror exemplis, quorum me turba fatigat?* and Henderson *ad loc.*, Eur. *Phoen.* 751 'To recite the name of each [sc. of the champions] would be a great waste of time' (often interpreted as a hit at Aeschylus' *Septem*). There is also a hint of the commonplace that all tradition (even what treats of the gods) is in the keeping of the poets (*Am.* 3.12.21–40).

138 ~ 2.58 *lateri conseruisse latus,* Prop. 2.2.12 *uirgineum ... composuisse latus,* Tib. 1.8.26 *femori conseruisse femur,* Catull. 69.2 *tenerum sup posuisse femur. latus* virtually = 'body' by synecdoche (cf. *OLD* s.v. 1b).

141 lato ... mari 'out at sea'; a mere strait ought to be beneath his notice. For *latus* predicative cf. e.g. *Am.* 1.7.8 *lata per arua* 'far and wide over the fields' and McKeown *ad loc.*

proelia misce: a cliché; cf. *Met.* 5.156 *proelia miscet,* Lucret. 4.1013 *p. miscent,* 5.442 *p. miscens,* Virg. *G.* 3.220, *Aen.* 10.23 *p. miscent, Aen.* 12.628 *p. miscet; G.* 2.282–3 *miscent p.*

142 ~ Gallus (*FPL* p. 99, *FLP* p. 263) *uno tellures diuidit amne duas,* of the river Hypanis (Vib. Sequ. 77 Gelsomino). There may be a discreet echo in O.'s verse of Gallus' rather heavy-handed patterning (VAbBa ~ aBVAb). Cf. 16.107–14n.

143 te ... magnum 'great god that you are'; 129n.

145 turpe deo pelagi ... terrere 'it is a shameful thing for the seagod to frighten'; the inf. is treated as a neuter noun (17.24n.). Cf. 185.

146 'that distinction (sc. of yours, *ista*) is beneath (even) the meanest pond', compendious comparison (18.69n.).

147 nobilis etc.: 99–100n. In Musaeus it is Hero who is 'heiress of Zeus-engendered blood' (Διοτρεφὲς αἷμα λαχοῦσα, 30); see Introd. p. 14.

148 a ... Vlixe: Poseidon's (Neptune's) persecution of Odysseus (Ulysses) motivates the first part of the *Odyssey*.

suspecto 'hated'; the word often connotes more than mere suspicion. Cf. 20.173, Livy 31.47.1 *sinus Euboicus ... suspectus nautis* 'disliked by sailors'.

149–50 Another variation on the one soul in two bodies theme (18.125–6n.).

149 -que 'and so' (*OLD* s.v. 6a).

natat ille, sed '(for) though it is he that swims, yet ...'.

150 pendet 'floats' but also 'is uncertain', 'depends' (sc. on your goodwill) (*OLD* s.v. *pendeo* 9, 11a, 13b).

151 sternuit en lumen: the sudden spluttering of the lamp recalls Hero to her surroundings. *en* (Heinsius) is a necessary correction of *et* (MSS), an inopportune connective which has clearly intruded from the next verse; cf. 153 *ecce*. For a sneeze as a favourable omen for lovers cf. Catull. 45.8–9 and Fordyce *ad loc.*; the same conceit as here in an epigram by O.'s contemporary Marcus Argentarius (*A.P.* 6.633 = *GP* 1365–8; see Gow–Page *ad loc.*).

nam: postponed only here in *Her.*; cf. Bömer on *Met.* 9.669, Norden (1916) 403. See 16.26n.

153 merum ... instillat: as a libation in response to the omen (cf. Prop. 4.3.60, cit. next n.), but also as an excuse for the old nurse to have a swig herself ('ill-timed realism' Purser). Cf. *F.* 2.579–80 *uina quoque instillat; uini quodcumque relictum est | aut ipsa aut comites, plus tamen ipsa, bibit*. Old women, esp. of the confidante/go-between/procuress type, were notoriously addicted to the bottle; cf. e.g. O.'s Dipsas (*Am.* 1.8) and Herodas' Gyllis (1.78–87).

154 'cras ... erimus plures' 'there will be three of us', but also perhaps 'we shall be dead'; for *plures* = 'the majority' in this

178 COMMENTARY: 19.155–159

sense see *OLD* s.v. 2b, Otto s.v. *plures*. The omen, like most, is ambiguous: cf. Prop. 4.3.60 (Arethusa) *seu uoluit tangi parca lucerna mero* and Butler–Barber, Camps *ad loc.*

-que: 17.159n.

155 The irony continues. *euinco* of overcoming navigational hazards also at *Met.* 14.76 (Bömer *ad loc.*), 15.706, *Tr.* 1.10.33; *lapsus* implies a smooth and easy transit (*OLD* s.v. *labor*[1] 1a), but also has connotations of failure and death (7).

156 toto corde recepte 'welcomed right into my heart'; cf. 16.13–14n. Elsewhere in O. it is *animus* not *cor* that is used in similar phrases: 6.55 *uirum ... tectoque animoque recepi*, *A.A.* 2.407 *Thyestiaden animo thalamoque recepit*, *Met.* 9.278–9 *illam* | *... thalamoque animoque receperat Hyllus* and Bömer *ad loc.*, 14.78 *excipit Aenean ... animoque domoque*. With *cor* it is usually Love who is the lodger: 11.26 *nescioquem sensi corde tepente deum*, *Am.* 2.9.2 *o in corde meo desidiose puer*. In a different context one would take *toto corde* = *toto pectore* 'wholeheartedly' (208n.). For the expression here cf. Musaeus 156 (Aphrodite) ἐνὶ κραδίηι θέτο πάσηι 'put him (Milanion) in all her heart'. The coincidence suggests a common original.

157 The Roman elegists ring many changes on the idea of the lover as soldier and love as warfare (Lier (1914) 33–4, Spies (1930) 45–73); see in particular O.'s celebrated *Militat omnis amans* (*Am.* 1.9; McKeown *ad loc.*).

socii desertor Amoris 'deserter from Love's alliance'. Amor (Cupid) is generally figured as C.-in-C. of the army in which the lover is a private (McKeown on *Am.* 1.2.32) rather than as a comrade in arms: *socius Amor* = *Amor qui sociat* ('cuius nos societatem iniimus' Loers). For the image of desertion cf. Tib. 2.6.5–6 *ure, puer, quaeso, tua qui ferus otia liquit,* | *atque iterum erronem sub tua signa uoca* and Murgatroyd *ad loc.*

158 medio, 161 medias, 167 medium: on such rhetorically unmotivated repetitions see 16.150–2n.

158 medio ... toro 'in a solitary bed'; cf. *Am.* 1.5.1–2 *aestus erat, mediamque dies exegerat horam;* | *apposui medio membra leuanda toro* and McKeown *ad loc.*

159 quod timeas non est: 79n.

159–60 Venus ipsa fauebit etc.: 16.23, 24nn. Cf. Musaeus 248–

50 (Leander to himself) 'What care you for the surge? | Do you not know that Cypris is offspring of the sea, | And is mistress over the deep and over our sufferings?' (Whitman) and Kost, Gelzer *ad loc.*

aequore nata 'seeing that she is born of the sea'.

161 libet ... saepe 'I am often minded'.

162–4 Another conceit in some danger of being done to death (127n.). The generalizing *solet* sharpens the rhetoric.

164 uastis: hardly 'wide', given both the known facts and the words *breuis unda* at 142; but even if the word is allowed its connotation of 'desolate', 'dreary' (*OLD* s.v. 2) it does not seem especially apt for the Hellespont.

167 at 'Well then' (*OLD* s.v. 10a).

diuersi 'from our different sides' (*OLD* s.v. 1c).

coeamus: 67n.

168 obuia ... oscula demus 'let us meet and kiss', a good ex. of neat Ovidian Latinity.

169 atque ita 'and having done so' (18.115n.).

quisque = *uterque*, as at *Met.* 4.79–80 (Pyramus and Thisbe) *partique dedere | oscula quisque suae*, *Ex P.* 1.10.44 (two brothers) *suppliciter uestros quisque rogate deos*; cf. K–S 1 648, H–S 201. Cf. 174n.

171–2 i.e. 'utinam uel hic pudor, qui nos clam amare cogit, (*amori cedere uellet*), uel amor famae (i.e. pudori)' (Housman, *CP* 546). The alternative interpretation, taking *timidus famae* together ('our love which fears public opinion') and *cedere* absolute, destroys the point, which is that shame and love are in conflict with each other (next n.). Cf. *Met.* 1.618–19 *pudor est qui suadeat illinc, | hinc dissuadet amor*, Musaeus 98 'love drove out shame' and Kost *ad loc.*

173 'As it is, love (*calor* = amor) and shame (*reuerentia* = pudor) are equally matched.'

male res iunctae: cf. *E.S.* 121 *non ueniunt in idem pudor atque amor*, *Met.* 2.846–7 *non bene conueniunt nec in una sede morantur | maiestas et amor* and Bömer *ad loc.*

174 quid = *utrum*, as at 20.124, 21.63, Virg. *Aen.* 12.719; cf. Shackleton Bailey on Cic. *Att.* 16.8 (418).1, K–S 1 655, H–S 201.

sequar: deliberative subj.

in dubio est 'I know not' (16.140n.).

175–6 See 16.347n.

Colchos: 'Colchis' (18.157–8n.).

176 impositam ... tulit 'took her on board and made off with her'; *tulit = abstulit* (*OLD* s.v. *fero* 35a).

177 Idaeus ... adulter 'the adulterer from Ida' i.e. Paris. This was his standing epithet in Euripides; cf. 16.53n. Hero might have paused to reflect that neither of her examples is exactly propitious.

Lacedaemona: acc. of motion towards (18.157–8n.).

179 quod amas 'your beloved' (16.85n.).

180 'it would be troublesome (even) for ships to cross as often as you do by swimming'; see Housman, *CP* 417–18.

181–2 'Yet please, please ... fear the sea even as you despise it'; see 17.165n. The repeated *sic* and the periphrasis with *facito* lend emphasis to her plea. For the omission of *ut* after *facito* cf. 16.263–4n.

183 arte laboratae [= Virg. *Aen.* 1.639] **merguntur** 'though carefully constructed are (nevertheless) sunk'; *tamen* is not essential (16.238n.) to signal the concessive sense of the participle.

184 plus ... posse 'are of greater avail' (*OLD* s.v. 8b).

185 quod ... hoc: the inf. is treated as a neuter noun (145n.).

natare 'swim', but also 'swim for it', i.e. 'be shipwrecked': Prop. 3.7.8, 3.12.32, 4.1.116, Juv. 10.257.

186 exitus 'their means of escape' (*OLD* s.v. 2b), but also 'their fate', 'their end' (4, 3b); understand *nautis* dat.

fractis puppibus 'if their ships are wrecked', abl. abs.

187 cupio etc. 'I wish my urging (sc. that you should be cautious) not to carry conviction.'

188 sis ... precor: 16.5n.

ipse 'unprompted'.

189–90 excussa ... bracchia 'those arms which have swum so many strokes'; cf. *Met.* 5.596 *excussa ... bracchia iacto.* This use of *excutio* is Ovidian (Bömer *ad loc.*); cf. of flying *A.A.* 1.235 *pennas uelociter excutit udas* and Hollis *ad loc.*, *Met.* 6.703.

189 per undas, 191 ad undas, 199 per undas, 207 in undis: cf. 158–67, 16.150–2, 279–80nn.

192 nescioquo ... hebet: Reeve's correction (Reeve (1973) 331) differs in effect by only two letters from the reading of P. *Hebeo* is an uncommon word, occurring elsewhere in O. only as a variant at *Tr.* 4.1.48 (*hebeto* 4x) and not attested before the Augustan age (Williams on *Aen.* 5.395–6; only there in Virgil, *hebeto* 2x). *nescioquo* 'mysterious', 'unaccountable'.

193 hesternae ... imagine noctis 'last night's vision'; cf. *Met.* 9.474 *tacitae ... noctis imago*, [Ov.] *Am.* 3.5.31, 33 *nocturnae ... imaginis. imago* (120x in O.) here practically = 'dream'. No dream figures in Musaeus, though Hero 'divined' Leander's fate (332) when he failed to appear; cf. Pohlenz (1913) 7–8, suggesting that it was a feature of the Hellenistic original. The dying dolphin may have been suggested to O. by the Greek epigrammatists who exploited the idea for pathetic effect (Anyte, *A.P.* 7.215 (*HE* 708–13); Antipater of Thessalonica, 7.216 (*GP* 163–8); Archias, 7.214 (*GP* 3724–31)). It was a recognized symbol in dream-interpretation: 'Seeing a dolphin out of the sea is not auspicious, for it means that you will witness the death of someone very dear to you' (Artemidorus, *Onirocritica* 2.16).

194 piata: the dream is treated as an omen or portent sent by a god or power that can be propitiated by sacrifice. *pio* is almost invariable in the poets for prose *expio* (Bömer on *Met.* 8.483).

195 sub auroram 'towards dawn'. *auroram* is Heinsius' correction of MS *aurora*; O. consistently uses the acc. with *sub* in this sense (*OLD* s.v. 23a; for abl. see *ibid.* 8). Cf. *Met.* 4.79 *sub noctem* and Bömer *ad loc.*, *A.A.* 2.315 *sub autumnum* (*autumno* some MSS).

dormitante lucerna ∼ 18.31, 19.35 *uigilantia lumina*; *dormito* only here in O. With the coming of day the lamp may be allowed to relax its attention, to 'nod off': Hor. *A.P.* 359 *quandoque bonus dormitat Homerus.* Cf. 46n.

196 A traditional belief: Moschus, *Europa* 5 and Bühler *ad loc.* (p. 52 nn. 4, 5), Hor. *Sat.* 1.10.32–3 *Quirinus | post mediam noctem uisus, cum somnia uera*.

197 digitis cecidere ... remissis ∼ *Met.* 4.229, 5.399, Prop. 4.8.53.

198 nostra: 'suspectum' Palmer, but his *sera* is unconvincing. *noster = meus* is so common that the variation in number *nostra ... dedi* is unremarkable; cf. e.g. 16.13–14 *nostra ... me*, 27–30 *attulimus ... inuenimus ... mihi ... nos ... meae*, 35 *peto ... nostro*, 159–60 *tulissem ... nostra*, 165–6 *ego ... nobis*, 171–2 *nostram ... deprecor*, 219–20 *nostris | experior* etc.

199 hic 'thereupon' (*OLD* s.v. *hic*² 6); cf. *A.A.* 1.143, 2.585, Catull. 10.24, 44.13, Virg. *Aen.* 1.728, Hor. *Sat.* 1.9.7 and Lejay *ad loc.* It is tempting however to read *huc* (with *nantem*).

delphina: Gk acc.; the poets almost invariably use the Gk forms of the word (*OLD* s.v. *delphinus* headn.). Cf. Appendix.

200 non dubia ... fide 'there was no mistaking it'.

201 ∼ Musaeus 339 'She saw her husband, a dead body flayed by the tide-rocks' (Whitman).

202 uita ... deseruit: cf. Enn. *Ann.* 37 Sk. (Ilia on her dream) *uita corpus meum nunc deserit omne*. On the polysyllabic ending see Introd. pp. 22–3.

203 quidquid id est, timeo = Virg. *Aen.* 2.49 (Laocoon on the Wooden Horse). A dry Lucretian formula (3.135, 5.577, 1252) takes on an ominous resonance from the Virgilian reminiscence.

nec 'so do not'; cf. 16.309n.

204 nec nisi tranquillo 'and only if it is calm'.

bracchia: it is not only his arms that he entrusts to the sea; this seems an implausible synecdoche (16.21n.). Read *corpora*? *bracchia* has occurred in the same *sedes* at 184, 190, and words of this scansion were readily confused by copyists (17.119n.).

205 si tibi non parcis 'if you will not spare yourself'; the present tense is perhaps analogous to that at e.g. 14.74 *nox tibi, ni properas, ista perennis erit*, *Met.* 6.208–9 *cultis | arceor, o nati, nisi uos succurritis armis*, where the apodosis expresses a threat or (here implied) a warning (Bömer *ad loc.*, Blase (1903) 109–10); but it is tempting to emend to *parces*.

206 numquam nisi te sospite 'only if you (too) are safe'; cf. 16.2n.

erit (Wω) is less obvious than *ero* (PGς) and rhetorically stronger – 'the girl you love ...'; cf. 20.228n. and Thompson (1993) 261 n. 16.

207 'The weakened seas offer hope of an early calm'; for *frango* = 'diminish', 'abate' cf. *Tr.* 1.2.108 *uictaque mutati frangitur unda maris*, *OLD* s.v. 6a. Contrast Hor. *C.* 2.14.13–14 *carebimus | fractis ... rauci fluctibus Hadriae* ('*fractis* ... suggests dangerous reefs' N–H). Bentley's *stratis* (cf. Plan. λωφησάντων?), for which he compared 7.49 *strata ... aequaliter unda*, is not a clear improvement. For *spes* + *in* with abl. see *OLD* s.v. 1c.

tamen: the adversative is not inappropriate, but it is tempting to read *tandem* 'at long last'.

208 tum 'when that happens'.

tuto pectore 'in safety (cleave the waves) with your breast', but perhaps also 'with confident heart'; for *tutus = securus* see *OLD* s.v. 2b, but there are no other exx. in O., who uses the word more than 150x. The better-supported reading *toto pectore* 'whole-heartedly' (*A.A.* 2.536, *Ex P.* 1.8.63, 3.1.39, *OLD* s.v. *pectus* 4b) suits only mental or emotional exertion. Cf. 156 *toto corde* and n.

pectore finde: Leander as ship again. The words, however, do not imply that he used the breast-stroke; the previous references to arm-movements indicate something like the crawl, which was indeed the stroke principally favoured by ancient swimmers (Mehl, *RE* Suppl. v 855.22–43, Housman on Manil. 5.423–5).

uias: 16.22n.

XX
Acontius to Cydippe

1 pone metum: an arresting beginning, which may be authorial, but it seems more probable that here too an introductory couplet has been lost (17.1, 18.1–2, 19.1–2, 21.1nn.). As the text stands, Acontius does not name Cydippe until line 107 or himself until the very end of his letter (239). The couplet supplied as introduction by a handful of late MSS is not O.'s (Kirfel (1969) 80–2).

hic 'in this case' (*OLD* s.v. *hic*² 5), 'this time round'.

2 promissam: sc. *in matrimonium* (*OLD* s.v. *promitto* 2b). The word sums up his whole case.

3 perlege 'read it to the end'; cf. 16.12, 4.3 *perlege quodcumque est: quid epistula lecta nocebit?* Cydippe has good reason to be wary of missives that come out of the blue.

sic: *si perleges* (18.46n.)

4 i.e. *quod* (sc. *corpus tuum*) *si ulla parte dolet, ego quoque doleo*; *quod dolere* 'the feeling pain of which' is the grammatical subject of the clause, *meus est dolor* the predicate. For the sentiment cf. 233–4, 18.125–6, 19.149–50nn.

5 ora (ω) gives straightforward sense; cf. *Tr.* 4.3.50 *auertis uultus et subit ora rubor*. *ante* (PG5) is preferred by e.g. Showerman–Goold, but entails two ellipses: (i) of the reference, sc. 'even before reading it'; (ii) of an object for *subit*. For (i) cf. *A.A.* 1.277–8 *conueniat maribus ne quam nos ante rogemus, | femina iam partes uicta rogantis aget*, *TLL* s.v. 130.62–8); for (ii) (*subeo* absolute) see *OLD* s.v. 11 fin.

COMMENTARY: 20.6–12

in aede Dianae: cf. 21.105 and Introd. pp. 4, 15.

6 ingenuas connotes 'the fair complexion associated with free birth' (Shackleton Bailey (1956) 16); cf. McKeown on *Am.* 1.7.50, Fedeli on Prop. 1.4.13–14. Cf. 97, 21.111–12n.

7 coniugium pactamque fidem: cf. *Met.* 9.722 *coniugium pactaeque... taedae*, *Her.* 6.41 *heu ubi pacta fides, ubi conubialia iura?* Cf. 40n.

non crimina 'nothing dishonourable'.

8 debitus ... coniunx 'your destined husband', sc. owed to you by fate (*OLD* s.v. *debeo* 4). Cf. 7.103 *debita coniunx*, Virg. *Aen.* 8.374–5 *Pergama ... debita* and Fordyce *ad loc.*

adulter 'philanderer'; neither is married.

9 licet repetas 'recall if you will'; equivalent to a polite imperative.

demptus ab arbore fetus: the periphrasis probably signals the learned poet's awareness that his sources differed as to the identity of the fruit, which is conventionally referred to as an apple. *malum* (209, 237, 21.107) and *pomum* (239, 21.123, 145, 216) cover any orchard fruit, and the Diegesis to Callimachus is similarly vague (Z2–3 μήλωι καλλίστωι); Aristaenetus (1.10.26) specifies a quince Κυδώνιον ... μῆλον (cf. *ibid.* 34 on its scent). For what it is worth, the skin of a quince would be easier to write on than that of most apples. On its bridal symbolism cf. Plut. *Coni. praec.* 1. See 21.215–16n.

ab arbore: according to Aristaenetus (1.10.25–6) in the grove of Aphrodite. The apple was heavily charged with erotic symbolism (for μῆλα = 'breasts' see LSJ s.v. II.1) and was a traditional lover's gift. By throwing one at Cydippe Acontius was declaring his love; cf. Virg. *Ecl.* 3.64 *malo me Galatea petit lasciua puella* and Clausen *ad loc.* – but not *more bonis solito* (21.127)! On the apple motif see also Introd. pp. 15 n. 60, 19 n. 74.

10 me iaciente 'when I threw it'.

11 spondere 'that you promise': the present tense emphasizes that the oath is still binding. [T.]* For *spondeo* of giving or taking in marriage see *OLD* s.v. 1b. Of course to use the word of Cydippe's involuntary pledge is thoroughly disingenuous; cf. 29 *feci sponsalia* and n.

12 te potius etc.: i.e. I had rather you remembered it (and married me) than that she should have to (and punish you for not marrying me) (Ruhnken, Loers).

---

* See Preface, p. x.

13 cupio: Bentley's correction of MS *timeo*, which 'stultifies the whole passage' (Housman, *CP* 418). This is the most satisfactory of the emendations that have been proposed (Watt (1995) 93-4), but the corruption is difficult to account for.

idem ... illud 'that same thing'; *TLL* s.v. *idem* 202.22-7, H-S 188.

14-16 Cf. *A.A.* 3.473-4 *mora semper amantes | incitat* (but there with the rider *exiguum si modo tempus habet*), *Met.* 4.60 *tempore creuit amor*.

14 flamma: cf. 56 *flammae*, 17, 42 *ardor*, 119 *incendia*, 170 *ignibus*. This recalls Paris (16.49-50n.); cf. Hintermeier (1993) 113 n. 32.

15 tempore longo: in Callimachus this must have been well over a year, since Cydippe fell ill four times, the second time for seven months (fr. 75.16-20 Pf.). Acontius employed the interval in wandering through the woods, bemoaning his fate, and carving his name on the trees (frr. 72-3, Aristaen. 1.10.51-9); O. makes him adopt the more practical course of coming to Naxos, hanging around the back door of the house, and ingratiating himself with the help (129-32). See Introd. pp. 16-17.

16-17 dederas tu ... tu dederas: the chiastic repetition underlines his total lack of scruple; Cydippe had 'given' nothing of her own free will.

17 meus ... ardor = *ego ardens*; cf. 17.73-4n.

hic 'this passion of mine' gives good sense, but it is tempting to emend to *hinc* [T.], 'it was because of this that my passion has trusted you'.

19 praesens ut erat 'being actually there'; for *ut erat* cf. 16.121n. So Callim. fr. 75.22-7 Pf. (Apollo to Cydippe's father): 'A solemn oath by Artemis frustrates your child's marriage. For my sister was not then vexing Lygdamis, neither in Amyclae's shrine was she weaving rushes, nor in the river Parthenios was she washing her stains after the hunt; she was at home in Delos when your child swore that she would have Acontius, none other, for bridegroom' (Trypanis). Like the false gods of Israel (1 Kings 18:27), the Olympians were not omnipresent. Contrast the (Stoic) Zeus of Aratus: 'full of Zeus are all the streets and all the market-places of men; full is the sea and the havens thereof' (*Phaen.* 2-4, tr. Mair).

20 mota ... coma 'by nodding her head' (16.42n.), sc. that of her statue.

dicta tulisse 'received your words', a sense of *fero* apparently otherwise attested only at Stat. *Theb.* 11.252 *mugitum hostilem summa tulit aure iuuencus* (see Venini *ad loc.*). (Purser's parallels are for *fero* = 'obtain' (*OLD* s.v. 36d) and are irrelevant.) Planudes' προσδεδέχθαι probably renders *notasse* (ς), which gives good sense but looks like a banalization. *probasse* (Heinsius from MSS now untraceable) misrepresents the role of the goddess, which is that of witness (12, 18). After *uerba* in 19 *dicta* is otiose and may be corrupt: *signa dedisse* Slichtenhorst.

21 dicas ... licebit 'you are welcome to say', sc. *per me*; cf. 71–2. O. uses *licebit* and *licet* indifferently in such phrases for metrical convenience: cf. Bömer on *Met.* 2.58.

21–2 nostra ... fraude ... fraudis nostrae: cf. 16–17n.

23 uni: Burman emended to *unum*, 'my sole object was ...'; but *uni* gives excellent sense, and it is the assurance that Cydippe is 'the only girl in the world' that is calculated to placate her. See Thompson (1993) 258, citing *inter al. A.A.* 1.42 *elige cui dicas 'tu mihi sola places'*.

24 te (Bentley) is rhetorically stronger than *me* (MSS), 'win over' (*OLD* s.v. *concilio* 2) sc. *mihi*, rather than 'commend' (3) sc. *tibi*.

25 non ego ...: sc. *sum* (17.253n.).

26 Cf. Prop. 2.1.4 *ingenium nobis ipsa puella facit*, *Am.* 3.12.16 *ingenium mouit sola Corinna meum*. *sollers* is a favourite word of O.'s (14x): see McKeown on *Am.* 1.8.87–8.

27–30 ~ Callim. fr. 67.1–4 Pf. 'Eros himself taught Acontius the art, when the youth was ablaze with love for the beautiful maiden Cydippe – for he was not cunning – that he might gain for all his life the name of a lawful husband' (Trypanis). Love's traditional role as teacher (Pfeiffer *ad loc.*) had been previously hijacked by O. *in propria persona* at *A.A.* 1.1–30; now he brings him on in Romanized guise as counsel learned in the law devising a watertight 'contract' for Cydippe to be bound by.

27 si quid tamen egimus 'if indeed I played any part in the matter', i.e. I can claim no credit, since all I have done is write out words put together by Love. The qualification is awkwardly placed and awkwardly expressed, but Palmer's alternative reading 'if I have gained anything' gives worse sense and dubious Latinity.

si ... tamen 'if indeed', 'if after all' (*OLD* s.v. *si* 8b); cf. 32.

a se (Nisbet *ap.* Thompson) gives pointed sense, taken up and varied by *dictatis ab eo* eqs. (29). Neither *a me* (P) nor *arte* (Gω) can be convincingly defended.

28 astrinxit: cf. 16.321–2 and n.

29 dictatis: cf. *CIL* IV 1928 = Diehl 1 *scribenti mi dictat Amor monstratque Cupido.* | *a peream, sine te si deus esse uelim,* Am. 2.1.38 *carmina purpureus quae mihi dictat Amor.* 'The word has a slight legalistic/bureaucratic flavour, appropriate to a *iuris consultus*' [T.], citing Suet. *Tib.* 22, *Nero* 32.

ab eo 'it was at his dictation', emphatic. The oblique cases of *is* are used sparingly by the poets (Axelson (1945) 70–3); of the twenty-three instances of *is* used in the oblique cases in *Her.*, fifteen are in 16–21 (Knox on 7.15). Virgil has *eo* 3x (Harrison on *Aen.* 10.101), Ovid 11x, of which five in his elegiacs: *Her.* 12.69, 20.29, 240 (see n.), *F.* 4.146 (adjectival), *Ex P.* 1.2.99 (Platnauer (1951) 117).

feci sponsalia 'I betrothed us'; *sponsalia* is a technical term, tendentiously (not to say anachronistically) abused by Acontius, for there had to be two parties to a betrothal (Berger s.v.). The only other occurrence of the word in poetry is at Juv. 6.25.

uerbis: the repetition from the previous verse may be purely inadvertent (cf. 16.150–2n.), but it can be defended for the emphasis: 'yes, it was in words dictated by him ...'.

30 The syntax is ambiguous: either (i) 'by consulting Love I became cunning in the law' (*uafer* + gen. on the analogy of e.g. *callidus, peritus*) or (ii) 'I became cunning through jurisconsult Love' (*consulto ... iuris* = *iuris consulto* (*OLD* s.v. *ius²* 2a), instrumental abl. or abl. abs.). Possibly, as Purser suggests, '*iuris* goes with both *consulto* and *vafer* [amphibole: Bell (1923) 293–303], Love being my Counsel learned in the law I became cunning therein.'

32 si tamen: 27n.

quod ames 'what a man loves', generalizing 2nd person subj. (*NLS* §119); cf. *A.A.* 1.741 *non tutum est, quod ames, laudare sodali.* Cf. 16.85n.

33–4 'See, another written message, but now it is a plea that I send; here is another "trick" for you to complain of'. There is always an unprincipled edge to Acontius' rhetoric.

35 si noceo ... nocebo ~ Callim. *A.P.* 12.118.6 (*HE* 1080) (a lover apologizing for his behaviour) εἰ τοῦτ' ἔστ' ἀδίκημ', ἀδικέω 'If this is a crime, then I'm a criminal' [T.] *noceo* = both 'harm' and *nocens sum* (*OLD* s.v. *nocens* 2). Acontius, however, is distinctly unapologetic. *quod amo* is ambiguous = 'by loving you', but also 'the one I love' (16.85n.).

36 teque, peti caueas tu licet, usque petam 'and I shall persist in wooing/harassing you, though you take precautions against being wooed/harassed'. The general sense of the line is clear, the details disputable. (i) *petere* is used ambiguously, no doubt deliberately so; what Acontius describes as pressing his suit (*OLD* s.v. 10b,c), Cydippe views as persecution (2). (ii) The construction of *caueo* + inf., except with the imperative (*Ex P.* 3.1.139–40 *caueque | spem festinando praecipitare meam*; unique in O.), is rare; in the poets at Prop. 2.17.17 *dominam mutare cauebo*. Since, however, *caueo* + acc. and inf. (active and passive) is attested in the jurists (*TLL* s.v. 638.27–50), it would suit the legalistic tone of Acontius' letter to read *te* (ς) rather than *tu* (PGω); but the anaphora *te ... te* is pointless and inelegant. (iii) *usque* (ς), picking up *sine fine*, is rhetorically stronger than *ipsa* (Gς: *ipse* Pω), but has the air of plausible tinkering. For *caueo* = 'provide for/against', 'stipulate', etc. in legal contexts see *OLD* s.v. 7.

37 per gladios etc. ~ 17.246. The contrast is specious; Acontius' original 'letter' has 'carried off' Cydippe (from her intended husband) no less forcibly than Paris or Theseus carried off Helen.

38 scripta ... caute littera 'a letter written with due care'; *caute* covers both the present letter, couched, as he would have her believe, in terms of studious moderation (cf. *A.A.* 2.167 *pauper amet caute*), and the message on the apple, written 'advisedly' [T.], as dictated by his attorney (cf. *A.A.* 1.457 *littera Cydippen pomo perlata fefellit*; for *littera* = 'writing' see *OLD* s.v. 5a). See 16.174n.

mihi goes with *crimen erit*, 'am I to be called a criminal?'

39 faciant possim: 16.263–4n.

nodos: the familiar image of the bonds of love (4.135–6 *illa coit firma generis iunctura catena | imposuit nodos cui Venus ipsa suos*; see N–H on Hor. *C.* 1.13.18) is given a legal flavour: cf. Juv. 8.50 *qui iuris nodos et legum aenigmata soluat* and Courtney *ad loc.*, Gell. 13.10.1 *ea ... praecipue scientia ad enodandos plerosque iuris laqueos utebatur*, Hor. *Sat.* 2.3.69–70 *adde Cicutae | nodosi tabulas, centum, mille adde catenas*. Cf. 45, 85–6nn.

40 nulla ... parte: 18.147n.

fides: the word connotes (*inter al.*) the ideas of a guarantee (*OLD* s.v. 2), credit (5), honour (6), sincerity (7), credibility and reliability (9); here the legal sense 'honest keeping of one's promises' (Berger s.v.) is uppermost. Acontius' wish exposes his own lack of *fides*, in its reciprocal sense of trust in another (10, 12b), and his distorted notion of the thing, which ought of its nature to be voluntary, *libera*.

41 cliuo sudamus in imo 'I haven't begun yet'; cf. *Rem.* 394 *principio cliui noster anhelat equus*, a proverbial phrase: Petron. 47.8 *nec adhuc sciebamus nos in medio, quod aiunt, cliuo laborare*, Otto s.v. *clivus*.

43 sit: sc. *quamuis*.

capi, captabere 'won ... wooed'; for *capto* in this sense cf. e.g. *Am.* 1.10.28 *non aries placitam munere captat ouem*, *A.A.* 1.351–2 *sed prius ancillam captandae* (Itali: *captatae* MSS) *nosse puellae | cura sit*, 403, *Met.* 11.768 and Bömer *ad loc.* The same play on words at Plaut. *Amph.* 821, Ter. *Hec.* 73 [T.].

44 exitus in dis est: an ironically pointed concession to conventional piety (Hom. *Il.* 17.514, 20.435 'but these things lie on the knees of the gods', Pindar *Ol.* 13.104–5, *al.*), for Acontius knows that Diana will exact fulfilment of the oath. For *in* cf. *Met.* 7.23–4 *uiuat an ille | occidat, in dis est* and Bömer *ad loc.*, *OLD* s.v. 26b.

sed capiere tamen 'but won you will be'; cf. Prop. 2.8.28 *tu moriere tamen.* Of the other seven Ovidian exx. of *tamen* ending a pentameter (Platnauer (1951) 41), four are in *A.A.* 1.

45 partem: sc. *retium*.

retia: the metaphor of 39–40 is given a new turn. For the lover as hunter, fowler or fisherman cf. *A.A.* 1.45–8 and Hollis *ad loc.*; here it is Love himself who spreads the snares. Cf. Lucret. 4.1146–8 *nam uitare, plagas in Amoris ne laciamur, | non ita difficile est quam captum retibus ipsis | exire et ualidos Veneris perrumpere nodos*, and for the earlier history and diffusion of the image Kenney (1970*d*) 386–8 = (1986) 257–9 (and p. 265). Cf. Hintermeier (1993) 111 n. 20.

46 'and he has spread more of them for you than you think'; *quae* is connective (*NLS* §230 (6)), *plura* predicative. The threat of force that follows is a stratagem only in the sense that it might be expected, in terms of Ovidian psychology, to appeal to Cydippe's subconscious longing to be raped: cf. *A.A.* 1.673–6 *uim licet appelles: grata est uis ista puellis; | quod iuuat, inuitae saepe dedisse uolunt. | quaecumque est Veneris subita uiolata rapina, | gaudet, et improbitas muneris instar habet.* It is certainly of a piece with O.'s characterization of Acontius.

47 artes ... arma: cf. *F.* 1.13 *Caesaris arma canant alii; nos Caesaris aras* etc.

48 in ... tui cupido ... sinu 'in those arms that long for you'; *sinu* = both 'embrace' and 'heart' (*OLD* s.v. 2b, 5).

ferere 'carry off' = *auferere* (*OLD* s.v. 35a).

49 non (*is*) **sum qui** 'I am not the kind of man who ...', generic-consecutive subj. (*NLS* §§157 (2), 230 (3)).

reprehendere: as most did; cf. Introd. pp. 5–6, 19. Propertius (2.3.35–8) and O. himself (*A.A.* 3.253–4) had allowed that Paris had good reason to do what he did; here self-reference, an authorial glance back at the first pair of the double epistles, may be suspected. 'The situations of Acontius and Paris are very similar: both attempt to displace a rival who has a better legal claim to the beloved, and both have divine support – Artemis and Aphrodite respectively' [T.]. See Introd. p. 19.

50 'and (I cannot blame) him who, to be a husband, played the man', exploiting two if not three senses of *uir* (*OLD* s.v. 1c, 2a, 3). Cf. *Met.* 9.722–3 *coniugium pactaeque exspectat tempora taedae, | quemque uirum putat esse, uirum fore credit Ianthe, A.A.* 1.524 *si quis male uir quaerit habere uirum.*

uir posset ut esse ~ Callim. fr. 67.3–4 Pf. (cit. 27–30n.).

51 nos quoque – : sc. I am willing to brave the consequences, be they what they may, of following Paris' example. *quoque* implies a parallelism with Paris that is, critically considered, tenuous. Paris' death was in a sense a requital for the rape of Helen and its aftermath (Soph. *Phil.* 1425–7), but it did not happen until he had possessed her for ten years; Acontius is boasting that he is prepared to perish in the attempt. Again, he appears to be echoing Callimachus: Aristaen. 1.10.20–1 'Thus wounded (by Eros) you straightway, beautiful Acontius, decided that the choice lay between marriage or death'. Cf. 167, 16.275–6, 18.195–6nn.

mors: for the death penalty for rape or abduction in Greek, Roman and declamatory law see Bonner (1949) 89–91.

52 ut 'though'.

53 nata esses 'You should have been born'; Watt's correction (Watt (1995) 94) solves the textual difficulty elegantly and economically; for the predicative expression cf. *Am.* 2.14.19 *cum posses nasci formosa*. Accepting MS *aut esses* entails inferring an unexpressed alternative: either (i) '(Either I must be allowed to assert my claim) or you should be less beautiful'; or (ii) 'Either you should be less beautiful

COMMENTARY: 20.55–57   191

(or you should not be surprised at being wooed so shamelessly)' [T.]. For (i) *aut* = 'otherwise', cf. 10.112, 12.13, 16.313, *Am.* 2.16.17 (cit. below); the ellipse is harsh but *aut* is hardly (*pace* Heyworth (1984) 105) 'meaningless'. (ii) can hardly be defended as the text stands; possibly a couplet which also began with *aut* has been lost after 54 through parablepsy. For the jussive/optative plpf. subj. cf. e.g. 10.77 *me quoque, qua fratrem, mactasses, improbe, claua, Am.* 2.16.17 *aut iuuenum comites iussissent ire puellas* ... (*NLS* §111).

peterere modeste '(in that case) you would be wooed less high-handedly'; *nata ... minus* functions as the protasis to a conditional clause (K–S II 166, H–S 657, Bömer on *Met.* 9.490). Cf. 67n.

modeste: in O. only here and at *F.* 2.607, *Ex P.* 1.2.65 (cf. *E.S.* 99 *modestius*), otherwise before the Silver Age only in comedy and satire (ix: Hor. *Sat.* 1.2.50). See 16.174n.

55–60 In Callimachus the lovers were equally matched in beauty, 'both beautiful stars of the islands' (fr. 67.8 Pf.); cf. Aristaen. 1.10.3–9, though there as elsewhere he has evidently embroidered his model (55–6, 59nn.). This catalogue of the charms of the beloved is characteristic of Latin elegy, and of O. in particular: *Am.* 1.5.19–22 and McKeown *ad loc., A.A.* 1.621–2 *nec faciem nec te pigeat laudare capillos* | *et teretes digitos exiguumque pedem, Met.* 1.497–502, *F.* 2.763–4, and for a general conspectus see Kost on Musaeus 63–6.

55–6 Cf. e.g. *Am.* 2.16.44 *oculos, sidera nostra, tuos, Met.* 1.498–9 *igne micantes* | *sideribus similes oculos,* 3.420 and Bömer *ad loc.,* Prop. 2.3.14 *oculi geminae, sidera nostra, faces.* The original image of the lovers themselves as stars (previous n.) has evidently been transposed, so to say, into the Latin elegiac mode. In Callimachus the single reference to eyes that survives (fr. 67.21 Pf. ὄθμασιν) probably pertains to Acontius, not Cydippe (Pfeiffer *ad loc.*).

56 flammae causa ... meae: cf. e.g. Prop. 1.1.1 *Cynthia prima suis miserum me cepit ocellis* and Fedeli *ad loc., Her.* 12.36 *abstulerunt oculi lumina nostra tui, Am.* 3.11.48 *tuos oculos, qui rapuere meos*; but the idea is familiar from the love poetry of all ages. Aristaenetus is lyrical: 'In her eyes danced not the three Graces of whom Hesiod tells, but a hundred' (1.10.5–7). This too may be his own embroidery, but cf. Musaeus 63–5 and Kost *ad loc.* with Strato, *A.P.* 12.181, suggesting an older common source.

57 flaui ... eburnea: conventional traits; fair-skinned blondes were generally admired, no doubt for their rarity. See the comprehensive n. of Pease on Virg. *Aen.* 4.590.

59 decor et uultus 'the beauty of your face', hendiadys. Cf. Callim. fr. 67.13 Pf. 'a face resembling dawn'.

sine rusticitate pudentes: seemingly, if Aristaenetus may be trusted, another trait transferred from Callimachus' description of Acontius: 'his eyes were bright, as befitted his beauty, but stern (φοβεροί), as befitted his sobriety (ὡς σώφρονες)' (1.10.7–8). On *rusticitas* as a pejorative term on the lips of a lover cf. 16.222n.; on quadrisyllabic nouns in this *sedes* cf. 16.52n.

60 Thetidi (possessive dat.) is Heinsius' correction of MS *Thetidis*; the verse can well do with one less sibilant (and cf. 132n.). Nice feet, like nice hands, were admired in gods as well as human beings: ἀργυρόπεζα 'silver-footed' is Thetis' stock epithet (11x) in the Iliad. The recurrence of the comparison in Rufinus (*A.P.* 5.48.4, 94.2 = 19.4, 35.2 Page) suggests a lost Hellenistic original [T.].

quales uix rear 'such as I should scarcely think', generic subj.

61 cetera etc.: cf. *Am.* 3.2.35–6 *suspicor ex istis et cetera posse placere | quae bene sub tenui condita ueste latent*, *Met.* 1.502 *si qua latent, meliora putat*, 6.491–2 *repetens faciem motusque manusque, | qualia uult fingit, quae nondum uidit*. This, of course, is no way to address a respectable girl [T.].

62 opus: he appraises her as if she were a work of art (*OLD* s.v. 9b); cf. *Am.* 1.7.51–2 *astitit illa amens albo et sine sanguine uultu, | caeduntur Pariis qualia saxa iugis* eqs., *Met.* 4.673–5 (Andromeda) *nisi quod leuis aura capillos | mouerat et tepido manabant lumina fletu, | marmoreum ratus esset opus*, Kenney on Apul. *Met.* 4.32.2, 5.22.5–7. So Heliodorus describes Chariclea on her first appearance in his novel (1.2.2 and Maillon *ad loc.*). Cf. McKeown on *Am.* 1.5.19–22.

63–4 i.e. *non est mirabile si, hac forma compulsus, pignus uolui* eqs. This ex. of Ovidian hyperbaton was overlooked by Housman (16.177n.).

64 pignus ... uocis ... tuae 'a pledge (in the shape) of your words (*OLD* s.v. *uox* 7a)', gen. of definition or identity. Cydippe rightly insists that it was only her voice, not her mind, that swore (21.141–4). Her words cannot properly be called a *pignus*, which is a form of contract (Berger s.v.). Again, Acontius relies on legalistic bluff.

66–7 'Let it be (allowed) that it is by my wiles that you have been won; I shall put up with the odium so long as by doing so I reap the

COMMENTARY: 20.68-73   193

reward that it (the *inuidia*) has earned'. *passo ... dentur*, sc. *modo* (cf. 53n.). *sua*, like *suus* (68) = 'appropriate', 'due' (*OLD* s.v. B12); cf. 12.133 *o iusto desunt sua uerba dolori*.

puella is ironic, 'poor little thing'; cf. 21.115–16n.

patiar, passo: O. is fond of this form of polyptoton (21.11n.) whether in a subordinating construction, as here or at 73, *Am.* 1.2.52 (McKeown *ad loc.*); or with copula, as in the famous verse *F.* 3.21 *Mars uidet hanc uisamque cupit potiturque cupita*; or in asyndeton, as at *Am.* 2.11.22 ... *credite: credenti nulla procella nocet*, *Met.* 6.579–80 ... *gestu rogat, illa rogata | pertulit ad Procnen*. Cf. H–S 812–13, Bömer on *Met.* 6.656 (uncritical).

68 The declamatory logic – that something must be allowed to a criminal if his crime is sufficiently heinous – is psychologically apt. Acontius, as O. presents him, is obsessive to the verge of insanity.

69 Hesionen Telamon ... cepit: in the standard version of the story Telamon received Hesione from Hercules as a reward for his help in storming Troy, of which her father Laomedon was king (Apollod. *Bibl.* 2.6.4.1–4): cf. *Met.* 11.216–17 *nec pars militiae Telamon sine honore recessit | Hesioneque data potitur*. Unless O. is following another (lost) version, the example is less clearly relevant to Acontius' case than that of Achilles.

Briseida cepit Achilles: at the sack of Lyrnessus (Hom. *Il.* 2.689–91). In *Her.* 3 O. had portrayed her as deeply in love with her captor; cf. Hom. *Il.* 19.298–9 and Edwards *ad loc.*, Prop. 2.20.1 *quid fles abducta grauius Briseide?*, N–H on Hor. *C.* 2.4.3.

70 nempe is heavily (and speciously) logical, 'and of course'. O. is fonder of the word (35x) than the other Augustans (McKeown on *Am.* 1.9.25–6, Knox on 2.36), and Acontius has a particular penchant for it (94n., 191).

uictorem ... uirum 'her conquering hero'; for adjectival *uictor* see *OLD* s.v. 3, H–S 157–8.

secuta: sc. *est*. In fact of course they had no choice.

71–2 irata licebit, irata liceat: the heavy-handed anaphora underlines her helplessness and Acontius' excitement at the prospect of allaying her indignation in bed: cf. *A.A.* 2.459–62 *oscula da flenti, Veneris da gaudia flenti: | tum pete concubitus foedera: mitis erit*. On *licebit* see 21n.

73 facimus, factam: 67n.

74 placandi ... tui: cf. Plaut. *Truc.* 370 (to a woman) *tui uidendi copia est.* The construction is otherwise, strictly speaking, unparalleled (Ter. *Hec.* 372 (also to a woman) *eius uidendi cupidus* is explained as based on false analogy; cf. *Phorm.* 880, cit. below); the usual explanation is that the genitive forms of the personal pronouns *mei, tui,* etc. are neuters from *meum, tuum,* etc., so grammatical gender overrides sex. In that case this gerundival construction must be distinguished from the (commoner but still archaic) gerundal construction with nouns, of the type of Plaut. *Capt.* 1008 *lucis ... tuendi copiam* (see Lindsay *ad loc.*), Enn. *Scaen.* 210 J. *nauis incohandi exordium,* Lucret. 5.1225 *poenarum ... soluendi tempus* (see Munro *ad loc.*). For the various explanations offered see Roby lxviiif., Bennett I (1910) 448, Bell (1923) 92–3 (Prop. 3.21.3 a false example), K–S I 744–6, H–S 374–5, *NLS* §206 n. (iii). Heinsius pronounced *placandae* a solecism – 'Latine vix dicitur'; cf. however Ter. *Phorm.* 880 *potestatem eius adhibendae* (emended away by Bentley) and Ov. *Her.* 11.106 *amissae memores sed tamen este mei,* styled 'constructio ad sensum' in Housman's unpublished lecture notes (cf. Madvig on Cic. *Fin.* 1.60). As Roby lxviii points out, these constructions are found principally with *copia* and nouns of similar meaning; *placandi* might therefore still have sounded acceptable to the ears even of an Augustan reader as set phraseology.

modo: 18.51n.

75–90 An abrupt switch from the macho to the masochistic mode of elegiac love and to the familiar theme of the *seruitium amoris,* the enslavement of the lover to his mistress: see Copley (1947), Lyne (1979), Murgatroyd on Tib. 1.5.5–6. In O. cf. *Am.* 1.7.63–6 *at tu ne dubita (minuet uindicta dolorem) | protinus in uultus unguibus ire meos; | nec nostris oculis nec nostris parce capillis: | quamlibet infirmas adiuuat ira manus, A.A.* 2.451–4 *ille ego sim, cuius laniet furiosa capillos; | ille ego sim, teneras cui petat ungue genas; | quem uideat lacrimans, quem toruis spectet ocellis, | quo sine non possit uiuere, posse uelit.*

75 ante tuos ... uultus 'in your sight'.

flentem: sc. *me;* for the construction of *licet* with acc. + inf. see *OLD* s.v. 1b.

76 suis 'that belong with them', sc. the *uerba;* cf. 66–7n. Palmer proposed *sua,* comparing 14.67 *lacrimae sua uerba sequuntur,* but *suus* frequently connotes a mutual relationship (Housman, *CP* 502–3, 936–7). *meis* (ς) is possible, but lacks point. Cf. 18.172n.

78 ad tua crura 'to your knees', traditionally clasped by suppliants: 4.153–4 *uicta precor genibusque tuis regalia tendo | bracchia*, Met. 9.216–17 *dicentem genibusque manus adhibere parantem | corripit Alcides* and Bömer *ad loc.*, Kirk on Hom. *Il.* 1.512–13.

79 tua iura: 16.321–2n.

uoca: sc. *in ius* (*OLD* s.v. 4c, Berger s.v. *In ius vocatio*).

cur arguor absens?: an absent party usually lost his case by default (Berger s.v. *Absens, absentia*); Acontius is now protesting that he is being deprived of his legal rights. Cf. 91–2.

80 ~ 3. 154 *domini iure uenire iube*, sc. *me* (16.118n.) Like a slave, the elegiac lover must instantly obey the peremptory summons of his mistress: *A.A.* 2.225–30, esp. 228 *tum quoque pro seruo, si uocat illa, ueni.*

81–2 Cf. Prop. 3.8.5–6 *tu uero nostros audax inuade capillos | et mea formosis unguibus ora nota*, *Am.* 1.7.63–6, *A.A.* 451–2 (cit. 75–90n.).

83 fortasse must be taken with the *ne*-clause (hyperbaton).

83–4 timebo etc.: a perversion of the conventional wish to spare the beloved pain (Virg. *Ecl.* 10.48–9, Tib. 1.1.67–8) – mawkish, but again psychologically plausible; the dividing line between sado-masochism and drooling sentimentality is thin.

84 ista 'your' (*OLD* s.v. 1a).

85–6 'No need, however, of physical chains; my love for you will bind me.' Images of chaining and servile punishment (a Tibullan rather than an Ovidian theme: Murgatroyd on Tib. 1.5.5–6) shade into that, already encountered, of the (intangible) bonds of love. For *uinctus* cf. *Rem.* 529–30 *mollior es neque abire potes uinctusque teneris | et tua saeuus Amor sub pede colla premit*, *F.* 4.223–4 *Attis | turrigeram casto uinxit amore deam*, Tib. 1.1.55 *me retinent uinctum formosae uincla puellae*, 1.9.79 *tum flebis cum me uinctum puer alter habebit* ... , [Tib.] 3.11.13–14 *uel seruiat aeque | uinctus uterque tibi uel mea uincla leua*, 3.19.21–3 *tuus usque manebo, | nec fugiam notae seruitium dominae, | sed Veneris sanctae considam uinctus ad aras* (*OLD* s.v. *uincio* inadequate), 212n.

87 bene 'thoroughly' (*OLD* s.v. 13a).

uolet sustains the personification of *ira* in *se ... satiauerit*; *uoles* (Heinsius, rec. Goold) is no improvement.

88 ~ 19. 4 *non patienter amo* and n.

89 ferre: sc. *me. ferri* (Ruhnken) neatly eliminates the ellipse, but the omission of personal pronouns in o.o. (cf. e.g. 16.261n.) is too common to be reckoned an anomaly. Had Juvenal read this epistle? cf. 5.170–1 *omnia ferre | si potes, et debes.*

91 reus ... agor: more legal language (cf. 79n.); cf. *Am.* 1.7.22

egit me lacrimis ore silente reum and McKeown *ad loc.*, *OLD* s.v. *reus* 3d, e.

92 non ullo ... tuente 'since I have no defence counsel' (*OLD* s.v. *tueor* 4b).

perit 'is lost'; *pereo*, as often, functions as the passive of *perdo*. For *perdo causam, litem*, etc. see *OLD* s.v. 5.

93 The sense required by the context must be something like 'granted that what I wrote was a dirty trick (*iniuria*) ...'. *hoc* cannot be construed with *scriptum ... nostrum*, which must refer to the message on the apple, not to the letter Cydippe is now reading. None of the corrections proposed merits printing, even as a *pis aller*. Heinsius thought the couplet spurious, but line 94 is faultless, and without it the transition from 92 to 95 would be very abrupt.

94 nempe 'yet to be sure' (*OLD* s.v. 1d); cf. 7on. The word qualifies *habes*, not *queraris* (Housman, *CP* 417); it occurs in the pentameter in this *sedes* also at *Am.* 2.6.20, *A.A.* 2.616, *Her.* 9.70, *Tr.* 2.260.

95 falli sophistically exploits the different senses 'break an oath' (*OLD* s.v. 5c) and 'elude' (7a). It is not Acontius who has been deceived but the unfortunate Cydippe (97 *decepta*!), and it is the height of impudence to represent himself and the goddess as equally aggrieved.

quoque qualifies *Delia*; see Housman on Lucan 9.463, Shackleton Bailey (1956) 175–6, *OLD* s.v. headn.

Delia: Diana, born and especially worshipped (with her brother) on Delos. Delia in this sense was a Virgilian innovation: Clausen on *Ecl.* 7.29, Bömer on *Met.* 1.454.

95–6 non uis 'refuse' (*OLD* s.v. *nolo* 1b).

97 decepta 'on being duped', causal.

rubebas: 6n.

98 memori condidit aure 'heard and remembered'.

99 omina 'unpleasant possibilities' (*OLD* s.v. 2b), i.e. the sort of thing suggested by the stories shortly to be alluded to [T.]. Mentioning or envisaging misfortune is liable to make it happen.

re careant 'lack realization', not come to pass. For *res* = 'reality' see *OLD* s.v. 6, but this phrase is unparalleled.

nihil est uiolentius etc.: Aristaen. 1.10.65–7 'They say that this goddess is dreadfully provoked by all transgressions, oath-breaking most particularly'. Cf. Callim. *H.* 3 (Diana).122–35 and Bornmann *ad loc.*, fr. 96 and Dieg., Pfeiffer *ad loc.*, the latter certainly a case of *laesum numen*, a man who boasted of being a better hunter than the goddess.

100 numina: poetic pl., as at e.g. *Am.* 1.8.86 *commodat in lusus numina surda Venus*, 2.8.18, *Met.* 3.290–1, *al.*

quod nolim: like *re careant*, a deprecating gesture.

101–3 testis ... testis: for the anaphora cf. 17.193, Tib. 1.7.9–12.

101–2 'Witness the Calydonian boar, savage, but not so savage as Althaea was found to be towards her son' = *ut illo saeuior in natum (esse) reperta sit parens*; the word-order throws *natum* and *parens* into relief. For the limiting or stipulative construction with *sic ... ut* cf. 17.165n. Diana sent a gigantic boar to ravage Calydon in return for a slight put upon her by its king Oeneus. In a quarrel over the disposal of the boar's hide Althaea's son Meleager killed her brothers and was killed by her in revenge (*Met.* 8.273–97, 420–525). Mention of the boar is entirely apt, that of the sequel irrelevant to Acontius' argument; more 'exuberans abundantia' (16.23n.), this time in the form of mythological embroidery. Perhaps a sly self-reference, 'for further details see the *Metamorphoses*'? It does not help to excise the couplet (Heinsius): without it *et* in 103 lacks a reference, and Cydippe in her reply alludes to Oeneus (21.179).

Calydonis aper: one would expect *aper Calydonius* vel sim.: cf. e.g. Callim. *H.* 3 (Diana).218–19 Καλυδωνίου ... κάπροιο, *Met.* 8.324 *Calydonius heros, al.* Cf. also however Callim. fr. 621 Pf. τέρας Καλυδῶνος [T.]. On the general preference in Latin for the possessive adj. over the identifying gen. see Löfstedt 1 (1942) 107–24, Kenney (1993) 459–60.

103–4 'Witness Actaeon, once believed to be a wild beast by those with whom he had previously killed wild beasts.' Actaeon, having inadvertently surprised Diana bathing, was turned into a stag and torn to pieces by his own hounds (Callim. *H.* 5 (Bath of Pallas).107–18, *Met.* 3.138–252).

105 superba parens: Niobe boasted of having more children than Leto (Latona), mother of Apollo and Diana. They killed her children, and she was turned to stone (Hom. *Il.* 24.602–17, *Met.* 6.146–312).

saxo per corpus oborto (= *Met.* 10.67), a vivid and specifically

Ovidian usage of *oborior* (*OLD* s.v. 1c); the stone 'rises up' to occupy (not merely 'cover', *OLD*) the body.

106 nunc quoque: an aetiological formula of which O. is fond: *Am.* 3.13.21 *nunc quoque per pueros iaculis incessitur index*, *A.A.* 1.133–4 *scilicet ex illo sollemni more theatra* | *nunc quoque formosis insidiosa manent*, *F.* 1.113, 388, *al.* (15x), *Met.* 1.235, 2.706 and Bömer *ad loc., al.*, Myers (1994) 66 and n. 22; characteristically varied in O.'s handling of the legend in *Met.* 6.312 *lacrimas etiam nunc marmora manant*. So Homer on Niobe: *Il.* 24.614–17 νῦν δέ που ἐν πέτρῃσιν κτλ. 'And now somewhere among the rocks ... though a stone, she broods on her troubles'; cf. e.g. A.R. 1.1061–2, 2.524–7.

Mygdonia: a learned epithet for 'Phrygian' (N–H on Hor. *C.* 2.12.22, Bömer on *Met.* 2.247), probably by synecdoche (16.21n.); the Mygdones were a people of N.W. Asia Minor. The rock traditionally identified with Niobe was on Mt Sipylus: 'Niobe from close up is a rock and a stream, and nothing like a woman either grieving or otherwise; but if you go further off you seem to see a woman downcast and in tears' (Pausanias 1.21.5, tr. Levi). Cf. Bömer on *Met.* 6.146–312 (pp. 50–2).

extat '(is still) to be seen' (*OLD* s.v. 3a), a reading found by Burman in two MSS and placed by him in the text, where it remained until it was removed by Merkel. In O.'s account she was sitting down when the metamorphosis occurred (*Met.* 6.301–2), and *exto* is *vox propria* in aetiological contexts: *Met.* 13.569–70 *locus extat et ex re* | *nomen habet*, 14.73 *scopulum qui nunc quoque* [N.B.] *saxeus extat*. *astat* (MSS) can however be defended as virtually equivalent to *stat* (*Met.* 3.78 and Bömer *ad loc.*), which can = simply 'be situated' (*OLD* s.v. 13a); cf. Sen. *Ag.* 376–7 Zw. (394–5 Tarrant) *stat nunc Sipyli uertice summo flebile saxum.*

107 Cydippe: only now named (1n.).

108 causa ... mea 'for my own sake', a well-attested idiom (*OLD* s.v. 18a), found however in O., who uses *causa* over 300x, only here and restored by conjecture at 198 (see n.).

109–10 ~ Callim. fr. 75.10–12 'In the morning the oxen were to tear their hearts seeing before them reflected in the [lustral] water the sharp blade [i.e. they were destined for the pre-nuptial sacrifice]. But in the afternoon an evil pallor came upon her; the disease seized her ...', 16–19 'A second time the couches were spread; a second time the maiden was sick for seven months with a quartan fever. A third time they thought of marriage; a third time again a deadly chill settled on Cydippe' (Trypanis), Aristaen. 1.10.81–8.

109 est ... est: the anaphora, accentuated by the verse ictus, is pointless and displeasing. Palmer's *dicendum tamen. hoc, hoc est ...* eliminates the anomaly and satisfyingly raises the emotional temperature; the corruption is easily explained by the loss of one *hoc* through haplography followed by interpolatory patching, a classic sequence. However it is open to serious objection on metrical grounds, since O. does not favour a sense-pause after a 2nd-foot diaeresis (Ott (1974) 49).

hoc est ... quod 'this is why'; cf. *Met.* 12.607–8 *quod Priamus gaudere senex post Hectora posset | hoc erat* and Bömer *ad loc.*, Virg. *Aen.* 2.664–5 *hoc erat, alma parens, quod me per tela, per ignes | eripis*, Prop. 2.24.17 *hoc erat in primis quod me gaudere iubebas?*, Shackleton Bailey (1956) 112–13.

110 ipso nubendi tempore ~ Lucret. 1.98 *nubendi tempore in ipso*, an ironical echo of the sacrifice of Iphigenia, another victim of Artemis.

saepe: three times (21.157–8, Callim. Aristaen. *locc. cit.* 109–10n.). Cf. 21.161–2 and n.

111 consulit ipsa tibi 'she is going out of her way to protect your interests' (*OLD* s.v. *ipse* 7). Even for Acontius it is a bit rich to tell Cydippe, purporting to be speaking for Diana, that what she is going through is all for her own good.

neu = *et, ne* (16.71n.).

112 'and she wishes you to be made well (*OLD* s.v. *saluus* 3) while keeping faith (7b)', i.e. without breaking your oath; cf. *Ex P.* 1.2.146 *non potes hanc salua dissimulare fide.*

113 existere perfida 'to prove yourself forsworn' (*OLD* s.v. *exsisto* 2b). Acontius chooses his words to suggest that she is wilfully perjuring herself.

115 parce mouere 'forbear to provoke'.

116 si patiare 'if you would allow (her to be)'; *fieri ... potest* is equivalent to *fiat* (cf. 16.162n.).

117 corrumpere 'allow to be wasted', an ex. of the idiom by which Latin says 'do' for 'allow to be done' (Kenney on Lucret. 3.490 and *Addenda* (p. 250)). Cf. 21.93–4n.

118 'your beauty must be kept intact for me to enjoy.'

fruenda: passive gerundive, as usual with verbs that take an instrumental abl. (*NLS* §207 (3) *Note*, K–S I 733). Cf. *A.A.* 1.433 *multa rogant utenda dari*.

119 ad nostra incendia nati 'born to set me ablaze'; cf. 16.123, *A.A.* 2.301 *astiterit tunicata: 'moues incendia' clama*. For *natus* + *ad/in* = 'made/meant for' see *OLD* s.v. *nascor* 14, N–H on Hor. *C.* 1.27.1.

120 subest 'waits below' (*OLD* s.v. *subsum* 2a); the blush is, so to say, on call.

lenis ... rubor 'gentle blush' (Showerman–Goold), 'soft red hue' (Palmer). For this use of *lenis* in the context of colour no close parallels are forthcoming (*TLL* s.v. 1144.77ff.). *leuis* is reported in two MSS (and probably awaits detection in others; in some scripts the two words are very difficult to distinguish), and was printed by Palmer in his text. It is frequently used of fine skin (*OLD* s.v.² 2), but the sense and the balanced phrasing require a word that characterizes *rubor* itself. The red–white contrast was an obligatory feature of such descriptions: *Am.* 3.3.5–6 *candida, candorem roseo suffusa rubore | ante fuit: niueo lucet in ore rubor*, *Met.* 3.423 *in niueo mixtum candore ruborem* and Bömer *ad loc.* and on 6.46–7, Booth on *Am.* 2.5.35–42, Kost on Musaeus 58–9.

121 hostibus etc.: cf. 16.219n. The chief enemy, hinted at in *si quis*, is Cydippe's official fiancé, shortly to be apostrophized.

si quis '(for) anybody who ...' = *cuiuis qui*.

repugnat: see 17.137n.

122 inualida te 'when you are ill'.

123 ex aequo: 16.87n.

uel te nubente uel aegra 'whether you are getting married or lying ill'. None of the weddings actually comes off; *nubente* is in effect conative present.

124 quid = *utrum* (19.174n.).

125–6 ~ Callim. fr. 74 Pf. (Acontius speaking) 'shameless I, why have I imposed upon you this fear?' (Trypanis), Aristaen. 1.10.64–5 'Unlucky that I am, why have I brought this fear upon you?' In Callimachus the emotional spotlight was focussed throughout on Acontius himself: Introd. p. 16.

125 maceror 'I am distressed'. The word originally meant 'soak' or 'steep', hence 'weaken'. It is used of the effects of love by Horace (*C.* 1.13.8 and N–H, West *ad loc.*, *Epod.* 14.16), only here by O.

quod sim: subj. as referring to what he is thinking (cf. 19.45n.).

126 puto must belong to the *quod*-clause (so, rightly, Showerman–Goold), but (i) it is otiose (ii) it should idiomatically be *putem* (on the attraction of verbs of saying and thinking into the subj. in o.o. see *NLS* §242 n. (ii), H–S 548, Löfstedt II (1956) 129 n. 2). *pudet* (though shame is not one of his most prominent characteristics) would give much more pointed sense: for the construction with acc. + inf. and omission of *me* cf. *Met.* 1.758–9 *pudet haec opprobria nobis | et dici potuisse et non potuisse refelli*, *Ex P.* 4.2.3–4 *cuius adhuc nomen nostros tacuisse libellos | ... pudet*.

127–8 'and I pray that her perjury may fall on my head'; elsewhere in O. *quaeso* is parenthetic, as at 16.296, where the weaker sense 'please' is clearly required. The choice is between accepting the anomaly, with or without the addition of *ut* (*in caput ut* Ehwald; cf. *OLD* s.v. *quaeso* 2b) or removing it by emendation. Hollis (1989) ingeniously proposed '*in'que 'caput nostrum dominae periuria' clamo | 'eueniant; poena tuta sit illa mea'*; which also eliminates what some have seen as an awkward change of person from 2nd to 3rd (125–6/127–8) and back (127–8/129–30) [T.], and introduces a specifically Ovidian idiom in the treatment of *-que* (17.159n.).

in ... caput nostrum ... periuria ... eueniant: the expression is unusual: (i) with *euenio* = 'happen to' the common construction is with dat. (16.219n., *OLD* s.v. 3b); with *in* + acc. at Cic. *Fam.* 2.10 (86).1 (the only other classical ex.: Shackleton Bailey *ad loc.*). (ii) it is properly the penalty and not the offence that should be invoked.

128 poena ... mea 'through my punishment', instrumental abl.

129 quid agas 'how you are' (*OLD* s.v. 21f); cf. 21.19–20n.

ad 'near'.

130 'I furtively prowl about in my anguish'; cf. 15, 21.51–2nn., Introd. p. 17. By bringing Acontius to Naxos O. transforms him into a familiar figure of Roman elegy, the *exclusus amator*, jealously watching the comings and goings of his rival and torturing himself with visions of what is happening inside; cf. e.g. *Am.* 1.4.61–70, 3.11.11–16.

huc illuc ... eo: cf. *Am.* 3.8.7–8 *cum bene laudauit* (sc. his poetry), *laudato ianua clausa est: | turpiter huc illuc ingeniosus eo.*

dissimulanter: a rare adverb, found in O. only here and at *A.A.* 1.488, then in poetry only in Ausonius; cf. 16.174n.

131 subsequor ancillam: 16.259n.

famulumue (Heinsius) for *-que* (MSS); though *-que* is not infrequently disjunctive in sense (Fordyce on Catull. 45.6), *-ue* is here more natural.

132 cibi: 'the small and frequent nourishments of a rich [*sic*: *lege* sick [T.]] person, and by parity of reasoning *somni* the short sleeps taken during the day as well as in the night' (Palmer). This is overly ingenious: *somnus* is used indifferently in sing. and pl. (*OLD* s.v. 1a), and O. elsewhere uses *cibus* in the pl. without distinction of sense, e.g. *Am.* 1.4.34, 2.6.30, *A.A.* 3.755, *Her.* 11.28, *al.* Other things being equal he avoids ending the first half of a pentameter with a syllable that is long 'by position' as would be the case with *somnus quid* (here accentuated by rhyme) (Hilberg (1894) 447).

profuerint ... quid tibi 'what good they have done you', internal-cognate acc.

133–4 At *A.A.* 2.319–36 O. recommends the lover to take advantage of his mistress's illness: *tunc amor et pietas tua sit manifesta puellae; | tum sere quod plena postmodo falce metas* (321–2). Acontius' fantasy is illogical: if he were her betrothed she would not be ill.

133 medicorum iussa ministro 'give you your medicine'; *iussa* = 'prescriptions'.

134 effingo: cf. 139. The word (nowhere else in O.) must mean 'stroke', 'caress', a sense paralleled only at *Cons. Liv.* 138 *effingoque manus oraque ad ora fero?*, an obvious imitation. Cf. *F.* 5. 409 *saepe manus aegras manibus fingebat amicis.*

insideo ... toro 'sit on the bed', the natural thing in the circumstances and not (*pace* Dr Thompson) a sign of Acontius' shamelessness, since *assidet* at 137 does not necessarily imply sitting by *the bed* (see n.). Edd. generally read *assideo* (Heinsius from an unspecified 'Regius') as *vox propria* of attendance at a sickbed (137), but the corruption of this obvious word to the unexpected *insideo* (only here in O.) seems unlikely.

136 quem minime uellem 'the last person I should want' (defining relative), i.e. her official fiancé.

COMMENTARY: 20.137–143

137 assidet aegrae: the dat. is usual of the invalid (*OLD* s.v. *assideo* 1c); the words need not imply that he, unlike Acontius, is imagined as keeping a respectful distance (134n.). Cf. 141.

138 cum superisque: this placing of *-que*, here metrically convenient, is in fact standard, though not invariable, (prose) usage in such phrases (K–S 1 583); cf. 21.19–20n. The sentiment recalls the rebuke delivered by a Vice-Chancellor of the University of Cambridge (Dr G. E. Corrie) to the Eastern Counties Railway in 1851, that their plans to run Sunday excursions were 'as distasteful to the authorities of the University as they must be offensive to Almighty God'.

139 i.e. while feeling her pulse; cf. *Met.* 10.289 *saliunt temptatae pollice uenae*, Virg. *G.* 3.460 *salientem sanguine uenam. salientem* = 'throbbing', *pollice* = *digitis* (17.266n.).

140 per causam: sc. *illam* 'on that pretext'. The normal (prose) construction is with gen. (*OLD* s.v. 5a) or pronominal adj.; cf. Livy 1.49.5 *perque eam causam occidere ... poterat* eqs. In poetry the phrase (always absolute) only here and at *Tr.* 2.451–2 *saepe, uelut gemmam dominae signumue probaret, | per causam meminit se tetigisse manum* < Tib. 1.6.25–6 (see Owen, Murgatroyd *ad locc.*).

141 forsitan: probably to be taken ἀπὸ κοινοῦ with both verbs; *oscula* hardly mark an advance in audacity.

142 merces ... ista 'that reward of yours'; he turns to apostrophize his rival.

plenior 'more generous'; cf. *Ex P.* 1.8.23 *quid enim tibi plenius optem?* O. is fond of *plenus* (120x).

suo 'that earned it' (66–7n.).

143–4 Acontius launches into an extravagant legalistic recital of his claims. Cydippe is first figured as real property, an estate, the produce of which the rival is trying to intercept. See, for a discussion of the legalities apparently alluded to, Hollis (1994), who suggests that Acontius is denying entitlement to usufruct with access.

praecerpere: sc. before the rightful owner, Acontius.

sepem: this is Heinsius' correction of MS *spes/spem*, printed with some hesitation. *spes* is acceptable in itself, referring both to *messes* (*Met.* 15.113 *spem ... anni*, Virg. *G.* 1.224 *anni spem*) and to the hopes of a lover; but the pl. is unexpected, and the repeated *quis* suggests that the legal/agricultural imagery ought to be sustained in the pentameter. For *sepem* cf. *A.A.* 3.562 *cingenda est altis sepibus ista seges* (sc. the novice lover). Palmer commented 'I should rather have expected *per sepem*; for a man has a right to go *up to, as far as*, another man's boundary'; however for *ad* = 'up to and into' cf. *OLD* s.v. 1a, 20.10 *ad ... manus*, and such phrases as *ad urbes* (12.127, 16.33, 19.169), *ad aures* (11.71, 12.137, 18.79). In the light of this objection, Hollis (1994) emends to *saeptum* (the pl. perhaps more likely in a poet?); however, *saepta* are properly paddocks for animals rather than cornfields, to which his argument requires the reference to be. Damsté's *segetem* is supported by *A.A.* 3.562 (cit. above), and though further from the transmitted text it solves any possible difficulty with *ad*.

145 meus est: the usual (and obvious) phrase for asserting a legal claim to ownership: 12.157–8 *uix me continui quin dilaniata capillos* | *clamarem 'meus est' iniceremque manus*, *Am.* 1.4.40 *dicam 'mea sunt' iniciamque manum*, and McKeown *ad loc.*, Virg. *Ecl.* 9.4 *'haec mea sunt: ueteres migrate coloni'*. The words anticipate the identification of Cydippe as a chattel (150n.).

turpiter: 16.174n.

148 istud 'what you are doing now'.

149 uacuis 'that has no (legal) owner', also (of a spinster or widow) 'single' (*OLD* s.v. 9a, c); cf. 154 *non uacat*.

uindicet 'claim', another word with a legal flavour (*OLD* s.v. 1), favoured by O. along with its cognates *uindex, uindicta* (Kenney (1969) 253–5); cf. e.g. 8.7–8 *'quid facis, Aeacide? non sum sine uindice' dixi*; | *'haec tibi sub domino est, Pyrrhe, puella suo'*. The subj. is generic.

150 si nescis: 16.246n.

dominum: an ironical reversal of roles from 80 *dominae more* (Frécaut (1972) 133).

res ... ista 'that property'; Cydippe is both farm and chattel. Cf. Gaius, *Inst.* 2.13 (*res*) *corporales hae sunt, quae tangi possunt, uelut fundus, homo* (slave), *uestis, aurum, argentum* (Kenney (1969) 255).

151 nec = *et, ne* (cf. 152n.) 'and don't take my word for it'.

recitetur formula pacti 'let us have the actual terms of the agreement read out', the language of an advocate in court demanding the production of documents (*OLD, Berger* s.vv.). To style Cydippe's involuntary oath a *pactum* is of course outrageous.

152 neu = *et, ne* (16.71n.).

fac ipsa legat: thus once more (this time knowingly) committing herself; cf. 213n. For the construction cf. 16.263–4n.

153 tibi nos, tibi, dicimus '*you*, yes it's *you* I'm talking to'; cf. *Met.* 9.119–22 *Nessoque paranti | fallere depositum 'quo te fiducia' clamat | 'uana pedum, uiolente, rapit? tibi, Nesse biformis, | dicimus: exaudi nec res intercipe nostras'* and Bömer *ad loc.* on the legalistic rhetoric. A colloquial idiom (Hofmann (1951) 125–6).

154 hic: in his overheated imagination he is there in the room, confronting his rival.

155 quod habes et tu 'though you too have': 17.43, 51nn.

gemini uerba altera pacti 'the text of another agreement like mine', i.e. the official marriage contract. *gemini* = 'identical' (*OLD* s.v. 3), sc. in substance. *altera* belongs in sense with *pacti* by enallage (16.107n.).

156 non erit idcirco 'is not for that reason, as you will find …' (16.186n.).

157–8 This is not an argument that (at least in the case of a girl of Cydippe's age) would have cut much ice at Rome either in law or in practice: cf. Catull. 62.27–8 *conubia … | quae pepigere uiri, pepigerunt ante parentes*, 60–1 *pater cui tradidit ipse, | ipse pater cum matre, quibus parere necesse est.* Though that poem 'present[s] to us a wedding such as could not be celebrated anywhere in the ancient world' (Fraenkel (1955) 7 = (1964) 98), this sentiment must be contemporary. So Hermione clearly has no voice in either of her betrothals: *Her.* 8.31–4 *me tibi Tyndareus, uita grauis auctor et annis, | tradidit: arbitrium neptis habebat auus. | at pater Aeacidae promiserat inscius acti: | plus patre, quo prior est ordine, pollet auus.* See Berger s.v. *Matrimonium*.

157 primus ab illa 'first (but only) after her', i.e. second; on *a* see 16.98n.

158 propior 'more closely related'; cf. 3.28 *ille gradu propior sanguinis, ille comes*, 16.328 (*OLD* s.v. 3a), but also perhaps glancing at the idea that one is one's own best friend: Ter. *Andr.* 636 *proximus sum egomet mihi*, Otto s.v. *proximus*. This is very Ovidian: *Met.* 14.679–80 (the disguised Vertumnus to Pomona on himself) *neque enim sibi notior ille est | quam mihi* [T.].

159, 161 haec et iurauit … haec et periura 'she swore as well … she (fears to be called) forsworn as well'. Cydippe too has made a promise, but it was in the form of an oath; she too fears to be called deceitful, but in her case deceit means perjury. For *et* = 'also' qualifying a single word see *OLD* s.v. 5a, *TLL* s.v. 907.64ff. The expression is difficult to parallel exactly, but the two instances support each other, and the rhetoric is effective. No convincing parallels for *se iurauit* (ς, rec. e.g. Showerman–Goold) are forthcoming.

162 hic ... ille 'the former ... the latter' (Shackleton Bailey (1956) 279); the rhetoric implies the question 'Is deceit worse than perjury?'.

163 denique introduces a clinching argument.

ut ... possis 'so as to be able to compare the hazards on either side'. *amborum pericula* = *ambo pericula* = *utrumque periculum*; cf. Virg. *Aen.* 6.540 *partis ... se uia findit in ambas* and Norden *ad loc.*, Arusianus, *GLK* VII 455.10 *ambobus pro utrisque*, citing *Aen.* 1.458.

164 respice ad euentus: basely pragmatic: Cic. *Rab. Post.* 1.1 *hoc plerumque facimus ut consilia euentis ponderemus et, cui bene quid processerit, multum illum prouidisse, cui secus, nihil sensisse dicamus, Her.* 2.85–6 *'exitus acta probat'; careat successibus opto, | quisquis ab euentu facta notanda putat,* Otto s.v. *eventus* 2. The pl. here is purely for metrical convenience.

cubat 'is on a sickbed' (*OLD* s.v. 1c); cf. 173 *iaceas*.

ualet: her father's good health does not really arise from what has happened; once more logic is sacrificed to antithesis [T.].

165 'It is, moreover, in different states of mind that we engage in contest.' *certamina* pl. for metrical convenience.

166 i.e. you have less to hope for and I more to fear. These are the emotions which conflict and predominate in elegiac love: 9.42 *speque timor dubiae spesque timore cadit,* 13.124 *spes bona sollicito uicta timore cadit,* 16.377, Prop. 3.17.11–12 *semper enim uacuos nox sobria torquet amantes: | spesque timorque animos uersat utroque modo,* al.

167 petis ... repulsa: though both words belong to the vocabulary of electioneering, it is doubtful whether the metaphor is relevant here: of the twelve instances of *repulsa* in O. six (*Am.* 2.19.6, *A.A.* 1.346, 3.580, *Met.* 13.967, 14.42, 15.503) refer to amatory rebuffs.

ex tuto: i.e. you have nothing to lose, not being in love. The point is not so much that Acontius pretends to know how the other feels, as that his is the real (elegiac) love at first sight, not what the partners to an arranged marriage might or might not (168 *forsan amabis*) come to feel for each other. See 16.87n.

grauior ... morte: 51n.
168 id ... quod: 16.85n.
quod ... forsan amabis, amo 'what you perhaps *will* love, I do'; inflexion makes the point.
170 debueras: 16.162n.
ipse 'of your own accord' (*OLD* s.v. 7).
171 nunc 'as it is, however' (*OLD* s.v. 11a).
ferus hic: he now turns back to address Cydippe. The rival is *ferus* because he (wilfully, as Acontius would have it) persists in holding her to the engagement contracted by her father on her behalf, so endangering her life. It is with more reason that she calls Acontius himself *ferus* (21.60).
pugnat 'persists in fighting'.
iniqua 'unequal', i.e. which he cannot win (*OLD* s.v. 3a), rather than 'unjust'.
172 ad te ... redit 'comes back to you'; i.e., since he will not budge, though he has not a leg to stand on, I shall show that the initiative now rests with you. The expression, though prosaic (*OLD* s.v. *redeo* 4a), is in keeping with Acontius' hectoring tone, as is the use of Cydippe's name; the better-attested reading *ad quid ...?* is both pedantic *and* pointless.
173–5 hic ... hunc ... hoc 'it is *he* ... *him* you should ... it is *his* doing'; sc. so by throwing him over you can at one stroke set everything right (but only you can do it). The polyptoton (21.11n.) (+ 177 *hunc*, s.v.l.: see n.) adds to the effect.
173 iaceas 'lie ill' (*OLD* s.v. 2c); cf. 164 *cubat*.
suspecta Dianae 'viewed askance by Diana', dat. of agent. For *suspectus* in a strong sense cf. 19.148n.
174 si sapias 'if you knew what was good for you', a colloquial phrase of which O. is fond; cf. 17.257–8n.
176 'and indeed (*OLD* s.v. *atque* 2c) I wish that he who is responsible for them might die instead of you'. If anybody has set these events on foot (*OLD* s.v. *moueo* 17a) it is Acontius himself. *cadat* has overtones of sacrifice (*OLD* s.v. 9b): Cydippe is a victim of Diana's anger.
177–8 'If you reject him, you will not be loving someone whom the goddess damns, and you straightway, then I, will be saved.' The transmitted text poses several difficulties. (i) It is not clear whether

the apodosis to the *si*-clause begins after *reppuleris* or after *amaris*. (ii) The tense of *amaris* (fut. pf.) is awkward. (iii) The sense of the pentameter is absurd: Acontius cannot be made to say 'you will be all right – at all events I shall'. (iv) Though *certe ego* is an Ovidian cliché (19.81n.), the elision of the long vowel in *certe* in this *sedes* is unexampled (Platnauer (1951) 88). Of the various attempts at correction (Thompson (1993) 258–9; Watt (1985) 57) none meets all these points satisfactorily; the text printed here is offered as an economical *pis aller*. Dilthey condemned lines 175–8 as spurious, and this couplet certainly would not be missed if the MSS did not offer it.

hunc is Hollis's correction (*ap*. Thompson) of MS *quem*, neatly eliminating an ineffective and substituting an effective anaphora (cf. 173–5n.)

nec ... amabis ... et ... ero: retaining *et*, which there is no reason to emend away, entails that the apodosis begins with *nec*, and in that case *amabis* (one MS) gives better sense and a neater construction than *amaris*: cf. (i), (ii) above; so Thompson (1993) 260. For *nec ... et* cf. Plaut. *Pseud.* 1135, Ter. *Eun.* 965; otherwise apparently a prose usage (K–S II 48, *OLD* s.v. *neque* 8a; Ov. *F.* 5.530 is doubtful, Manil. 4.96 irrelevant).

et tu: sc. *salua eris*.

tunc 'then', 'after you', adopted *ex. gr.* from Housman (*CP* 419), who reads *(continuo per te tunc e.s.e.)*; *tecum* would make the point more neatly, but though Propertius elides a syllable in *-m* 9x in this *sedes* (Platnauer (1951) 88 n. 2), O. only elides a short open vowel (*ibid*. n. 3). For the sense cf. 4n.

180 fac modo ... colas: i.e. *modo si colas* (16.263–4, 18.51nn.); for pres. subj. protasis + fut. indic. apodosis cf. 17.47–8n.

polliciti conscia templa 'the shrine that witnessed your vow', shorthand for 'the shrine of the goddess who witnessed ...'; *templa* is poetic pl.

181–2 Conventional and admirable sentiments, hard to take from this speaker – but we are not meant to sympathize with Acontius. Cf. Helen on abstinence and self-control (17.98n.).

181 boue mactato 'in the sacrificing of oxen' (16.42, 18.139–40nn.), collective sing.

182 et sine teste 'even without witnesses'. He continues his unscrupulous exploitation of the theme of *fides* (40, 186nn.).

183–4 ~ Prop. 1.1.27 *fortiter et ferrum saeuos patiemur et ignes*, *Rem.* 229 *ut corpus redimas, ferrum patieris et ignes*, *Am.* 3.11.8 *saepe tulit lassis sucus amarus opem*.

aliae ... aliis 'some ... others'.

ferrum ... ignes ... sucus: surgery, cautery, drugs.

tristem ... amarus: then as now it was generally believed that medicines had to be nasty to do any good. For *tristis* of taste and smell see *OLD* s.v. 8b.

185 nil opus 'no need whatever'; *nil* is adverbial (*OLD* s.v. *nihil* 11). A common phrase in O.: McKeown on *Am.* 1.2.21–2.

186 A full-blown ex. of O.'s favourite figure, syllepsis (18.57n.), *serua* being used both of physical preservation and of keeping faith (*OLD* s.v. 9a, 4a), as at *Tr.* 5.14.20 *et pariter serua meque piamque fidem*.

teque ... meque: 4, 177–8, 233–4nn.

datam: *deceptam* or *extortam* would be nearer the mark.

187 ignorantia: also at *Met.* 7.92, Lucret. 6.54, otherwise not found in poetry before the Silver Age, and then rarely. Ignorance of the law was not generally a valid defence; the categories for which it might on occasion be allowed included women (Berger s.v. *Ignorantia iuris*).

188 exciderant animo ... tuo 'you had forgotten' (*OLD* s.v. *excido*[1] 9b), sc. when she allowed herself to be betrothed to the rival.

foedera lecta 'the fact that you had read out the bond' (18.139–40n.). *foedera* is poetic pl.

189–90 '(Well,) you have been reminded now by what I say as well as by the misfortunes which you always undergo each time you try to break faith'; on text and interpretation see Housman, *CP* 480. For *cum* = 'as well as' cf. 138 *cum superis*. Feeling that an adversative was needed, Maehly proposed *at monita es* (νῦν δὲ Planudes); but 'remind' rather than 'warn' is wanted after 188.

191 his quoque uitatis 'even if you escape these perils' (*OLD* s.v. *quoque* 4a).

nempe rogabis: a statement, not a question (Dörrie, Showerman–Goold): 'you will certainly still find yourself praying to her' (*OLD* s.v. *nempe* 1d).

192 luciferas: a stock epithet of Diana as moon-goddess, cf. 11.46 *noua luciferos Luna mouebat equos*; here an etymologizing allusion to the Roman goddess Lucina, with whom she was identified in her capacity as goddess of childbirth: *F.* 2.449–50 *gratia Lucinae: dedit haec tibi nomina lucus, | aut quia principium tu, dea, lucis habes* and Frazer *ad loc.*, 3.255 *dicite 'tu nobis lucem, Lucina, dedisti'*, 6.39–40, Maltby (1991) s.v. *Lucina*. Cf. 231–2n.

afferat ... manus: O. nowhere else uses the phrase, which generally connotes violence (*OLD* s.v. *affero* 9b). Here with *luciferas* the connotation is one of help, as with *auxilium, opem* et sim. (*OLD* 4d).

193 quae sint audita: sc. *ante*, when she read the oath.

194 partus 'birth' rather than 'child', picking up *partu* (191).

eat 'proceed', here practically = 'come'; for *eo* used with the emphasis on arrival cf. 2.52 (of tears) *quaque iubentur, eunt?*, 13.1–2 *mittit et optat amans quo mittitur ire salutem* eqs., *Am.* 1.4.15–16 *cum premet ille torum, uultu comes ipsa modesto | ibis ut accumbas* ... , 1.5.11–12 *qualiter in thalamos formosa Semiramis isse | dicitur*, *F.* 5.655–6, Virg. *Aen.* 2.375 *uos celsis nunc primum a nauibus itis?* (*itis* pro '*uenitis*' Serv.), *OLD* s.v. 5a.

197 non agitur de me 'We are not talking about me' (*OLD* s.v. *ago* 39b).

198 causa ... tua 'because of you' (cf. 108n.). Housman's restoration (*CP* 419, 578–9) of *uita ... tua* (ς). *uitae ... tuae* (ω) gives acceptable grammar (cf. e.g. *Met.* 1.623 *anxia furti*) but inferior sense: *causa ... tua* elegantly restates and varies *non agitur de me*. This is a good illustration of the principle '*impossibilis lectio uerae propior*': an evidently corrupt and ungrammatical reading is a more reliable pointer to the original than a superficially plausible 'correction'.

199–200 cur ... fleuere ... ?: the question answers itself in the pentameter: it is because they are in the dark that she is ill and they despair of her life.

te dubiam 'when you were in a critical state'; *dubiam* sc. *uitae*; cf. 21.31n.

201 et cur ignorant? 'and why *are* they in the dark?' The indic., picking up *ignaros*, makes the point forcibly; *ignorent* (Heinsius) 'why should they ... ?', inexplicably preferred by edd., weakens it.

licet 'there is nothing to stop you'.

202 nil ... ruboris 'nothing that you need blush for', gen. of definition/the rubric. For *rubor* = 'shame' cf. *A.A.* 3.83 *Latmius Endymion non est tibi, Luna, rubori*, *Tr.* 3.7.26 *causa ruboris eram*, *OLD* s.v. 2b. *pudoris* (ς) is less concrete and expressive.

203 ordine 'in order', 'from first to last'; cf. *Met.* 5.335 *refer ordine*

COMMENTARY: 20.204–209

carmen, 14.473 *referam tristes ex ordine casus*, *OLD* s.v. 8b. Of the 59 instances of *ordo* in O. 50 are in the abl. sing. (cf. Lucret. 28/37, Virg. 35/42, Lucan 11/16, Val. Flacc. 13/16, Statius 42/61).

fac referas: 16.263–4n.

ut 'how' (*OLD* s.v. 1c).

204 pharetratae: as a stock epithet for Diana, the archer-goddess, first used by O.: *Am.* 1.1.10 and McKeown *ad loc.*, *Met.* 3.252, *Tr.* 4.4.64. Cf. 21.173.

dum facit: cf. 207 *miror*; the indic. is sometimes retained in *dum*-clauses in o.o. (to which the indirect question with *ut* is syntactically equivalent; cf. 209–10). Cf. *Am.* 2.11.49–52, *Met.* 4.776–7 *id se sollerti furtim, dum traditur, astu* | *supposita cepisse manu*, 783–5 *aere repercusso formam aspexisse Medusae,* | *dumque grauis somnus colubrasque ipsamque tenebat,* | *eripuisse caput collo* and Bömer *ad locc.*, *NLS* §221 n.(iv), Roby §1784 (*c*).

205–8 The classic *coup de foudre*: Theoc. 2.82 'I saw, and madness seized me, and my hapless heart was aflame' (tr. Gow) > Virg. *Ecl.* 8.41 *ut uidi, ut perii, ut me malus abstulit error!*, A.R. 3.962–5 (Medea meets Jason) and Hunter *ad loc.*, *Met.* 2.574 *uidit et incaluit* (= 3.371, *F.* 2.307), 4.673–7 *uidit Abantiades ... trahit inscius ignes* | *et stupet et uisae correptus imagine formae* | *paene suas quatere est oblitus in aere pennas*, Prop. 4.4.21–2 *obstipuit regis facie et regalibus armis,* | *interque oblitas excidit urna manus.* Cf. 16.135–6, 18.55–104 and nn.

205 te conspecta subito 'the moment I saw you'.

si forte notasti = *Met.* 9.538. In her reply Cydippe implies (disingenuously?) that she was too busy sightseeing to have noticed him (21.103–4).

206 restiterim: 16.135n.

fixis ... genis 'with my gaze riveted on you'; cf. 11.10 *siccis ... genis* 'dry-eyed', *OLD* s.v. *gena* 2.

207 nota certa furoris is in apposition to what follows.

208 deciderint: perhaps as he raised his hands in admiration [T.].

umero pallia lapsa meo: the pallium was often worn fastened and draped over one shoulder, but the sing. *umero* is probably poetic, elegantly complementing the poetic pl. *pallia*.

209 nescioqua 'somehow', 'from nowhere', as it would have seemed to her (*OLD* s.v. *nescio* 7a).

uenisse uolubile 'came rolling', *uolubile* predicative; the narrative modulates smoothly into acc. + inf.

210 'bearing deceitful words in cunning signs'. *doctis* and *insidiosa* reinforce each other; this sort of pleonasm is standard poetical rhetoric (cf. e.g. 184 *tristem ... amarus*). For *doctus* = 'skilfully expressed' cf. Lucret. 2.987–8 *et sapere et doctis rationem reddere dictis | non ex seminibus sapientibus atque disertis* (*sapere* ~ *sapientibus*, *doctis* ~ *disertis*), Enn. *Ann.* 250 and Skutsch *ad loc.* The word would be especially apt for an inscription in verse (Fordyce on Catull. 35.17): see 21.107n.

211 quod (sc. *malum*) **quia** = *et quia id*; on the connective use of the relative see *NLS* §230 (6).

212 uinctam ... fidem: 39, 40nn. For the metaphorical use of *uincio* here see *OLD* s.v. 3a.

213 scripti sententia quae sit 'what the words say', a second invitation (cf. 152) to commit herself once again.

214 lecta tibi quondam '(the words) once read by you', *tibi* dat. of the agent.

215 nube: sc. *illi*.

216 quem fore: sc. *generum*.

217 quisquis is est: as he promptly goes on to tell her, he is by no means a bad catch; so in Callimachus (frr. 67.7, 75.30–3 Pf.).

placet ante 'is already pleasing to', but *placet* is disingenuous; the arrangement only 'pleases' the goddess in the sense that it is, in virtue of the oath, divinely ordained (*OLD* s.v. 5c.).

218 si modo mater erit 'if only she proves to be a (real) mother' (16.186n.). The point is underlined by the chiasmus and the shift of the metrical ictus: *erit mátér ... mátér erit*.

219 ut is found only in one late MS but is generally and rightly (*pace* Thompson (1993) 260) preferred to *et* by edd. on syntactical grounds. The ellipse of *ut* in such constructions is very common in O. (16.5, 263–4nn.), but with *uideto* is otherwise unexampled in classical poetry. The additional emphasis imparted by *et* (all other MSS) 'that she also enquires' is unnecessary with *sed tamen* and the emphatic fut. imper. *uideto* (19.87n.) 'but *do* make sure ...'.

qui 'who I am'; *qui* is found only in two MSS, but is preferable to *quis* on euphonic grounds (Coleman on Virg. *Ecl.* 1.18; cf. 6on.). Generally in O.'s text the MSS (for what it is worth) tend to support *qui* in comparable cases.

uideto is both better attested and better in sense than *iubeto*; even

Acontius cannot tell Cydippe to give orders to her mother. The imperative is grammatically equivalent to the protasis of a conditional clause (16.163n.).

220 uobis consuluisse 'that she has the best interests of your family at heart': cf. 217n. and Callim. fr. 75.50 Pf. 'From that marriage a great name [sc. the family of the Acontiadae] was fated to arise'.

221–2 insula ... cingitur Aegaeo ... mari 'There is an island lying in the Aegean'; about 12 miles E. of Sunium. Callimachus' learned historical and mythological excursuses (frr. 75, 32–7, 54–63 Pf.) are merely hinted at. The expression is Homeric: cf. e.g. *Od.* 4.354–5 'There is an island in the sea-waves off Egypt, they call it Pharos', 7.244, 15.403–4, *al.*, Virg. *Aen.* 3.692–6 (Ortygia) *Sicanio praetenta sinu iacet insula* eqs., 8.416–22 *insula Sicanium iuxta latus Aeoliumque | erigitur* eqs. and Williams, Gransden *ad locc.*

221 quondam qualifies both adjj. (amphibole: 30n.). The nymphs were once Corycian, since their original home was the Corycian cave on Parnassus (*Met.* 1.320 and Bömer *ad loc.*, Aesch. *Eum.* 22–3, Soph. *Ant.* 1128–9, A.R. 2.705, 711, *al.*); and Ceos was once both famous on their account and frequented by them (*OLD* s.v. *celeber* 5b, 1a), since its recorded history began with their migration thither when they were evicted from the cave by a huge lion (Callim. fr. 75.56–7 and Pfeiffer *ad loc.*).

222 Cea: sc. *insula*, from the Gk. adj. Κεῖος; for the adj. cf. *Met.* 10.120 *Ceae ... gentis*, Callim. fr. 75.32–3 Pf. ὁ Κεῖος | γαμβρός (Acontius), and for the fem. *tout court* of the island *Met.* 7.368 and Bömer *ad loc.*, Virg. *G.* 1.14. The usual Gk name was Κέως (f.).

223–4 nec ... despectis arguor ortus auis 'and I cannot be accused/convicted of coming of negligible stock'; the litotes (16.225n.) implied by the negative expression conveys a proud boast. Callimachus had been more circumstantial (fr. 75.32–7 Pf.). *arguar* [T.] is attractive; cf. 220 *inueniet*.

225 sine crimine mores 'a blameless character'; cf. e.g. *Am.* 1.3.13 and McKeown *ad loc.*, 16.307–8n.

226 amplius utque nihil 'and even though there were nothing besides' = *et ut nihil amplius esset*, ellipse plus hyperbaton. For *amplius* = 'further' see *OLD* s.v. 3.

227–8 'Even unsworn you should have sought such a husband; once you had sworn you should have accepted even a husband who was not such.' Anaphora, polyptoton and chiasmus added to hyperbaton accentuate the logical dilemma: either way she has no choice but to accept.

iurata ... iuratae: the pf. part. of *iuro* in the middle sense = 'having sworn' is usual from Plautus onwards (*TLL* s.v. 677.25ff.; *OLD* unhelpful).

227 appeteres is jussive (*NLS* §110), as the parallelism with *habendus erat* dictates. Cf. 53n.

228 iuratae: dat. of agent with the gerundive.

erat (most MSS) is more pointed than *eram* (Nodell, Bentley), as conveying a (bogus but characteristic) suggestion of objectivity (Thompson (1993) 261). Cf. 19.206n.

229 in somnis 'in a dream' (*OLD* s.v. 1c, Austin on Virg. *Aen.* 2.9). Dreams played an important part in both literature and real life, and were sometimes resorted to by declaimers in want of a plausible motivation: Sen. *Contr.* 2.1.33, 7.7.15 *erat autem ex somniatoribus Otho: ubicumque illum defecerat color, somnium narrabat*. It is therefore possible that O. intends a stroke of satire at Acontius' expense [T.]. It seems, however, simpler to read the couplet as a variation on the stock 'night and day motif' (16.101–2 and nn.). Hero's dream (19.193–204) is rather different.

iaculatrix: only here and at *Met.* 5.375, *F.* 2.155 *iaculatricemque Dianam*. As well as bow and arrows (204) she carries throwing-spears, the hunting weapon *par excellence*.

230 uigilem 'in my waking hours'. Cf. 16.101.

231–2 alterius ... alterius 'the latter ... the former', chiastic structure.

nocuere ... noceant 'wound' (as conventionally of inspiring love) ... 'slay' (in good earnest). Sudden deaths of women in Homer are commonly attributed to Artemis (*Il.* 19.59–60 and Edwards *ad loc.*), a vestige of her original role as 'a patron of women's life in all its phases' (Guthrie (1950) 103). Cf. 192n. O. glances at Callim. fr. 70 Pf. 'but the archer himself [sc. Acontius], feeling the point of an arrow from the bow of another' (Trypanis); cf. Aristaen. 1.10.14–17, expanding the conceit of the biter bit. See 21.209–12n.

233–4 A further variation on the 'one soul in two bodies' theme (4n.).

miserere meique tuique: cf. Prop. 2.28.41–2 *si non unius, quaeso, miserere duorum: | uiuam, si uiuet; si cadet illa, cadam,* Am. 2.13.15–16 *huc adhibe uultus et in una parce duobus: | nam uitam dominae tu dabis, illa mihi.*

quid dubitas? 'Why hesitate?'

235 cum iam: either 'when the day shall come that ...' (cf. Virg. *Aen.* 12.821–2 *cum iam conubiis pacem felicibus (esto) | component, cum iam leges et foedera iungent* ...) or 'as soon as' (*Rem.* 125–6 *aggrediar melius tum cum sua uulnera tangi | iam sinet* ...).

data signa sonabunt 'the sounding signals will be given'; so Showerman–Goold, adroitly glozing over the awkwardness of *data*, which with *sonabunt* is wholly superfluous (*signa sonabunt* = *signa dabuntur*). It may have ousted a word such as *rata* (Cuperus, prob. Bentley; but cf. 240), *pia* or *bona*. These signals, whatever they were, must refer to the proceedings in Delos (next n.), not to the wedding, which of course would take place on Naxos. For trumpets signalling or accompanying a sacrifice cf. Varro, *L.L.* 5.117 *tubicines sacrorum,* 6.14 *sacrorum tubae, F.* 3.849–50 and Frazer *ad loc.*, Calp. Sic. 1.68, *CIL* x 5393. That being so, *sonarint* (fut. pf.) would consist better with *tincta ... erit*; but in the general uncertainty textual tinkering is hazardous.

236 uotiuo sanguine (= 21.93): the sacrifice which is to accompany the dedication vowed to Artemis in the next couplet.

237 ponetur 'will be set up' (*OLD* s.v. 2b, 8c), *vox propria* of dedications: cf. *E.S.* 183 *grata lyram posui tibi, Phoebe, poetria Sappho.* Such dedications are a commonplace of love-elegy: cf. e.g. *Am.* 1.11.27–8 and McKeown *ad loc.* Apples, golden or other, are among the dedications recorded at Delos and elsewhere; this one is uniquely appropriate.

238, 240 scripta ... SCRIPTA: cf. 16.150–2n.

239 HVIVS must refer in sense to the model, not to the original fruit (enallage: 16.107n.); so Showerman–Goold 'By this image of the apple'. See next n.

240 IN EO: sc. *pomo*, the original. On *eo* see 29n.; though it is striking that two of the five instances in O.'s elegiacs are in this epistle, here it seems to suit the rather plain style appropriate to such an inscription. Cf. next n.

RATA: on the avoidance by the elegists of a short open vowel in this *sedes* see 18.172n.; this is the only ex. cited by Platnauer (1951) 65 of a neuter pl. pf. part. so placed. The effect here may be deliberate; certainly the word carries great emphasis as the last word of the letter proper, prophesying the accomplishment of Acontius' desires. Cf. 21.14n.

242 clausaque ... sit: sc. *ut*, understood from *ne* in 241; cf. Juv. 13.35–7 ... *cum | exigis a quoquam ne peieret et putet ullis | esse aliquod numen templis* and Courtney *ad loc.*, K–S II 563–4.

consueto ... sibi fine 'by the ending usual to it', sc. *epistulae*; cf. *Ex P.* 2.7.18 *per sibi consuetas semper itura uias*.

uale: not only 'goodbye', the conventional subscription, but also literally 'be well'; as she can be, but only by complying with his desires.

xxi
Cydippe to Acontius

1 pertimui ~ 20.1 *pone metum* and n.; whether the undeniably effective plunge *in medias res*, echoing sound as well as sense, is authorial is here too a moot point. The introductory couplet found in two late MSS is not O.'s (Kirfel (1969) 83–4).

sine murmure: she had read the oath aloud because her nurse, who picked the apple up, being (presumably) illiterate, asked her to do so (109–110). Though reading aloud was usual in antiquity, and Greek and Latin literature was written to be listened to, silent reading was by no means unknown (Knox (1968)).

2 inscia 'unwittingly'; cf. 135–50. For *iuro* + acc. cf. 16.321n.

3 captasses iterum 'you would have tried to ensnare me a second time'; cf. 20.43n.

fateris 'declare' (*OLD* s.v. 2a), but also 'confess' (1b), implying that he should be ashamed of himself.

4 'that for me to have been promised once was enough'; *esse* does double duty (amphibole: 20.30n.).

5 dura 'hard-hearted', the usual word for an obdurate mistress, and thus perhaps already implying that she acquiesces in this peculiar courtship.

7 omnia cum faciam 'Do what I will' = [Ov.] *Nux* 121 (*OLD* s.v. *omnis* 7b). *cum* = 'although'.

8 iusta plus ... parte [= Virg. *G.* 1.35] 'more than is fair' = *plus iusto* (cf. 3on., 170). For *pars* = 'proportion' see *OLD* s.v. 2d; cf. *Tr.* 3.3.16 *plus in nostro pectore parte tenes* 'more than your (due) half of my heart', and Luck *ad loc.*

9 credi 'to be believed', passive of a person (*OLD* s.v. 5a).
memori ... ira ~ Virg. *Aen.* 1.4 *saeuae memorem Iunonis ob iram*, *Met.* 12.583 *memores ... iras*, 14.694 *memorem ... Rhamnusidos iram*.

10 'She hardly did as much for her beloved Hippolytus.' Hippolytus was a paragon of chastity, devoted to the service of Diana. His stepmother Phaedra, having failed to seduce him, committed suicide, leaving a letter in which she falsely accused him of raping her. His father Theseus prayed to Poseidon to destroy him. In the most familiar version of the story Diana could not or would not save him from death (Eur. *Hipp.*, Hor. *C.* 4.7.25–6); however, in a variant exploited elsewhere by O., she set him up anew as the Italian god Virbius (Callim. fr. 190 and Pfeiffer *ad loc.*, Virg. *Aen.* 7.765–77, Ov. *Met.* 15.492–546).

in Hippolyto 'in the matter of Hippolytus' (*OLD* s.v. *in* 42).
11 melius 'more fittingly'.
uirgo ... uirginis: cf. *Met.* 2.579–80 *mota est pro uirgine uirgo | auxiliumque tulit*; on O.'s predilection for such inflexional variation (polyptoton) see Kenney (1993) 460–1. *uirgo* 'being herself a virgin', predicative.

uirginis annis: marriage being the expected destiny of most freeborn women, virginity and youth are automatically equated.

13–144 On the textual basis of this part of the epistle see Introd. p. 26.

13 causis non apparentibus 'for no apparent reason', circumstantial-concessive abl. abs.

14 'and nothing the doctor can do helps me in my weariness'. For substantival *medens* see *OLD* s.v. On the postponement of *et* see 16.26n.
ope: the acc. sing. and pl. and abl. sing. of *ops* tend in O. to gravitate to this *sedes*; *ope* 23x (cf. 18.172, 20.240nn.).

15–16 'How wasted away you must imagine her to be who can scarcely pen this answer to you, how sallow the limbs that she can scarcely raise on one arm!' *puta* gives a more forceful exclamatory expression than *putas*, which must be read as a question; but O. was not a television reporter ('Just how distressed were you, Mrs Lincoln ...?'). So Dido (7.183–6) and Canace (11.3–6) picture themselves as they write.

17 huc timor accessit 'To this (situation) is added the fear ...'; for *huc* (Heinsius) cf. e.g. *Am.* 3.7.37 *huc pudor accessit facti*, Cic. *Rosc. Am.* 9 *huc accedit summus timor*. *nunc* (MSS) implies a contrast which is not readily extracted from the context.

conscia nutrix = *Rem.* 637, *Met.* 9.707; see 18.97n. She alone in the family knows about the oath (109–10).

18 colloquii ... uices 'our correspondence'; cf. *Ex P.* 2.10.35 *uicibus ... loquendi*, *Tr.* 4.4.79 *uice sermonis*, Virg. *Aen.* 6.535 *uice sermonum*, *OLD* s.v. *uicis* 4a.

19–20 'She sits outside the door, and when people ask how I am, so that I can write in safety, she tells them "She's in her room, asleep".' The punctuation adopted is that of Watt ((1995) 94); the credit for seeing that *intus* belongs with what follows, not with *quid agam*, is Thompson's ((1993) 261); see below. He punctuates ... *rogantibus (intus | ut possim tuto scribere) 'dormit' ait*; but after *rogantibus* it would have been easier for readers of an unpunctuated text (for whom O. was writing) to understand the next word as direct speech than as the beginning of a subordinate clause or parenthesis.

quid agam 'how I am' (20.129n.). If the words bear this, their natural and obvious sense in the context, *intus* cannot be construed with them (Thompson, *loc. cit.*). For the placing of *-que* cf. 20.138n.

21 mox 'eventually', 'in due course'; cf. Servius on Virg. *G.* 1.24 *mox ... id est postea* (*OLD* inadequate).

secreti longi causa optima 'the most plausible pretext for my prolonged seclusion', in apposition to *somnus*.

22 tarda ... mora 'because it has gone on so long', causal abl.

23 iamque 'and finally'.

quos non admittere durum est '(those) whom it would be difficult for her to keep out'.

24 ficta: the signal is 'feigned' because she does not really need to clear her throat but only pretends to do so. For *fictus* = 'lying' cf. *Met.* 13.9 *tutius est igitur fictis contendere uerbis*, *F.* 6.507–8 *Bacchas | instimulat fictis insidiosa sonis* (Kenney (1970*b*) 181). Critics who do not find this explanation satisfactory have generally emended to a word meaning 'arranged': e.g. *dicta* (Burman), *pacta* (Palmer), *certa* (Kenney); alternatively *fida* (Watt (1985) 57).

25 sicut erant: like *ut erat* et sim. (16.121n.) an Ovidian cliché; cf. e.g. *Am.* 2.5.45 *sicut erant (et erant culti) laniare capillos* ... , *Met.* 3.178 *sicut erant nudae ... nymphae* and Bömer *ad loc.*

uerba imperfecta: the artistic use of elision is a device associated rather with Virgil than with O., but the elision of *uerba* before *imperfecta* here undeniably reinforces the sense.

26 tegitur ... rapta 'is snatched up and hidden'; cf. *A.A.* 3.240 *rapta bracchia figit acu*, Juv. 4.76 *rapta properabat abolla*, 6.514. *rapta* (Kenney (1970b) 181–2) reinforces the impressions of hurry and agitation conveyed by *properans* and *trepido*. *rupta* (Thompson (1993) 261–2) suggests tearing the letter (*littera* is here the physical object, the papyrus itself) rather than breaking off the act of writing; cf. *Am.* 3.1.57–8 *quid cum me* (Elegia) *munus natali mittis, at illa | rumpit* eqs. Edd. generally read *coepta* (Dilthey) for the impossible MS *cauta*, but the sense 'unfinished' is required rather than '(just) begun'.

27 inde ... repetita 'taken out again thence', i.e. *e sinu.*

28 'You can see for yourself the toil it costs me', i.e. you have only to look at the writing. Naugerius' *sis* for MS *sit* is not an improvement: 'the personification of *labor* which *sis* produced sits awkwardly alongside line [29]' [T.].

29 'May I die if you have shown yourself worthy of it'. For *peream si* cf. 17.183n.; for *eras* – 'you (always) were (and are)' – cf. *Am.* 1.6.64 *sollicito carcere dignus eras* and Barsby *ad loc.*, Hor. *Ep.* 1.4.6 *non tu corpus eras sine pectore* and Mayer *ad loc.*, Kenney on Apul. *Met.* 4.34.4; cf. the analogous use of *conueniebat* (Lucret. 1.881) and *decebat* (*ibid.* 885, Ov. *Met.* 3.540–2). See Blase (1903) 149–51. Cf. 206n.

30 melior iusto 'kinder than (what) is just'; cf. 170 *grauius iusto*, 12.11 *plus aequo, E.S.* 47 *plus solito, al.*

ero 'I shall prove myself', sc. by going on with the letter. Rhyme of this kind with a word not in grammatical agreement, though uncommon in O., is not unexampled: e.g. *A.A.* 1.426 *nunc opus esse sibi, nunc bene dicet emi, Tr.* 1.8.22 *uocem populi publicaque ora sequi*, 2.118 *grande tamen toto nomen ab orbe fero* [T.]. *ego* (Naugerius), when used by O. to end a pentameter, carries an emphasis lacking here: cf. e.g. 53–4, 6.148 *non quia tu dignus, sed quia mitis ego, Am.* 1.7.32 *ille deam primus perculit; alter ego.*

31 ergo té propter 'So, it seems that (*OLD* s.v. *ergo*² 4) it's *your* doing'. For *propter* following the word it governs (anastrophe) cf. *Ex P.* 4.14.15, the only other instance – and that only partially parallel – in O. Here he was clearly influenced by Virgil, whose Dido in her bitter tirade against Aeneas uses *te propter* twice (*Aen.* 4.320–1). On di- and trisyllabic prepositions in anastrophe see K–S I 586–7, and cf. 172, 17.87n. *propter* was generally avoided in the higher genres of poetry (Axelson (1945) 78–81; 11x in O.).

incerta salutis 'given over for dead'; *salus* here = 'survival' (*OLD* s.v. 2 *fin.*) rather than 'health'. For the gen. of respect cf. *Met.* 15.438 *dubio ... salutis, Tr.* 3.3.25 *dubius uitae*, Apul. *Met.* 5.28.3 *dubium salutis, OLD* s.v. *incertus* 9.

32 commentis ... tuis 'because of your schemes/tricks', causal abl. *Commentum* (subst.) occurs 3x in O., once in Statius (*Ach.* 1.624 *timidae commenta parentis* < *Met.* 13.38–9 *timidi commenta retexit* | *Naupliades animi*), otherwise only in Comedy and prose; the passive part. *commentus* only in O. (5x).

doque dedique: cf. *A.A.* 1.93, *Met.* 2.409 *redit itque, F.* 1.126 *it redit, Tr.* 5.7.14 *itque reditque*, all meaning exactly the same thing. On the fallacy of calling this sort of expression *hysteron proteron* and on the need to shake off 'the lineal habit of mind' when reading literary Latin see Postgate (1907–8) 167; cf. Bell (1923) 270–1, H–S 698–9.

-que ... -que: 16.96n.

33–4 'This, it seems is the reward I am vouchsafed for the beauty that is proud of your praise, and to have pleased you is my ruin.' It is more effective to read the couplet as a single heavily ironical statement in the form of theme and variation still qualified by *ergo* (31) than, as generally taken by edd., as two questions.

te laudatore: causal-instrumental abl. abs.

placuisse nocet: for the idea that beauty can be a curse cf. e.g. *Met.* 2.572 *forma mihi nocuit*, Apul. *Met.* 4.34.5, and Bömer, Kenney *ad locc.* It was a commonplace of popular philosophy (Juv. 10.289–345).

35 fuissem: 17.23n.

36 culpatum 'by being faulted', but also with a concessive nuance: though unpraised she would nevertheless be well and happy.

ope: 14n.

37 nunc 'as it is' (*OLD* s.v. 11a).

certamine uestro: it is a little hard on the other poor lad, who has no idea of the true situation (39n.), to implicate him in the responsibility, but Cydippe is naturally intent on portraying herself as an innocent victim [T.] – and she can hardly arraign Diana, who is the real upper millstone. Cf. 53–4.

38 proprio uulneror ipsa bono 'I am wounded by my own beauty', seemingly an ironic transferral and adaptation to Cydippe's predicament of Callim. fr. 70 Pf., referring to Acontius, 'but the archer himself, feeling the point of an arrow from the bow of another ...'; cf. Introd. p. 16, 209–10n. For *bonum* of physical charms cf. *A.A.* 2.113 *forma bonum fragile est*, 17.134n.

39 dum neque tu cedis nec ... putat ille 'By your refusing to yield, and his not imagining ...'; *dum* is causal (*OLD* s.v. 4).

nec se putat ... secundum 'and he has no idea that he is not first in the field', not 'nor ... deems him second to you' (Showerman–Goold, and so the other translators). It would ruin the plot for him to be party to the secret, and lines 193ff. clearly indicate that he is not, though he senses that something is amiss. *secundum*, sc. *cuiuis alteri*; cf. *OLD* s.v.² 6b, 11b.

40 'each of you obstructs the other's hopes', a pithy and elegant chiasmus.

41–2 Cf. *Am.* 2.10.9–10 *erro, uelut uentis discordibus acta phaselos | diuiduumque tenent alter et alter amor*, *Met.* 8.470–3 *utque carina, | quam uentus uentoque rapit contrarius aestus, | uim geminam sentit paretque incerta duobus, | Thestias haud aliter dubiis affectibus errat*.

certus 'steadily' (*OLD* s.v. 14a), adverbial, to be taken ἀπὸ κοινοῦ with *aestus et unda*.

aestus et unda 'the set of the sea', 'the current' (the Mediterranean is virtually tideless); currents are independent of the wind.

refert agrees grammatically with the nearest element of the subject (16.362n.), but the two nouns constitute a hendiadys, expressing a single idea.

43 caris optata parentibus: sc. but not by me? O.'s readers must have recollected the recurrence of *optatus* in the context of marriage in Catullus' *Peleus and Thetis* (64.22, 31, 141 *sed conubia laeta, sed optatos hymenaeos*, 328 *optata maritis*, 372 *optatos ... amores*; cf. 66.79). *caris* connotes the dutiful daughter, but the reservation which lurks in Cydippe's words may be another hint (5n.) that in spite of herself she is drawn to this violent suitor and will eventually yield to him.

44 immodicus ... ardor: some kind of fever; cf. 60 *tabe*. In Callimachus the first sickness is epilepsy, the second a quartan fever, the third a deadly chill (fr. 75.12–19 Pf.). The phrase would equally well characterize Acontius' love (cf. 20.17, 42).

pariter 'simultaneously' (*OLD* s.v. 4a).

adēst 'consumes', from *adedo*; cf. *Am.* 1.15.41 *cum me supremus adederit ignis* ... This form also at Lucan 6.267 (N–W III 615).

45 ei (Heusinger) is preferable to *tunc* (one late MS) or *nunc* (ρ) as providing a construction for *mihi*, which otherwise must be taken as dat. of disadvantage and is awkward with *nostras* following. *nec* (cett.) makes no sense.

45–6 crudelis ... Persephone ... pulsat acerba 'cruel Persephone knocks before her time'. *acerba* is predicative; O. generally respects the 'rule' forbidding the use of two attributive adjj. with one noun (16.45–6n.). Persephone, Queen of the Underworld, is often figured as the messenger of death (Hor. *Sat.* 2.5.109–10, [Tib.] 3.5.5, *al.*); this knock at the door is clearly inspired by Hor. *C.* 1.4.13–14 *pallida Mors aequo pulsat pede pauperum tabernas | regumque turres*. For *acerbus* of premature death see *OLD* s.v. 4. Cf. 157–72n.

47 iam pudet 'By now I am ashamed'; this has happened more than once (20.110, 113–14). However Francius' *et pudet* is tempting: cf. *Ex P.* 4.15.29 *et pudet et metuo*, *Her.* 17.177 *et libet et timeo*. More drastic is *iam pridem timeo* (Watt (1989) 68).

quamuis mihi conscia non sim 'though I feel no guilt' (*OLD* s.v. *conscius* 3a, 4a).

48 '(I fear) that people will think I have deserved the displeasure of the gods'; *offensos meruisse = offensos merito habere* (201–2n.).

49–52 aliquis ... alter ... pars 'some ... others ... others', poetic variation for the standard *alii ... alii ... alii*.

51–2 A plausible touch; since Acontius has been seen practically picketing the house (20.129–30), tongues have naturally wagged.

neue ... credas: 16.363n.

ueneficiis 'spells'; cf. 6.149–50 *uultus | quos ... ueneficiis abstulit illa suis*, *Rem.* 249–52, 289–90, *OLD* s.v. 1a. On magic in Latin poetry see McKeown on *Am.* 1.8.5–18.

53–4 pace ... summota 'you have banished peace'; for the personification cf. Virg. *Aen.* 11.133 *pace sequestra*, Hor. *C.S.* 57–9 *Pax*

... *redire* ... *audet*, F. 1.121–2 *cum libuit Pacem placidis emittere tectis,* | *libera perpetuas ambulat illa uias*, 281–2.

plector ego = 7.82 (Dido to Aeneas); O. clearly had in mind Hor. *Ep.* 1.2.13–14 *hunc amor, ira quidem communiter urit utrumque;* | *quidquid delirant reges, plectuntur Achiui.*

55 dic mihi: Bentley's correction of MS *dicam* gives satisfactory sense, and the corruption is more easily explained (*dicm̄* > *dicam*) than is the case with *dic age* (van Lennep, edd.). For *dic mihi* introducing a question cf. 2.27 *dici mihi, quid feci* ...?, Clausen on Virg. *Ecl.* 3.1.

ne: Naugerius' correction again gives good sense; though *me* (MSS) can be defended as ironic (cf. 145), it is not really wanted after *mihi*. However, whatever text is adopted, there is something of a disparity between this weighty adjuration and the purely rhetorical question that follows.

solito ... tibi 'that is usual with you'.

56 For the argument cf. 18.40n. The fut. indic. is idiomatic in such rhetorical questions (cf. e.g. Juv. 1.119 *quid facient comites* ...?, 2.65–6 *sed quid* | *non facient alii* ...?, al., Bömer on *Met.* 3.465); but O. may have written *faceres* (cf. 18.40 and for the corruption 16.103 *faceres* Heinsius: *facies* MSS; Kenney (1979) 399 and n. 18)). *facies* generalizes the question, *faceres* relates it pointedly to Cydippe: 'What would you be doing to me if you hated me, when you treat me like this in "love"?' See next n.

57 quod amas: 16.85n.

sapienter amabis ~ 2.27 *s. amaui, A.A.* 2.501, 511, 3.565 *s. amabit, Rem.* 745 *s. amasset*; but here the sense is '(in that case) you will love your enemies – it's the logical course' [T.]. The fut. has quasi-imperatival force; cf. e.g. *Am.* 2.2.37–8 *obicies ... deme, Met.* 5.414 *nec longius ibitis* and Bömer *ad loc.*, Blase (1903) 116–18, Bennett I (1910) 39. This is rhetorically effective, and there is no need to consider emending to *amares* (cf. previous n.).

58 uelle uelis 'you must bring yourself to wish'. No satisfactory parallels have been adduced for the pleonasm (see Housman, *CP* 420; Löfstedt II (1956) 183). However, none of the suggested emendations is really convincing; the best is *posse* (Burman on Prop. 3.13.21), for which cf. *Met.* 10.25 *posse pati uolui* (Diggle (1972) 37–8).

For an analogy, if not a parallel, with the transmitted text cf. *Ex P.* 1.5.18 *mensque pati durum sustinet aegra nihil* 'cannot bear ... to endure'. Cf. 121n.

59–61 aut ... aut: she continues to counter Acontius' legalistic assault with her own (rather feeble) brand of declamatory logic (cf. 63–4n.).

60 indigna tabe perire 'to waste away and die undeservedly'.

61 tibi: dat. of the agent with *rogatur*.

62 'that influence you boast of doesn't exist'; in fact he has made no such claim, emphasizing that it is entirely up to her to placate Diana. However, she affects to disbelieve him: he got her into this mess, let him get her out of it. Palmer's *iactes* (? 'for you to boast of') would not dispose of the difficulty, if there were one. For *te iactas* cf. 17.251.

63–4 The alternatives posed in 59–62 are neatly summarized. It suits Cydippe's (pseudo-)logic better to punctuate *non uis placare Dianam* and *non potes* as statements, equivalent to the protases of a conditional clause, rather than as questions (*pace* Thompson (1993) 262).

elige quid fingas 'Choose which story you'll tell'; either way he is bound to be lying. *quid = utrum* (19.174n.). For the hectoring tone cf. Sen. *Contr.* 6 *exc.* 3.1 *elige ut aut patrimonio careas aut scelere*. The dilemma is a basic weapon of the logical armoury; cf. 139–42n.

65–114 The portion of the *Aetia* in which Callimachus described Acontius' stratagem has not survived; Aristaenetus' narrative is relatively brief (1.10.24–45). Cydippe's recollection of those carefree hours contrasts with and adds to the bitterness of her present situation. The style is 'swift, fresh and picturesque' (Wilkinson (1955) 109).

65–6 Cf. 4.67–8 *tempore quo nobis inita est Cerealis Eleusin, | Cnosia me uellem detinuisset humus* and see 16.5n. All such wishes look back to the celebrated opening lines of Euripides' *Medea*: 'Would that Argo had never sailed to Colchis ...'; see Pease on Virg. *Aen.* 4.657–8 *felix, heu nimium felix, si litora tantum | numquam Dardaniae tetigissent nostra carinae*.

67 difficili ... sidere 'under an evil star', abl. of attendant circumstances; for this astrological sense of *sidus* cf. 8.88 *quod mihi, uae miserae, | sidus obesse querar?*, *Am.* 3.12.3–4 *quod ... putem sidus nostris occurrere fatis | ... querar?*, *OLD* s.v. 6a, and cf. *hora sinistra* in the next verse (theme and variation). *sidere* is Bentley's correction of MS *ae-*

quore, which can only mean that the voyage was stormy, which, though roundabout, it apparently was not and which in any case would have been irrelevant. For the corruption cf. 17.119n. and 17.60 (*sanguine* some MSS for *nomine*), Housman on Manil. 1.416.

69–70 quo pede...?: i.e. did I on setting out stumble or make some other inauspicious movement, such as stepping forward with the wrong (for the Romans the left) foot? Cf. 17.159n., *Am.* 1.12.3–4 *omina sunt aliquid: modo cum discedere uellet, | ad limen digitos restitit icta Nape*, Petron. 30.5, Juv. 10.5 *dextro pede*, and McKeown, Smith, Courtney *ad locc*. The repeated *quo pede* conveys her obsessive retrospection.

limine: abl. of separation.

70 '... did I board the swift painted ship'. *texta ratis* 'the fabric (*OLD* s.v. *textum* 2) of the ship' is an epic-style periphrasis for *ratis* (itself a poetic word: *OLD* s.v. 2a), with which both *picta* and *citae* belong in sense (enallage: 16.107n.), allowing an elegant 'Golden' disposition of the stock epithets: abVAB (16.107–14n.). Cf. Catull. 64.10 *pinea coniungens inflexae texta carinae*. *tetigi* = 'got on to' (*OLD* s.v. 7a) rather than 'trod' (sc. the deck: so Palmer, Showerman–Goold).

71 tamen: the head wind can now be recognized as an (ostensibly bad) omen that might just have aborted the trip; to that extent (only) luck was on her side.

71–2 aduerso ... secundus: playing on the literal ('contrary ... following') and figurative ('unfavourable ... favourable') senses of the words. A similar conceit at 5.49–50 *a quotiens, cum te uento quererere teneri, | riserunt comites! ille secundus erat*.

carbasa: in the contest of wind a natural synecdoche (16.21n.) for the ship, like the more familiar *puppis*; cf. *Rem.* 531 *referant tua carbasa uenti*, Val. Flacc. 1.8, *Her.* 2.11–12 *saepe putaui | alba procellosos uela referre Notos*, Eng. 'six sail of the line' et sim.

72–3 ille secundus erat: this kind of repetition from the end of one verse to the beginning of the next (epanalepsis) is characteristic of epic, usually for emotional effect (Norden on Virg. *Aen.* 6.164); for O.'s elegies see Platnauer (1951) 33–5. For more discreet exx. see 16.249–51 (*pectora*), 18.101–2 (*oscula*). Here the emphasis seems a trifle heavy-handed: the point hardly needs a whole couplet by way of footnote. More 'molesta abundantia'? cf. 113–14n.

73–4 referebat ... impediebat 'tried to bring back ... to hinder', inceptive-conative impf. (*NLS* §200 (ii), Blase (1903) 148–9).

76 The line is by no means 'inane' (Palmer): Cydippe bitterly reflects that she has enough solid grounds for complaint without wasting words on this well-worn theme (18.185–6n.). Her trouble is a lover who is only too constant.

77 loci fama: it was a place of pilgrimage, celebrated for a great annual festival in honour of Apollo and Diana. O.'s readers might also recollect that Delos was the subject of Callimachus' fourth Hymn (see Hutchinson (1988) 36–40 on this unusual poem).

properabam 'I was all agog' (*OLD* s.v. 3b).

Delon: *delum* MSS, but O. would certainly have used the Greek form. Cf. 81–2, where *Tenon* is secured by metre.

78 'and I thought the ship I was voyaging in a sluggish one;' *ignaua* is predicative. From Naxos to Delos is barely 20 miles: see 81–2n.

80 uento lintea parca dari 'that too little sail was being set'; *parca* is predicative.

81–2 A glance at the map will show that the direct voyage from Naxos to Delos does not take one past Andros and Tenos, and only by a stretch of language past Myconos. It seems that the ship bucketed around the Aegean for several days (cf. 83–4); but a head wind would have taken her S., not N.W., of her destination. Much ink has been spilled on the problem; the simplest solution is that O. liked the sound of the names and sacrificed geographical accuracy to poetic atmosphere. Cf. e.g. the lists of the islands overflown by Daedalus and Icarus (*A.A.* 2.79–82, *Met.* 8.220–2), though in these the geography is, broadly speaking, correct, and the movements of Minos' fleet (*Met.* 7.460–6 and Bömer *ad loc.*).

82 candida: islands in the poets are conventionally 'bright' or 'shining'; Hor. *C.* 1.14.19–20 *nitentis* | ... *Cycladas* and N–H *ad loc.* Here there is an allusion to the etymology of the name: δῆλος = 'bright', 'conspicuous'. Cf. Callim. *H.* 4 (Delos).52–3 '... sailors gave you your name, because you no longer floated obscure (ἄδηλος) ...', Antipater of Thessalonica, *A.P.* 9.421.5–6 (*GP* 235–6) ἥ ποτε λευκή | Δῆλος 'Delos once so bright' and Gow–Page *ad loc. in ... meis oculis* may be a discreet pointer: 'there before my eyes was Delos, as plain as its name implies'. On O.'s predilection for etymological wordplay see McKeown (1987) 45–61.

COMMENTARY: 21.83-93 227

83 quid me fugis?: Virgil uses *fugiens* = 'elusive' of Italy, the Trojans' goal (5.629, 6.61, not noticed by *OLD*; cf. 3.496 *arua ... Ausoniae semper cedentia retro*); O. wittily appropriates his language to recall the legend that Delos was a floating island until anchored as a reward for giving sanctuary to Leto (100n.); cf. Virg. *Aen.* 3.75-6 and Williams *ad loc.* [T.].

84 'Surely you are not still moving about over the high seas?'; i.e. have the poets got it wrong after all?

85-6 Theme and variation: the prosaic *prope luce peracta* 'when day was almost done' is restated in an inflated periphrasis in the high epic style (18.111n.).

85 institueram etc. 'it was sunset before I was standing'; the plpf., as often in poetry, is equivalent to an impf.; cf. 117, *A.A.* 2.129 *litore constiterant* 'they were standing on the shore'. Cf. 17.23n.

86 Cf. e.g. *F.* 2.73-4 *proximus Hesperias Titan abiturus in undas | gemmea purpuris cum iuga demet equis* eqs.

uellet 'was on the point of' (16.122n.).

87 A hint of authorial irony? Whatever changes the poets ring on the theme, one sunrise is, after all, very like another.

88 comuntur: sc. *ab ancilla*. At this stage her mother merely supervises, reserving for herself (89-90) the finishing touches.

89 crinibus: so ed. Venet. 1481 and most edd.; cf. *E.S.* 73-6 *ecce, iacent collo sparsi sine lege capilli, | nec premit articulos lucida gemma meos; | ueste tegor uili, nullum est in crinibus aurum, | non Arabum noster dona capillus habet*, for which this passage was clearly the model. Pace Thompson (1993) 262-3 a tiara seems more appropriate to Cydippe's *grande tenue* than anklets (*cruribus* MSS). The object being to attract admiring attention, 'the emphasis on the hair' (Thompson *ibid.*) is no more than one would expect. Cf. *Am.* 3.13.25 *uirginei crines auro gemmaque premuntur*.

91 grata is more pointed than *sacra*; cf. *Met.* 10.230-1 (Venus speaking) *sed quid loca grata, quid urbes | peccauere meae?*, Hor. *C.* 1.35.1 *o diua gratum quae regis Antium* and N-H *ad loc.* There were shrines to other gods on the island, but those to whom Delos was (especially) dear were of course Apollo and Diana. It is ironical though inevitable that Cydippe should begin the day by propitiating the goddess she is fated to offend.

93-4 tingit ... ingerit: of course she does not perform these messy operations herself but has it done for her by the priests (20.117n.). Cydippe naturally prefers sightseeing.

93 uotiuo sanguine = 20.236.

94 Cf. *F.* 4.638 *sectaque fumosis exta dedere focis*.

95 sedula: a traditional epithet of nurses (*Met.* 10.438, Hor. *A.P.* 116, *al.*), but here ironical: 'it was precisely because the nurse was so attentive that she spotted the apple with the oath on it, with unfortunate consequences for Cydippe' [T.].

altas quoque ... in aedes 'inside the lofty temples (themselves) as well', sc. from the courtyard in which the sacrifices were conducted. *altas* is Wakefield's correction of MS *alias*, which would imply that the sacrifices had taken place inside – something which a moment's thought will show to be unlikely.

97–102 Apart from the two central attractions (99–100) O. does not particularize the many sights to be seen on Delos, so preserving the timeless character of the story. Porticoes, evidences of royal munificence, and statues abounded in all the great sanctuaries and cult-centres.

98, 99 et: 16.26n.

99 aram: supposed to have been built by Apollo from the horns of wild goats killed by his sister (Callim. *H.* 2 (Apollo).60–3 and Williams *ad loc.*).

100 arbore: the tree which Leto (Latona) clutched in the agony of childbirth: Hom. *H.* 3 (Apollo).117–18, Ov. *Met.* 13.634–5 *duasque | Latona quondam stirpes pariente retentas, al.* The MSS read *de qua*, which gives acceptable Latin, the construction with *nitor* being on the analogy of *pendeo + de* et sim.; but after *de* in a totally different sense in line 99 the expression is awkward. Palmer's *te* (also, independently, Damsté) solves the problem with great economy: O. is fond of apostrophe, which here reflects the special awe attaching to this holiest of relics. For the incorporation of the antecedent *arbor* (voc.) into the relative clause cf. e.g. 3.147–8 *me petat ille tuus, qui, si dea passa fuisset, | ensis in Atridae pectus iturus erat, Am.* 2.2.4 *illa qua Danai porticus agmen habet,* 2.16.25–6 *nec (timeam) quae submersis ratibus saturata Charybdis | fundit et effusas ore receptat aquas, F.* 6.395–6 *forte reuertebar ... illa | quae Noua Romano nunc Via iuncta foro est,* Lucret. 1.152–4 *multa in terris fieri caeloque tuentur | quorum operum causas nulla ratione uidere | possunt* and Munro on 1.15, Hor. *Sat.* 1.4.2 *alii quorum comoedia prisca uirorum est,*

COMMENTARY: 21.101–112

Juv. 3.91 *ille sonat quo mordetur gallina marito*, H–S 564. Cf. 17.237 *cruentam* and n.

101 neque enim ... -ue ... -ue: a prose writer would say *nam ... neque ... neque* or *non enim ... aut ... aut*. For the metrical convenience of repeated *-ue* cf. 16.96n.

102 quicquid 'everything that'.

103 spectans ... spectabar: cf. *A.A.* 1.99 *spectatum ueniunt, ueniunt spectentur ut ipsae*, *Am.* 3.2.5 *tu cursus spectas, ego te*; but the girls at the theatre and the Circus are supposed to know what they are in for. Cf. 11n.

106 tutior: because belonging to a virgin goddess (cf. 11).

107 carmine: cf. 110 *magne poeta*. Callimachus' version has not survived; Aristaenetus (1.10.37–8) gives a prose paraphrase μὰ τὴν Ἄρτεμιν Ἀκοντίωι γαμοῦμαι '(I swear) by Artemis I shall marry Acontius' (= *Dieg.* as supplemented from Aristaen.: Pfeiffer p. 71). *carmine* may also carry a suggestion of witchcraft (*OLD* s.v. 1b) [T.]; cf. 51–2n. *tali* 'the following' (*OLD* s.v. 2b).

109 mirataque 'perlege' dixit: in Aristaenetus she speculates excitedly on where it came from and rhapsodizes over its beauty and scent (1.10.28–36). Her wonder as to 'what girl can have let it fall from her bosom as she jumped up (μετέωρος)' (29–30) is strikingly reminiscent of Catull. 65.19–24 *ut missum sponsi furtiuo munere malum | procurrit casto uirginis e gremio, | quod miserae oblitae molli sub ueste locatum, | dum aduentu matris prosilit, excutitur, | atque illud prono praeceps agitur decursu, | huic manat tristi conscius ore rubor* (N.B. the blush: 111–12n.), pointing to a common origin in Callimachus (Daly (1952) 98–9).

110 magne poeta ~ 19.90 *magnus ... natator*.

111–12 Cf. 20.5–6, 97. Cydippe's blush was evidently a feature of Callimachus' narrative: Aristaen. 1.10.42–5 'Her face became as red as if there were a bed of roses on her cheeks, just as red as her lips'. So in Nicander's similar story of Hermochares and Ctesylla (Ant. Lib. 1.2). Cf. for the expression 11.35 *erubui gremioque pudor deiecit ocellos*, *Am.* 2.8.16 *uidi te totis erubuisse genis*. These are the natural reactions of a modest girl meeting her lover (cf. e.g. Hypsipyle and Jason at A.R. 1.790–1) – but this is a very different kind of lover's meeting.

112–13 sensi ... tenebam: the tenses are descriptive: realization comes in a flash (emphasized by the metre: *sénsi | me*), then she stays transfixed.

113–14 lumina ... lumina: not a standard type of epanalepsis (72–3n.), and where occasionally found elsewhere in O., not as a rule markedly emphatic. Here it effectively conveys Cydippe's resentment at having her own eyes made to act as the instruments (*ministra*) of Acontius' design.

113 ueluti: *(de)figo* in this sense is not usually qualified in this way either by O. or by other writers (*OLD* s.v. 3); cf. 242. Cf. however Tac. *Ann.* 1.68.2 *milite ... quasi ob metum defixo*; and for similar apologies for metaphors by Lucretius see Kenney on 3.131. Hardly an argument for non-Ovidian authorship (Palmer); cf. 16.33, where the word is almost equally otiose.

115–16 Cf. 2.63–4 *fallere credentem non est operosa puellam | gloria: simplicitas digna fauore fuit* and Barchiesi *ad loc.*

aut ... -ue: cf. Lucret. 3.616, Virg. *Aen.* 1.369–70, 10.93, *TLL* s.v. *aut* 1570.72ff., H–S 522.

tibi: dat. of agent after *parta est*.

uir ... uirgine: cf. Virg. *Aen.* 1.493 *audetque uiris concurrere uirgo* (Penthesilea: 118n.), *Met.* 4.681–2 *nec audet | appellare uirum uirgo*. *uir* 'you, a man', predicative.

quid ... laudis 'what (kind of) renown', gen. of definition/the rubric.

elusa uirgine 'by tricking a (poor) girl', instrumental abl. abs.; cf. 122 *puella*, 18.139–40, 20.66–7nn.

117–24 Cydippe, like Hero (19.137), has read the poets and is primed with apposite *exempla*. To have worsted Penthesilea, Hippolyta or Atalanta really was something to boast about.

117 constiteram: sc. in the battle-line (*OLD* s.v. *consisto* 6b). For the tense see 85n.

sumpta peltata securi: an axe and a light shield (*pelta*) were the standard Amazonian equipment.

118 Penthesilea: Queen of the Amazons, killed in battle by Achilles, who fell in love with her when the helmet was removed from her corpse: Prop. 3.11.15–16 *aurea cui postquam nudauit cassida frontem, | uicit uictorem candida forma uirum* (cf. Monteverdi's *Il combattimento di Tancredi e Clorinda*). A hint not to push matters to extremes? Cf. 120n.

119 Amazonio caelatus balteus auro 'an Amazon belt engraved with gold', i.e. with engraved gold ornament. *Amazonio* belongs in sense with *balteus* (enallage: 16.107n.).

COMMENTARY: 21.120–128

120 Hippolyte: another Amazon Queen. One of Hercules' labours was to possess himself of her sword-belt or girdle (*balteus*). In some versions of the story he killed her, in others he gave her to Theseus to wife as a reward for his assistance. In the manner of the learned poet O. leaves the allusion open: it does not affect Cydippe's point, that she is defenceless and Acontius a coward.

121 uerba ... uerba dederunt: an untranslatable play on the literal and transferred senses of *uerbum* (for *uerba dare* see 16.239n.). 'Putidum hoc & minime Nasonianum' thought Burman; Loers was more tolerant: 'mihi vero, licet in elegantiis non posuerim, tamen ab huius poetae ratione non abhorrere [videtur]'. *Equidem in elegantiis pono:* the pun neatly encapsulates the point on which Cydippe's argument turns: see below, 133–50nn., Introd. p. 17. It is precisely *words* – mere words devoid of intention – by which she has been entrapped. Cf. for the word-play 58n.

122 parum prudens = *imprudens*, incautious and taken unawares (*OLD* s.v. 2a, 4a).

dolis: *doli* Heinsius, taken with *parum prudens* 'not forewarned of deceit'; cf. 5.150 *deficior prudens artis ab arte mea, OLD* s.v. *prudens* 1b. If that was what O. wrote, corruption to *dolis* was inevitable.

123 Schoeneida: 16.265–6n. Since death was the penalty for losing the race, here too the point is Acontius' cowardice.

124 'I suppose you will make yourself out to be a second Hippomenes'; *scilicet* is heavily ironical – some Hippomenes this!

125 fuerat melius 'it would have been better' (16.162n.).

puer iste 'that boy of yours', the one you keep on about.

126 faces: he had referred to Cupid's arrows (20.231) and to the fire in his heart (20.14, 17, 56, 170), but not to torches. This can only be pure inadvertence on O.'s part.

127 '... as is usual with good men, not to taint what you hope to gain (*OLD* s.v. *spes* 4) by dishonesty (in the manner of acquiring it)'. A general precept (cf. *A.A.* 1.642 *fraus absit* as one of the rules of a virtuous life), tailored to the circumstances; Acontius is spoiling what might have been something beautiful. Cydippe is recurring to his words at 20.21–2; even though his *fraus* must in the end succeed, will she ever forget what he has made her suffer?

128 exoranda ... non capienda ~ *Met.* 5.415–16 *roganda, | non rapienda, fuit. capienda* 'caught')(132 *capi* 'won', context determining sense.

129 ea: i.e. what he has now, belatedly, declared in his letter (20.219–28). Why did he not come forward openly like an honest man?

132 '... if I might have been (16.162n.) won by hearing a (proper) proposal (*OLD* s.v. *condicio* 2, 3, 4)?', sc. on such terms as those. The point is specious; her hand was already promised when he first saw her (Kenney (1970*c*) 400 and n. 44, Introd. p. 15 n. 61.

133–50 She meets him on the legal(istic) plane. Her argument turns on the conflict between words and intention, the letter and the spirit, familiar in the schools of declamation as the *status ex scripto et ex sententia* (Kenney (1970*c*) 401–2: *status* = Gk στάσις, the pivotal issue of a legal or declamatory case). Her pleading would carry more weight if that to which it is an answer had had any legal force to begin with, which of course it does not. No Roman court would have regarded her oath as binding (Kenney *ibid.* n. 48), but Diana was not amenable to human law. It is, however, a splendid example of the sort of exercise on which O. and many of his readers had cut their rhetorical teeth.

133 iurandi formula iuris 'an oath in set terms', prosaic technical language. Exact wording was important in Roman litigation: *formula cadere* = to lose a case through using the wrong *formula* (*OLD* s.v. 6c).

134 lingua ... testificata 'the fact that my tongue called to witness' (18.139–40n.) ~ 20.160.

praesentem ... deam: 20.19n.

135 quae iurat, mens est etc.: an allusion to the notorious (and much misrepresented) words of Euripides' Hippolytus 'My tongue swore, my mind is unsworn' (*Hipp.* 612) = Cic. *Off.* 3.108 *iuraui lingua, mentem iniuratam gero* (see 137n.).

nil coniurauimus illa 'I have shared in no oath with my mind' (so Timpanaro *ap.* Kenney (1979) 421), an unexampled use of *coniuro*. Of the suggested corrections *nil tum iurauimus* (one late MS) is perhaps preferable to *nil nos i.* (Bentley) or *sed nil i.* (Palmer), but all seem fussy in comparison. Cf. 143n.

135–6 illa ... illa: cf. 72–3n.

136 illa ... sola 'only the mind'.

137–8 'It is deliberate choice, a conscious decision of the mind, that constitutes an oath; the only valid obligations are those incurred by an act of will.' Sound moral and legal doctrine, weightily expressed through theme and variation; Ehwald's and Palmer's unargued condemnation of the couplet does them no credit.

137 -que 'that is', epexegetic (18.157–8n.); cf. Cic. *Part.* 38 *facta et euentus aut consilii sunt aut imprudentiae*. On the metre see 16.337n.

animi sententia = *Met.* 9.588; cf. Virg. *Aen.* 1.582 *quae nunc animo sententia surgit?*, 5.748, 9.191, Cic. *Off.* 3.108 *non enim falsum iurare periurare est, sed quod 'ex animi tui sententia' iuraris ... id non facere periurium est* (there follows the quotation from Euripides), *OLD* s.v. *sententia* 1c. O. had probably read the *De officiis* (Kenney (1958) 207 n. 2).

138 iudicii uincula 'obligations of (belonging to, implied by) a conscious decision', descriptive or characterizing gen. (18.63n.); *uinculum* belongs to the legal vocabulary (Berger s.vv. *Obligatio, Vinculum*).

139–42 Another argument in the form of a dilemma (63–4n.).

139 si ... uolui 'If it was my conscious wish'.

140 exige ... debita iura 'exact the rights which are owed to you', legalistic language.

141 sine pectore uocem 'sound devoid of sense' (*OLD* s.v. *pectus* 3b, 4a); cf. 16.307–8n.

142 '(then) what you have is useless, (merely) words bereft of any real force'; *uerba* is predicative and emphatic. For the ellipse of 'only' cf. 17.134n. *suis*: that is rightfully theirs, that they ought to have (*OLD* s.v. B 11, 12).

143 non ego etc.: it was not I (i.e. my mind, my will) that swore, only the words, echoing and varying line 135.

144 'I should not have had to name you as my husband in that way'; she had 'read' his name in the oath and so had (involuntarily) 'chosen' him; *legendus* neatly epitomizes the manner of the deception (Schawaller (1987) 206).

145–248 This part of the text is transmitted only in the Parma edn of 1477 (π). See Introd. p. 26, and for a full discussion Kenney (1979).

145–8 Her *reductio ad absurdum* is no more than an exaggerated reflection of the sort of tactics actually recommended by Cicero to the speaker who is pleading for *aequitas* and against the strict letter of the law: *Inv.* 2.140 *deinde nullam rem neque legibus neque scriptura ulla, denique ne in sermone quidem cotidiano atque imperiis domesticis recte posse administrari, si unus quisque uelit uerba spectare et non ad uoluntatem eius, qui ea uerba habuerit, accedere*.

145 alios (π) should not be corrected to *alias*; her sarcastic point is that if the trick has worked on her, it will work on anybody, not just on other girls.

succedat epistula pomo 'let a letter take the place of an apple'; cf. 17.33 (*OLD* s.v. *succedo* 4a, 5a).

146 si ualet hoc ... aufer 'If this principle holds good, (use it to) carry off ...'; understand *hōc* (abl.) with *aufer*. For *ualere* = 'be legally valid' see Berger s.v., *OLD* s.v. 9.

ditibus (Heinsius) is rhetorically more effective (cf. 147 *reges*) than *diuitis* (π) though grammatically there is little to choose. *ditibus* is dat. of disadvantage, common with verbs meaning 'remove'.

147 fac iurent: 16.263–4n.

149 maior es hoc 'This makes you greater'; *hōc* (abl.) 'by virtue of this (principle)' picks up *hoc* from 146.

ipsa ... Diana: on whom you palm off the responsibility. This is hardly an exaggeration: Acontius *has* converted the goddess into a mere instrument in his hands by engineering the taking of the oath in her sanctuary and in her presence. She has no choice but to exact fulfilment, and Acontius, having in effect outwitted her as well as Cydippe, is in truth 'much greater' than she.

150 tua ... littera 'whatever you write'.

tam praesens ... numen: cf. Ps. 46:1 'God is our hope and strength, a very present help in trouble', *OLD* s.v. *praesens* 3.

151–2 'Having said all this, having firmly refused you, having effectively pleaded my case, (yet) ...'; for concessive *cum* + pf. indic. cf. *Am.* 3.8.5–7 *cum pulchre dominae nostri placuere libelli, | quo licuit libris, non licet ire mihi; | cum bene laudauit, laudato ianua clausa est*, Tib. 2.6.14 *cum bene iuraui, pes tamen ipse redit*, K–S II 349. This is the turning-point in Cydippe's letter; now begins the retreat that eventually becomes a rout (Bopp (1966) 102, 133; Kenney (1979) 429).

me tibi ... negaui: see *OLD* s.v. *nego* 2c.

firma 'stoutly', adverbial.

promissi ... mei 'concerning my promise', gen. of definition.

153 Letoidos 'daughter of Leto (Latona)': *Latoidos* π, edd., but the usual Gk form is Λητωΐς (Callim., A.R.), and there is no reason for O. to have adopted the Doric form in Λᾱ-. Cf. *Met.* 7.384 *Letoidos* MSS, 8.278 *Latoidos* MSS, corr. Burman; and on *Le(a)toius* Luck on *Tr.* 3.2.3f., on *Le(a)tous* Bömer on *Met.* 6.274. O. appears to have introduced *Letois* to Latin poetry; after him the name occurs only in Statius (*Theb.* 9.834 *Latoida* MSS, corr. Klotz) and Ausonius (*Epigr.* 58.2 Green) [T.].

154 suspicor: she has not so far committed herself to believing everything that Acontius has told her; cf. the reservations expressed or implied in lines 9, 13, 53. The word must be emphasized and glossed in reading: 'I do indeed begin to believe ...' (Kenney (1979) 418–19).

inde = *ab ea* (*ira*).

155 nam 'For otherwise'.

socialia sacra 'the marriage ceremony'; *socialis* in this sense is another Ovidian innovation.

156 nupturae ... languida membra cadunt 'on the point of being married I languish and faint'; for *membra* cf. 16.224.

157–72 This description is heavily indebted to a favourite topic of Hellenistic epigram and the novel, the bride who dies on her wedding day (Kenney on Apul. *Met.* 4.33.4, Lattimore (1962) 192–4). Cf. Aristaen. 1.10.85–6 'Her parents were faced with a funeral instead of a marriage'; Shakespeare, *R. & J.* 4.5.84–90.

157 mihi ... positas 'put up for me'.

159–60 'and reluctantly do the lamps so often replenished by his lazy hand revive, reluctantly is the flame of the torches which he waves stirred into life.' Text and interpretation are problematic. (i) The use of *infundo* = 'fill' can be paralleled in Latin only from technical writers (*OLD* s.v. 2). However, no convincing emendation has been proposed; and one may compare for the construction *fundo, perfundo* + acc. = 'drench by pouring' (*OLD* s.vv. 3, 2a) and the analogous use of Gk ἐγχέω 'fill by pouring' (LSJ s.v. II); cf. Diggle (1972) 38. (ii) Lamps are not known to have played a part in marriage ceremonies, though they are a natural concomitant of festivity. (iii) The change of subject from the lamps to Hymenaeus himself has been thought awkward. (iv) *corripit* (π) in 160 gives no acceptable sense; what Hymen does with torches is brandish them. *concutit* (Burman) is the best correction; cf. *Am.* 1.2.11–12 *uidi ego iactatas mota face crescere flammas | et uidi nullo concutiente mori, Met.* 4.758–9 *taedas Hymenaeus Amorque | praecutiunt*, Catull. 61.14–15 *manu | pineam quate taedam.* (v) Even with this emendation the phrase resists easy construction: *manu pigra* has to be understood ἀπὸ κοινοῦ with *concutit* and *uix* taken with *moto igne* (the emphasis falling as not infrequently on the grammatically subordinate participle), '(with sluggish hand) he waves the torches (so that) their flames (are) (only) reluctantly stirred into life', circumstantial-associative abl. abs.

161–2 portray the splendour of Hymen's attire, contrasted with the scene that greets him. *saepe* 'again and again' picks up *ter* (157); Cf. 20.110n.

161 stillant unguenta capillis ~ Tib. 1.7.51 *nitido* [cf. 166] *stillent unguenta capillo*.

162 'and the robe with which he sweeps the ground (*OLD* s.v. *traho* 14a) is bright with saffron dye', *splendida* predicative.

164 cuncta (Francius) is what the sense requires; *multa* (π) implies that not everything was funereal, which weakens the rhetoric. After *multo* (162) and *cultu* the corruption was all but inevitable.

167–8 The couplet was transposed by G. Meynck to this position, giving a more natural sequence of events: the god's immediate reaction of shame at finding himself so inappropriately accoutred, followed by the gestures of renunciation into which it is translated.

consurgere: Hymenaeus, identified with his own hymn (cf. Bion, cit. 165–6n. ἑὸν μέλος), is ashamed to 'arise' joyfully. If this is the conceit intended, it is, though in itself not too far-fetched to be Ovidian, very abruptly introduced; and parallels for *(con)surgo* in this sense are lacking. Burman's *consistere* 'hold his ground'(?) gives adequate sense; better is *considere* (Watt *per litt.*) 'take his place', sc. at the feast. *os ostendere* (Watt (1995) 95) is apt and ingenious, but the corruption is difficult to account for.

rubor: cf. *F.* 1.342 *rubri ... fila croci*, *Am.* 2.6.22 *tincta ... rubro Punica rostra croco;* the red colour of the stamens used of the whole flower (synecdoche: 16.21n.) and hence of the dye. See Bömer on *Met.* 3.150, 509–10, 10.1.

165–6 Cf. Bion, *Lament for Adonis* 87–90 'Hymenaeus extinguished all his torches on the doorpost, shredded his wedding-garland, and no longer sang his own "Hymen" but "aiai".'

sua deductas: Cuperus' and Francius' easy correction of *suas deducta* (π), unconvincingly defended by Heinsius and Palmer. *deduco* as O. elsewhere uses it = 'let down' (of clothes, hair, etc.) is not really *vox propria* for this action, and *detractas* (Burman) is tempting; cf. *Am.* 1.6.67 *non laetis detracta corona capillis*, *Met.* 9.771–2 *crinalem capiti uittam* *nataeque sibique* | *detrahit*. However, for the sense 'pull off' cf. perhaps Plaut. *Truc.* 479 *soleas mihi deduce* (Geppert: *duce* MSS).

169 uae miserae = 3.82, Virg. *Ecl.* 9.28; cf. Ter. (*passim*) *uae misero mihi*, Catull. 64.196 *uae misera*, Ov. *Ibis* 205. *uae* was felt as colloquial; elsewhere in O. only at *Am.* 3.6.101, *Medea* fr. 2 (*s.u.l.*; see Lenz *ad loc.*), once each in Virgil and Horace (N–H on Hor. *C.* 1.13.3).

torrentur febribus: cf. Callim. fr. 75.16–17 Pf. 'a second time the maiden was sick for seven months with a quartan fever (πυρί)' (Trypanis).

170 grauius iusto 'heavier than it ought to be' (3on.), i.e. the bedclothes feel heavier than they really are.

171 'And I see my parents looking down at me in tears'; cf. for a much more mannered version of the idea *Ciris* 347–8 *noctem illam sic maesta super morientis alumnae* | *frigidulos cubito subnixa pependit ocellos* and Lyne *ad loc.* For this 'patient's-eye' view cf. Humbert Wolfe's 'misty memory of ... faces bending round the boy's bed like a clumsy frieze of angels in an Italian picture' (*Now a stranger* (London 1933) 28).

172 One of the stock conceits of the 'death on her wedding-day' theme (157–62n.); cf. e.g. 6.41–2 *ubi conubialia iura* | *faxque sub arsuros dignior ire rogos?*, Erinna, *A.P.* 7.712.5–6 (*HE* 1793–4), Meleager, *A.P.* 7.182.7–8 (4686–7), Antipater of Thessalonica, *A.P.* 7.185.5–6 (*GP* 161–2), Sen. *Contr.* 6.6, *al.*, Kost on Musaeus 308. For the two torches symbolizing marriage and death cf. Prop. 4.11.46 *uiximus insignes inter utramque facem.*

face pro thalami: 17.87n.

173 laboranti 'in my sickness' (*OLD* s.v. 6a) ~ Callim. fr. 75.17 Pf. ἔκαμνε; but O.'s readers were also bound to recollect Horace's invocation of Diana as the goddess *quae laborantes utero puellas* | *ter uocata audis adimisque leto* (*C.* 3.22.2–3).

picta ... laeta pharetra: 20.204n. Deities are often described as 'rejoicing' in their attributes or manifestations of worship, etc.

174 salutiferam ... opem: Apollo was the god of medicine and healing. *salutifer* is first attested in O.

iam seems to lack point, and the assonance -*am iam* is no ornament to the line. Perhaps *tu:* 'do *you* (take it on yourself to) perform your brother's functions'. Gods did not normally encroach on each other's activities: *Met.* 3.336–7 *neque enim licet irrita cuiquam* | *facta dei fecisse deo*, *Am.* 1.1.7–12.

176 titulum mortis habere meae (= 7.76, *E.S.* 190) 'to have the "credit" for my death' (*OLD* s.v. *titulus* 7b).

177–80 ~ 20.101–6 (see nn.). Cydippe and her family are innocent of any such offence against the goddess. Language and tone recall Prop. 2.28.9–12 (why is his mistress ill?) *num sibi collatam doluit Venus? illa peraeque | prae se formosis inuidiosa dea est. an contempta tibi Iunonis templa Pelasgae, | Palladis aut oculos ausa negare bonos?* [T.].

178 uultus ... tuli 'directed my gaze' (*OLD* s.v. *uultus* 3a).

labra 'bathing-place', in this sense an Ovidian innovation, a calque on Gk λουτρά [T.].

179 de tot caelestibus: i.e. *de tot caelestium aris*; the expression is analogous to compendious comparison (18.69n.).

180 uestra: yours and Apollo's. Both had joined forces to kill Niobe's children.

181 periuria legi 'I (merely) read a false oath', a boldly condensed but perfectly intelligible and effective restatement of line 143. See Kenney (1979) 420–1 and cf. 135n.

182 'and chose an inauspicious text with which to prove that I could read'. *docta* = 'literate'; cf. *A.A.* 1.428 *littera poscetur, ne didicisse iuuet (disco = doceri), Tr.* 2.343–4 *ei mihi, quo didici? cur me docuere parentes | litteraque est oculos ulla morata meos? in* = 'in respect of' (*OLD* s.v. 41, 42).

183–8 She now returns to Acontius, again taxing him with the inconsistency of his conduct (59–64). O.'s readers would, unbidden, recall the classic example of Telephus, whose wound was healed by Achilles with rust from the spear that had inflicted it: *Rem.* 43–4, 47–8 and Henderson *ad locc. feras, prosint*: jussive subjj.

185–6 π reads

cur quae succenses quod adhuc tibi facta puella
    non tua sed fieri ne tua possit agis.

When the obvious corrections of *facta* to *pacta* and *sed* to *sit* have been made, sense may be restored in two ways: (i) Reading *quae succenset ... agit* 'Why does she who is so angry because the girl that is pledged to you is not yet yours, act to prevent her from being yours?' (ii) Reading *qui* (Hickey) or *quia* (Diggle) *succenses ... agis* 'Why do you who are so angry ...?' Against (i) it has been objected that the reappearance of Diana in the 3rd person in an apostrophe to Acontius is awkward and upsets the sequence of thought (Diggle (1972) 39–40). Against (ii) is the fact that anger is appropriate to Diana, not to Acontius. In fact the sequence of thought yielded by (i) is pointed: the implied answer to her questions in this and the following couplet is 'Because of what *you* have done.' It is Acontius who is responsible for Diana's behaviour, as she has already sarcastically pointed out (149n.). If she dies, it will be his doing, not Diana's. The slightly elliptical connexion of thought would be improved by transposing the couplet to follow line 188 (Hollis *ap*. Thompson).

187 'All your hopes depend on my living.'

188 saeua ... diua: 19.7n.

189–206 Cydippe's official betrothed does not figure in the action either in the extant fragments of Callimachus or in Aristaenetus, and is almost certainly O.'s creation, though a hint may have been taken from Callimachus' passing mention of the boy with whom Cydippe must ritually 'sleep her prenuptial sleep' (fr. 75.1–3 and Pfeiffer *ad loc.*). As he comes to life in Acontius' fevered imagination (20.135–70) he is a stock literary figure, the elegiac rival, a source of jealous fantasizing. Now Cydippe portrays him as he really is, a bewildered boy who is quite out of his depth in the situation in which he finds himself, vaguely aware that there is something badly wrong, but too unsure of himself to insist on his rights or to demand an explanation. In the plot as O. has reshaped it he becomes the catalyst; it is he who by his innocent intrusion has motivated the peripety in the emotional drama by which Cydippe finally succumbs to Acontius' ruthless importunity (cf. Bopp (1966) 141). The revelation that in spite of herself she is in love with this man is managed with extraordinary economy and delicacy: 'pulcra est amoris modo enascentis suique vix dum conscii tecta significatio' (Dilthey (1863) 95). Lines 203–6 show that the game is finally up: what follows is a rearguard action (see Kenney (1970*c*) 402–4).

189 uxor 'as wife', predicative.

190 superposita ... manu 'by laying a hand on me', an oddly weighty phrase. *superpono* is found only here and at *Tr.* 3.1.47 in Latin poetry.

191 quantum 'as much as', 'to the extent that' (cf. 233–4n.).

ipse 'without my reminding him'. Dilthey's correction of *ipsi* (π) gives acceptable sense, but the combination of postponed *sed* with enjambment is unOvidian. *aegrae* (Heinsius) is neat (cf. 20.137), but unlikely with *aegra* just preceding; *usu* 'by custom', taken with *quantum permittitur*, (Hollis *ap*. Thompson), deserves consideration.

193 π reads

> et quoque iam nescio quid desensisse uidetur.

There are two problems: (i) The simplest way to restore metre and sense to the beginning of the verse is to delete *quoque*, which has nothing to refer to. (ii) The missing word after *de* has been variously supplied: *de te* (Heinsius) is more pointed than the vague *de me* 'about my feelings' (Ald.¹), given the background of rivalry; the boy has heard the gossip (51–2). Palmer's *de se* 'of his own accord' cannot be defended on the analogy of *de suo* (*OLD* s.v. *suus* B5b), and the proximity of *sensisse* demands that *de* = 'about'.

195 minus audacter blanditur 'his endearments [not 'flatteries'] become hesitant'; on *audacter* see 16.174n.

195–6 'and it is only rarely that he tries to kiss me, and when he calls me "my own" his voice is timid'; *rara*, *timido* are predicative.

appetit is Palmer's correction of the impossible *accipit* (π); for other conjectures see Thompson (1993) 263–4 (add *occupat* Watt (1995) 95).

197 sensisse: sc. *eum*.

198 uertor (Francius) 'I turn over' is what the sense requires; *uersor* (π) = 'toss and turn', as at *Am*. 1.2.4 *lassaque uersati corporis ossa dolent*. Cf. 16.233 *uersa ceruice recumbo*.

199 'I sham sleep by closing my eyes', instrumental abl. abs. On *lumine* see 16.37–8n.

200 'and when his hand tries to touch me I push it away'.

reicioque: 16.216n.

201–2 'and he (finds that he) has offended me though himself innocent of offence'. For the expression cf. 48 (and n.), *Tr*. 4.1.46 *nec iratos sentit* (sc. *se*) *habere deos*, Cic. *Att*. 14.19.4 *nolo te illum iratum habere*, *Fam*. 2.18.2 *fratres ... te nolo habere iratos*; and for the evolution of the construction with *habeo* + pf. part. to equivalence with the pf. active see Bennett 1 (1910) 439, H–S 319–20, Coleman (1977) 113–16. It is unnecessary to take *habeo* = 'holds that', understanding *esse* (Thompson (1993) 264); the young man's awareness of her feelings is implied by his reactions. See also 233–4n.

203 illa simultas 'that hostility'. *simultas* is Heinsius' bold correction of *uoluptas* (π); but *ista* (π) cannot = 'this (here)' (cf. 17.226n.) and must be emended to *illa* (Kenney). A simpler remedy is to read *me* for *te* (Thompson (1993) 265). This is neat and economical, but the sense is unsatisfactory: it is not Acontius' pleasure at what is happening that might be calculated to please her but (if anything) her consciousness of being desired by both men. Lines 199–202 sufficiently betray her inner feelings; O.'s nuances do not need to be spelled out. For other proposals see Kenney (1979) 421, Thompson *loc. cit.*

204 sensus ... meos 'my feelings' (*OLD* s.v. 7), only here in O. in this sense.

205–6 quod nisi lenta foret (sc. *ira mea*) etc. 'But were it not that my anger is slow to stir (cf. 3.22 *ira ... lenta tua est*), it is you ... who should incur it.' This drastic rewriting of *at mihi lingua foret* (π) is printed *exempli gratia*: *nisi lenta* is due to Watt ((1995) 95–6), who suggests *at nisi lenta forem* (*forem* Gronovius), sc. *in ira* (cf. 17.249). For other proposals see Kenney (1979) 421; add *si mens aequa foret* (van Lennep).

205 iustius: 16.174n.

206 dignus eras = 29 (see n.), but perhaps simply equivalent to *esses* (17.23n.)?

207–26 Acontius wishes to see her – but how sadly changed he would find her from what he remembers! Her illness has made her a fright: perhaps on seeing her he will regret his cleverness. This is an implicit plea to him to fly to her side and comfort her; now there can be no going back. The final stages of Cydippe's yielding, from these hints to the overt avowal of 240 *do ... libens in tua uota manus*, though the state of the text obscures some of the details, are delicately and adroitly managed.

207 scribis ut ... liceat 'you ask leave' (*OLD* s.v. *scribo* 13c); cf. 20.79–84, 133–4.

208 inde 'from where you are'.

209–12 vary and embellish a conceit exploited by Callimachus (cit. 20.231–2n.). The original paradox, that the wounds which Acontius inflicted on men he now receives from a girl (Introd. p. 16), was irrelevant to his character as redrawn by O. It is now Cydippe's 'wound', inflicted by the trick with the apple, which is the occasion for typically Ovidian (McKeown (1987) 45–61) bilingual etymological word-play (Kenney (1979) 422).

209 Acontius: Callimachus and Aristaenetus (1.10.14–17) evidently allude to the derivation of the name from ἀκόντιον 'javelin' (cf. 212 *ut iaculo*). Similarly with Virgil's Aconteus 'Javelinman', called *acer* and hurled to his death like a missile (*Aen.* 11.612, 615–17; cf. Hardie (1986) 178 n. 61); the name recurs at Thallus, *A.P.* 6.91.1 (*GP* 3408) as, appropriately, dedicating spears (cf. Gow–Page *ad loc.*). Such 'speaking' names are common in Greek and Latin epic.

210 quod faciat 'such as deals', consecutive-generic subj.

acumen habes 'you are sharp by name and sharp by nature'; *acumen* = 'point' and 'wit' (*OLD* s.v. 1, 4).

211 uulnere tali 'just such a wound', sc. as those you are equipped to deliver (Kenney (1979) 422).

212 scriptis ... tuis 'your composition' (*OLD* s.v. 5). The pl. is metrically convenient, but may be sarcastic; cf. 110 *magne poeta*.

213 anne ut (Heinsius) 'surely not to ...?' (*OLD* s.v. *an* 1a, b). Neither *sane* (π) 'to be sure' nor *sane ut* (Burman) 'doubtless to' (*OLD* s.v. 7) strikes quite the right note; pathos rather than irony is required.

214 uideas has as its object *miserabile corpus*, with which the rest of this verse is in apposition.

magna (Dilthey) is the most favoured correction of the impossible *bina* (π), an intruder from 17.242 (also at 4.66, *Rem.* 158); cf. 110 *magne poeta*. *uana* (Meurig Davis) is also possible, but here irony is not out of place. For the pl. cf. *F.* 6.611 *templum, monimenta parentis*, Virg. *Aen.* 6.26 *Minotaurus ... Veneris monimenta nefandae, al.*

215–20 These are, ironically, the classic symptoms of love-sickness: 3.141 (Briseis) *abiit corpusque colorque*, 11.27–8 (Canace) *fugerat ore color, macies adduxerat artus, | sumebant minimos ora coacta cibos*, *Met.* 9.536 (Byblis) *et color et macies et uultus*, *A.A.* 1.729 *palleat omnis amans*, 733 *arguat et macies animum* and Hollis *ad loc.* O. appears to have transferred them from Acontius to Cydippe: cf. Aristaen. 1.10.51–2 'His limbs wasted away, he pined in his despair, his complexion and look were wan.'

215–16 qualem etc.: a traditional image from Sappho (fr.

105a,b L–P) onwards, but usually the fruit is red and the comparison flattering. For Cydippe's pallor cf. *A.A.* 3.703–5 (Procris) *palluit, ut ... | ... quae ... suos curuant matura Cydonia ramos*; if the fruit in this case was a quince (20.9n), they are in fact yellow, which is apt enough for a fever patient (and cf. *OLD* s.v. *pallor* 1a); but this apparent touch of realism is somewhat compromised by what follows (see nn.).

216 refero: with *mente, animo* et sim. the usual word is *repeto*, which may be what O. wrote here; cf. *Ex P.* 4.15.37 *semper inoblita repetam tua munera mente, OLD* s.v. 6b.

217–18 Now she is as white as a newly carved marble statue. Again a traditional literary comparison: e.g. *Am.* 1.7.51–2 *astitit illa amens albo et sine sanguine uultu, | caeduntur Pariis qualia saxa iugis* and McKeown *ad loc.* For the favourite red–white antithesis see 20.120n.

nec: 16.348n.

sublucent 'glow from underneath'; at its only other Ovidian occurrence the word = 'glimmer' (*Am.* 1.5.5 and McKeown *ad loc.*).

219–220 Now her complexion is compared with the condensation on a silver vessel filled with ice-water. No parallel for this extraordinary image is forthcoming; it has been praised ('this admirable simile' Palmer), but it seems more appropriate to leprosy than to a wasting fever – to say nothing of the implausibility of putting it into Cydippe's mouth.

221–4 uideas ... negabis ... dices ... remittes ... cupies: 17.47–8n.

222 '... nec ...' dices = *et 'non ...' dices* (16.83n.).

(*non*) **est ... ista petita** 'this is not the girl I wooed'.

223 ne sim tibi uincta 'so that I may no longer be bound by you' (? rather than 'to you'). *uincta* is apparently Micyllus' correction (1543) of *uita* (π), and was approved by Heinsius, citing 20.212 (q.v.). However, *iuncta* (one MS) has been preferred by most edd. (not e.g. Loers) since Heinsius absent-mindedly installed it in his text, and, though it does not reinforce the legal phraseology as *uincta* does, it allows *tibi* to be construed more straightforwardly.

224 illud: sc. *promissum.*

225 ut is superfluous (16.263–4n.) and its postponement here slightly awkward. Delete?

226 quae ... legam 'for me to read', final relative clause.

227–8 π reads

sed tamen aspiceres uellem prout ipse rogabas
et discas sponsae languida membra tuae.

There is no case for deleting the couplet (Palmer, Reeve (1973) 336 n. 7): its general sense and its function as a protasis to the next couplet are clear – 'But in fact I wish you *could* see me as I now am: in spite of yourself you would be moved to pity.' There are three problems: (i) *prout* is impossibly prosaic; (ii) *discas* is in the wrong tense, and the sense 'learn to recognize' difficult to parallel satisfactorily; (iii) she is not as yet his *sponsa*. (i) is solved comparatively easily (though the corruption is not easy to account for) by *uelut* (Francius) or *quod ut* (Bentley). (ii) and (iii) would be neatly dealt with at one stroke by *quam dicis* (Hollis (1991) 90), if the resulting syntax (*quam dicis sponsae* = *eius quam sponsam dicis*) could be satisfactorily paralleled. If *sponsae* cannot be glossed in some such way it must be explained as uttered in a spirit of ironical resignation (see below). For discussion of other attempts at emendation see Fisher (1970) 198–200, Kenney (1979) 422–3; add *lecto instans* Courtney (1974) 298–9, *despicias* Watt (1995) 96.

aspiceres uellem: 16.5n.

sponsae ... tuae 'your "betrothed", as you call me and I suppose I must call myself' (Kenney (1979) 423). He has not used the word, but his whole letter is predicated on the position that her oath constitutes a betrothal: cf. 20.11 *inuenies ... id te spondere quod opto*.

229 'though your heart be harder even than iron ...'; *et* is Heinsius' correction of *ut* (π), introducing a qualification of this stock comparison (Otto s.v. *ferrum* 1, N–H on Hor. *C.* 1.3.9) that is usual only in paired phrases, as at *Met.* 14.712–13 *durior et ferro, quod Noricus excoquit ignis, | et saxo, quod* ... , Prop. 1.16.30 *sit licet et ferro durior et chalybe*. Heinsius' alternative solution *ut ... iam* is accepted by several edd., but the phrase *ut iam* = 'even supposing' is not divided in this way (Fisher (1970) 200). For concessive *cum* + subj. see *OLD* s.v. *cum*² 7a.

230 'you would yourself ask pardon for my words', i.e. you would pray the goddess to release me from my vow; cf. *Met.* 6.32–3 *cede deae ueniamque tuis, temeraria, dictis | supplice uoce roga*. After the future tenses at 221–4 (see n.) it is tempting to read *petes* (ed. Venet. 1492).

231–2 'And, to keep you fully informed, (I may tell you that) en-

COMMENTARY: 21.233–234

quiries are even now being made from the god who prophesies at Delphi as to how I may regain my health.' Mention of her father's embassy to the oracle (Introd. p. 17), is brought in aptly enough: if Acontius could see her he would intercede with Diana, but meanwhile assistance is being sought from the goddess's brother. In such circumstances resort to an oracle was the obvious course (*Met.* 11.410–13, Walsh (1970) 202 and n. 3).

ne tamen ignores: an epistolary formula: Hor. *Ep.* 1.12.25 *ne tamen ignores quo sit Romana loco res* ..., Cic. *Fam.* 5.7.3 *ac ne ignores quid ego in tuis litteris desiderarim* etc. *tamen*, as commonly in O., is connective rather than adversative (16.39–40n.).

ope qua 'by what means', introducing an indirect question depending on *quaeritur.*

fata canente: for *fata cano* = 'prophesy' cf. e.g. *Ibis* 246, Hor. *C.* 1.15.4–5 and N–H *ad loc.*, *OLD* s.v. *cano* 8a. For the abl. in *-e* cf. 16.11–12n.

233–4 'He too, (himself) a witness, complains, so far as wandering rumour whispers, that somebody has omitted (and is still omitting) to keep faith.' This rumour has come to her ears while she has been writing her letter, which from time to time she has had to lay aside to receive visitors (21–6). For the intervention *ab extra* into the psychological drama cf. Introd. p. 19, Kenney (1979) 427. Here it is essential to O.'s treatment: the revelation that the Delphic oracle itself is on Acontius' side is the last straw. She now has no option, after a last futile flight of sarcasm, but to yield.

The text of 233 printed here is a restoration *ex. gratia* of what stands in π, *et quoq; nescio quantum nunc u. f. s.* (Kenney (1979) 423–4; see also Fisher (1970) 201–4).

nescioquem: Fisher's correction of the vulgate *nescioquam* introduces an appropriate note of oracular obscurity. In Callimachus the god describes the situation precisely to her father (fr. 75.26–7 Pf.); as O. adapted the story the ambiguity is essential. Cf. 13.93–4 *sors quoque nescioquem fato designat iniquo,* | *qui primus Danaum Troada tangat humum.*

quantum etc.: for this limiting sense cf. e.g. *Met.* 3.461–2 *et, quantum motu formosi suspicor oris,* | *uerba refers,* Her. 16.137, al.

neglectam ... habere fidem = *neglexisse f.* (201–2n.). In the exx. of this construction offered by Fisher (1970) 202 n. 30 most of the participles are predicative rather than perfective, but cf. *F.* 3.50 *raptas fratri ... habebat opes* (= *eripuerat*), 6.600 *sceptra ... socero rapta ... habet* (= *eripuit*). Here it has a continuative force.

testis: the vow was made to his sister on his own sacred island.

235–6 π reads

> hoc deus & uates hoc & mea carmina dicunt
> at desunt uoto carmina nulla tuo.

The sense required must be something like '(235) Everything conspires against *me*, (236) whereas *you* lack no support. (237–8) How do you do it ...?'. In 236 *carmina* cannot be convincingly defended; *numina* (Dilthey; cf. 17.119n.) gives good sense: both Apollo and Diana are on Acontius' side. In 235 Bentley's restoration is printed *faute de mieux*, with the substitution of *ei mihi* (Kenney: *et mihi* Burman) for his *edita*, rightly objected to by Fisher (1970) 204 (q.v. for further discussion). For the position of *ei mihi* see 17.246n. That his threefold *hoc ... hoc ... hoc* is correct is suggested by the obvious reminiscence of the verse by Theodulf of Orleans, a Carolingian poet well acquainted with O., *Carm.* 28 (*Contra iudices*).451–2 *hanc deus, hanc uates, hanc leges, hanc quoque princeps | percensent* (for other echoes of *Her.* 20 and 21 in Theodulf see Dilthey (1885) 21 n. 9); but what O. actually wrote is past recall.

deus ... uates ... carmina: Apollo, the Pythia, the words of the oracle, which would have been delivered in verse. The anaphora would perhaps have more force if the reference were to three different agencies, but there has been no suggestion of any other prophecies (taking *uates* pl. = 'seers'), and *carmina* cannot be convincingly identified with either Acontius' letter or Cydippe's.

at 'whereas' (*OLD* s.v. 1b, 2a).

desunt 'fail to support' (*OLD* s.v. 2).

237–8 Her last jibe harks back to 145–50; perhaps he has got the better of Apollo as well as of Diana?

nisi si 'unless it is that', Housman's simple correction (*CP* 421) of *nisi forte noua* (π); cf. 17.151n.

noua ... littera: cf. 150n. How many more such potent texts has he got up his sleeve?

quae capiat 'such as to ensnare', final-consecutive subj.

lecta 'by (merely) being read'.

239–42 No amount of emendation will remedy the discontinuity of thought in these lines, and it seems probable that the end of the roll or the last leaf of the codex on which they once stood was so severely damaged that some text has been lost. Accordingly lacunae are postulated both before and after 239–40; the argument will originally have proceeded (e.g.):

(238a–b) Well, it seems that you have indeed got the gods in your pocket,

(239–40) and that being so, I must surrender.

(240a–b) I have sent the nurse for my mother/My mother has appeared, and she cannot be excluded;

(241–2) and so I have told her everything.

(See Kenney (1979) 425.)

239 teque tenente deos 'and since you (evidently) hold sway over the gods ...' (*OLD* s.v. *teneo* 9b).

240 libens perhaps connotes the frame of mind proper to one acquiescing in the will of the gods rather than glad acceptance: cf. Virg. *Aen.* 3.438 *cane uota libens* and Williams *ad loc.*, *OLD* s.v. 1 *init.* (votive inscriptions).

in tua uota 'to fulfil your desires' (16.282n.).

241 fassa ... sum matri: exactly as counselled by Acontius (20.201). In Callimachus she tells her father, but only after he has learned about the oath (though not the details) from the oracle (fr. 75.38–9 Pf.). On O.'s handling of this part of the story see Kenney (1979) 427–8.

242 ~ 111–14. Acontius had told her that she had nothing to be ashamed of, which is true enough so far as the *deceptae foedera linguae* are concerned; what fills her with shame and confusion is her consciousness that she has after all been seduced by this violent and unscrupulous courtship.

lumina ... plena pudoris 'my gaze overcome with shame' (*OLD* s.v. *plenus* 4a).

243 cetera cura tua est ~ Callim. fr. 75.40–1 Pf. λοιπόν, Ἀκόντιε, σεῖο μετελθεῖν | ... ἐς Διονυσιάδα 'As to the rest, Acontius, it is for you to go ... to Naxos'. It naturally falls to him to discuss with her family the arrangements for their marriage.

plus hoc quoque uirgine factum 'even this is more than an unmarried girl should have done', a highly condensed expression for which no exact parallel has been adduced. It is probably best explained by taking *plus* as adverbial, *hoc* as subject of *factum* (*est*), equivalent to *hoc feci ultra id quod uirginem decet* (Hunt (1975) 224). For the comparative abl. with *plus* cf. *Am.* 2.6.62 *ora fuere mihi plus aue docta loqui* (i.e. *ora plus docta fuere quam auis est*), *Met.* 11.336–7 *mihi currere uisus | plus homine est* (i.e. *plus quam hominis est/quam hominem decet*).

244 quod 'namely that', picking up *hoc*.

loqui: cf. 18 *colloquii ... uices, A.A.* 1.467–8 *sit tibi* (when writing to your mistress) *credibilis sermo consuetaque uerba, | blanda tamen, praesens ut uideare loqui*. For a well-brought-up girl to write a letter to a strange man was hardly less compromising than meeting him [T.].

245–6 ~ 20.241, 17.265–6.

246 officium longius ... negat 'will no longer do its duty'; *longius* is adverbial (16.174n.).

247–8 'Nothing is left except for my letter to add (the usual wish for) good health, which I desire will now be mine along with (my marriage to) you', i.e. *quid restat, nisi ut ascribat littera nostra* (*id*) *uale, quod cupio mihi tecum contingere?* She picks up and returns on him Acontius' words at 20.233–5 (N.B. *contigerit*). *uale* is equivalent to *salutem accipe* (cf. 16.1–2) and is treated as a neuter noun: cf. 13.14 *uix illud potui dicere triste uale, Tr.* 3.3.87–8 *accipe supremo dictum mihi forsitan ore, | quod, tibi qui mittit, non habet ipse, uale, al.* (Kenney (1970*b*) 183–5).

iam 'now at last', emphatic.

Addenda

xvii 13 sane: only here and (*s.v.l.*) at 21.213 (see n.) in O., and before him in poetry only at Catull. 10.4, 43.4, Virg. *Aen.* 10.48, where the obvious banalization *procul* should not be preferred (Axelson (1945) 94). Cf. 17.213n. on *qui?*

xxi 149 multum (π) is to be preferred to *multo* (edd.) as avoiding a third abl. sing. For the usage of Latin poets in this respect see J. Diggle, 'Notes on the text of Ovid, *Heroides*', *C.Q.* 17 (1967) 141–3.

APPENDIX

GREEK PROPER NAMES IN *HEROIDES* 16-21

Like other Latin poets, Ovid exploited to the full the sounds and associations of Greek proper names. Perhaps more than most he was alive to their metrical convenience (cf. Kenney (1973) 126–7). The following *catalogue raisonné* (of what may be thought to be significant instances only) illustrates his practice in the double epistles. What chiefly emerges is the utility of these names as affording (i) dactylic terminations (ii) final long syllables not available in Latin.

* = 'saves' the metre

1. *Feminines in* -a
    Achaia   16.187 (n.), 17.209
    Aethra   16.259 (-*an* (n.)), 17.150 (-*ă*), 267 (-*an*)
    Andromeda   18.151 (-*ān*)* (n.)
    Cassandra   16.121
    Cea   20.222 (n.)
    Deianira   16.268
    Hippodamia 16.266, 17.248
    Idyia   17.232 (n.)
    Leda   17.55
    Penthesilea 21.118

Note. Variation in the quantity of the final vowel in these names to suit the metre was one of the counts urged by Lachmann against Ovid's authorship (Lachmann (1876) 59). Cf. however *A.A.* 1.53 *Andromedān*, 3.35 *Ariadnă*, 1.28 *Ascră*, *Am.* 1.7.17 *Cassandră*, *Her.* 5.138 *Idă*, *Am.* 2.4.42 *Ledă*, *A.A.* 1.511, *Rem.* 743 *Phaedrā* (nom.), *A.A.* 1.744 *Phaedră*. Cf. Clausen on Virg. *Ecl.* 8.30, suggesting that -*ān* is an Ovidian innovation.

2. *Feminines in* -as
    Ilias   16.338 (-*ades*)
    Pallas   16.65 (-*ade*), 168 (-*ade*), 19.44 (-*ade*)
    Plias   16.175 (-*ada*), 18.188
    Troas   16.185 (-*ades*)

APPENDIX

3. *Feminines in* -e

Alcyone	19.133*
Amymone	19.131*
Calyce	19.133* (n.)
Chalciope	17.232*
Clymene	16.259 (-*en*)*, 17.267 (-*en*)*
Crete	17.163 (-*en*)
Cydippe	20.107*, 172*, 202*, 21.123 (-*en*)
Helene	16.281*, 287*, 17.134 (-*ae*, perhaps to avoid another sibilant?)
Helice	18.149 (-*en*)*
Helle	18.141 (abl.), 19.123 (-*es*), 128 (nom.)*
Hermione	16.255 (-*es*)
Hesione	20.69 (-*en*)
Hippolyte	21.120 (abl.)*
Hypsipyle	17.193*
Laodice	19.135*
Oenone	16.97 (-*es*, s.v.l.), 17.196 (-*en*)
Persephone	21.46*
Phoebe	20.229
Pleione	16.62 (-*es*)
Sparte	16.189 (-*en*), 191*, 17.209*

4. *Feminines in* -is

(a) *Adjectives*

Atracis	17.248 (n.)
Bistonis	16.346
Parrhasis	18.152
Sestis (?)	18.2 (n.)
Taenaris	16.30, 17.6 (cf. 16.276 *Taenaria*)

(b) *Patronymics*

Athamantis	18.137 (-*idos*)
Briseis	20.69 (-*ida*)
Dardanis	17.212 (-*ides*)
Erecthis	16.345 (-*ida*) (n.)
Letois	21.153 (-*idos*) (n.)
Leucippis	16.329 (-*idas*)
Minois	16.349 (-*ida*) (cf. 17.193 *Minoia uirgo*)

GREEK PROPER NAMES

Oebalis	16.128 (*-i*) (n.)
Phasis	16.347 (*-ida* (n.)), 19.176 (*-ida*)
Schoeneis	16.265 (*-ida*), 21.123 (*-ida*)
Tyndaris	16.100 (*-i*), 308 (*-i*), 17.118 (*-idos* (n.))

Cf. 16.83, 17.254 *Pari*. See McKeown on *Am.* 1.2.47–8, N–W I 443–5.

5. *Masculines and feminines in* -os

Abydos	19.30 (*-on*)*
Andros	21.81 (*-on*)
Arctos	18.149 (*-on*)
Delos	21.77 (*-on*) (n.)
Menelaos	17.249 (*-on*) (cf. 16.205, *al. Menelaus*). See N–W I 191–207
Myconos	21.81 (*-on*)
Tenos	21.81 (*-on*)*

Occurrences of names of this form in the nominative are not listed.

6. *Others*

Alcyon	18.81 (*-es*)
Arctophylax	18.188*
Boreas	18.39 (*-ā* voc.), 209*, 21.42*
Ceyx (?)	18.81 (*-os*) (n.)
Cres	16.350 (*-tas*)
Hecataeon	19.133 (*-one*) (n.)
Lacedaemon	16.131 (*-one*), 19.177 (*-ona*)
Palaemon	18.159 (*-ona*)
Theseus	17.33 (*-ea*)
Tyro	19.132*

Cf. 19.199 *delphina*.

WORKS CITED BY SHORT TITLE

Standard commentaries referred to by the name of the commentator (e.g. 'McKeown on Ov. *Am.* 1.14.33') are not included in this list.

Adams, J. N. (1982). *The Latin sexual vocabulary*. London.
Anderson, W. S. (1973). 'The *Heroides*', in Binns 49–83.
Appel, G. (1909). *De Romanorum precationibus*. Giessen, repr. New York 1975.
Austin, C. and Reeve, M. D. (1970). 'Notes on Sophocles, Ovid, & Euripides', *Maia* n.s. 22: 3–18.
Axelson, B. (1945). *Unpoetische Wörter. Ein Beitrag zur Kenntnis der lateinischen Dichtersprache.* (Skrifter utgivna av Vetenskaps-Societeten i Lund 29.) Lund.
 (1958). 'Der Mechanismus des ovidischen Pentameterschlusses', in Herescu 121–35.
Belfiore, Elizabeth (1980–1). 'Ovid's encomium of Helen', *C.J.* 76: 136–48.
Bell, A. J. (1923). *The Latin dual & poetic diction. Studies in numbers and figures.* Oxford.
Benedum, J. (1967) *Studien zur Dichtkunst des späten Ovids*. Diss. Giessen.
Bennett, C. E. (1910), (1914). *Syntax of early Latin*. I *The verb*. II *The cases*. Boston.
Bentley, R. *See* Hedicke.
Berger, A. (1953). *Encyclopedic dictionary of Roman Law*. (Trans. American Philosophical Society n.s. 43, 2.) Philadelphia.
Bersmann, G. (ed.) (1582). *P. Ovidii Nasonis Opera*. Leipzig.
Binns, J. W. (ed.) (1973). *Ovid*. London.
Bischoff, B. (1961). 'Hadoardus and the manuscripts of classical authors from Corbie', in (ed.) S. Prete, *Didascaliae. Studies in honor of Anselm M. Albareda* 41–57. New York.
Blase, H. (1903). *Tempora und Modi*, in (ed.) G. Landgraf, *Historische Grammatik der lateinischen Sprache.* III *Syntax des einfachen Satzes*. Leipzig.
Bonner, S. F. (1949). *Roman declamation in the late Republic and early Empire.* Liverpool.

WORKS CITED

Bopp, Heike (1966). *Inscia capta puella. Akontios und Kydippe bei Kallimachos und bei Ovid*. Diss. Münster.

Burman, P. (ed.) (1727). *P. Ovidii Nasonis Opera Omnia*. 4 vols. Amsterdam.

Casson, L. (1971). *Ships and seamanship in the ancient world*. Princeton.

Ciofanus, H. (1582). *P. Ovidii Nasonis Epistulae Heroides ... emendatae, & obseruationibus illustratae*. Antwerp.

Clark, S. B. (1908). 'The authorship and the date of the double letters in Ovid's Heroides', *H.S.C.P.* 19: 121–55.

Coleman, R. (1977). 'Greek influence on Latin syntax', *Trans. Philol. Soc. 1975*: 101–56.

Coles, R. A. (1974). *A new Oxyrhynchus Papyrus: the Hypothesis of Euripides' Alexandros*. B.I.C.S. Suppl. 32. London.

Copley, F. O. (1974). '*Servitium Amoris* in the Roman elegists', *T.A.P.A.* 78: 285–300.

Courtney, E. (1965). 'Ovidian and non-Ovidian Heroides', *B.I.C.S.* 12: 63–6.

—— (1974). 'Problems in Ovid's Heroides', *Mnem.* 27: 298–9.

—— (1989). 'Emendations in Ovid', *S.O.* 64: 125–9.

Dale, A. M. (ed.) (1967). *Euripides Helen*. Oxford.

Daly, L. W. (1952). 'Callimachus and Catullus', *C.P.* 47: 97–9.

Diggle, J. (1972). 'Ovidiana', *P.C.P.S.* 18: 31–41.

Dilthey, C. (1863). *De Callimachi Cydippa*. Leipzig. [Includes critical text of *Her.* 20–21.]

—— (1885). *Observationum in epistulas heroidum Ovidianas particula* 1. Progr. Göttingen.

Dörrie, H. (1960), (1972). *Untersuchungen zur Überlieferungsgeschichte von Ovids Epistulae Heroidum*. (Nachr. d. Akad. d. Wissenschaften in Göttingen, Phil.-Hist. Kl. 1960, 5 (Teil 1), 7 (II); 1972, 6 (III).) Göttingen.

—— (ed.) (1971). *P. Ovidii Nasonis Epistulae Heroidum*. (Texte und Kommentare 6.) Berlin and New York.

D'Orsi, L. (1968). 'Un graffito greco di Stabia', *P. d. P.* 23: 228–30.

Dover, K. J. (1978). *Greek homosexuality*. New York.

Ehwald, R. (ed.) (1903). *P. Ovidius Naso. 1 Amores* etc. Leipzig.

Eklund, S. (1970). *The periphrastic, completive and finite use of the present participle in Latin. With special regard to translation of Christian texts in*

Greek up to 600 A.D. (Acta Universitatis Upsaliensis. Studia Latina Upsaliensia 5.) Uppsala.

Ernout, A. and Meillet, A. (1959), (1960). *Dictionnaire étymologique de la langue latine.* 4th edn. 2 vols. Paris.

Fedeli, P. (1972). *Il carme 61 di Catullo.* (Seges 16.) Fribourg.

Fischer, Uta (1969). *Ignotum hoc aliis ille novavit opus. Beobachtungen zur Darstellungskunst Ovids in den Heroides unter besonderer Berücksichtigung der Briefpaare her. 16 and 17 (Paris und Helena) und her. 20 and 21 (Acontius und Cydippe).* Diss. Augsburg.

Fisher, Elizabeth (1970). 'Two notes on the *Heroides*', *H.S.C.P.* 74: 193–205.

Fowler, D. (1987). 'Vergil on killing virgins', in (edd.) M. Whitby, *et al., Homo Viator. Classical essays for John Bramble.* Bristol and Oak Park, Illinois.

Fraenkel, E. (1955). 'Vesper adest (Catullus LXII)', *J.R.S.* 45: 1–8 = *Kleine Beiträge zur klassischen Philologie* (Rome 1964) II 87–101.

Fränkel, H. (1945). *Ovid. A poet between two worlds.* (Sather Classical Lectures 18.) Berkeley and Los Angeles.

Frécaut, J.-M. (1972). *L'esprit et l'humour chez Ovid.* Grenoble.

Gelzer, T. (ed.) (1975). Musaeus, *Hero and Leander*, in Callimachus, *Fragments* ed. C. A. Trypanis (Loeb Classical Library) 289–389, 421–2. Cambridge, Mass. and London. [Musaeus tr. by C. Whitman.]

Goold, G. P. (1965). '*Amatoria critica*', *H.S.C.P.* 69: 1–107.

Guthrie, W. K. C. (1950). *The Greeks and their gods.* Boston.

Guttmann, K. (1890). *Sogenanntes instrumentales* ab *bei Ovid.* Progr. Dortmund.

Hall, Edith (1989). *Inventing the barbarian.* Oxford.

Häussler, B. (1968). *Nachträge zu A. Otto* [q.v.] ... Darmstadt.

Hardie, P. R. (1986). *Virgil's Aeneid. Cosmos and Imperium.* Oxford.

Haupt, M. (1875–6). *Mauricii Hauptii Opuscula.* 3 vols. Leipzig.

Hedicke, E. (1905). *Studia Bentleiana* v: *Ovidius Bentleianus.* Progr. Freienwalde.

Heinsius, D. (ed.) (1629). *Pub. Ovidii Nasonis Opera.* 3 vols. Leiden.

Heinsius, N. (ed.) (1661). *Operum P. Ovidii Nasonis editio nova.* 3 vols. Leiden. [Heinsius' commentary is incorporated with additions in Burman, q.v.]

WORKS CITED

Hellegouarc'h, J. (1964). *Le monosyllabe dans l'hexamètre latin. Essai de métrique verbale.* (Etudes et commentaires 50.) Paris.

Henry, J. (1873–89). *Aeneidea, or critical, exegetical and aesthetical remarks on the Aeneis.* 4 vols. London, Edinburgh and Dublin.

Herescu, N. I. (ed.) (1958). *Ovidiana. Recherches sur Ovide.* Paris.

Heyworth, S. J. (1984). 'Three notes on the *Heroides*', *Mnem.* 37: 103–9.

Hilberg, I. (1894). *Die Gesetze der Wortstellung im Pentameter des Ovid.* Leipzig.

Hinds, S. (1993). 'Medea in Ovid: scenes from the life of an intertextual heroine', *M. & D.* 30: 9–47.

Hintermeier, Cornelia M. (1993). *Die Briefpaare in Ovids Heroides.* (Palingenesia 41.) Stuttgart.

Hofmann, J. B. (1951). *Lateinische Umgangssprache.* 3. Auflage. Heidelberg.

Hollis, A. S. (1989). 'Ovid, *Heroides* 20.127–30', *L.C.M.* 14: 4.

—— (1991). 'Ovid, *Heroides* 21.229–30 and Callimachus, fr. 67.3–4', *L.C.M.* 16: 90–1.

—— (1994). 'Rights of way in Ovid (*Heroides* 20.146) and Plautus (*Curculio* 36)', *C.Q.* 44: 545–9.

Holmes, N. (1995). '*Gaudia nostra*: a hexameter-ending in elegy', *C.Q.* 45 (forthcoming).

Hopkinson, N. (ed.) (1988). *A Hellenistic anthology.* Cambridge.

—— (ed.) (1994). *Greek poetry of the Imperial period. An anthology.* Cambridge.

Housman, A. E. (ed.) (1938). *D. Iunii Iuuenalis Saturae.* Cambridge.

Hunt, J. M. (1975). Review of Dörrie (1971), *C.P.* 70: 215–24.

Hutchinson, G. O. (1988). *Hellenistic poetry.* Oxford.

Jacobson, H. (1968). 'Ennian influence in *Heroides* 16 and 17', *Phoenix* 22: 299–303.

—— (1974). *Ovid's Heroides.* Princeton.

Jocelyn, H.D. (ed.) (1967). *The Tragedies of Ennius.* (Cambridge Classical Texts and Commentaries 10.) Cambridge.

Jouan, F. (1966). *Euripide et les légendes des Chants Cypriens.* Paris.

Kenney, E. J. (1958). 'Nequitiae poeta', in Herescu 201–9.

—— (1959). 'Notes on Ovid: II', *C.Q.* 9: 240–60.

—— (1961). Review of Dörrie (1960), *Gnomon* 33: 478–87.

—— (1969). 'Ovid and the law', *Y.C.S.* 21: 241–63.

(1970a). Review of Kirfel, *C.R.* 20: 195–7.

(1970b). 'Notes on Ovid: III', *H.S.C.P.* 74: 169–85.

(1970c). 'Love and legalism: Ovid, *Heroides* 20 and 21', *Arion* 9: 388–414 = (tr. G. Luck) 'Liebe als juristisches Problem', *Philol.* 111 (1967) 212–32.

(1970d). 'Doctus Lucretius', *Mnem.* 4, 23: 366–92 = (ed.) C. J. Classen, *Probleme der Lukrezforschung* (Hildesheim 1986) 237–65 [with *Addendis addenda*].

(1973). 'The style of the *Metamorphoses*', in Binns 116–53.

(1979). 'Two disputed passages in the *Heroides*', *C.Q.* 29: 394–431.

(1983). 'Virgil and the elegiac sensibility', *I.C.S.* 8: 44–59.

(ed.) (1984). *The Ploughman's Lunch. Moretum: a poem ascribed to Virgil.* Bristol.

(1992). Introduction and notes in A. D. Melville (tr.), *Ovid. Sorrows of an exile.* Oxford. [Pbk 1995.]

(1993). 'Ovidiana', *C.Q.* 43: 458–67.

(1995). '"Dear Helen ...": the *pithanotate prophasis*?', *Papers of the Leeds International Latin Seminar* 8: 187–207.

Kinsey, T. E. (1979). 'The meaning of *interea* in Virgil's *Aeneid*', *Glotta* 57: 259–65.

Kirfel, E.-A. (1969). *Untersuchungen zur Briefform der Heroides Ovids.* (Noctes Romanae 11.) Bern and Stuttgart.

Klemm, J. (1889). *De fabulae quae est de Herus et Leandri amoribus fonte et auctore.* Diss. Lepizig.

Knox, B. M. W. (1968). 'Silent reading in antiquity', *G.R.B.S.* 9: 421–35.

Knox, P. E. (1986). *Ovid's Metamorphoses and the traditions of Augustan poetry. P.C.P.S.* Supplement 11.

(ed.) (1995). *Ovid Heroides. Select epistles.* Cambridge.

Kost, K. (ed.) (1971). *Musaios Hero und Leander.* (Abh. zur Kunst-, Musik-, und Literaturwissenschaft 88.) Bonn.

Kraus, W. (1950–1). 'Die Briefpaare in Ovids Heroiden', *W.S.* 65: 54–77.

Lachmann, K. (1876). *Kleinere Schriften zur classischen Philologie*, ed. J. Vahlen (*Kleinere Schriften* II). Berlin.

Lattimore, R. (1962). *Themes in Greek and Latin epitaphs.* Urbana, Illinois.

Leyhausen, J. (1893). *Helenae et Herus Epistulae Ovidii non sunt.* Diss. Halle.

Lier, B. (1914). *Ad topica carminum amatoriorum symbolae*. Progr. Stettin, repr. New York and London 1978.
Loers, V. (ed.) (1829). *P. Ovidii Nasonis Heroides et A. Sabini Epistolae*. Cologne.
Löfstedt, E. (1942), (1956). *Syntactica. Studien und Beiträge zur historischen Syntax des Lateins*. I *Über einige Grundfragen der lateinischen Nominalsyntax*. 2. Auflage. Lund–Leipzig–London. II *Syntaktischstilistische Gesichtspunkte und Probleme*. Lund.
Luck, G. (1961). *Die römische Liebeselegie*. Heidelberg.
Lyne, R. O. A. M. (ed.) (1978). *Ciris. A poem attributed to Vergil*. (Cambridge Classical Texts and Commentaries 20.) Cambridge.
   (1979). 'Servitium Amoris', *C.Q.* 29: 117–30.
Mack, Sara (1988). *Ovid*. New Haven and London.
McKeown, J. C. (ed.) (1987). *Ovid: Amores*. I *Text and Prolegomena*. Liverpool and Wolfeboro, New Hampshire.
Maehler, H. (1982). 'Ein fragment eines hellenistischen Epos', *Mus. Phil. Lond.* 7: 109–18.
Maltby, R. (1991). *A lexicon of ancient Latin etymologies*. (ARCA 25.) Leeds.
Meiggs, R. (1982). *Trees and timber in the ancient Mediterranean world*. Oxford.
Meijer, F. J. A. M. (1990). 'Ovide, *Héroides* XVI 112 et la construction navale romaine', *Mnem.* 43: 450–2.
Merchant, W. H. P. (1967). 'Ovid, *Heroides* 16.117', *C.R.* 17: 262–3.
Merkel, R. (ed.) (1852). *P. Ovidius Naso*. I *Amores* etc. Leipzig.
Micyllus, J. (ed.) (1549). *P. Ovidii Nasonis ... Opera quae uocantur amatoria*. Basle.
Müller, L. (1894). *De re metrica poetarum Latinorum praeter Plautum et Terentium libri septem*. 2nd edn. St. Petersburg and Leipzig.
Myers, K. Sara (1994). *Ovid's Causes. Cosmogony and aetiology in the Metamorphoses*. Ann Arbor.
Naugerius, A. (ed.) (1515). *P. Ovidii Nasonis uita ... Heroidum epistulae* etc. Venice.
Norden, E. (ed.) (1916). *P. Vergilius Maro Aeneis Buch VI*. 2. Auflage. Leipzig and Berlin.
Ott, W. (1974). *Metrische Analysen zu Ovid, Metamorphosen Buch I*. (Materialien zu Metrik und Stilistik 7.) Tübingen.

Palmer, A. (ed.) (1898). *P. Ovidi Nasonis Heroides with the Greek translation of Planudes*. [Completed by L. C. Purser.] Oxford.
Papanghelis, T. D. (1987). *Propertius: a Hellenistic poet on love and death*. Cambridge.
Parker, H. N. (1993). 'Sappho schoolmistress', *T.A.P.A.* 123: 309–51.
Pfeiffer, R. (ed.) (1949), (1953). *Callimachus.* I *Fragmenta.* II *Hymni et Epigrammata*. Oxford.
Platnauer, M. (1951). *Latin elegiac verse. A study of the metrical usages of Tibullus, Propertius & Ovid*. Cambridge.
Pohlenz, M. (1913). 'Die Abfassungszeit von Ovids Metamorphosen', *Hermes* 48: 1–13.
Postgate, J. P. (1907–8). 'Flaws in classical research', *P.B.A.* 3: 161–211.
Purser, L. C. *See* Palmer.
Rand, E. K. (1925). *Ovid and his influence*. (Our debt to Greece and Rome 13.) London–Calcutta–Sydney.
Reeve, M. D. (1973). 'Notes on Ovid's *Heroides*', *C.Q.* 23: 324–38.
Richmond, J. A. (1965). 'A note on the elision of final $\breve{e}$ in certain particles used by Latin poets', *Glotta* 43: 78–103.
Riley, H. T. (tr.) (1919). *Ovid's Heroides* etc. London.
Ripert, E. (1921). *Ovide. Poète de l'amour, des dieux et de l'exile*. Paris.
Sabot, A.-F. (1981). 'Les Héroides d'Ovide: préciosité, rhétorique et poésie', *ANRW* II 31.4: 2552–2636. Berlin and New York.
Schawaller, Doris (1987). 'Semantische Wortspiele in Ovids Metamorphosen und Heroides', *Grazer Beiträge* 14: 199–214.
Schott, G. (1957). *Hero und Leander bei Musaios und Ovid*. Diss. Cologne.
Schulze, W. (G.) (1894). *Orthographica et Graeca Latina*. Marburg. References are to the edn pubd Rome 1958 (Sussidi Eruditi 14).
Sedlmayer, H. S. (1880). 'Die Aufeinanderfolge gleicher oder ähnlicher Versschlüsse bei Ovid', *W.S.* 2: 293–5.
Segal, C. P. (1969). *Landscape in Ovid's Metamorphoses. A study in the transformation of a literary symbol*. (Hermes Einzelschriften 23.) Wiesbaden.
Shackleton Bailey, D. R. (1956). *Propertiana*. Cambridge.
Showerman, G. and Goold, G. P. (1977). *Ovid, Heroides and Amores*. 2nd edn rev. G. P. Goold (Loeb Classical Library). Cambridge, Mass. and London.
Sommer, F. (1948). *Handbuch der lateinischen Laut- und Formenlehre. Eine*

Einführung in das sprachwissentschaftliche Studium des Lateins. Heidelberg.

Soubiran, J. (1966). *L'élision dans la poésie latine*. (Études et commentaires 63.) Paris.

Spies, A. (1930). *Militat omnis amans. Ein Beitrag zur Bildersprache der antiken Erotik*. Diss. Tübingen, repr. New York and London 1978.

Stinton, T. C. W. (1965). *Euripides and the Judgement of Paris*. (Soc. Prom. Hell. Stud. Supplementary Paper 11.) London = *Collected papers on Greek tragedy* (Oxford 1990) 17–75.

Tarrant, R. J. (1983). 'Ovid', in (ed.) L. D. Reynolds, *Texts and transmission. A survey of the Latin classics* 257–84. Oxford.

Terpstra, J. (ed.) (1829). *P. Ovidii Nasonis Heroides*. Leiden.

Thompson, P. A. M. (1993). 'Notes on Ovid, *Heroides* 20 and 21', *C.Q.* 43: 258–65.

Thompson, S. (1955–8). *Motif-index of folk-literature*. Rev. and enlarged edn. 6 vols. Copenhagen.

Tracy, Valerie A. (1971). 'The authenticity of *Heroides* 16–21', *C.J.* 66: 328–30.

van Lennep, D. J. (ed.) (1812). *P. Ovidii Nasonis Heroides et A. Sabini Epistolae*. Amsterdam.

Vessey, D. W. T. C. (1969). 'Notes on Ovid, *Heroides* 9', *C.Q.* 13: 349–61.

Walbank, F. W. (1967). 'The Scipionic legend', *P.C.P.S* 13: 54–69.

Walsh, P. G. (1970). *The Roman novel*. Cambridge.

Washietl, J. A. (1883). *De similitudinibus imaginibusque Ovidianis*. Diss. Vienna.

Watt, W. S. (1985). 'Ovidiana', *Mus. Helv.* 42: 56–60.

(1989). 'Notes on Ovid, Heroides', *R.F.I.C.* 117: 62–8.

(1995). 'Ovidiana', *Mus. Helv.* 52: 90–107.

Wentzel, G. (1890). 'Die Entführung der Helene', in ΕΠΙΘΑΛΑΜΙΟΝ *Wolfgang Passow und Helene Passow* dargebr. von F. Spiro und G. Wentzel I–LVIII. Göttingen.

White, Diana G. (1968). 'Ovid, *Heroides* 16.45–46', *H.S.C.P.* 74: 187–91.

Wilkinson, L. P. (1955). *Ovid recalled*. Cambridge.

(1963). *Golden Latin artistry*. Cambridge.

Williams, G. (1968). *Tradition and originality in Roman poetry*. Oxford.

INDEXES

References are to lemmata in the Commentary.

1 Latin words

a (= 'next to'), 16.98, 18.69, 20.157; (instrumental), 16.279–80
Achaia (prosody of), 16.187
Actaeus (= 'Attic'), 18.42
adedo, 21.44
adhuc (referring to future), 18.169
ambo, 20.163
antemnae, 16.113
applico(r) (construction of), 16.128
atque ita, 18.115, 19.169
aueo, 17.114
aut ... -ue, 21.115–16

barbarus (= 'Trojan'), 17.64
bona (= 'charms'), 17.134

caueo (+ inf.), 20.36
causa (in abl. + possessive adj.), 20.108, 198; (in phrase *per causam*), 20.140
Cea (sc. *insula* = Ceos), 20.222
commentum, commentus, 21.32
coniuro (unique use of), 21.135
cor (= 'intelligence', uniquely in O.), 17.101–2
cum (concessive + pf. indic.), 21.151–2

debeo (= 'leave unpaid'), 16.105
decipio (= 'beguile' w. time as obj.), 19.55. Cf. *diluo, fallo*
decus (+ gen. in periphrastic expression), 17.54
demo (+ *ex*), 18.103–4
dico (construction of *ne dicam*), 16.287; (*dic mihi* introducing question), 21.55
diluo (w. time as obj.), 19.14. *Cf.*
decipio, fallo
do (reciprocal), 16.225
doctus (= 'skilfully expressed'), 20.210; (= 'literate'), 21.182
dum (causal), 21.39; (+ indic. in o.o.), 20.204

effingo, 20.134
ei mihi (position in verse), 17.246, 21.235–6
eo (= 'proceed', i.e. 'act'), 16.269; (= 'come'), 20.194; (ironical), 17.57–8
et (adversative), 16.346; (= 'also', qualifying single word), 20.159, 161; (postponed), 16.26
euenio (construction of), 20.127–8
ex (w. neuter adj. to form adverb), 16.87, 160, 20.123, 167

facio (+ *ad* = 'suit'), 16.192
fallo (w. *iura* as obj.), 16.286; (= 'beguile' w. time as obj.), 19.38. See also *decipio, diluo*
fero (= 'receive' words et sim.), 20.20
fides, 20.40
forem (= *essem*), 16.36
futurus eras (= *esses*), 17.68

habeo (+ pf. part. = pf. active), 21.48, 201–2, 233–4
hebeo, 19.192
Hero (inflexion of), 18 Superscription
hic ... ille, 20.162

idem illud (= 'that same thing'), 20.13
ignorantia, 20.187

INDEX: LATIN WORDS

Ilion, Ilios (gender and inflexion), 16.49, 17.240
illud (euphemistic), 16.161
imago (O.'s use of), 16.45–6; (= 'dream'), 19.193
immansuetus, 18.37
in (+ acc.) (= 'to further'), 16.282, 21.240; (w. *iurare*), 16.321–2; (+ abl.) (causal), 17.249; (= 'in the case of'), 21.10; (*in dubio esse* et sim.), 16.140, 17.178, 19.174; (compounded w. pf. part.), 18.37
iners, 16.314, 18.110, 122
infirmo, 17.127
infundo (+ acc. = 'fill'), 21.159–60
interea, 16.89
is (oblique cases of in poets), 20.29, 240
isto (= 'thither'), 18.205
-itas (quadrisyllabic nouns in), 16.52
iuratus (in middle sense), 20.227–8

labra (= λουτρά), 21.178
laudatrix, 17.126
lenis (of colour), 20.120
lentus, 16.228, 18.58
Letois (orthography of), 21.153
libo, 16.161
licet (used interchangeably w. *licebit*), 20.21, 71–2; (+ subj. equivalent to polite imperative), 20.9

materia, 16.148
memini (+ *cum*), 19.85–7
mixtus (adjectival), 16.151–2
modo (= *si modo*), 18.51, 147, 20.180
mora (= 'distraction'), 19.10
morator, 19.70

nec (adversative), 16.189, 348, 19.107, 203; (inferential), 16.309; (= *et ne/'ne'/'non'*), 16.15, 83, 21.222; (= *ne ... quidem*), 17.109–10, 233. See also in General Index conjunctions, postponed
nec ... et, 20.177–8

nempe, 16.292, 20.70; (position in verse), 20.94
neque ... -que ... -que, 19.119–20
neque enim ... -ue ... -ue, 21.101
neue (anticipatory), 16.363; (= *et, ne*), 16.300, 363, 18.67, 19.97–8, 20.111, 21.51–2
nil opus, 20.185
nisi si, 17.151, 21.237–8
nomen habere, 16.143–4
non (+ imper.), 17.164
non quo (+ subj. of attributed reason), 17.37
nullus (emphatic), 16.350
nympha (= 'wife'), 16.128

obmurmuro, 18.47
oborior, 20.105
odiosus, 19.21–2
ops (cases, position in verse of), 21.14
opus, 16.269–70
ordo (abl. sing. of in poets), 20.203

Pallas (= olive oil), 19.44
pars (*nulla parte* = 'in no respect'), 18.147; (= 'proportion'), 21.8
pereo (as passive of *perdo*), 20.92; (*peream si*), 17.183, 21.29
Phasis (= Medea), 16.347
pollex (= *digiti*), 17.266, 19.26, 20.141
pono (w. *tempus* et sim.), 19.10
possum (in indic. w. potential sense), 16.162, 17.92. 18.13–14
pronurus, 17.206
propter, 21.31

quaeso (construction of), 20.127–8
-que (adversative), 19.119–20; (disjunctive), 19.116; (epexegetic), 18.157–8, 19.149, 21.137; (attached to 1st word of o.r.), 17.159, 19.154, 20.127–8; (to 2nd word of phrase), 20.138, 21.19–20. See also in General Index conjunctions, postponed
-que ... -que, 16.96, 21.32

qui (= 'who'), 20.219; (abl. = 'how'), 17.213
qui, quae (in 'assessing' relative clause), 17.29; (connective), 20.46
quianam, 16.223
quid prohibet et sim., 17.42
quis (= *uter*), 19.174, 20.124, 21.63–4
quisque (= *uterque*), 19.169
quod (= 'as to the fact that'), 17.43, 51, 143, 251, 261, 18.41, 173, 20.155; (= 'why' in *hoc est quod* et sim.), 20.109
quod amo et sim., 16.85, 18.153, 179, 19.179, 20.32, 35, 21.57

rapidus, 18.37
repugno (construction of), 17.137, 20.121

scires, 16.78
sedeo (of a virtuous matron), 17.16
Sestus, 18.1–2
sic (in prayers), 16.282, 18.46
sic ... ut/ne (in stipulative sense), 17.165, 19.87–8, 181–2, 20.101–2. See also *ut ... sic*
similis (construction of), 16.30
sine (in adnominal phrases), 16.307–8, 20.225, 21.141
spes tua (= *tu qui speras*), 17.74
sponsor (fem.), 16.115–16

sub (+ acc. = 'just before'), 19.195; (= *in*), 17.94
subitus (adverbial), 18.160
suspectus (in strong sense), 19.148, 20.173
suus (= 'appropriate'), 20.66–7, 76, 142; (emphatically positioned), 16.315; (of mutual relationship), 20.76; (referring to logical rather than grammatical subj.), 19.111; (= 'rightfully theirs'), 21.142

tamen (ending pentameter), 20.44; (implying concessive sense), 16.238, 19.57; (= δέ), 16.39–40, 115–16, 21.231–2

uae, 21.169
uale (treated as neuter noun), 21.247–8
uolo (= 'be about to'), 16.122, 21.86; (= 'consent'), 16.157, 21.139
ut (omitted after *facio, malo* et sim.), 16.5, 263–4; (understood from preceding *ne*), 20.242; (= *utinam*), 19.115. See also *sic ... ut/ne, ut ... sic*
ut erat et sim., 16.121, 20.19, 21.25
ut ... sic (concessive), 17.71, 109–10, 241–4. See also *sic ... ut/ne*

2 General

ablative
  absolute, nuances of: causal, 17.155, 266, 20.92, 21.33–4, 239; circumstantial, 16.224, 275–6, 17.124, 259, 19.48, 20.206, 21.13, 159–60; concessive, 21.13; conditional, 16.2, 205, 19.186, 206, 20.191; descriptive/characterizing 19.90; instrumental, 17.3, 19.48, 124, 20.20, 30, 21.33–4, 115–16, 190, 199; stipulative, 16.162, 20.112;
  temporal, 16.217, 220, 221, 18.57, 111, 19.195, 20.10, 122, 123, 205; equivalent to relative clause, 16.168, 18.36
  adverbial, 16.377–8, 18.38
  of attendant circumstances, 21.67
  of cause, 16.178, 17.214, 21.22, 32
  of comparison, 17.222, 18.7, 25, 19.106, 21.30, 243
  descriptive/characterizing, 16.302, 18.144, 19.90, 134

of duration of time, 16.215, 317, 18.27–8, 193
instrumental, 20.128; of person, 17.49–50, 19.102, 20.30; w. *ab*, 16.279–80
locative, 16.131
of measure of difference, 19.76
of price, 16.172
of respect, 18.147
of separation, 16.155, 18.103–4, 21.69–70
'*uiae*', 16.118, 18.58, 19.31–2
w. *causa* (*mea, tua*, etc), 20.108, 198
in -*e*: of 3rd decl. adj., 16.279–80; of present participle, 16.11–12

accusative
exclamatory, 16.302, 17.145, 19.111
of extent, 18.71–2, 21.191, 233–4
internal, 16.145, 297, 321, 20.132
of motion towards, 17.163, 18.157, 19.177
appositional phrase in, 18.163

adjectives
adverbial, 21.41–2, 151–2
two attributive w. one noun, 16.45–6
predicative, 16.155, 21.45–6

adverbs
Ovid's use of, 16.174
formed from *ex* + adj., 16.87
treated as indeclinable noun, 18.180
nil as adv., 20.185

Aesacus, 16.49
Alcidamas, 16.303–6
Alexander (= Paris), 16.360
amphibole, 20.30, 221, 21.4
anachronisms, 16.33, 92, 151–2, 198, 293, 305, 17.7, 64, 87, 98
anaphora, *see* repetition
Apollonius, 16.348, 18.61–4, 133
apostrophe
metri gr., 16.267–8
pointed, 21.100
apposition, phrases in, 18.163–4, 20.55–6, 207, 21.21, 214

Aratus, 20.19
arguments
a minori, 18.40, 21.56
by dilemma, 21.63–4, 139–42
by *reductio ad absurdum*, 21.145–8
Aristaenetus, 20.9, 15, 51, 55–60, 56, 59, 99, 109–10, 125–6, 231–2, 21.65–114, 107, 109, 111–12, 157–72, 209, 215–20
Aristophanes, 16.249–54
Aristotle (?), 16.161

Bion, 21.165–6

cacemphaton, 16.372, 18.175
Callimachus, 16.348, 18.7, 42, 62, 150, 20.9, 15, 19, 27–30, 35, 50, 51, 55–60, 55–6, 59, 99, 109–10, 125–6, 217, 220, 221, 223–4, 231–2, 21.38, 44, 65–114, 77, 82, 99, 109, 111–12, 169, 173, 189–206, 209–12, 209, 233–4, 241, 243
Cassandra, 16.107–24, 121, 123–6, 125
Catullus, 16.37–8, 111–12, 18.62, 107–8, 181–2, 19.37, 45–6, 20.157–8, 21.43, 70, 109
Cicero, 16.105, 17.126, 183, 18.112, 181–2, 19.10, 20.127–8, 21.135, 137, 145–8
comparatives formed from participles, 18.45, 19.83
'compendious comparison', 18.69, 19.146; *cf.* 21.179
compounds formed from *in-* + participle, 18.37
concord
participle agrees with nearer noun, 16.87
sing. verb w. compound subject, 16.362, 17.160, 19.132, 21.41–2
verb takes number of predicate, 16.52
conditional clauses
protasis expressed as statement,

21.63-4; by imperative, 16.163, 19.4, 8; by jussive subjunctive, 18.193; as wish, 20.53
'*sit . . . erit*' type of, 17.47-8, 21.221-4
See also Index of Latin words s.v. modo
conjunctions, postponed: general, 16.26; *aut*, 19.12; *et*, 16.26, 92, 19.110, 114, 160, 21.14, 98, 99; *nam*, 19.151; *nec*, 16.348, 18.6, 132, 212, 21.217-18; *-que*, 16.216, 18.94, 214, 21.200; *sed*, 16.191, 17.95, 18.180, 19.72, 109; *sed tamen*, 17.184
Cypria, 16.19, 41, 53-88, 107-24, 118, 121, 126-7, 187, 279-80, 303-6, 343

Dardania (= Troy), 16.57-8
dative
  of advantage, 17.235-6, 18.96; of disadvantage, 17.179, 187, 21.146
  of the agent, 16.30, 211, 281, 17.55, 19.63, 129, 136, 20.214, 228, 21.61, 115-16
  of motion towards, 16.88
  predicative, 17.39, 147, 160
  possessive, 20.60
  w. *similis*, 17.30
diffuse or negligent writing, 'molesta abundantia', et sim., 16.17, 23, 49-50, 50, 85, 125, 212, 246, 352, 17.63, 116, 18.49-50, 175, 20.101-2, 21.72-3, 126
Dioscuri, 16.153, 343
distribution of adjective-noun phrase, 19.7, 21.188. *See also* word-order
'do' for 'allow to be done', 20.117, 21.93-4
dreams, 16.43-50, 19.59, 193, 20.229

elegiac motifs, 16.220, 247-8, 255-6, 259, 285-94, 321-2, 17.35, 41, 79-80, 81-2, 88, 185-8, 256, 18.37-46, 19.9-14, 37-8, 80, 20.46, 75-90, 80, 81-2, 85-6, 130, 133-4, 166, 21.5, 189-206
ellipse, words or ideas 'understood'
  of conjunction, 16.82
  of idea of 'even', 18.8; 'only', 16.299, 17.134, 21.142, 238; 'other', 18.72
  of negative, 19.98; of positive, 20.242
  of object of verb, 16.118, 17.185, 187, 20.80
  of personal pronouns, 16.261, 17.113, 185, 201, 18.32, 20.80, 89, 215
  of subject of o.o., 21.197
  various, 16.199-200, 17.34, 209-10, 218, 19.15-16, 113-14, 122, 171-2, 186, 20.5, 53, 216
  of parts of *esse*, 16.129-30, 191, 325, 17.2, 13, 104, 181-2, 253, 18.3, 88, 19.7, 129, 143, 20.25, 70, 226; of *fiet*, 18.187, of *quamuis*, 16.238, 19.183, 20.43; of *si*: w. *modo*, 18.51, 147, 20.180; w. *liceat*, 18.66; w. protasis expressed as imperative, 16.163; as statement, 21.63-4; as stipulation, 18.193, 20.66-7; as wish 20.53
See also paratactic (coordinating) constructions; word-order, ἀπὸ κοινοῦ
enallage, 16.107, 111-12, 17.79-80, 18.133, 144, 20.155, 239, 21.70, 119
Ennius, 16.42, 43-50, 45-6, 47-8, 91, 96, 107-14, 111-12, 123-6, 143-4, 223, 361, 17.213, 237-8, 19.202
epanalepsis, 16.249-51, 18.101-2, 21.72-3, 113-14, 135-6
epicisms, 16.42, 17.54, 21.70, 72-3, 85-6
Euripides, 16.51-2, 54, 90, 91, 179, 187, 191, 249-54, 255-6 299-304, 333-8, 361, 17.77-8, 109-

10, 119, 18.97, 19.9–14, 21.65–6, 135

finite verb expressed w. participle + *esse*, 16.57–8, 151–2

Gallus, 16.107–14, 19.142
gender, feminine: of male bird, 17.56; of *sponsor*, 16.115–16
genitive
  defining, 17.114, 18.133, 19.11, 20.64, 202, 21.115–16, 151–2
  descriptive/characterizing, 18.63, 21.138
  objective, 16.60, 293, 323, 17.19, 123
  partitive, 16.143–4, 17.28, 101–2, 19.23
  possessive, 16.293, 19.54
  of price, 19.97–8
  of respect, 21.31
  for adjective: attributive, 17.87, 21.172; possessive, 20.101–2
  w. *similis* 17.30
geography, cavalier treatment of, 18.49–50, 21.81–2
gerundive, 20.74
Greek proper names, 16.62, 175, 187, 259, 267–8, 345, 17,118, 248, 18.2, 81, 151, 19.129, 21.77, 153. *Cf*. 19.199 *and see also Appendix*

Hellenistic epigram, 21.157–72, 172
hendiadys, 16.23, 183, 223, 20.59, 21.41–2
Herodotus, 16.51–2, 126–7
Hesiod, 16.24, 37–8, 341, 17.104
Homer, 16.22, 64, 83, 96, 111, 113, 126–7, 186, 199–200, 255–6, 257, 259, 263–70, 263–4, 291, 299–304, 354, 357–8, 360, 376, 17.64, 220, 252, 18.7, 8, 46, 57, 66, 69, 103–4, 163–4, 19.132, 148, 20.44, 60, 69, 106, 221–2, 231–2
Horace, 16.113, 114, 150, 182, 17.23, 18.36. 19.9–14, 33–4, 46, 195, 196, 207, 20.39, 125, 21.45–6, 53–4, 91, 173, 231–2
hysteron proteron (so called), 21.32

Ida, Mount, 16.53, 109, 203–4, 303–4, 19.177
imagery and symbol
  dolphin, 19.193
  erotic: apple or quince, 20.9; bonds of love, 20.39, 85–6, 212; fire of love, 16.49–50, 124, 125, 18.85–6, 89–90; heart as lodging-place, 19.156; Love as hunter, 20.45; military, 17.256, 19.157; property (beloved as), 20.143–4, 145, 150
  Paris as firebrand, 16.45–6, 123–6, 164
  ship: connoting recklessness, 16.107–24; Leander as, 18.6, 148, 207–8, 215, 19.47, 208
imperative
  'future' form, 19.87, 20.219
  in protasis of condition, 16.163, 19.4, 8, 20.219
  w. *non*, 17.164
indicative, *see* mood
infinitive
  as neuter noun, 17.24, 19.145, 185
  inf. phrase as subject of clause, 20.4
irony, authorial, 16.22, 41, 53–6, 84, 89, 125, 164, 172, 182, 198, 249–54, 257, 263–70, 263–4, 279–80, 281, 291, 303–4, 340, 357–8, 375, 376, 377–8, 17.54, 104, 146, 18.31, 55–104, 75, 156, 19.17–18, 154, 155, 177, 20.44, 21.87, 95

Laomedon, 16.182
legal language, 16.115–16, 245, 321–2, 17.107, 194, 206, 18.110, 20.29, 30, 36, 38, 39, 40, 64, 79, 91, 92, 143–4, 145, 149, 150, 151, 187,

266   INDEX: GENERAL

21.133–50, 133, 138, 140, 146, 223
litotes, 16.18, 225, 373, 20.223–4
Lucretius, 19.203, 20.110
Lycophron, 16.47–8, 49, 109, 17.22, 191, 18.139–40

Menelaus, 16.129–30, 249–54, 257, 263–70, 301, 302, 303–6, 357–8, 17.109–10, 169–70
metonymy, 19.44, 21.167–8
metre
  anapaestic words, sequence of, 16.101
  caesura at 3w, 16.67
  descriptive use of, 21.112–13
  diction and metrical convenience, 16.33–4
  elision: at caesura, 16.337, 21.137; of -ē, 19.81; of iambic word, 16.97; of monosyllabic pronoun, 19.29–30; reinforcing sense, 21.25; prodelision, 18.169, 19.29–30
  imparting emphasis, 20.218
  monosyllables, hexameters ending in, 16.71
  open short vowel ending pentameter, 18.172, 20.240
  polysyllabic word ending pentameter, 16.290, 17.16, 19.202
  prosody: of *Achaia*, 16.187; of final -*o*, 18.203; of final syllable of 1st half of pentameter, 20.132; of *periit* et sim., 19.128
  sense-pause after diaeresis in 2nd foot of hexameter avoided, 20.109
  -*que* postponed *metri gr.*, 16.216
'mind's eye', 16.101
mood
  indicative: in apodosis of past unreal condition, 17.23, 21.206; connoting potentiality or obligation w. *possum* etc., 16.162,
17.92, 169–70, 186, 18.13–14, 19.130, 20.170, 21.125, 132; retained in *dum*-clause in o.o., 20.204, 207; future in rhetorical question, 21.56
  subjunctive: deliberative, 19.174; generalizing 2nd person, 17.192, 20.32; giving assumed or attributed reason, 19.45, 107; reflecting thought of speaker, 20.125, 126; jussive, (present) 21.183–4, (imperfect) 20.227, (pluperfect) 20.53; perfect of 'cautious assertion', 16.189, 17.109–10, in question, 16.7; stipulative w. *ut*, 17.165; w. *quod* = 'as to (presumed) fact that', 17.43; w. *non quo* = 'not because (as you might think)', 17.37
  See also relative clauses
Musaeus, 17.191, 18.27–8, 31, 36, 42, 55–104, 57, 61–4, 66, 83, 89–90, 97, 103–4, 105, 106, 148, 149–56, 163–4, 197, 207–8, 19.9–14, 21–2, 99–100, 147, 159–60, 171–2, 193, 201, 20.56

neuter
  characterizing a person, 19.91
  in phrases of type *ultima Ponti*, 18.157–8
  infinitive treated as neuter noun, 17.24, 19.145, 185; ditto quoted word, 18.180; ditto *uale*, 21.247–8
  quod amo/ames, 16.85, 20.168
Nicander, 21.111–12
novel, motifs from, 16.333–8, 18.66, 20.62, 21.157–72
number
  plural, 'poetic': *certamen*, 20.165; *cibus*, 20.132; *corpus*, 17.253; *cultus*, 16.195–6; *currus*, 17.203; *euentus*, 20.164; *exemplum*, 17.214; *fatum*, 19.106, 118; *foedus*, 20.188;

lumen, 18.31; *nomen*, 18.139–40; *numen*, 20.100; *otium*, 19.102; *pallium*, 20.208; *pectus*, 16.249, 251, 20.198; *scriptum*, 21.212; *somnus*, 20.132; *templum*, 20.180; *uelum*, 16.113; *uerbum*, 16.10; *uia*, 16.22, 18.60, 19.52, 21.68; *uultus*, 16.37–8
singular: collective: *bos*, 20.181; *fluctus*, 19.121; *miles*, 16.368; *Plias*, 18.188; *pollex* (= *digiti*), 17.266, 19.26, 20.139; 'poetic': *lumen*, 16.37–8; *umerus*, 20.208
variation of *metri gr. et sim.*, 16.195–6, 19.62, 198
nurse as confidante, 18.97, 19.153, 21.17, 19–20, 109

Oenone, 16.97–8, 128, 17.195–8, 196
'one soul in two bodies', 18.125–6, 19.149–50, 20.4, 233–4
orthography, 16.345, 17.55
oxymoron, 17.259

paratactic (coordinating) constructions: w. *facio*, 16.263–4, 17.158, 18.204, 19.181–2, 20.39, 152, 180, 203, 21.147; w. *malo* et sim., 16.5, 18.21, 21.65–6, 227–8; w. *mando*, 16.303–4; w. *precor*, 19.188; w. *uideto* (?), 20.219; other, 16.79
participles
 comparative of, 18.45, 19.83; superlative, 17.71, 18.37, 19.131
 equivalent to relative clause, 16.6, 60, 168, 19.73
 expressing main idea though grammatically subordinate, 21.159–60
 future: in periphrastic construction, 17.68, 18.11; predicative, 17.158;
 in *ab urbe condita* construction, 18.139–40, 20.188, 21.134
 nuances of: causal, 16.3, 24, 17.22, 129, 155, 19.15, 159–60, 20.97; concessive, 16.238, 19.183, 21.36, 239, 21.13, 36; conditional, 16.2, 205, 341, 19.186, 206, 20.191; instrumental, 17.3, 20.20, 181, 21.190, 199, 237–8; predicative, 17.158; proleptic, 19.77; volitive, 18.212
perfect: compounded w. *in-*, 18.37; contemporaneous in aspect, 16.42, 17.3, 19.37, 48, 90, 124; in periphrastic constructions: + *esse*, 16.151–2; + *habere*, 21.48, 201–2, 233–4
present: abl. sing. of, 16.12; conative, 20.123; in periphrastic construction + *esse*, 16.57–8
See also ablative, absolute
passive
 in reciprocal (middle) sense, 19.93
 of *credo* (personal), 21.9
'patterned' verses, 16.107–14, 17.265–6, 19.37–8, 37, 49, 142, 21.70
personification: of anger, 20.87; cloud, 19.123; peace, 21.53–4, ships, 16.122
Philoctetes, 16.279–80, 363–4
Phrygians, 16.198
Pindar, 16.121, 123–6
pleonasm, 18.113, 20.210, 21.58
'polar' expressions, 16.143–4
polyptoton, 20.66–7, 173–5, 227–8, 21.11, 103
predicative expressions, 16.10, 88, 155, 233, 265–6, 269–70, 332, 367, 17.3, 27, 53, 55, 60, 107, 126, 158, 18.56, 58, 94, 160, 173, 195, 19.77, 119–20, 129, 141, 20.46, 53, 209, 21.11, 45–6, 78, 80, 115–16, 142, 162, 189, 195–6, 222
prepositions
 in anastrophe, 17.87, 21.31, 172
 w. *sine* in adnominal phrases, 16.307–8, 20.225, 21.141

Propertius, 16.187, 253–4, 17.116, 126, 18.200, 19.37–8, 21.118, 172, 177–80
prosaic/colloquial/technical expressions, 16.57–8, 105, 128, 17.29, 37, 69, 127, 151, 165, 183, 213, 18.181–2, 19.10, 87–8, 181–2, 20.74, 127–8, 153, 172, 174, 177–8, 242, 21.159–60
See also legal language

relative clauses
  characterizing, 17.29
  connective, 20.211
  consecutive-generic, 16.180, 208, 218, 17.44, 47–8, 100, 19.79, 159, 20.49, 60, 149, 21.210
  defining, 20.136
  final-consecutive, 16.115–16, 134, 301, 17.202, 231, 18.146, 19.15–16, 21.226, 237–8
  incorporating antecedent, 17.237–8, 21.100
  repetition
    not rhetorically motivated, 16.150–2, 279–80, 19.10, 158–67, 189–207, 20–109, 238–40
    pointed (anaphora), 20.16–17, 21–2, 71–2, 101–3, 159–61, 173–5, 177–8, 227–8, 21.235–6
rhyme, 21.30
ring-composition, 16.220

self-reference, 17.196
similes and comparisons, 16.251–2, 20.55–60, 55–6, 21.215–16, 217–18, 219–20
simple for compound verb, 19.194
'speaking' names, 17.231–2, 21.209
Statius, 16.286, 20.20, 21.32
subjunctive, *see* mood
subordinate clause dependent on sub. cl. following, 17.9–10, 19.29–30
superlatives formed from participles, 17.71, 18.37, 19.131
syllepsis, 18.57, 126, 19.13, 20.186

synecdoche, 16.21, 18.11, 19.138, 204, 21.71–2

tenses
  descriptive use of, 21.112–13
  future: w. force of imperative, 21.57; of probability, 16.186, 188, 206, 357–8, 368, 17.47–8 (?), 60, 106 (?), 20.156, 218; in rhetorical questions, 21.56
  imperfect: inceptive-conative, 21.73–4; (subjunctive) for plpf., 16.103, 156–8, 18.43–4; = 'was and is', 19.130, 21.29, 206
  pluperfect: for impf., 17.23, 91, 21.35, 85, 117; jussive, 20.53
  perfect: 'gnomic', 17.190 (?), 19.109; inf. for present, 16.203–4, 352, 17.98, 169–70, 18.95; (subjunctive) in question, 16.7; in statement, 16.189, 17.109–10
  present: conative (participle), 20.123; continuative, 16.209–10, 20.11; for impf. (?), 17.24; in protasis of cond. clause expressing threat or warning (?), 19.205
  sequence of breached, 17.24
  variation of in narrative, 16.225–6
'theme and variation', 16.111–12, 147, 17.101–2, 18.157–8, 19.97–8, 21.33–4, 67, 85–6, 137–8
Theodulf of Orleans, 21.235–6
Theseus, 16.153, 161, 17.21
third person used by speaker of himself, 16.357–8, 19.206, 20.228
Thucydides, 16.151–2, 18.75
Tibullus, 16.216, 18.166, 19.37–8, 80, 20.85–6, 21.161

Virgil, 16.57–8, 67, 111–12, 150, 164, 177, 223, 357–8, 372, 375, 17.5, 139–40, 189, 200, 220, 18.25, 55, 59, 89–90, 115, 157–8, 197, 200, 19.31–2, 183, 203, 20.95, 221–2, 21.9, 31, 65–6, 83, 209

word-order
  ἀπὸ κοινοῦ, 16.150, 317, 321–2,
    17.127, 249, 253, 18.3, 19.7, 11,
    24, 112, 171–2, 20.141, 21.41–2,
    159–60, 205–6 (?)
  chiastic, 16.147, 17.151–2, 173–4,
    20.16–17, 21–2, 218, 227–8,
    231–2, 21.40
  emphatic/expressive, 16.11–
    12, 173, 315, 361, 19.99–
    100, 20.101–2, 218, 227–8,
    21.40
  hyperbaton, 16.82, 134, 177 (?),
    17.109–10, 18.1–2, 191, 19.15–16,
    29–30, 86, 20.63–4, 83, 94, 95,
    101–2, 226, 21.214
  'hysteron proteron', 21.32
  Achaia tota et sim. ending
    hexameter, 17.209; *nempe, sedes*
    of in pentameter, 20.94; *tamen*
    ending pentameter, 20.44
  See also conjunctions, postponed;
    distribution of adjective-noun
    phrase; 'patterned' verses
word-play, verbal ambiguity 16.13–
    14, 17, 25, 49–50, 98, 104, 123–
    6, 124, 172, 232, 320, 340, 17.3,
    145, 181, 265–6, 18.43–4, 74,
    85–6, 96, 130, 207–8, 208,
    19.67, 150, 167, 185, 186, 20.30,
    36, 38, 43, 48, 50, 95, 112, 231–
    2, 242, 21.3, 71–2, 115–16, 121,
    144, 210
  etymologizing, 16.173, 17.9–10,
    20.192, 21.82, 209
  See also irony, authorial

zeugma, *see* syllepsis

CPSIA information can be obtained at www.ICGtesting.com
Printed in the USA
LVOW08s2251180816
500949LV00001B/10/P